THEORETICAL
APPROACHES
TO PERSONALITY

Barry D. Smith
UNIVERSITY OF MARYLAND

Harold J. Vetter
UNIVERSITY OF SOUTH FLORIDA

PRENTICE-HALL, INC.
Englewood Cliffs, New Jersey 07632

Library of Congress Cataloging in Publication Data

Smith, Barry D.
   Theoretical approaches to personality.

   Includes bibliographies and index.
   1. Personality. I. Vetter, Harold J., (date)
II. Title.
BF698.S566   155.2   81–8694
ISBN 0–13–913491–3   AACR2

Editorial/production supervision and interior design by Cathie Mick Mahar
Cover design by Miriam Recio
Manufacturing buyer: Edmund W. Leone

Printed in the United States of America

10 9 8 7 6 5 4 3 2 1

Prentice-Hall International, Inc., *London*
Prentice-Hall of Australia Pty. Limited, *Sydney*
Prentice-Hall of Canada, Ltd., *Toronto*
Prentice-Hall of India Private Limited, *New Delhi*
Prentice-Hall of Japan, Inc., *Tokyo*
Prentice-Hall of Southeast Asia Pte. Ltd., *Singapore*
Whitehall Books Limited, *Wellington, New Zealand*

To our parents:
Clinton T. and Gretchen D. Smith
Gladys L. Vetter

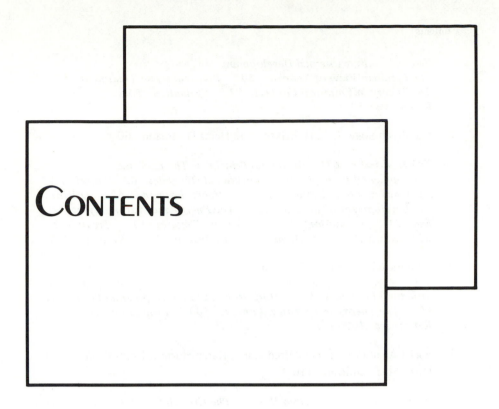

CONTENTS

V   BEHAVIORAL AND COGNITIVE APPROACHES   191

8   Stimulus-Response Learning Theory: John Dollard and Neal Miller   193

9   A Behavioral Approach: B. F. Skinner   213

10   Cognitive Theory: George Kelley   237

11   Social Learning Theory: Albert Bandura, Walter Mischel, and Julian
Rotter   249

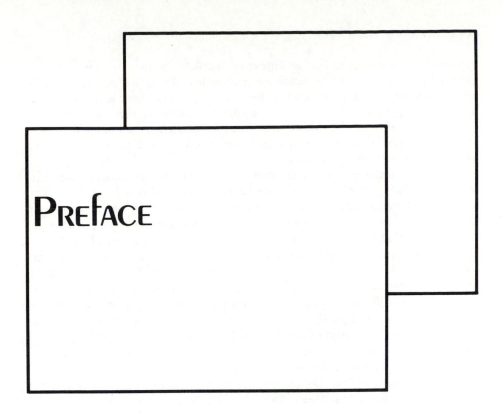

PREFACE

Perhaps the most fascinating scientific study ever undertaken is that of human personality and behavior. Why do people behave as they do? How do patterns of behavior become established and how do they change? Why do you become depressed, angry, happy, or anxious? How do people develop patterns of abnormal behavior and how can such behavior be effectively treated?

The psychology of personality is the intriguing study that will provide us with the answers to all these questions and has already provided at least partial answers to some. Our knowledge of human personality functioning is based largely on the major theories of personality and the research done to test and extend these theories. Through systematic theory and research, we have learned more about human personality and behavior in the past eighty years since Freud published his first book than in all the preceding centuries.

Our approach to the study of personality in this book has been to provide a thorough coverage of each of the major theories of personality. In selecting the major theories, we have chosen those that have had the most significant impact on the field and that are of greatest current importance to our understanding of personality. We have attempted to write about each theory in such a way that the coverage is at once basic and advanced. It is basic in that an understanding of the theories presented requires no prior knowledge of personality theory. At the same time, we have attempted to provide an in-depth coverage of most theories that is comprehensive enough to permit advanced study of the theory and its ramifications.

The detailed statement of any given theory without attention to other topics related to the theory would be a cold, sterile exercise. It will thus be seen that each theory chapter also discusses the historical origins of the theory and the biographical background of the major theorists, covers research associated with the theory, provides a critical evaluation of the approach, deals with applications of the theory, where relevant, and compares the theory with others. The latter two approaches are quite unusual in personality texts. However, we believe they add to the comprehensiveness and interest of the theory. Thus, for example, we discuss not only Freudian theory but how Freud applied his theory to an understanding of the causes of neurosis and how psychoanalytic therapy is carried out. In addition, Freudian theory is compared with others as to the similarities and differences of many of its major constructs. The final chapter goes even further in providing a more comprehensive intercomparison of the various theories.

The reader will note that the organization of each theory chapter is similar but not identical to that of the others. This is because we have attempted to follow the same basic format in presenting each approach without forcing the theory to fit coverage guidelines not suited to that theory. To aid the reader in understanding, evaluating, and intercomparing the theories, we have also provided, in Chapter 1, a useful set of guidelines as to the major constructs and postulates found in the various approaches.

The coverage provided in the present work has been greatly enhanced by the contributions of a substantial number of individuals. We are particularly indebted to the theorists whose work we have presented. Every living theorist provided a careful and helpful review of the chapter on his own work. Included in this group were Carl Rogers, Neal Miller, B. F. Skinner, Erik Erikson, Albert Bandura, Raymond Cattell, and Hans Eysenck. Each provided many useful suggestions concerning the coverage of his work and, in several cases, new, unpublished work was brought to our attention and has been included in the book. In addition to these special chapter reviews, we are indebted to a substantial group of reviewers, each of whom carefully reviewed several chapters, and in some cases, the entire book. Included among these reviewers were Drs. Dene Berman (Wright State University), Margaret E. Fitch (Hendrix College), Jesse E. Gordon (University of Michigan), Leslie Horst (San Diego State University), Rosina Lao (East Carolina University), Elaine Nocks (Furman University), John P. Lombardo (State University of New York at Cortland), and James Uleman (New York University). Each of these reviews was most helpful in revising the manuscript, and the overall work has profited greatly from the efforts of these reviewers. The book was also greatly facilitated by the numerous colleagues who were kind enough to answer questions, read chapters, and make suggestions and by the many graduate and undergraduate students who have read and commented on the various chapters. Throughout the process of writing, revising, and producing the book, we have been most impressed with the expertise and professionalism of our Psychology Editor, John Isley, and the entire Prentice-Hall editorial staff, including Marilyn Coco, Richard Kilmartin, Cathie Mick Mahar, and Gertrude Glassen. Their help is greatly appreciated. Finally, we are indebted to the three secretaries—Irma Nicholson, Josephine Shaffer, and Linda Schwartz—without whose long hours of hard labor there would yet be no manuscript.

Barry D. Smith
Harold J. Vetter

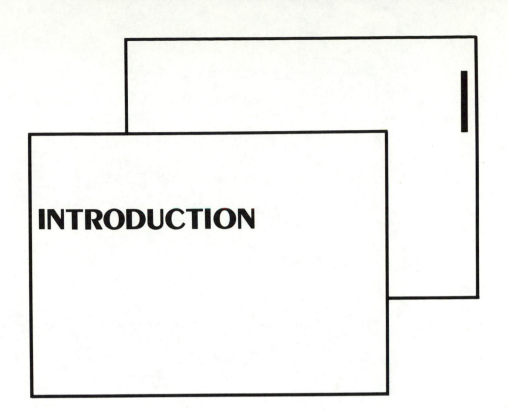

INTRODUCTION

Theory and Research in Personality

Before beginning our discussion of specific theories of personality let us consider briefly the term itself and its various meanings. An examination of the literature discloses that personality has been viewed as both a construct and an area of inquiry. The statement that personality is a construct immediately recognizes that it is something that is not directly observable but must be inferred from observed events. The view that personality is an area of inquiry indicates that psychological science, while never hoping to find an absolute or substantive definition of the term *personality* will best advance by pursuing both theoretical and empirical investigations of personality.

PERSONALITY AS A CONSTRUCT

The term *personality* derives from the ancient Latin, *persona*, and the medieval Latin, *personalitas*. The original meaning of these words is mask, a reference to the external appearance of the individual. Carl Jung, whose theory we will discuss, used the term *persona* to identify explicitly the individual's public personality, in the sense of the lines from T. S. Eliot's "Love Song of J. Alfred Prufrock":

> There will be time, there will be time
> To prepare a face to meet the faces that you meet . . .

This meaning did not, however, stand alone for long, because *persona* came to mean a variety of things, including the persons of the Trinity and any important individual, such as a parson. In addition, the term came to connote the inner characteristics and qualities of the individual as well as his or her external guise. Boethius was thus led to his classical definition: *Persona est substantia individua rationalis naturae* ("A person is an individual substance of a rational nature") (Muller 1888).

As we consider more recent definitions of personality, their relationships to the original meanings will become apparent.

Three Definitional Classes

If we search the literature on personality, we find literally hundreds of definitions of the term, each based on the personal and theoretical biases of the respective author. Allport (1961) distinguished three classes under which all or most of these definitions can be subsumed.

The first class, *external effect* approaches, makes use essentially of the mask connotation. Personality is seen as consisting of certain qualities of the individual as these are perceived by an observer; personality is the effect that a given individual has on others and often refers to his or her social competence or appeal. If we define personality as the overall effect the individual has on other people, we have an example of an external effect definition. Allport pointed out that we may risk confusing personality with reputation. The difficulty with external effect definitions, of course, is that they do not define or deal with the inner person so that predictions about the individual's behavior must be made entirely through knowledge of the social impression he or she creates.

The second class of definitions treats personality as an *internal structure*—an existing, objective entity. These are essentialist definitions; proponents of this view insist that personality is not a mere mask but an extant psychological or psychophysical structure. Such definitions view personality as an aggregate of innate and learned characteristics, processes, systems, or traits, either psychological or physical, or both, which are often organized into some dynamic whole. In one definition Linton (1945, p. 84), for example, says "Personality is the organized aggregate of psychological processes and states pertaining to the individual."

While the internal structure class probably contains the largest number of definitions, some psychologists have objected to this approach on the ground that the postulated internal structure cannot be directly observed and hence is not accessible to scientific study. This is a statement of the positivist view, which holds that only those things which can be defined in terms of specific, observable operations are admissible to science. Thus, personality can be defined only with reference to actual operations, such as scores on personality tests or reports by trained observers. By way of example, personality might be defined as "the most adequate conceptualization of a person's behavior in all its detail that the scientist can give at a moment in time" (McClelland, 1951, p. 69). There is no such thing as personality as an entity apart from the specific operations employed in scientific investigations. We shall discuss the problems and ramifications of operationalism later in this chapter.

Personality as a System of Constructs

Viewing the foregoing discussion of definitions of personality from a somewhat positivistic perspective, we can conclude that personality is a construct and a complex system of constructs. When viewed as an entity, an existing internal structure, personality is itself a construct in that it must be inferred from observations of behavior. At the same time, for a given theorist, personality usually consists of a number of specific subparts, each of these being itself a separate construct. Thus, we will see that Freud spoke of an id, an ego, and a superego, which together form the structure of personality. Jung described archetypes and complexes existing in the collective unconscious and the personal unconscious. And Allport employed a dynamic organization of psychophysical systems, including traits and attitudes. These will, of course, be discussed in detail when we consider the individual theories. The point to be made here is that each component of the personality must be inferred from observations of behavior, and each is, therefore, a construct.

Approaching personality and its components as constructs, we must reach the conclusion, shared with others (Bischof 1970; Hall and Lindzey 1978; Sarason 1972), that *personality is not an existing substantive entity to be searched for but a complex construct to be developed and defined by the observer*. There can never be, therefore, a single, generally agreed upon definition. Rather, personality must be defined by the observer with respect to a particular theoretical orientation and in terms of the particular concepts, postulates, and data language that constitute a given theory. The reader will thus find in the chapters that follow numerous definitions of personality, each implied by and consonant with a particular theoretical orientation.

PERSONALITY AS AN AREA OF INQUIRY

Apart from efforts to discover substantive or to develop theoretical definitions of personality, we may view the field of personality as an area of investigation. This point of view recognizes two types of inquiry, theory and research. Although considerable emphasis will be placed on research relevant to the various theories, the primary concern of the later chapters is the analysis and synthesis of theories. Since the use of theory as a method of inquiry will be detailed later in this chapter and throughout the book, let us briefly consider here the role of research.

We may differentiate for purposes of the present discussion two types of research. The first, which may be called *theory-based research,* involves studies conducted in order to test specific hypotheses deduced from a formal theory. The second type of research, *empirically based research,* is exploratory research in which no formal theory provides the hypotheses to be tested. Exploratory research is often done when no available theory deals adequately with the particular variables of interest to the investigator. Both types of research have advantages and disadvantages. Theory-based research has the advantage of being generated within a logically consistent framework. This means that a program of related empirical investigations can systematically expand the knowledge of the science, while at the same time determine the validity of hypotheses and, therefore, of the theory. Empirically based studies, on the other hand, are of great value in that they may provide the data base upon which a formal theory can be built. The possible contribution of such exploratory research to the science is, however, often dampened by the relative lack of organization and integration of the field of study.

THE STRUCTURE OF A THEORY

The principal purpose of this book is to present the reader not only with a detailed discussion of the major theories of personality but also with evaluations of the theories and some comparisons of the major points of various theories. In order to accomplish the goals of evaluation and comparison, it is first necessary to consider just what a scientific theory is—and what it is not. With the structural properties in mind, we will be better prepared to discuss and understand specific theories.

It is of interest to observe that every science is replete with a variety of theories. Since no definition indicates that an area of endeavor, in order to be a science, must have theories, we may ask why the theory-building phenomenon pervades all sciences. The answer may lie in the definition of theory. We may define a scientific theory as an *organized set of concepts designed to mediate prediction and explanation in a particular area of empirical observation.* As the definition states, theory simultaneously serves the functions of organization and mediation; this dual purpose is the basis for the usefulness and, indeed, necessity of theory in science.

FUNCTIONS OF A THEORY

Let us now be more specific about the major functions of a theory. We may view a theory as having two major functions with respect to empirical observation:

1. A theory provides a logical framework for the incorporation and integration of empirical observations previously seen as disparate. The results of a number of exploratory studies done by different scientists may often appear to be lacking in

agreement. The theorist recognizes that certain principles appear to underlie the otherwise conflicting findings and may construct or begin to construct a theory integrating the available empirical observations.

While the theorist must incorporate as much research evidence as possible, he or she is also constrained to conform to the principle of *parsimony*. This venerable principle of theory construction states that the theory should explain the phenomena of interest in the simplest possible fashion. Complexities should not be introduced unnecessarily, and, in fact, a concerted effort should be made to avoid unnecessary complexity. We should hasten to point out, however, that in evaluating a theory, adherence to the principle of parsimony must be pitted against the adequacy with which the theory explains and predicts the phenomena of interest. The application of this principle can be carried too far, to the extent that the theory will be simple but relatively useless.

2. A theory provides and generates, within a logically consistent framework, new hypotheses which can lead to *systematic* empirical research. It is with regard to this second function that a theory makes its greatest contribution to science, for it is here that the organizational and mediational functions reach fruition. The parsimonious integration of known empirical data is, of course, important, but a science advances primarily through a process of constantly adding and integrating new observations. A theory provides a logical structure within which scientific knowledge can be expanded systematically. The mechanism for such systematic expansion derives from the general theory of testable hypotheses that lead the scientist to carry out research. The resulting empirical observations may then be incorporated into a given theory and may, in fact, lead to its modification.

COMPONENTS OF THE THEORY

Having noted the functions which a theory may serve for science, we must now consider how a theory can be constructed in order to carry out these functions. What follows is a brief consideration of the terms of a theory and the ways in which they operate to produce a systematic integration and expansion of scientific knowledge. The interested reader will find more detailed discussions, as well as other viewpoints, in a number of sources (Braithwaite 1953; Cohen and Nagel 1934; Conant 1947; Feigl and Brodbeck 1953; Feigl and Sellers 1949; Frank 1949; Nagel 1961).

Primitive Terms: The Data Language

A formal theory contains a number of terms which are defined with reference to other more basic terms within that theory. At the most basic level, however, the theory should have some terms which are not defined by further reduction. Specifically, there should be some terms which are widely used in the field of which the theory is a part, terms which would be defined in the same way by theorists of different orientations. Theorists in physics, for example, might use the term *temperature* in their theory. This term would not need to be further defined within the theory, since physicists are widely agreed upon the definition of temperature and its measurement by one of several mathematically interrelated scales. Such terms, which are used with the same meaning throughout a given field, form the empirical foundation of the theory and are called *primitive terms.* Collectively, the primitive terms are referred to as the *data language* of the theory.

The principal function of the data language is to avoid the ultimate circularity which inheres in any purely formal theoretical system. Some mathematical systems, such as projective geometry, are totally circular, since all terms are defined by reference to other terms within the system. The result is that the theory has no empirical foundation and, therefore, is not a testable theory in the usual sense. While such formal systems are useful to mathematicians, they are of little help to the scientist who wishes to predict and study empirical phenomena. Thus, the more solid and the more neutral the data language of a theory, the more adequate is that theory for predicting the phenomena of interest.

Theoretical Constructs

A *construct* is an explanatory concept which is not immediately and directly observable. It is usually a label for a hypothesized relationship between an object and an event. A theoretical construct is used by a theorist as a logical inference to fill in the gaps in the explanation and prediction of empirical data. It should be pointed out that a construct is not the only type of concept. In common usage, a concept refers to a class of objects or events that have common properties, such as *tree, dog,* and *building.* Common constructs include such relative abstractions as *democracy, love,* and *patriotism.* Theoretical constructs in personality psychology are exemplified by *self-concept, ego,* and *anxiety.* It is notable that constructs are more complex than other concepts in that the constructs specify relationships rather than merely descriptions.

To be maximally useful in a theoretical system, a construct must be stated unambiguously and employed in such a way that it is possible to define it in terms of observable events. That is, the theorist should provide or readily permit an operational definition of each construct in the theory. When a construct is stated in terms of an operational definition, it is measurable, and, to the extent that its constructs are measurable, a theory is testable.

Propositions and Predictions

One function of a theory is to predict certain phenomena; we may identify two types of propositions which are used to implement the predictive function. The first, the *hypothesis,* is a relatively specific prediction about some empirical relationship. In its most common form, it is the hypothesis which forms the direct propositional link between theory and data. The second type of proposition, the *postulate,* is a more general statement concerning relationships with which the theory is concerned. There are usually relatively few postulates in a given theory, and it is often possible to derive a number of specific hypotheses from single postulates or combinations of postulates.

The propositions of the theory may be seen as performing three important functions. First, they state the functional relationships among variables. Second, it is only through hypotheses that a theory can be tested experimentally. If only very general, nontestable postulates are possible, the theory must exist in scientific limbo, since it is not possible to determine whether its postulates are empirically tenable. In general, the more capable a theory is of generating testable hypotheses, the more readily it can be evaluated and, if necessary, modified or extended. A final function of propositions is in mediating the observation of previously unobserved empirical relationships. By functioning in this way, the hypothesis allows the theory to carry out its function of expanding scientific knowledge.

Relational Rules

We have thus far viewed a theory as comprising a formal structure and empirical base. The formal structure consists of a number of constructs and propositions, while the empirical base includes the primitive terms of the theory as well as relevant empirical evidence. To complete the theory we need two sets of relational rules, one to interrelate the various aspects of the formal theory and the other to relate the theory to its empirical base. The former is called the *syntax* of the theory, the latter the *semantics.* The syntactical rules formulated by the theorist state how the various constructs and propositions of the theory are related to one another. Together such rules give structure to the theory, where otherwise there would be only a disjointed array of terms. The semantics are rules which relate the theory to data. The relationship is most importantly expressed in the form of operational definitions of the constructs in the theory. An *operational definition* refers primarily to the specification of measurement processes that will define a given construct. Where operations for the measurement of the construct are clearly specified, the meaning of the construct will be relatively unambiguous. More important, it is only through the specification of operational definitions that a theory can be subjected to an empirical test.

As an example of an operational definition, consider anxiety, which appears as a major theoretical construct in a number of personality theories. A given theorist might define anxiety as a general feeling of apprehension or fear in which the object of the fear is unknown or indefinite. This definition gives us a fairly clear idea of how the theorist views anxiety but does not permit us to test his or her hypotheses about anxiety; we must first tie the term down empirically. If we decide to define anxiety operationally as the score obtained by a subject on the Taylor Manifest Anxiety Scale (Taylor 1953), we have provided a definition of the construct in terms of an observable measurement operation and can test the theorist's hypotheses about anxiety.

THE THEORY

With the components of a theory at hand, we can now, by way of summary, describe the theory as a whole. The theory is ideally composed of a number of relatively general postulates, each of which is a statement of the functional relationships of certain variables and each of which involves one or more of the constructs of the theory. Each construct, as well as each other major term of the theory, is defined by reference to other terms within the theory. Exceptions are the primitive terms, which are defined, if at all, by reference to terms or observations external to the theory. The various constructs, terms, and propositions within the formal theory are interrelated by the syntax of the theory. Through the application of syntactical rules, hypotheses concerning relatively specific empirical relationships are deduced from the postulates of the theory. If hypotheses are anchored semantically to the data language and constructs are operationally defined, various provisional definitions may be provided for use on an exploratory basis. Depending upon results of empirical investigations, the theory may be extended through the formulation of new postulates, or the deduction of new hypotheses, or both; or the existing postulates, hypotheses, or syntax of the theory may be modified to incorporate the new empirical observations within a logically consistent framework. Through the deduction and testing of hypotheses, the theory may lead to new empirical observations and, in that way, aid in the expansion of scientific knowledge.

Unfortunately, many theories—including many personality theories—do not conform closely to the structure outlined above. Constructs are often not defined, or even readily definable, in operational terms. Verbal definitions of constructs and other terms in the theory may be ambiguous, inconsistent, or even nonexistent. Relational rules may be unspecified, weak, or too general to be useful. And the theory as a whole may not, even in its original formulation, be capable of consistently explaining and predicting existing, relevant empirical relationships. We will discuss the evaluation of theories later in this chapter.

WHAT A THEORY IS NOT

A Phenomenon of Nature

We must note first that a theory is not a given or natural phenomenon. It is not a discovery but rather a creation of the theorist. It is developed out of his or her interpretations of empirical results and is subject to the biases of both the theorist and any scientist who later interprets the theory. Theorist biases are based, in general, on the personal and professional experience of the theorist, and they influence the theory in every aspect and at every point in its development.

A Law

Theories—or their postulates—may or may not become laws, depending upon the definition of law. If law is defined as a final and irrevocable empirical relationship, a theory can never become a law. If, however, as is more common in science, law is defined as a well-established empirical relationship which has been repeatedly observed, a theory or postulate can become a law. In this latter sense, a law is simply a theoretical proposition which has received widespread experimental support. There is no implication that the relationship is absolute or irrefutable, and there is the continuing recognition that the law originated as a theoretical proposition or perhaps simply as an empirical observation.

WHY DIFFERENT THEORIES?

We have noted that the construction of theories is a phenomenon which seems to pervade all science. It is legitimate to ask, then, why this should be so. Why can we not simply perform relevant empirical observations in a systematic fashion, without the necessity for theory, and answer each empirical question factually, rather than theoretically? Do other sciences, in fact, as we have stated, rely on theory for the advancement of the science?

An Example from Physics

To illustrate the use of theory in an older, more "exacting" field than that of personality, let us consider an example from physics and attempt to draw relevant analogies to theories of personality. Despite its relative age and scientific precision, physics does rely heavily on theories to deal with phenomena that are not precisely understood in terms of factual, experimental knowledge. A good example is the area of light transmission, where an early theory held that light travels through space in the form of waves. Newton later rejected the wave theory in favor of a particle theory, which holds that light does not travel in waves but rather as a set or series of particles emitted by the light source. Many studies were done in an attempt to compare the two theories. Following the completion of some of these experiments, Einstein did offer a partial resolution of the controversy by introducing his concept of the photon, which may be seen as a light particle that travels in waves. Even the Einstein formulation, however, is not entirely satisfactory, and the phenomenon of light transmission is still open to further research and theoretical formulation. The point is that physics, like psychology, needs theories in order to organize its bodies of knowledge and provide bases for gaining further knowledge.

Theories of Personality

Let us now again ask why we have different theories of personality. Light, which we can so easily control by drawing a shade, flipping a switch, or admitting it briefly through a camera shutter, might seem quite simple and readily explainable without the necessity for a variety of theories. Yet we have seen that light is so complex as to have been the center of a theoretical controversy extending over some three centuries, and it is still unresolved. How much more complex, then, is the human personality? How much broader the scope of phenomena to be predicted and explained? How much more numerous and diverse the empirical observations to be integrated? But why, specifically, despite differences in complexity of phenomena, is it not possible to arrive at a single, consistent explanation of light or personality?

Empirical Variance. Most theories, whether of light, personality, or other phenomena, are based on empirical observations. To the extent that these observations vary, the resultant theories may vary. While empirical observations may differ for a variety of reasons, two principal factors in variation are the control of variables and the degree of precision of measurement. In order for a given experiment to test a hypothesis or demonstrate a relationship adequately, all variables which might affect the outcome of the experiment must be either systematically manipulated, held constant, or measured. Only to the extent that such control is accomplished does the experiment demonstrate a given relationship. The variables requiring control depend upon both the general area of investigation and the particular hypotheses being tested. Physicists studying the phenomena of light transmission have found it necessary to control such variables as the temperature and intensity of the light source, which can be manipulated or held constant, and the motion of the earth, which can be measured. Psychologists testing theories of personality have found it necessary to control such variables as the age, sex, socioeconomic status, and length of hospitalization of subjects, to name but a few.

Even when the control of variables is adequate, precision of measurement of dependent variables may be a factor in empirical variance. If the experimenter wishes to determine the relative improvement of patients under several types of psychotherapy, he or she may have to rely either on the opinions or ratings of psychologists and psychiatrists or upon the often unreliable results of projective techniques. In other cases, where dependent measures involved well-constructed personality inventories, or such measures as reaction time or physiological responses, precision may be higher. But even with these measures, the degree of precision varies considerably from one experiment to another and even within the same experiment.

Theorist Bias. A second major reason why we have a variety of personality theories is that each scientist, despite his or her attempts to interpret data objectively, is influenced by personal pretheory biases. Perhaps the most important factor affecting bias is the theorist's background, including the books and articles read and the course material studied. The theorist's background also includes research experience and, in the case of the personality theorist, experience with patients in the clinical situation. In addition, the personality theorist's own background and personality structure are likely to influence the nature of the theory that he or she develops.

THE EVALUATION AND COMPARISON OF THEORIES

Having discussed some of the characteristics and functions of theories, we are now in a position to evaluate and compare a number of personality theories. Any given theory may be assessed in terms of its formal, or structural, properties and its empirical properties. Any two or more theories may be compared and contrasted according to these two sets of properties and, in addition, in terms of a number of specific issues concerned primarily with the postulated attributes of the human personality.

Structural Properties

In our discussion of theory construction, the emphasis was placed on the description of the properties of an ideal theory. Since, obviously, not all theories of personality will attain this ideal, it is useful to consider some specific questions that might be asked in evaluating the formal attributes of a given theory.

1. Data Language
   a. Does the theory have a data language? That is, are an adequate number of primitive terms specified?
   b. Is the data language neutral, not unduly influenced by the biases of the theorist?
   c. Are the primitive terms clearly and explicitly defined by reference to terms outside the theory?
2. Theoretical Constructs
   a. Are constructs stated and defined unambiguously?
   b. Are definitions operational or merely verbal?
   c. If operational definitions are not supplied, are classes of operations stated or implied in order to make operational definitions readily derivable?
3. Propositions
   a. Are postulates clearly and explicitly stated, or must they be deduced from the general writings of the theorist?
   b. Are hypotheses specifically stated, or must they be derived?
   c. Do the stated postulates and hypotheses provide adequate specification of functional relationships among variables which constitute the theory?
   d. Are hypotheses readily amenable to empirical tests?
4. Relational Rules
   a. Is an adequate set of syntactical rules clearly specified?
   b. Are the interrelationships of major theoretical variables made adequately explicit through the application of syntax?
   c. Do the semantics of the theory clearly relate the theoretical variables to empirical data?

Empirical Properties

Far more important than the adequacy of its formal properties is the empirical value of the theory. A theory which closely approximates the structural ideal and contributes little to the expansion of scientific knowledge is of far less value than the poorly constructed theory which nevertheless pushes the frontiers of science a few steps forward.

In evaluating the empirical contribution of a theory, we must consider both the adequacy with which the theory integrates existing experimental evidence and the ability of the theory to generate further research. The scientist who sets out to construct a formal theory ordinarily has available to him or her a reasonably large body of empirical data. In evaluating a theory, it is essential to determine the extent to which the theory is able to explain or "post-dict" existing data. In addition, we will be interested in the ability of theory to generate scientific research and hence, potentially, to expand scientific knowledge.

The stimulation of research may be accomplished in two ways. First, the theory may generate research formally, that is, through the statement of postulates and hypotheses. If the hypotheses are amenable to empirical test, the amount of research stimulated will depend largely on the importance placed upon the theory by the scientific community. The second way to stimulate research is through the heuristic influence of the theory, which may take any of several forms. The theory may suggest to other scientists particular directions or ideas for research, not providing specific hypotheses but merely serving as an impetus. The theory may open a general area of scientific inquiry that has received little previous attention. In this way, the theory may stimulate not only a variety of research efforts but also, eventually, even the development of other theories (for example, the influence of Freud's theory on the development of Jungian and neoanalytic theories). Finally, a theory may generate research, in the process of which new scientific leads concerning phenomena only indirectly relevant to the theory may be obtained.

Issues and Attributes

The above formal and empirical considerations involve a value dimension, on which a theory may be called relatively *good* or *poor* in comparison with either the ideal as a standard, a normative standard established by all related theories, or with any other given theory. It is also profitable to compare theories as to their treatments of a number of neutral, nonevaluative, theoretical issues. As compared with formal and empirical properties, these neutral issues are relatively specific to theories of personality and have been elsewhere referred to as substantive attributes (Hall and Lindzey 1978).[1]

The Origins of Personality. Two major questions which must be answered by any personality theory are where personality comes from and by what mechanisms or processes it exists or develops. Several related issues are involved in a consideration of these questions. First, theories differ as to the postulated relative importance of *heredity* and *learning* in the development of personality. Most theorists agree that both hereditary and learning factors are involved, but their differences in emphasis on the two factors are great. Those who place relatively great stress on the individual may actually inherit a substantial proportion of the personality in the form of knowledge or predispositions to respond to specific objects or situations in

[1]While we have chosen a somewhat different approach from theirs, we—and indeed the entire field of personality—are indebted to Calvin S. Hall and Gardner Lindzey (1978) for their recognition and excellent treatment of the substantive attributes of personality theories.

particular ways. Another maintains that through the provision of other predispositions or the control of particular aspects of the maturational process, or both, heredity may greatly influence the kinds of personality-relevant learning that will take place. The greater the degree of control which heredity exerts over learning, the less important is seen the learning process. A third way in which heredity is seen to operate is by providing and controlling a number of specific physiological or primary drives, such as hunger and thirst, upon which the learning of secondary drives may be based. A final argument is that heredity may indirectly influence personality development by controlling or partially controlling such important factors as intelligence and ability.

While their degree of emphasis varies markedly, all theorists have agreed that learning does influence the development of personality. In some theories learning serves only to modify slightly the inherited maturational process. In others its importance is implicit in many aspects of development. In still others learning is the single most important factor in the developing and functioning of the personality, and the learning process receives explicit and detailed treatment. When the learning process is specified, theories may differ as to the nature of that process. One major position holds that learning involves primarily the operation of hedonism and its modern counterpart, reinforcement. The hedonic hypothesis states simply that people learn those behaviors which allow them to attain pleasure and avoid pain. In its basic form, this hypothesis may be traced to the ancient Greek philosphies of Plato and Aristotle, the Cyreniac philosophy of Aristippus, and to the Epicurean school. It is seen again during the Renaissance in the psychological hedonism of the British associationists and utilitarians, including Hobbes, Hume, Locke, Bentham, and J. S. Mill. And it appears once more in Thorndike's (1911) Law of Effect, which says, in essence, that acts followed by satisfaction are more likely, and those followed by dissatisfaction are less likely, to be repeated (that is, learned). In its modern, "strong" theoretical form, the reinforcement hypothesis holds that *only* those acts followed by drive reduction (pleasure, satisfaction) will be learned. A *reinforcer* is then defined in some theories as anything which, when it follows an act or response, increases the probability of occurrence of that response.

A second learning process hypothesis states that it is not reward or reinforcement that is important for learning but rather the close temporal proximity of the stimulus and response. Advocates of this *principle of contiguity* or association hold that reward (drive reduction) is not a necessary condition for learning. If reinforcement does aid the learning process, it is only because the reinforcer introduces a new situation that prevents the contiguously learned stimulus-response configuration from being unlearned. While some theorists have employed either the reinforcement or the contiguity hypothesis to the exclusion of the other, there are others who quite explicitly postulate within the same theory the operation of both principles.

A third approach to understanding how personality is learned has been to specify that a process of imitation, identification, or modeling is central to personality development. Learning takes place when the child observes an adult or older child engaging in a certain kind of behavior and proceeds, then, or on some subsequent occasion, to imitate the behavior.

A second issue concerning the origins of personality involves the question of the postulated developmental process. Even theories which are in essential agreement as to the importance and mechanisms of learning may differ as to whether personality development is smooth and ongoing or broken into a series of relatively discrete steps or stages. In the latter viewpoints the postulated stages usually follow a rough chronological sequence, with specific events and developments taking place at each stage. All stages may be contained within the childhood years, or stages may extend through the teens and even into adulthood. The particular stages that are postulated by a given theorist may be based on: (1) a physiological maturational process; (2) a psychological maturational process; (3) the occurrence of specific learning situations; (4) a social learning process; or (5) some combination of these. On another dimension, the sequential stages may be totally dependent, the occurrence of a given stage necessitating the completion of the preceding stage; partially dependent, in that each stage is influenced by the events (for example, learning) of earlier stages; or totally independent.

A further question deals with the continuity of personality development, raising the issue of whether or not a single set of major developmental principles can account for the continuous development of personality from birth through adulthood. Some theorists suggest that the adult personality represents such continuity, while others propose discontinuity, arguing that the personality of the adult is relatively independent of the developmental processes that carried the person through childhood.

A fourth major differentiator of personality theories is the importance given to early life experiences in personality development. Some theorists place great emphasis on early experience. The personality structure, its characteristics and functioning, are seen as being totally or largely set during the early years, and later psychopathology may be predisposed at this time. On the other side are theorists who explicitly deny the importance of early life. These theorists postulate continuous development and change in personality throughout life or hold that all behavior (and hence the inferred personality) is primarily a function of current factors. There are also, of course, those theorists who postulate that both early experience and later, including current, factors influence personality and behavior.

Motivation. The fact that an organism, including a human, is not constantly quiescent implies the presence of some force or forces which impel the organism to activity. Such forces may be collectively referred to as the *motivation* of the organism. Essentially all theories agree that the organism is motivated, but they divide on at least three major dimensions on the question of how it is motivated. The first of these might be called the *time base* of the motivation. One group of personality theories holds that the individual is motivated principally by primary or secondary factors in his or her *past*. *Primary factors* are generally specified to be unlearned, physiological drives, which are, at least by implication, inherited, and which form part of the structural makeup of the organism. *Secondary factors* are *learned* drives or motives. These are usually more complex than the primary drives, but like those they serve to impel the organism to activity. Depending upon the theory, the secondary motives may or may not be learned on the basis of primary drives, may or may not require reinforcement for their learning and continuation, may be either more or less important than the primary drives, and may or may not *direct,* as well as activate, behavior.

Another theoretical approach to time base stresses the *teleological* character of motivation. In these theories man is viewed as a *purposive* creative, motivated to attain goals rather than to reduce drives. The operation of primary and secondary drives is not denied, but both are seen as merely serving the central purpose of goal attainment. The goals to be attained vary in number, origin, and type, and the mechanisms of goal attainment vary in type and specificity, but the time base is unmistakably future, and the quality of motivation, therefore, is definitely teleological. We would argue—not entirely without opposition—that there is also a third group of theories in which motivation is primarily based on the *present*. Here we refer principally to theories of the field type in which all behavior, and by inference motivation, is postulated to be a function of the field (external and internal environment) of the moment.

A second issue in motivation concerns the *number and centrality* of motivational concepts employed in each theory. Some theories utilize only one or two motivational concepts and place these at the center of theory. A second group of theorists makes motivation somewhat less central and specifies not one or two but many motives or motive systems. This enumerative, cataloging approach tends to suggest that only the motives that are specified activate behavior and closes the empirical door, at least partially, to the possibility of other nonlisted motives. A final approach is to specify few or no motives, with the implication that the number of possible motives is theoretically infinite.

A third important motivational issue is the *conscious-unconscious dimension*. This is the question of the individual's postulated awareness of motives. Some theorists propose that a large part of motivation is unconscious. Most such theorists hypothesize a psychic structure in which one or more subconscious reservoirs serve to store energy or information that is used in controlling the individual's motivation. The materials contained in such reservoirs may become subconscious in any or all of several ways: (1) unlearned, hereditary processes or information, or both, may be stored unconsciously from birth; (2) learning may actually take place unconsciously (never entering awareness); and (3) things learned consciously may be repressed (forced into the unconscious). A second group of theorists explicitly denies the existence of unconscious determinants of behavior, hypothesizing instead that all motives operate consciously. A third position permits the operation of both conscious and unconscious motives, usually stressing the importance of one over that of the other. One approach has been to postulate that the behavior of normal people is primarily under the control of conscious motives, while that of abnormals is dominated by unconscious motivation.

A final issue relevant to motivation is that of *free will* vs. *determinism*. Many philosophers of earlier centuries proposed that behavior is a function of man's free will to choose the behavior. The will to choose one's behavior freely was an important element in Aristotle's philosophy and was central in the work of St. Augustine. Immanuel Kant, the great German thinker of the eighteenth century, incorporated a concept of free will into a broader theory of behavior determination. He proposed that knowing, feeling, and willing are involved in human behavior. The alternative to free will is scientific determinism, which holds that all types of human behavior are causally determined and operate according to a set of scientific principles. Such principles can be stated as postulates and hypotheses in a scientific theory of human behavior and tested empirically in the laboratory. As we will see in studying the major theories of human behavior, a vast majority of psychologists and psychiatrists since Freud have held that determinism is a crucial assumption if one is to formulate a viable theory of human behavior.

Environmental Influences. A third general area of substantive differences among personality theories is concerned with the degree to which the influence of the external environment on personality is stressed and the particular ways in which the environment acts on the person. Depending upon the particular theory, any or all of at least three types of environmental influences may be postulated. First, the theorist may hypothesize the influence of cultural learning on personality structure and dynamics. This postulate recognizes the finding, in cross-cultural research, that personality patterns do tend to vary as a function of the culture in which the individual is raised. In particular, it appears that the culture may greatly affect the kinds of motives and goals that determine behavior. Second, the immediate social or interpersonal environment may influence behavior. Interpersonal interaction may be seen as both an important part of the learning that contributes to personality development and an agent of change in personality structure and dynamics. A third treatment postulates that the individual behaves at a given moment or across time as a function of his or her total psychological environment. The psychological environment is usually defined as consisting of all those external and internal factors that are capable of influencing the individual. A final approach suggests that a major determinant of human behavior is the immediate situation in which the person finds himself or herself at the time that behavior takes place. The emphasis here is on the role of the relatively objective external situation and on its impact on behavior; internal factors, that is, those within the personality, are not considered to be a part of the immediate situation. We will further consider the implications of situational positions below.

Individuality and Integrity of the Organism. Theories also differ in the degree of emphasis they place on the individuality or unique quality of the organism. While no theorist would deny that each person is an entity, some make the uniqueness of the individual a central postulate of their theories. Such theories hold that no two persons can have identical personalities and often, in fact, that no two acts of the same individual can be precisely identical. At the most basic level, the approach recognizes the essential complexity of the universe as applied to human behavior. The unique aspects of the individual are handled theoretically in either of two ways. In one approach, individuality is seen as a result of the operation of a virtually infinite number of different physical and psychological variables in both the person and the environment. This interpretation implies that the study of personality is, at best, many years in the future, pending the development of much more complex techniques than are now available. A second approach holds that individuality is due to the interaction and patterning of a relatively small number of variables. This position encourages research aimed at determining the precise variables and interactions that influence behavior in specific ways.

Related to the question of the unique aspects of the individual is the issue of wholism in contrast to what we might call segmentalism. The wholistic position asserts that in order to understand personality, we must consider the organism as a unitary whole. The segregation of the whole into component parts for purposes of experimental study is seen as more likely to lead to confusion than clarification. Two forms of wholism may be distinguished. The first, the organismic position, holds that all physical and psychological components and behavior of the organism or individual are interrelated. Any given behavior can be understood only in the context of the total organism, including both the organic and the psychological functioning of the individual. The second, or field approach, emphasizes the interrelatedness of the organism and its environment. Each aspect of behavior must be understood in the context of not only the integrated internal processes of the organism but also the environment surrounding the individual at the time of the act. The emphasis is usually on the external environment rather than on the internal functioning of the person.This segmentalistic position applies to essentially all theories not specifically espousing a wholistic approach. The correlation between the wholistic and uniqueness dimensions is apparent in that those theorists holding a wholistic position ordinarily also stress the individuality of the person.

The Trait-Situation Controversy

Most of the major theorists whom we will discuss have adopted the basic position that stable personality characteristics, or traits, account for most aspects of human behavior. Depending upon the particular theory in question, a given trait or characteristic may be largely the result of genetic factors, primarily represent learning experiences, or involve some combination of heredity and environment. In any case, the important point is that the trait represents a substantial degree of consistency in the personality and behavior of the individual, which extends across both time and situations. In the late 1920s and again in the late 1960s some psychologists questioned the validity of assuming that most behavior is a function of traits and suggested, instead, that the primary determinant of much human behavior may be the situation in which the behavior occurs. It has, in fact, been argued that there may be little consistency in individual behavior across situations, suggesting that trait concepts may not be particularly useful in predicting behavior. A third possibility, which may represent a partial and temporary resolution of the trait-situation controversy, is that most behavior results from the interaction of traits and situations.

Further Issues and Attributes. A further differentiator of personality theories is the relative use of terms and concepts from other disciplines. Some theorists rely entirely on psychological concepts in explaining and predicting behavior. Another group employs, with varying degrees of emphasis, concepts borrowed from other sciences. The issues are, first, whether or not such interdisciplinary anchoring (Hall and Lindzey 1978) is appropriate or necessary, and, second, what specific types of anchoring should be used and to what degree.

Theories may also be distinguished in terms of the use of two related personality attributes, self-evaluation and control centers. In some theories the structure and dynamics of personality revolve around the central idea that the individual constantly conceives of or evaluates himself or herself. The mechanism of this evaluative process is a self-concept, self-structure, or, simply, self, which perceives and construes itself in particular ways in relation to the environment. Each incoming stimulus or situation and each behavior of the individual is considered and evaluated in terms of its relationship to the self-concept. Other theories postulate no self-concept, and the self-evaluation process, if mentioned at all, is considered to be of minimal importance. The related question of control centers asks whether or not the theorist includes in the postulated personality structure a particular component which dominates others in determining personality dynamics and behavior. Some theories place control in one or two such centers, others spread the control over a large number of components, and still other theories change the control center as personality develops. In some theories the control center is the self or self-concept, while in others it may be some other component of the personality.

As specific theories are considered, it will become apparent that all do not deal equally well with all kinds of individuals. Another question we might then ask in comparing theories is to what population each theory applies. Does the theory deal most readily with the "normal" personality or the "abnormal" personality, and if the latter, to what type of abnormality does the theory best apply? A majority of theories to be discussed explain and predict the phenomena of abnormality more adequately than those of normality. In addition, the less disturbed forms of behavior of the neurotic are often explained more readily in theoretical terms than are the more severe and bizarre manifestations of the psychotic. Some theorists, however, have specifically concentrated their theoretical efforts on the normal individual to the exclusion of behavioral disorders.

We might finally ask of a theory, what is the nature of humans? What is the overall impression of human nature conveyed by the theory? Is it primarily a positive or a negative picture, or are equal elements of both types apparent? Are people basically good, bright, constructive beings, or are they primarily bad, rather dull, and destructive? Are they generally well-controlled, progressive, and normal, or are they impulsive, regressive, and abnormal? Are humans motivated only to gain pleasure and avoid pain or punishment, or are they capable of higher motives? If the emphasis is on pleasure and pain, which is primary? Does most learning occur in an effort to avoid punishment, or is a more positive, pleasure-seeking goal predominant? If emotions are stressed, does human nature include primarily such negative emotions as anger, hatred, and fear or more positive ones, such as joy, love, and elation? We could, of course, ask many other similar questions. The point to be made here is that, although most theorists do not explicitly define the nature of humans, careful study of their theories will nevertheless provide an impression of that nature.

A Comparative Approach to Personality Theory

We have discussed a number of formal, empirical, and substantive considerations in the evaluation of theories of personality. In the chapters that follow we will focus on the evaluation and comparison of theories in terms of their empirical and substantive properties, largely ignoring the formal properties. We take this approach for two principal reasons. First, as we have already seen, the empirical and substantive properties clearly have greater importance for the scientific progress of the field than do the formal properties of theories. Second, personality is such a young field that theorists have thus far had little time to consider carefully the development of formally adequate theories. They have been concerned, rather, with the development of theories which adequately reflect their standing on the major substantive issues and, in some cases, have concerned themselves with the extent to which the theory can be empirically tested and verified. An additional reason for the formal inadequacy of personality theory is that there are still very few primitive terms available, making this crucial aspect of the theory virtually impossible for the theorist to deal with adequately.

A Way of Viewing Theories

Before we go on to discuss our first theory, a word about the general content and organization of the chapters on theory may be helpful. In writing these chapters, we have attempted to provide reasonably consistent kinds of information about each theory and, at the same time, not to force the theory to conform to some rigid formula for its presentation. There are several topics that are covered systematically within most chapters, except in cases in which the theory simply does not lend itself to this type of coverage, and additional topics that are covered within certain chapters where they are particularly relevant to the theory in question.

Most theories are discussed in terms of their views on three major topics: structural principles, motivational dynamics, and origins and development of personality. *Structural principles* involve the basic constructs that comprise the personality, the way in which these constructs or structures interrelate, and the ways in which they function to influence behavior. The topic of *motivational dynamics* deals with those forces which are seen by the theorist as driving, activating, or motivating behavior. When we consider the *origins and development of the personality,* we are dealing with the theorists' views on the relative roles of genetics and environment in affecting personality development and structure, the developmental process, and the factors which affect development. The order in which these topics are taken up varies as a function of the particular theory discussed. In addition, our detailed discussion of the theory will sometimes be initially organized without reference to these three topics, and they will be discussed as a way of summarizing or providing an overview of the theory.

The various chapters also consistently provide brief biographical sketches of the major theorists and a brief treatment of the theory in an empirical context. The latter topic provides an overview of the types of research that have been done in connection with the theory and presents some of the results of important studies relevant to the theory. There is no intention, however, to provide an exhaustive coverage of the research relevant to any given theory, since often the body of available empirical evidence is massive.

In addition to these relatively consistent topics in each chapter, we will also take up special topics. In some cases, for example, we will discuss applications of the theory to particular areas of human behavior, while in other cases we will examine the theorists' approach to the treatment of psychological disorders.

REFERENCES

Allport, G. W. *Pattern and growth in personality.* New York: Holt, Rinehart & Winston, 1961.

Bischof, L. J. *Interpreting personality theories* (2nd ed.). New York: Harper & Row, 1970.

Braithwaite, R. B. *Scientific explanation.* London: Cambridge University Press, 1953.

Cohen, M. F., & Nagel, E. *An introduction to logic and scientific method.* New York: Harcourt, Brace, 1934.

Conant, J. B. *On understanding science.* New Haven, Conn.: Yale University Press, 1947.

Eliot, T. S. *Collected poems: 1909–1962.* New York: Harcourt, Brace, & World, 1963.

Feigl, H., & Sellers, W. (Eds.). *Readings in philosophical analysis.* New York: Appleton-Century-Crofts, 1949.

Feigl, H., & Brodbeck, M. *Readings in the philosophy of science.* New York: Appleton-Century-Crofts, 1953.

Frank, P. *Modern science and its philosophy.* Cambridge, Mass.: Harvard University Press, 1949.

Hall, C. S., & Lindzey, G. *Theories of personality* (2nd ed.). New York: Wiley & Sons, 1978.

Linton, R. *The cultural background of personality.* New York: Appleton-Century-Crofts, 1945.

McClelland, D. *Personality.* New York: Sloane, 1951.

Muller, F. M. *Biographies of words.* New York: Logmans, Green, 1888.

Nagel, E. *The structure of science: Problems in the logic of scientific explanation.* New York: Harcourt, Brace, & World, 1961.

Sarason, I. G. *Personality: An objective approach* (2nd ed.). New York: Wiley & Sons, 1972.

Taylor, J. A. A personality scale of manifest anxiety. *Journal of Abnormal and Social Psychology,* 1953, *48,* 285–290.

Thorndike, E. L. *Animal intelligence: Experimental studies.* New York: Macmillan, 1911.

PSYCHODYNAMIC
THEORIES

Psychoanalytic Theory:
Sigmund Freud

The history of world thought is dominated by those few creative geniuses who have reshaped human knowledge and values and hence the course of world events. Albert Einstein radically changed our understanding of the physical world. Karl Marx, as a socioeconomic evolutionist, forced many to rethink their understanding of the bases of society and the relationship of social class to economic laws. Charles Darwin showed the world that the human being is, in reality, an animal, representing merely a highly developed point on a lengthy evolutionary scale. Copernicus, a sixteenth-century astronomer, destroyed a centuries-old, worldwide belief that the earth is at the center of the universe.

Sigmund Freud stands equal with these and few other individuals in history in his impact on human thought. Before Freud most people believed that human behavior is governed by conscious processes and that individuals are basically rational, aware of the reasons for their actions, and function in a state of internal harmony. Freud demonstrated otherwise. The mind, he said, is like an iceberg, with only its tip—consciousness—showing above the surface. Below that surface, and forming the basis for most human behavior, is the unconscious mind, containing experiences and motivations which originate in childhood or earlier adult life and exist below the level of awareness. Moreover, Freud emphasized, much of our behavior is governed by irrationality and impulse, and we are often greatly influenced by strong but unconscious sexual and aggressive conflicts. The impact of Freud's creative new understanding of the functioning of human personality was tremendous. At first, he was treated as a professional and social outcast, whose radical new ideas were nontraditional and unacceptable. Like Copernicus and Darwin, Freud had delivered a powerful blow to the common beliefs about the human condition. Copernicus had shown that humans are not at the center of the universe; Darwin had theorized that the human is merely another animal, not an entirely unique biological being; and Freud had demonstrated that humans are impulsive, irrational, and conflicted, and not even aware of the true reasons for most of their behavior. The men who delivered these blows were no more quickly accepted than were the new ideas they created.

Despite the early ostracism he experienced, Freud, like Copernicus and Darwin, would have monumental impact on world thought. Indeed, Freud's theory reshaped many aspects of the social, cultural, and intellectual climate of the twentieth century. Some of his concepts have become firmly embedded in modern literature and popular culture, while others have been absorbed into the mainstream of psychiatric and psychological thought. As a result of Freud's work, numerous psychologists and philosophers have developed or modified related theories, incorporating Freud's concepts. Scientists have conducted a myriad of investigations to test his ideas and have thus contributed a massive new body of empirical knowledge. Sociologists, anthropologists, and historians, as well as psychologists and psychiatrists, have applied Freudian concepts in an attempt to understand phenomena in their respective fields. And "Freudianisms" have become a common part of our everyday language. We frequently speak of "Freudian slips," and "ego trips," of psychoanalyzing our friends and relatives, and of feeling defensive, conflicted, or anxious. Indeed, so pervasive is Freud's influence on our culture and language that it often goes unrecognized as such.

Before beginning to probe somewhat more deeply into the man and his theory, it should perhaps be noted that there are some rather serious obstacles confronting any attempt to provide a simple, straightforward, and totally accurate outline of Freudian personality theory. Freud's views on the origins, development, structure, and dynamics of personality are not readily accessible in a single handy source, but are scattered throughout his voluminous writings. Moreover, Freud constantly revised his ideas and recast his views in the light of newly acquired knowledge, with the result that conflicting, even contradictory, statements by Freud can be turned up on a wide variety of topics. Freud himself would probably have regarded this lack of internal consistency as evidence of the tentative, open-ended character of psychoanalytic theory, but it has proven to be a real trial for scholars seeking to formulate a cohesive, systematic version of Freudian personality theory.

Until he became incapacitated by the painful illness that eventually proved fatal,

Freud led a busy, active professional life and was a prolific author whose collected writings fill twenty-four volumes in the *Standard Edition*. Nearly a century's worth of further original scholarship and critical commentaries on psychoanalysis have generated an entire library of professional literature. We can do no more in a single chapter than selectively sample this body of work in order to present those elements of psychoanalysis which we consider essential for comprehending the fundamentals of Freudian personality theory. An obvious place to begin our discussion is with the theorist himself and those factors in his life that appear to have exerted important influences on his personal and professional development.

BIOGRAPHICAL SKETCH

Sigmund Freud was born on May 6, 1856, in Freiberg, a small town in the former Austrian province of Moravia, an area which is now part of Czechoslovakia. Freud was the progeny of his father's second marriage to a woman of half his age. The elder Freud, who was forty years old at the time Freud was born, was a none-too-successful wool merchant. Toward this rather strict and authoritarian person, the young Freud had ambivalent feelings of love and fear. But he was deeply devoted to his affectionate and protective mother—an attachment that may have had significant implications for his later development of the Oedipus theme as a part of the evolving system of psychoanalysis. About this relationship Freud later observed that, "A man who has been the indisputable favorite of his mother keeps for life the feeling of a conqueror, that confidence of success that often induces real success."

At the time Freud was four years old, his family moved to Vienna. In addition to the six children of his father's second marriage, Freud's large family included two older half-brothers, who were grown and had children of their own. The person with whom Freud had the closest ties, however, was a nephew of his own age. Freud later described him as the source of all his friendships and animosities. There was lively competition within the family for the attention and affection of the parents, and Freud experienced at firsthand the anger and resentment toward sibling rivals that figured so prominently in his theoretical interpretations of personality.

Freud was a precocious child. Despite the premium on space within the crowded household, a small room was found for Freud's exclusive use. It contained little more than a desk and narrow cot but boasted the luxury of an oil lamp, while the rest of the family had to make do with candles. His parents fostered Freud's intellectual development in every possible way, even denying his sisters the opportunity to study the piano, a common study for young women at that time, for fear the noise of their practicing might bother Freud's concentration. In high school, Freud was poor in mathematics and showed little interest in science but liked history and literature and excelled in languages. In addition to his knowledge of German and Hebrew, he attained a working command of Latin and classical Greek and acquired considerable fluency in French, Italian, Spanish, and English. He was especially fond of Shakespeare, whose works he had been reading in the original since he was eight years old.

When the time came to choose a career, Freud's decision to study medicine was prompted less by a desire to practice medicine than by his belief that the degree would allow him to pursue his new interest in scientific research. He entered medical school at the University of Vienna in 1873. For the next eight years, Freud's family scrimped and borrowed to put him through medical school. By the time he graduated in 1881, he had managed to gain a modest reputation as a physiological investigator under the direction of Claus and Brücke, who, nevertheless, advised him to abandon a career in scientific research. Perhaps a more persuasive argument for entering into medical practice, however, was Freud's difficult financial circumstance. He had become engaged to a young lady named Martha Bernays, but there were bleak prospects for an early marriage so long as Freud continued to subsist on loans from friends, relatives, and teachers. In a somewhat unchivalrous autobiographical passage, Freud blamed Martha for the fact that another investigator named Carl Koller, rather than he, received credit for discovering the local anesthetic properties of cocaine. We should record at this point that the man who was to be awarded the Goethe prize in 1930 had to pawn his watch and borrow enough money to get married.

Freud left the Institute of Cerebral Anatomy in 1881 and went into private practice as a clinical neurologist. During the next several years, he worked long hours with emotionally disturbed patients. He became friends with a colleague named Josef Breuer, who encouraged his patients to discuss their symptoms in a relaxed and permissive atmosphere. This "talking cure" represented a departure from the standard use of hypnosis as a technique in the treatment of emotional disorders. Freud grew frustrated with the limitations of hypnosis and spent a year of study in Paris with French psychiatrist, Jean Charcot, a leading expert on hypnosis. Freud's period of study with Charcot equipped him with a greater understanding of hypnosis in the treatment of the neuroses. He largely abandoned hypnosis in favor of Breuer's "talking cure," which became the principal basis for the development of Freud's *free association,* a technique for the exploration of unconscious processes and conflicts.

The years from 1890 to 1900 were lonely for Freud. Brücke became estranged because he was unable to accept Freud's views on the significance of sexual factors in the etiology of such emotional disorders as hysteria, although a series of three lectures that Freud delivered in 1896 on the same subject to the Doktor Kollegium, a group of general practitioners, was well received. He fared less well in the address he gave the following year to the Society of Psychiatry and Neurology in which he presented his theory on the role of parental seduction in neurosis. The chairman of this elite group, Krafft-Ebbing, dismissed the theory as "a scientific fairy tale." Even harsher criticisms were made by various medical and scientific organizations. Freud was vilified in the press. His doctrines were equated with pornography and seen as an attack upon the moral basis of Western civilization.

Freud stuck to his convictions with dogged persistence. He was helped by the support of a small but steadily growing band composed of young physicians and lay persons who listened to his ideas with increasing respect. In 1909, he was invited as a guest lecturer, along with Carl Jung of Switzerland, to the twenty-year founding of Clark University in Worcester, Massachusetts. Freud wrote, "As I stepped on to the platform at Worcester to deliver my 'Five Lectures on Psycho-Analysis,' it seemed like some incredible daydream: psycho-analysis was no longer a product of delusion, it had become a valuable part of reality." In the following year, further recognition came with the inauguration of the International Psycho-analytic Association.

In 1930, novelist Thomas Mann paid tribute to Freud as a leading influence in the history of modern thought. During that same year, the coveted Goethe prize was conferred upon Freud, an honor that he acknowledged was "the climax of my life as a citizen." In a few short years, the Nazi party and Adolf Hitler, implacable foes of everything Freud stood for, came to power in Germany, and their doctrines of "racial inferiority" became the prelude to the Holocaust. Freud remained in Vienna until the *Anschluss,* when the German armies marched in and put an end to Austrian independence. He shortly joined the ranks of other Jewish intellectuals who had been declared "enemies of the state." His ideas and views were officially proscribed, and the Nazi government conferred on him the honor of publicly burning his books. At the age of eighty-two, suffering from the constant pain of terminal cancer, he became a refugee from his native land. With the help of his long-time friend and later biographer, Ernest Jones, Freud found a haven in the city of London. There, in the modest home at 20 Maresfield Gardens where his daughter Anna continues to reside, he died on September 23, 1939. Stoic and uncomplaining, he worked at revising his theories until almost the very end.

BASIC CONCEPTS AND POSTULATES

It is, of course, impossible in a single textbook chapter to treat in detail all the many concepts, ideas, and applications of a theory that fills twenty-four volumes, even if one considers only the theorist's own writings. We will thus be forced to ignore most applications of Freudian theory and will be unable to trace the development of Freud's theoretical ideas, which changed periodically during the course of his career. Our efforts to understand the theory will be focused on a few major constructs and hypotheses and on several important extensions and applications of the theory.

A reasonably complete knowledge of basic Freudian theory can be acquired by understanding five major aspects of the theory. First, Freud emphasized the role of unconscious determinants of human behavior and showed how most major aspects of behavior are heavily influenced by motives of which we are unaware. A second central concept in the theory is that of the human being as an energy system in which all behaviors are a function of the ebb and flow of energy. Both physical and mental actions of all kinds require energy, and a limited quantity of energy is available to the individual at any given time. Third, the Freudian personality has a definite structure, and that structure involves three major constructs, the id, the ego, and the superego. Together, these three components of personality control human behavior. To understand the operation and interaction of these three structures, the levels of consciousness at which they exist, and their use of psychic energy is to understand largely how the Freudian personality functions. To broaden this understanding, it is helpful to know how the personality develops and what the implications of early life are for later life. Finally, we will see that anxiety and the defensive battle of the individual to fend off the anxiety are central to both the development and the functioning of personality. We must, therefore, know something about the sources of anxiety, its role in both normal and abnormal personalities, and the mechanisms used to defend against it. Once we have some understanding of these five major areas of the theory, we can treat briefly its applications to the understanding and treatment of neurosis.

THE UNCONSCIOUS

We all have consciousness or awareness of many things in our lives. You are aware right now that you are reading this book. If you pause briefly to inventory those additional aspects of life of which you are conscious, or can readily become conscious, the list is long: names and characteristics of family and friends; bodies of academic knowledge; rules, skills, and standings in various sports; technical skills that you have acquired; feelings of joy, anger, sadness, fear. The list goes on. Surely, this vast realm of awareness is the basis for most behavior. Your conscious feeling of anger leads you to strike out against another. An "A" in a difficult course causes you to feel joyful and celebrate. You choose a career in psychology, medicine, physics, or some other field for conscious, rational reasons of which you are aware. Are these correct statements of cause-effect relationships? No! Not according to Sigmund Freud. Consciousness, he said, despite its apparent scope, is only the tip of an iceberg. The bulk of those factors that influence important behaviors lies below the level of awareness in the *unconscious*. To understand the concept of unconscious motivation is to understand much of psychoanalytic theory.

A Pre-Freudian Unconscious

Freud was not the first to propose the existence of an unconscious psyche or mind. Schopenhauer (1819), in *The World as Will and Idea,* provided a version of the unconscious that is entitled to be regarded as modern. In Schopenhauer's philosophy, humans are seen as propelled by the urgings of the will, which corresponds to the unconscious. The principal components of the unconscious are instincts for self-preservation and sexual release, whose driving force is blindly irrational. Schopenhauer even noted the possible relationship of the unconscious to mental illness. In 1846, a book entitled *Psyche* by a physician named Carl G. Carus opened with the sentence: "The key to the understanding of the character of the conscious life lies in the region of the unconscious" (p. 1). Carus recognized the importance of the sexual functions and discussed some of the ways in which the unconscious is expressed in dreams. Von Hartman's *Philosophy of the Unconscious* (1868), published when Freud was twelve-years old, considered in detail no fewer than twenty-six aspects of unconscious mental activity. Other examples of the concept of unconscious functioning can be found before Freud, and, in fact, the concept was quite widely discussed by educated people prior to his work.

Freud's Concept of the Unconscious

That Freud did not "invent" or "discover" the unconscious need not detract from the significance of his contribution. He was the first theorist to develop a scientific, psychological theory of unconscious functioning and the first to make the unconscious a central component of the personality. He was also the first to integrate the concept of unconscious functioning into a much broader theory, with structural and dynamic components of the personality and their interaction carefully specified.

Freud proposed that there is a continuum of consciousness, ranging from acute awareness to deep unconsciousness. For conceptual convenience, Freud divided this continuum into three segments, the conscious, the unconscious, and the preconscious. In the schematic analogy of the psyche to an iceberg (Figure 2-1), only the smaller, *conscious* portion is visible. It contains everything of which we are aware at any given time and constitutes, for Freud, only one small part of our psychological life. Consciousness is unstable. Its contents change from moment to moment, and it is unimportant as a causal agent in behavior.

The *unconscious* contains the powerful drives which remain totally outside of awareness but are responsible for all important human behavior. Its contents are virtually barred from entrance into awareness, where they would constitute a real psychological danger to the individual. Only in a carefully masked, symbolic form can any materials from the unconscious ordinarily enter awareness. Nevertheless, the unconscious is the ultimate arbiter of all behavior—the repository of motives, wishes, desires, impulses, conflicts, processes, and dynamics that are presumed to constitute the mainsprings of human action. Behavior is not important in and of itself but only as a sign or symptom of unconscious functioning. The path between behavior or conscious thought and unconscious mental processes may be tortuous and difficult to understand, but it is nonetheless significant.

Between the conscious and the unconscious lies the preconscious, containing thoughts, memories, and perceptions that have minimal emotional significance and can, therefore, easily be brought into consciousness when they are made the focus of attention. When you are asked, for example, "What is your address?" you summon this information from the preconscious with no difficulty.

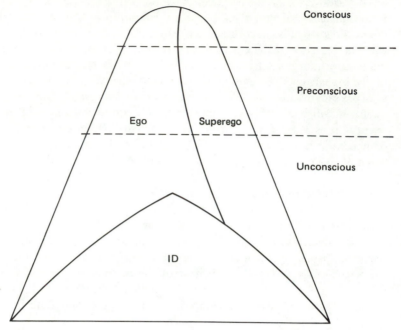

Figure 2-1 Levels of awareness and the structure of personality.

THE STRUCTURE OF PERSONALITY

Freud was a reasonably flexible theorist, willing to modify his own theory from time to time as he made new observations and reached new conclusions. His concept of a tripartite personality structure consisting of the three levels of consciousness outlined above was his focal theory only until about 1920. At that time, he revised the theory, hypothesizing a different three-part structure comprising the id, ego, and superego. He emphasized that these are hypothetical constructs, not actual structures in the brain. It should be noted that in proposing the new structure, Freud did not abandon his concept of unconscious motivation, and it can be seen in Figure 2-1 that there is an identifiable relationship between the dimension of consciousness and the new structural model of the psyche. The id is contained completely in the unconscious, while the ego and superego each have conscious, preconscious, and unconscious sectors. It is also important to note that there is a constant interaction, often involving conflict, among id, ego, and superego.

The Id

The id is present at birth and is the ultimate source of all psychic energy, even that which is later utilized by the other components of the personality. It is an extremely primitive structure and is unorganized, uninhibited, nonrational, and impulsive. It operates on the basis of the *pleasure principle,* which calls for the immediate reduction of any tension that may arise. The tensions arise from powerful drives, particularly sexual and aggressive drives, contained in the id and requiring gratification. Action to reduce these drives under the guidance of the pleasure principle is impulsive and indiscriminate, since the id is nonrational and amoral and does not experience fear.

Under the pleasure principle, tension is reduced using either reflex action or primary process. *Reflex action* involves the operation of an innate, automatic reflex mechanism to reduce some source of tension, such as blinking an eye or withdrawing a hand from a hot object. *Primary process* involves the formation of a mental image of some object known to satisfy a drive. A traveler stranded in the desert may eventually form an image of an oasis containing water, and this may temporarily satisfy the drive. The image is essentially a hallucination based on primary process. Psychotic hallucinations and dreams are other examples of this primitive form of drive satisfaction. Unfortunately, this method of satisfying needs is ultimately ineffective, since the id is incapable of distinguishing between the mental image of the satisfying object and the actual object itself. The person would literally die if he or she had to depend entirely on primary process to satisfy basic drives.

Ego

Effective satisfaction of important drives clearly requires some contact with external reality and some degree of logical reasoning or rationality. These are functions of the *ego,* which serves, in part, to satisfy the drives of the id. As we have seen, these impulses would lead to direct and immediate action with regard to consequences. The ego, however, acts to delay gratification of an id impulse until an appropriate object is located in the external environment. This delay function is termed the *reality principle.* It permits the realistic retrieval of actual objects to satisfy important drives and encourages the satisfaction of these drives without placing the individual in danger. There is thus, coupled with the reality principle, a *secondary process* on which the ego functions. This process involves the formulation of a plan of action, followed by the *reality testing* of this plan. For this reason, all cognitive abilities are under the control of the ego and available for use in secondary process. An an example of secondary process, the sexually aroused individual may carefully plan an approach to a particular member of the opposite sex, then test that plan. If it does not work well, it may be revised on future occasions.

The relationship of the ego to the id is, at best, a conflicted one. It derives its original existence from the id and continues to have as a major function the gratification of id impulses. It must also strive to prevent, or at least delay, the expression of id impulses which would otherwise endanger the individual physically or psychologically. It must thus selectively both block and satisfy the powerful drives of the id because its principal purposes are to keep the individual alive and healthy and to further the reproduction of the species.

Despite its conflicts with the id and, as we will see, with the superego, the ego also serves an integrative function in the personality. It mediates between the id and the superego and between each of these structures and external reality, attempting always to resolve conflicts, satisfy drives, and respond realistically and effectively to reality, while maintaining life.

Superego

The id and the ego account for the roles of biological drives and external reality in shaping our lives. What these constructs do not take into account is the influence of society on the individual. The superego performs this function. It is essentially an internalization of social and moral values learned primarily from the parents and forming an internal set of social controls over the behavior of the individual. In effect, the superego is an "in-dwelling parent."

The superego develops as the child inculcates, or introjects, social guidelines and structures. This learning process is a function of rewards and punishments by the parents for behavior. Basically, when the child is rewarded for an act, it tends to become part of the *ego ideal,* which consists of goals that the child may strive to achieve. Punishments, on the other hand, become the basis for the *conscience,* which defines for the individual those behaviors that are considered wrong or inappropriate. The emotional results of the operation of the superego are pride, when the ego ideal is satisfied, and guilt, when the conscience is violated. Given its moralistic and idealistic qualities, the superego attempts to impose its values on the other two psychic structures. It tries to block the powerful sexual and aggressive drives of the id, satisfaction of which often represents a violation of social mores. It also tends to block ego expression, since the reality striving of the ego is not necessarily always moral.

Intrapsychic Conflict

As we have already seen, the three psychic structures do not operate in isolation but rather interact continuously with one another. What, then, is the nature of this interaction? Freud's answer is that it is one characterized predominately by conflict among the three structures, termed *intrapsychic conflict.* The biological id strives constantly and impulsively to satisfy its drives, but to do so it must struggle with the reality and rationality of the ego and the morality of the superego. It should perhaps be emphasized that this intrapsychic conflict is characteristic of the normal personality, though certain aspects of conflict may also be responsible for the development of neurosis. As an example of conflict, consider the following: Hunger arouses tension in the id, which seeks immediate relief through the pleasure principle, delays eating (blocks id expression) until an appropriate food object is located. The superego may impose a further delay by dictating certain requirements (for example, no high calorie foods, no pork, no fish on Friday, no stealing of food). The conflict between the id and the other structures may, in this instance, be resolved when an appropriate object is located and consumed. More severe conflicts, however, may become an ongoing part of the unconscious personality.

ENERGY DYNAMICS AND THE INSTINCTS

One of the major issues in personality theory which we raised in Chapter 1 is the question of motivating or activating forces that drive the human organism and cause it to engage in behavior. Freud, in his theory of the id, ego, and superego, had a structure for the human personality but needed an explanation for behavior itself. What is it that activates the structure and allows it to function in such a way as to impel the human organism into overt behavior? He chose an energy model of motivation in which all activities are a function of the distribution, redistribution, and utilization of psychic energy. His energy theory grew out of the positivistic and deterministic philosophy of nineteenth-century science. In particular, Freud was heavily influenced by the theory of Ernst Brücke, a famous physiologist under whom he worked in medical school. Brücke, in turn, was the student of another famous physiologist, Johannes Muller, and as such had become acquainted with a fellow student of Muller's, the well-known physicist and physiologist Hermann von Helmholtz. Brücke and Helmholtz shared the view, a radical one at the time, that all active forces in the organism are physiochemical ones and that the ebb and flow of physical energy constitutes the best explanation for animal activity. Helmholtz published, in 1847, a famous paper on the conservation of energy, basically suggesting that energy is limited in quantity and is neither gained nor lost in a closed energy system. While the view was controversial in 1847, it had gained widespread acceptance by the time Freud entered Brücke's laboratory in 1876. Brücke taught Freud and Josef Breuer, another of his students, that metabolic processes provide physical energy, which is used for physical work, and that psychic energy derives from this physical energy to be used for mental activities.

Freud expanded upon the Brücke-Helmholtz theory and incorporated it into his overall theory of personality. He regarded the human body as a complex organic system that produces physical energy from the food it consumes and uses this energy to perform such functions as blood circulation, breathing, muscular exercise, and glandular activity; but the mind also performs a variety of functions, such as perceiving, thinking, and remembering, and these activities require psychic energy, differing in form, but not in kind, from physical energy.

Expanding upon the basic theory, Freud suggested that the human organism is an energy system that operates on the basis of two major principles, otherwise referred to as the first and second laws of thermodynamics. The first is the *law of energy conservation,* proposed earlier by Helmholtz and others, which holds that energy cannot be gained or lost from the total organism system, though it can be transformed from one state to another and can flow from one region of the energy system to another. An important derivative of the conservation principle is that the individual has a limited quantity of energy available for carrying out all activities. Thus, energy expended on one activity is temporarily gone from the system and cannot be expended upon another until it has been replenished through metabolic processes and sleep. For example, the mental energy you expend in studying for an exam diminishes your total energy supply and is not available when you turn to writing a paper for another course.

The second principle of the Freudian energy theory is the principle of equilibrium or entropy, otherwise known as the *second law of thermodynamics*. This law holds that an energy system, such as the human psyche, seeks a state of equilibrium or balance. In Freudian theory, this balance is achieved only through death.

Energy and the Instincts

If psychic energy can be transformed into physical energy and physical energy into psychic energy, there must be a mechanism for linking the two forms; that mechanism is the instinct. An instinct is basically an innate psychological excitation corresponding to some physical source of activation within the body. The somatic excitation, which originates in some temporary or recurrent tissue condition, is termed a *need,* while a mental excitation which represents this need psychologically is termed a *wish.*

The need–wish sequence is subsumed in the single term *Trieb,* which is literally translated as drive, suggesting that the wish or instinct supplies the propulsive force of personality and behavior. The drive or instinct is not the underlying tissue condition but rather the physical energy generated by that need and transformed into psychic energy as a mental representation or wish. The long-distance jogger, for example, may experience some tissue deprivation of water, leading to a thirst drive, which is mentally represented as a desire for water.

The Instinct Model

The instinct or drive model is a centrally important feature of Freudian theory. Freud held that all psychic energy—the driving force of life—is contained in and controlled by the instincts and further that *all behavior is influenced by the operation of the instincts.*

The instinct model is basically a *tension-reduction model* of motivation, similar to that seen in some modern drive and reinforcement theories. The instinct theory holds that the activation of a bodily need and its corresponding psychological wish cause a motivating state of tension that the organism must strive to reduce. The tension can be reduced by satisfying the need, which may, however, later recur. Tension, and the requirement that it be reduced, thus motivates all human behavior. The tension-reduction model is more formally expressed in Freud's definition of four major characteristics of an instinct: the source, aim, object, and impetus. The *source* is the physiological condition or need, such as the tissue changes caused by water deprivation. The *aim* is always to reduce the excitation arising from the activated need. The aim can be achieved by obtaining an *object,* which may be anything in the environment, including another person, or even something within the individual's own body, that satisfies the need. If the thirst need is activated through water deprivation, and the aim is reduction of thirst, a glass of water may be the object of the instinct. The *impetus* is basically the strength of the drive and is related to the amount of deprivation that has been experienced.

Given these characteristics of the instinct model, the operation of the instinct is straightforward. When a need arises, its aim, reduction, is immediately established, and it might be noted that the source and aim of any instinct always remain constant. The impetus of the instinct, which varies from time to time, influences the amount of effort to be devoted to reducing the drive. The object is sought, found, and consumed through the expenditure of psychic energy. The investment of energy in an object for purposes of satisfying a need is termed a *cathexis.* A simple example of object cathexis would be the expenditure of energy to obtain a drink from the refrigerator. More important, people may be cathected as objects, as when the young child becomes emotionally attached to its mother, forming a strong cathexis. In addition, energy may be invested and cathexis established with regard to a variety of aspects of life, such as a career, sporting activities, strong ideals, and the like. While a cathexis is formed by the ego in order to satisfy an instinctual drive, an *anticathexis* involves the investment of psychic energy to block the expression of an id instinct. The gratification of the instinct is thus prevented, and a conflict between the id and either the ego or superego exists. Anticathexis is the mechanism involved in the conflicts noted above in our discussion of the structural model.

The Major Instincts: Life and Death

Freud did not fix a total number of instincts. However, he did hypothesize two major groups of instincts, termed *Eros* and *Thanatos,* the life instincts and death instincts. The life instincts include those involved in individual and collective survival, such as hunger, thirst, and sex. The energy of the life instincts is termed *libido* and, like energy, more generally, it can be used in the cathexes and anticathexes established for the purpose of satisfying the life instincts. *Sex* is the life instinct to which Freud attributed the greatest importance in personality development. It is frequently involved in important conflicts and is the basis for some major cathexes that help to shape the personality.

The death instinct concept arose from Freud's view that the energy system of the living organism constantly seeks a state of equilibrium, which can only be achieved through death. Freud thus held that "the goal of all life is death" (Freud 1955b, p. 38). The importance of the death instinct lies in the nature of its manifestations in psychoanalytic theory. It is seen as underlying all aggressive and destructive forms of behavior, such as murder, suicide, hostility, cruelty, verbal abuse, and physical aggression. The appalling loss of 30 million lives in World War I convinced Freud that the aggressive drive, the derivative of the death instincts, is equally as significant in motivating human behavior as are the life instincts.

Instincts and the Adult Personality: Displacement

The adult personality is clearly complex and multifaceted, and human behavior, even within the same individual, is extremely varied. Yet, we have said that all behavior derives from the instincts, which may initially appear to operate in a simple and primitive form.

The apparent gap between the simplicity and primitiveness of the instinct model and the complexity and intricacy of the adult personality is bridged by the concept of *displacement*. The initial object of the infant's thirst drive may be milk, which satisfies the drive and reduces the need. Later, however, we find that the same individual can satisfy thirst with water, beer, soft drink, wine, and a variety of other liquids. Each of these has become an object choice of the thirst instinct through displacement, which occurs whenever the original object choice is blocked. If the infant cannot obtain milk, the infant will drink water, and, by the same process, other liquids. More important, the object choices of any instinct may be multiple and varied because displacement has occurred. Sexual needs, for example, can be gratified by heterosexual, homosexual, or autosexual activities. Moreover, sexual needs may be diverted into entirely different channels and, in that way, satisfied through what superficially appear to be nonsexual activities. The widely varied preferences, interests, and activities of the adult can be seen as largely a product of object displacements. The adult behavior is still motivated by the same instincts that drive the child, and these instincts have the same sources and aims as they do in the child. Only the object choices have changed.

Energy and Structure

The energy model and the structural model combine to provide a functioning personality in Freudian theory. All energy is originally contained in the id but is eventually distributed to the other two psychic structures as well. The three structures are seen as constantly in conflict and hence competing for energy, since energy is needed to carry out any activity. Basically, energy means "power," and thus the structure with the greatest amount of energy will be the most powerful in the personality. If the id had the most energy, behavior may be dominated by nonrational, impulsive acts. With the superego in control, highly moralistic behavior patterns may result. A dominant ego, so long as it is not too dominant, may lead to realistic behavior involving the regular and rational satiation of major instincts, while preventing the individual from entering into the dangers that might be caused by the discharge of some impulses. Freud hypothesized that in the normal adult personality the ego is the most powerful of the three structures, though it is by no means omnipotent.

Ego dominance is not an easy state to achieve, since all energy is originally contained in the id. The ego derives its original energy from the id through a process known as *identification*. It will be recalled that the id attempts to achieve drive satisfaction by forming an image of the needed object. The ego is capable of matching this image with a real object in the external world, and this matching process is termed identification. The ego then proceeds to cathect the object and hence satisfy the drive. Since this form of secondary process satisfaction takes place in the context of ongoing conflict among the psychic structures, the more difficult and dangerous impulses are blocked through anticathexis.

THE DEFENSE MECHANISMS OF THE EGO

We have noted that the ego serves both to satisfy and to block the impulses of the id and that it also serves to integrate personality. A further function of the ego, and one so important that it deserves separate treatment, is to defend against anxiety. When a person feels fearful, anxious, or "uptight" and there is no immediate way to cope with this feeling, there is a tendency to defend against the anxiety. The process of defense is a centrally important and complex one in the psychoanalytic personality and is theoretically under the control of the ego.

Anxiety

By the time most people reach adulthood, they have acquired at least some familiarity with the experience of anxiety. While individuals may differ with one another as to their exact feelings, they are likely to agree that anxiety is an unpleasant affective state characterized by nervousness and apprehension and that it has some features in common with fear. Unlike fear, which generally has a specific source, anxiety is vague, diffuse, and lacking in focus toward a particular object or situation. The person who experiences anxiety may claim that he or she feels frightened or uptight without having a rational reason for the fear.

Freud also regarded anxiety as a state or condition which possesses a special "character of unpleasure" with a particular quality of its own. Freud saw in the trauma of birth the prototype of all later anxiety experiences. As Schultz (1976) observes:

> The fetus in its mother's womb is in the most stable and secure of worlds, where every need is satisfied without delay. Suddenly, at birth, the organism finds itself thrust into a hostile environment. It must at once begin to adapt to reality, since its instinctual demands may not always be immediately met. The newborn's nervous system, immature and ill prepared, is suddenly bombarded with intense and diverse sensory stimuli. Consequently, the infant engages in massive motor movements, heightened breathing, and increased heart rate. (p. 27)

Birth trauma (the Greek word for "wound") constitutes the individual's first experience with anxiety. It establishes the pattern of feelings and reactions that will occur in the future whenever the individual encounters danger. At such times, the adult, regardless of age, experiences once again something of the demoralizing effects of infantile helplessness. One of Freud's followers, Otto Rank, was so impressed by the implications of this notion of birth trauma that he made it the key concept in his own theory of personality.

In his earlier theoretical formulations, Freud believed that anxiety resulted from the discharge of repressed somatic sexual tensions (libido). When libidinal excitation produces mental images that are perceived as dangerous, these ideas are excluded from consciousness by means of repression. The libidinal energy thus blocked from normal expression accumulates and is automatically transformed into anxiety or into symptoms that are anxiety equivalents. Freud later modified this interpretation in favor of a more generalized conception of anxiety whereby its functional utility to the ego was emphasized. Anxiety became the signal indicating the presence of danger. He distinguished three types of anxiety: reality anxiety, neurotic anxiety, and moral anxiety.

Reality, or objective, anxiety is roughly synonymous with fear. Its basis is external dangers in the real world: a bolt of lightning, hurricane winds, a robber with a gun, the voice on the telephone that warns of a bomb concealed somewhere on the premises. The unpleasantness of the resulting anxiety reaction, coupled with cues from its source, are generally sufficient to mobilize us into fleeing the dangerous situation or making some effort to protect ourselves from the threat posed by the situation. Reality anxiety serves the rational and functional purpose of guiding our behavior in response to a real external danger.

Neurotic anxiety, like objective anxiety, is characterized by feelings of apprehension and physiological arousal, but the source that evokes this reaction is internal rather than external. In essence, neurotic anxiety is the historical product of an aversive conditioning process which involves instinctual impulses and repression and commonly occurs in childhood. The sequence of events is represented by the paradigm shown in Figure 2-2. Since most of the cues associated with the

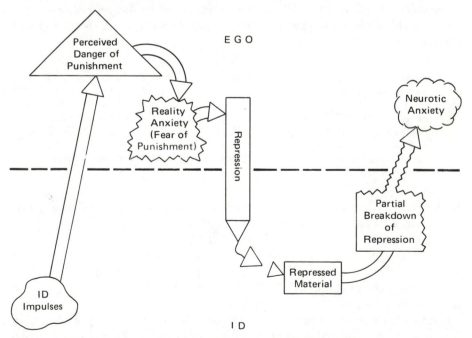

Figure 2-2 Freud's conception of the origins of neurotic anxiety.

punished impulses remain repressed, neurotic anxiety is experienced as "object-less," or, as in the case of the phobias, the relationship between the object that is feared and the original danger situation is not consciously recognized.

For Freud, anxiety is the fundamental phenomenon and the focal problem of neurosis. For the psychodynamic theorist, normal anxiety and neurotic anxiety are qualitatively different phenomena. According to May (1950):

> *Normal anxiety is, like any anxiety, a reaction to threats to values the individual holds essential to his existence as a personality; but normal anxiety is that reaction which (1) is not disproportionate to the objective threat, (2) does not involve repression or other mechanisms of intrapsychic conflict, and . . . (3) does not require neurotic defense mechanisms for its management, but can be confronted constructively on the level of conscious awareness or can be relieved if the objective situation is altered. (p. 194)*

Neurotic anxiety, according to this view, connotes a state of fear that is disproportionate to the precipitating cause of the fear or that exists without any discernible cause.

Moral anxiety, the third type, represents the pangs of conscience. The result of conflict between id and superego—between a forbidden instinctual impulse and moral inhibition and constraint—moral anxiety may reflect some basis in reality. If the individual has been punished in the past for violating the prohibitions of a moral code, he or she risks the possibility of further punishment. The feelings of shame and guilt thus serve adjustive functions.

It is clear that the three types of anxiety have different sources. Reality anxiety arises from stimuli in the external environment as perceived and interpreted by the ego. Moral anxiety or guilt is a product of the superego, and neurotic anxiety results from the operation of the id. It is important to note, however, that all three forms of anxiety are *felt* in the ego and that it is, therefore, the ego that must deal with the anxiety. It is also essential to understand that the extremely unpleasant state of vague fear that Freud termed anxiety is a powerful driving force in the personality. It is a major form of tension and motivation and, as such, requires that some action be taken to reduce it.

Mechanisms of Defense

When confronted with the threats to stability and integrity that are signaled by anxiety, the ego can either act to cope directly with the anxiety or can defend against it. If the source of the threat is some identifiable external stimulus, the ego can often cope with the anxiety by directly attacking or fleeing from this source. When, however, the anxiety arises from internal superego or id mechanisms, it is less susceptible to direct attack or coping and is more likely to trigger the operation of what Freud called the *mechanisms of defense*. These mechanisms operate either to distort the anxiety-producing impulse in such a way as to reduce its threat or to block the expression of the impulse entirely.

While there are a number of defenses, some of which we will define specifically, all share two major characteristics. They function entirely on the *unconscious* level, such that the individual never consciously decides to use a defense, and they deny, falsify, or *distort reality* to some degree. It should also be noted, that defenses are a part of the operation of the *normal* personality, though they are also seen in neurosis.

Repression. The most basic means by which the ego seeks to control id impulses is repression, the defense mechanism that operates to exclude from consciousness any dangerous impulses or thoughts. Through repression, the primitive impulse is forced back into the unconscious, and the delicate balance between the id and ego is thereby maintained. But the repressed idea or impulse is not completely eliminated; it makes continual efforts to return to consciousness via such other avenues as dreams and slips of the tongue. In a major work entitled *The Psychopathology of Everyday Life* (1914), Freud provided a wealth of examples of how apparently innocuous occurrences, such as the young woman with severe sexual conflicts who starts out to say "umbilical cord" and says, instead, "um*biblical* cord," reflect the twofold presence of the repressed idea or impulse and the partially failed repressive defense. Examples of the selective forgetting caused by repression are common. The college student may repeatedly forget where she has put her book or notes for the difficult, required math course she is taking. The businessman may have great difficulty recalling the details of a meeting with the boss in which he was criticized or fired. Or the individual having financial problems may have difficulty locating his or her checkbook on numerous occasions.

Freud believed that repression was basic to the operation of all other defense mechanisms. But the precariousness of the repressive defense means that other defensive efforts are required to assist the ego in its efforts at anxiety reduction.

Rationalization. This defense mechanism involves explaining unacceptable behavior in terms of some personally or socially acceptable motive, or, in general, making excuses to justify unacceptable behavior. The student who blames his or her poor grade on an incompetent teacher or a badly written textbook may be making an accurate and objectively supportable appraisal; on the other hand, this assessment may simply be a rationalization used to account for the failure. It is important to note that these rationalizations, like other defenses, are formulated at an unconscious level. The student does not make a conscious decision to distort the basis for the failure and is perhaps even less aware of the distortion than others who hear the account.

Sublimation. An individual may express an unacceptable motive by substituting socially and personally acceptable behavior for the direct expression of the motive. Thus, dancing might be considered a sublimation of sexual motivation, and attending hockey games or boxing matches might substitute for the direct expression of aggression. Such substitutions can be quite adaptive. Freud considered that one of the requirements for developing into a mature, responsible adult was the learning of effective sublimations for basic instinctual drives.

Displacement. Many motives do not possess a single goal but may have a hierarchy of goals. A motive is said to be displaced when a goal lower in the hierarchy is substituted for a higher goal. An individual who becomes angry at a police officer who is issuing a citation for a moving violation would surely be better off seeking another target; it may be, for example, the clerk at the checkout counter in the supermarket who would feel the brunt of displaced aggression. An eighteen-month-old child who was well known to one of the authors exhibited what seemed to be displacement by dunking a baby doll in the toilet not long after his new baby sister came home from the hospital. (He also rationalized this behavior by claiming that he was bathing the baby).

Compensation. Compensation is another form of substitution in which some personal shortcoming or inadequacy is overcome by intense efforts to become successful in a different or allied field of endeavor. Hence, a person who always wanted to excel at sports but was lacking in athletic prowess might become a famous sports commentator. Compensation, therefore, may have adaptive properties to the extent that it provides the motivation for becoming successful in some particular field. On the other hand, it can be seriously maladaptive in its consequences if the chosen field is equally unattainable for the individual in terms of basic competency. A person who experiences difficulties with abstract reasoning is ill advised to compensate by trying to become a successful mathematician; and a tone-deaf individual should avoid seeking a career as an opera singer (although such a handicap might not rule out success as a "rock" performer!).

Reaction Formation. An individual may defend against objectionable ideas or impulses by giving strong expression to opposite ideas or impulses. For instance, a person who is threatened on the unconscious level by the allure and fascination of pornography may become an avid supporter of censorship, or one who is fearful of losing in competitive situations may seek a career as a social activist working for the reform or overthrow of capitalism. Obviously, not all advocates of censorship or all opponents of the competitive aspects of capitalism adopt their positions because of reaction formation, but Freud believed that many such motives were actually defenses against anxiety.

Projection. In projection, a person defends against the recognition of unacceptable ideas, impulses, or personal characteristics in himself or herself by attributing them to others. Someone who harbors unacceptable feelings of hostility may deal with them by *projecting* these feelings upon colleagues, friends, or even family members, so that the hostility becomes justified as a reaction to someone else's (projected) hostility. (On an international note, Germany went to war in 1914 because the Kaiser claimed that his nation was "encircled" by enemies, a rationale that led historians to assert that there are no aggressive wars—only defensive wars.) Extreme forms of projection were considered by Freud to be the pathogenic factor in paranoid disturbances, leading to delusional beliefs of conspiracies, murder plots, and the like.

Identification. In identification, one adopts (interiorizes) the characteristics of an individual or individuals perceived as being more powerful, successful, or otherwise desirable than oneself. There is frequently a competitive aspect to this situation, that is, the weaker person attains a goal vicariously, through the person with whom he or she identifies. Freud believed that little boys were sexually attracted toward their mothers but that, rather than express this motive directly, they identified with their fathers, who were presumably seen as overwhelmingly powerful and threatening competitors. Through identification, however, the child was able to participate vicariously in the sexual favors accorded the father. Freud regarded identification as a crucially important factor in personality development because it is the means by which the child acquires adult behavior.

By means of these and other defense mechanisms, the ego attempts to keep the anxiety that is caused by emerging id impulses within tolerable limits. If the ego is successful in this task and instinctual energy has been displaced into socially acceptable and creative channels, personality matures normally in the Freudian view. If, however, the ego functions in a faulty manner or the displacement is not socially acceptable, Freud viewed this as a pathological process leading to neurotic or even psychotic behavior.

PSYCHOSEXUAL DEVELOPMENT

Freud conceived the development of each individual as dependent upon three principal sets of factors: (1) innate instinctual forces; (2) biologically determined developmental stages; and (3) environmental influences. Although all three sources of influence are important, the central factor in the human developmental process, as the term "psychosexual" implies, is the sex instinct. Implicit in this conceptualization is the assumption that development proceeds from the general to the specific. This progression means that children are *polymorphous perverse,* that is, they can derive pleasure from any bodily activity, but that this diffuse, and undifferentiated libidinal reactivity becomes successively concentrated within a particular area with the passage of time. Eventually, all sexual activity becomes subordinate to genital primacy.

As the infant matures, the sex instinct moves from one area of the body to another, causing the occurrence of a series of stages, each denoted by the primary erogenous zone that constitutes the major area for sexual satisfaction during that phase. During the pregenital phases of psychosexual development, the sexual life of the child represents a "series of independent activities of single-component impulses each seeking pleasure in a bodily organ" (Wolman 1960, p. 231). According to this scheme, psychosexual development can be divided into three periods: infantile sexuality (from birth to approximately five years), latent phase, and puberty. Infantile sexuality can further be divided into the oral, anal, and phallic periods, the latter culminating in the Oedipus complex, the "family romance" in which the child wishes to have intimate relations with the parent of the opposite sex and harbors antagonism toward the parent of the same sex.

The Neonate

Birth is a traumatic experience, the prototype of all later feelings of anxiety. The blissfully mindless nirvana of uterine existence is shattered; the infant is confronted within and without by stimuli which are beyond its capacity to handle. Nutrient processes which were formerly accomplished without discomfort or effort now become dependent upon the help of others. Cold, hunger, and pain occur and are followed by gratification, leading to the first relations of the infant and the world. The repetitive Freudian cycle of tension and tension reduction has begun. The maternal breast or the bottle are the first pleasurable objects the infant encounters, and the zone of pleasurable contact is the mouth and lips. Consequently, the oral stage of libidinal development is the first phase in the sequence, and it begins almost immediately after birth.

The Oral Stage

Libidinization of the mouth and lips comes about, in part, through the association between nursing and being fed and constitutes the basis for the *oral* stage. Manifestations of tension, such as restlessness and crying, quickly subside when the nipple is introduced. The expression of perfect contentment that the infant exhibits will never be regained in life, according to Freud, until the first experience of orgasm.

Actually, the preceding description is rather inferential, since Freud never devoted extensive attention to the specific mechanism by which oral sensations acquire pleasurable character in their own right. Although he maintained that the development of pleasure was anaclitic (that is, dependent) upon eating, he also seemed to believe that the oral stage of development was, to some extent, genetically determined. Sucking for nourishment provides the focal point of sexual pleasure in orality and constitutes the prototype for every type of sexual gratification noted in later life. Satisfaction is shown in the tendency of the infant to suck indiscriminately on any object, including its own thumb, and to engage in other types of spontaneous oral activity. The pleasurable character of the activity is also revealed by the decrease in restlessness that even nonnutritive sucking affords.

The child in early infancy does not discriminate between sensations within the body and those from without. Moreoever, it lacks comprehension of the relationship of its own behavior to the rewards that follow its occurrence. In the absence of such comprehension, actions are performed blindly, and the apparent ability of some actions to bring about gratification assumes a magical power in the child's perceptions. The term *primary narcissism* was introduced by Freud to refer to the absence of an external dimension in the psychological world of the infant and the total identification of pleasure with its own sensations. The oral stage ends with weaning, roughly at the end of the first year of life.

The Anal Stage

A shift from the mouth and lips to the anal area as the principal erogenous zone marks the transition from the oral to the *anal* stage of psychosexual development. Freud believed that this change is universal and occurs as a function of maturation. The pleasure experienced by the child and marking the anal zone as erogenous lies in the retention and expulsion of feces and can be increased by learning to delay bowel movements. Later psychoanalytic theorists have been disposed to interpet the oral-anal transition as due more to a shift of parental concern to matters of continence and cleanliness training than to the inexorable workings of maturation, but there is still agreement with Freud's contention that toilet training exercises a significant influence upon personality development. As Baldwin (1967) notes:

> *The mechanisms by which the experiences of the anal period affect personality are fundamentally similar to the mechanisms described for the oral period. Because of the interaction of the child's source of pleasure, his level of ego development, and the common experiences that occur during toilet training, various types of dispositions are initiated at this stage which shape the future development of the personality. (p. 359).*

The Phallic Stage

At about the age of four, the child's focus of libidinal gratification shifts to the genital area. This stage, therefore, has been designated the *phallic* period (from the Greek word *phallus,* meaning penis). This phallic, or early genital stage, confronts the child with a new set of problems and challenges. Chief among them is the *Oedipus complex* and its resolution.

As Freud indicates in *Beyond the Pleasure Principle,* his conceptualization of the universal "family romance," plus the name Oedipus complex and its derivation, came largely from the work of the philosopher Schopenhauer. Freud's theory depicts an eternal triangle, consisting of the child, the love object, who is the parent of the opposite sex, and the feared and hated rival, who is the parent of the same sex. Like the original characters in the play by Sophocles, the principals of this drama are compelled, not by the Fates but by biogenetic determinism, to portray their assigned roles: in the case of the boy, to lust after the mother and to hate the father; and in the case of the girl, to wish to submit to the sexual embrace of the father and to reject the mother. To be more specific, the boy initially adopts the mother as a love object and behaves seductively toward her. At the same time, he recognizes his father as a rival for the mother's affections and comes to fear that his father will punish him by cutting off his penis. This *castration anxiety* is a powerful drive and causes the boy to repress his sexual desire for the mother and identify with his father. Through identification, the boy begins to take on some of his father's behaviors and values, contributing to his sex-role identification as a male.

The female counterpart to the Oedipus complex is the *Electra complex*. The Electra complex begins as the girl discovers that she lacks a penis and wishes that she had one, a desire which Freud termed *penis envy*. Blaming her mother for the lack of a penis, she becomes hostile toward the mother and develops a sexual attraction toward the father, who has the desired organ. It takes little in-depth analysis of this theory to understand why Karen Horney took serious issue with it and why advocates for the equality of women think Freud is the penultimate male chauvinist.

According to Freud, the phallic stage is one of the most important in the formation of personality. It is at this time that the castration fear of the male and the penis envy of the female appear. It is also during this stage that the superego, said to be the heir of the Oedipus complex, comes to full formation. The child, denied direct biological fulfillment, typically solves problems by incorporating perceived parental attitudes as his or her own. The superego thus takes over control that was formerly external.

The Latent Phase

The turbulence of the phallic stage, with its castration anxieties, libidinal attachment to the same sex parent, and the introjection of the parental injunctions which form the kernel of the superego, is succeeded by the relative tranquility of the *latency* phase. The powerful libido, so direct and obvious in the phallic stage, is sublimated, and sexual energy is redirected into nonsexual, substitute activities. During this period of psychosexual development, there is a tendency to seek affectional attachments with members of one's own sex, and some of these may achieve a rather high level of emotional intensity, particularly among girls. There is also a continuation of some of the problems implicit in the Oedipal situation. For example, rebelliousness toward authority is seen as symptomatic of an underlying dependence and independence conflict with origins that antedate even the phallic stage.

Adolescence and the Genital Stage

With the psychological changes that usher in puberty, there is a reactivation of some features of the Oedipal period, and the *genital* stage begins. The developmental task of this period becomes the redirection of libido from its former relation to the parents to an external love object of the same sex. Also, there must occur an appropriate and effective resolution of conflict with the parent of the same sex.

The boy must overcome the exclusively male identification formed during the latency phase, during which libido was directed toward peer group members. Freud was of the opinion that boys typically undergo a period of homoerotic fixation upon some male figure—the hero worship which constitutes the male counterpart of the schoolgirl crush upon a classmate or teacher. These phenomena, in Freud's opinion, mark the return of sexual feelings repressed during the latency phase and provide a transition to heterosexual attachment.

The genital phase represents the culmination of psychosexual development. It is a confluence of sexuality and affection; the two merge and become one in the genitally mature individual. If adolescence, for Freud, was a matter of learning to be in love, the "final examination" for that learning is provided by the success or failure to achieve true genital sex and maturity. Love, marriage, and procreation were, in the Freudian view, the criteria for pass-fail.

Early Development and the Adult Personality

Freud was a strong advocate of the position that early developmental processes and events heavily predispose and influence the nature of the adult personality. The psychosexual staging process itself is based primarily on biological factors and is cross-culturally invariant in its sequencing, but the social experiences to which the child is exposed at each stage leave permanent impressions and thereby predispose the nature of the adult personality. A variety of character types are possible, depending upon significant events occurring during particular stages of development. *Fixation* at a particular stage occurs when developmental problems of that stage remain unresolved. *Regression* involves the reversion to an earlier developmental stage, a phenomenon that can occur when an individual is placed under stress. When fixations and regressions occur, the individual's behavior will be characterized by some of the attitudes and behaviors of the earlier stage. Frustration of the child's needs or overindulgence of those needs may be bases for fixations and regressions.

Each stage of development may serve as a basis for certain kinds of adult character types. For example, the sarcastic, argumentative, exploitative character of the *oral sadistic* adult results from frustration of the infant's need to chew and bite during the first year of life. Alteratively, an *oral passive* personality, involving a substantial degree of dependency on others during adulthood, may result from too much or too little stimulation during the oral stage. The *anal aggressive* personality involves destructiveness and cruelty and results from excessive rewards given during the anal stage for having regular bowel movements, while an *anal retentive* character results when toilet training is unusually harsh and involves such adult characteristics as stinginess and overconcern with orderliness and punctuality. Phallic fixation in the woman may result in a seductive, flirtatious approach to men, while a similar fixation in the male may produce a vain, overambitious individual. Finally, the *genital* character is, above all, a mature, responsible, heterosexual individual, who is an active and effective problem solver. This may sound like the ideal personality and, in Freudian theory, it is.

THE FREUDIAN VIEW OF NEUROSIS

While Freud's theory is a general theory of personality, his central clinical interest lay in the treatment of neurotic patients, and it was largely from his observations of these patients that his theory developed.

The term neurosis denotes a wide variety of behavior patterns, and there is not complete agreement on its meaning. It is basically a disorder in which the individual experiences high levels of continuing or recurrent anxiety and adopts defensive behavior patterns in order to reduce this anxiety. The result is a maladaptive life style, with symptoms ranging from anxiety panic attacks to depressions, phobias, compulsions, and hysteria.

In Freudian theory, the neurosis basically results from a severe conflict between the id and the ego, a conflict which invariably begins in early childhood. In fact, Freud held that neuroses are basically acquired only during childhood, even though the actual symptoms may not appear until adulthood.

While neuroses are viewed as disorders of the ego, they begin with activities in the id. Powerful aggressive or, more commonly, sexual impulses originating in the id seek direct and immediate satisfaction. Expression of these impulses may lead to punishment and hence anxiety, and the child may come to fear that parental love will be lost if these impulses continue to be discharged. As a result, the ego defenses are brought into play to strongly repress the dangerous id drives. If not allowed to discharge, the unconscious id impulses become increasingly powerful and more difficult to repress. A kind of pressure-cooker situation is set up in which the psychic energy of the id instincts exerts constant pressure for expression, while the ego employs its defensive energy to "keep the lid on." Partial breakdowns of repression may result in the experience of neurotic anxiety in consciousness, the anxiety serving as a warning signal to the impending danger of impulse expression. The impulses may continue to break through the defenses in a somewhat disguised form, so that the defensive behaviors are symbolic of the basis for the neurosis. For example, neurotic compulsive cleanliness may represent an attempt to deal with strong, repressed, anal impulses, while a neurotic (phobic) fear of snakes may signal a powerful underlying sexual conflict. One task of the psychoanalyst is to interpret the symbolic meaning of the symptoms as a partial means of understanding the basis for the neurosis and the best approach to treatment.

PSYCHOANALYTIC TREATMENT

Treatment of neurosis (and other disorders) is both a basis for and a product of psychoanalytic theory. Basically, the theory suggests that neurosis results from early childhood experience, develops over a long period of time, and is rooted in the unconscious. As a result, psychoanalytic therapy attempts to trace the unconscious bases for the neurosis back to childhood, and the therapy may be a long-term undertaking. The patient may be treated several times each week (even daily) for a number of years. The lengthy nature of a typical analysis reflects the goal of the therapy, which is to allow the patient to become consciously aware of his or her motives, thereby strengthening the ego, modifying the structure of personality, and changing the disturbing behavior patterns.

One of the major techniques used by the analyst is *free association*. In this approach, the patient is urged to talk freely, say whatever comes to mind, and hold back nothing. To this end, he or she is instructed to lie on a couch or sit in a chair and relax, eliminating all conscious screening and controls and reporting everything that enters awareness. Free association permits the disclosure of unconscious material, eventually revealing to analyst and patient the bases for the neurosis. In addition, it permits the analyst to interpret the patient's resistance to the expression of certain thoughts. The patient may hesitate, have his or her mind "go blank," or otherwise reveal resistance to the revelation of certain unconscious materials. Other signs of resistance are tardiness in arriving for sessions, finding excuses for missing sessions, or actually raising the possibility of terminating therapy early in the process. Resistances help the analyst understand those unconscious areas in which the patient is having the greatest difficulty.

A second approach used in psychoanalysis is the *interpretation of dreams.* Freud believed that repressed id impulses or conflicts, too dangerous to escape beyond the ego defenses during waking hours, are expressed in dreams. Even in the dream, however, these threatening impulses are available only in heavily disguised forms, such that the manifest content of the dream (that is, what the dreamer experiences) is only a symbolic representation of the underlying id conflict, which is termed the *latent content.* Freud interpreted dreams by understanding the latent content represented by certain dream symbols. For example, the penis is represented by poles, candles, or snakes, the vagina by pockets, tunnels, and the like, and sexual intercourse by staircases or ladders. The importance of dream interpretation is that it provides another inroad to the contents of the individual's unconscious.

Although psychoanalysis involves a variety of additional techniques and phenomena, we will discuss here only one further concept, that of *transference.* In transference strong feelings of love or hate, originally directed toward a parent or someone else in the patient's earlier life, will be displaced to the analyst. The patient's strong feelings toward the analyst are interpreted as transference and seen as representing important unconscious feelings toward another person. While a transference can be expressed directly to the analyst (for example, "I think I am falling in love with you," or "Why don't you ever pay attention to me?"), it can also occur in more disguised form in dreams or free association. Transference helps th analyst understand more about the patient's unconscious functioning and eventually aids the patient in gaining insight into important unconscious motives relating to his or her current functioning. As a result, transference is seen as essential to successful therapy, and the analyst encourages its development.

THE THEORY IN EMPIRICAL CONTEXT

Some aspects of nineteenth-century science were quite precise, and the experimental method was well known and widely used. Moreover, while undergoing his medical training, Freud was clearly exposed to the scientific method and had more than adequate opportunity to become an experimental scientist under the tutelage of Claus and Brucke. Bailey notes that, "If Freud had shown any inclination to use the experimental method, Brücke would surely have encouraged him" (1966, p. 86). Except for what Bailey calls an "abortive and amateurish effort" to test the effects of cocaine on muscular strength, however, Freud never again attempted to use the experimental method. It seems reasonable to conclude that Freud's aversion to the experimental method was more a function of Freud's personality and the subject matter he chose to study than a shortcoming of nineteenth-century scientific training. Freud once told his friend Fliess that he was not by temperament a man of science, an experimenter. He may have been helped toward this self-discovery by being assigned the task of dissecting four hundred eels while he was a student working at the Institute of Comparative Anatomy. Revelation (together with acute boredom) could have come as early as the three hundredth eel!

Empirical Origins of the Theory

Freud's views on personality were not the product of the laboratory but of the consulting room. Psychoanalysis was not only a theory of personality for Freud; it was a method of inquiry and an approach to psychotherapy. His theory of personality was constructed slowly, painstakingly, and bit by bit, through thousands of hours of contact with patients. During these sessions, he was not functioning as an aloof, detached observer but rather as someone seeking to help emotionally disturbed people explore their feelings, thoughts, and past experiences in an effort to obtain relief from subjective distress and an improvement in their ability to cope effectively with the sources of their distress. The data that form the basis of his theory were derived from his observations of the behavior, nonverbal as well as verbal, of patients in a clinical setting.

Freud's Scientific Method

Freud's scientific method for the testing and modification of psychoanalytic theory was the same as the methodology used to develop the theory. His general method was the case study. In carrying out a case study, the clinician delves deeply into the personality of an individual patient, using the methods that are part of the diagnostic and therapeutic regimens of the particular therapeutic approach being used. Freud saw many patients in the course of his career, and each of these was, in effect, a case study. To each case, he applied the methods of psychoanalysis and derived from these his observations relevant to the possible causes of the disorder. His observations then became the basis for testing and modifying the theory, which had originally been derived from observations of other cases.

The two principal methods of observation that Freud employed, were, as we noted earlier, free association and dream analysis. As the patient free associated, bringing up materials from the unconscious, the observations that Freud made and the conclusions he reached were applied not only to the treatment of that patient, but also to the development and testing of psychoanalytic theory. It is important to note that the nature of the theory was no doubt heavily influenced by the specific methods of observation employed. It may be recalled that Freud came upon the use of the free association method at a relatively early point in time, when he learned it from Breuer. Since Freud had not yet developed the major concepts that form the core of psychoanalytic theory, it appears that the free association method largely antedated the development of the theory itself. Had a different therapeutic technique—and hence a different observational method—been introduced, Freud might have arrived at somewhat different theoretical propositions.

Although Freud saw many patients, he actually published only six case studies after developing the basic concepts of psychoanalytic theory. By way of example, the Ratman (1955c) case involved an individual who was tortured by the strange obsession that his father and girl friend would be punished by having their buttocks gnawed by live rodents. A second example is that of "Little Hans" (1955a), a boy of five who was afraid he would be bitten by a horse if he ventured out into the street. A somewhat more detailed review of a third case may provide a flavor for Freud's clinical interpretatons.

The Schreber Case

Daniel Schreber was a judge, who wrote and published an autobiographical account of his experiences as a patient suffering from paranoia. Freud never met Schreber; his analysis was based entirely on Schreber's book. Two of Schreber's characteristically paranoid delusions centered on his belief that he was "the redeemer" and that he was being transformed into a woman. Freud's interpretation identified the motivation underlying these delusional beliefs as latent homosexuality; and he went on to hypothesize that the key factor in the pathogenesis of paranoid disorders was homosexuality. That is, Freud explained that sexual attraction toward members of one's own sex, which is objectionable and intolerable, is defended against by being replaced with its opposite: hostility. But the almost equally objectionable feelings of hatred or hostility are dealt with by projection, and now the paranoiac becomes the delusional center of a ring of enemies, what a later theorist called the "paranoid pseudocommunity."

Schatzman (1971), also using published materials written by Schreber's father, has provided an interesting and plausible alternative to Freud's interpretation. The senior Schreber, a recognized expert in child-rearing practices of that period, used his son as a guinea pig for experiments with disciplinary techniques that were little short of sadistic. Schatzman compared Schreber's paranoid fantasies with passages taken from his father's books and concluded that "Schreber did not imagine that he was persecuted; he was persecuted" (1971, p. 177).

The small number of case studies offered by Freud makes it nearly impossible to reach any conclusions concerning his more general approach in making and recording observations on individual patients as a basis for the development and modification of his theory. What does become clear is that the case-study method is much more useful as a basis for generating hypotheses than it is as an empirical basis for testing them. Each case is *sui generis,* a unique phenomenon that cannot be replicated, a story that will not recur, a life than cannot be relived. Despite Freud's unquestionable acumen as a clinical observer and genius as a creative theorist, he did not provide empirical tests of his hypotheses that have been generally acceptable to those outside the psychoanalytic movement.

Post-Freudian Empirical Developments

One heuristic value of psychoanalytic theory can be seen in the vast amount of interest it has generated among psychological researchers. It would be impossible, within the scope of a chapter such as this one, to do any justice to the body of empirical efforts that have been made on behalf of Freudian theory. Some research has focused on the outcome of psychoanalytic treatment, attempting to determine to what degree the therapy is successful. Other research has dealt with important events that occur during the process of treatment. Still other bodies of research have been concerned with the characteristics of psychoanalytic therapists as well as those of patients and with how these characteristics may affect the process and outcome of the therapy.

Despite all efforts, it has proven most difficult to conduct investigations that are at once well controlled and clinically meaningful. As a result, firm, empirically based conclusions concerning psychoanalytic treatment are nearly impossible to find. Perhaps the most formidable obstacle confronting the empirical validation of the Freudian approach—and the one that has thus far proven most refractory to any attempts at resolution—is that there is no single Freudian theory, only a large, incomplete, and sometimes contradictory body of Freud's writings. An attempted test of one aspect or version of the theory may not adequately take into account other aspects or versions and may thus suffer as a consequence.

Freud never doubted that his clinical observations constituted sufficient grounds for the verification of his ideas. This is graphically demonstrated in an anecdote related by Mackinnon and Dukes (1962) concerning the American psychologist Saul Rosenzweig and his correspondence with Freud. Rosenzweig had sent some reports to Freud in 1934 on the progress of studies he was conducting to investigate experimentally certain psychoanalytic concepts. Freud replied:

> *"I have reviewed with interest your experimental investigations for verifying psychoanalytic propositions. I cannot value these confirmations very highly since the abundance of reliable observations upon which these propositions rest makes them independent of experimental verification. Nevertheless, it [experimental verification] can do no harm." (p. 32)*

EVALUATION

Freud burst upon the world at a time when most human beings saw themselves as conscious, rational, planful, largely nonsexual beings, and suggested that instead people are unconscious, partially irrational, impulsive creatures whose sexuality is a major cause of motivation and conflict. He described children as lusting for their parents and made adults watchful of even simple slips of the tongue. No wonder that his theory has been one of the most widely and severely criticized of all theories in psychology. At the same time, it has been one of the most powerful and influential theories in the field. We will examine briefly a few of the major criticisms and the major positive values of the psychoanalytic approach.

Major Criticisms of the Theory

Lack of Precision and Parsimony. Many critics have noted that Freud's terms lack precision. They tend to be relatively broad concepts with multiple meanings. Moreover, these complex concepts lead to a theory that is lacking in parsimony and seems to take the most intricate route to an understanding of the simplest human behaviors. This complexity not only makes the theory more difficult to grasp but may slow progress in reaching higher levels of understanding.

Biology and Universality. Freud, it is argued by some critics, put far too heavy an emphasis on the biological bases of behavior, holding that the instincts of the id are ultimately responsible for all acts. In so doing, he made his theory universal, suggesting that the id applies equally to all humans. One effect of this emphasis is largely to ignore the possible differential influence of culture on personality, a point soon raised by cultural anthropologists and many psychologists. Although Freud's superego is shaped in its specifics by the particular culture in which the individual is raised, critics argue that this view does not go far enough toward allowing for differential cultural influences on behavior. One of the most direct reactions to this aspect of the theory has been the development of a series of social analytic theories, reviewed in Chaper 5.

Psychoanalytic Therapy. It has been suggested that psychoanalytic therapy is lengthy, expensive, and quite possibly ineffective. Many criticisms of the therapy have come from behaviorally oriented theorists, beginning with Hans Eysenck (1952). Eysenck's views of the differences between psychoanalytic and behavioral therapy clearly show his more positive view of the latter approach. He has also offered a controversial attack on psychotherapy as an ineffective means of modifying behavior. His early review of the literature on psychotherapy led him to the conclusion that there is basically no evidence for its effectiveness. The storm of controversies stirred by this view has led to further research in psychotherapy and to a number of replies to Eysenck's original critique. The issue remains unresolved, though both the criticisms and relevant research have been carefully summarized and evaluated (Bergin 1971).

Weak Empirical Qualities. Perhaps the most important criticism of Freudian theory has been that it lacks solid empirical qualities. Freud's original research, as we have seen, was basically case-study research involving clinical observation. Since such observation cannot be directly replicated and is necessarily based on a relatively small number of individual cases, it is widely considered to be a poor basis for testing theory. Subsequent work has often involved somewhat more precise correlational and experimental approaches, but much of this research has been lacking in controls, often due to the complexity of the theory itself and the difficulty in arriving at operational definitions of the major constructs. It is perhaps somewhat paradoxical to note that one of the great strengths of Freudian theory has been its ability to generate hundreds of studies that should increase our base of empirical knowledge, while one of its great weaknesses is that the extensive empirical efforts have seldom been precise enough to lead to firm and consistent conclusions.

Strengths of the Theory

In building psychoanalytic theory, Sigmund Freud constructed a great bridge, a triumph of intellectual architecture, that spanned the abyss between philosophy and psychology, linked the human mind and body, and permitted progressive travel from the nineteenth into the twentieth century. The massive girders of Freud's bridge proved more than adequate to support important aspects of a multitude of disciplines, wide enough to permit the construction of numerous "splinter" theories without substantially impeding the progressive development of the major theoretical artery, and strong enough to hold up under the weight of the criticisms that would come. Psychoanalysis also proved to be a shared language—a kind of *lingua franca*—that helped end the communication gap between the developing academic psychology and a movement that started as part of the medical profession.

Heuristic Value. We have already seen that the heuristic value of Freudian theory has been immense. It has been a stimulus for the development of many other theories and for the conduct of a huge volume of research. In the area of theory development, some theorists have merely expanded upon specific aspects of Freud's ideas, others have developed theories as a reaction against one aspect or another of the Freudian approach, and still others have adapted Freud's ideas to disciplines outside psychology and psychiatry, such as sociology, religion, political science, history, and anthropology. Freud's work has no doubt had greater heuristic scope than that of any other approach we will examine.

Application. Before Freud's time those who treated patients with emotional problems did so in an intellectual vacuum and without the benefit of any systematic theory to guide their work. Whatever the therapist did for the patient was done without knowing the reason why that particular approach might be of value. Sarnoff (1971) summarizes the impact of Freud's theory in this regard:

> *. . . Freudian concepts undoubtedly helped a great many clinicians to cope intellectually with the taxing challenges of their work; to impose cognitive order upon what might otherwise have utterly confounded them as a bewildering assortment of behavioral idiosyncracies. Indeed, Freudian theory at last gave clinicians a comprehensive system of explanation that went beyond the mere phenotypical diagnostic categories that had previously characterized the field of psychiatry. Moreover, while postulating discrete underlying psychological processes for various observable syndromes, Freud simultaneously proposed a theoretically consistent means of uncovering and changing them. (p. 3)*

Since giving early clinicians a set of theoretical guidelines for therapy, psychoanalysis has, of course, become a worldwide discipline and therapeutic technique. It is now systematically learned in psychoanalytic institutes all over the world and systematically applied by individual analysts to the treatment of their patients.

A Comprehensive View. Not only was Freud's theory the first scientific theory of human behavior, but it has also proven to be one of the most comprehensive overviews of human nature thus far developed. In the single, logical framework of his theory, Freud provides a structure of personality, a way of understanding the important influences on human behavior—biology, reality, and society—shows us how the person is motivated by unconscious forces to engage in important behaviors, demonstrates how both normal and abnormal behavior develop and function, and explains how the disordered individual can be treated in an effort to modify problematic behaviors. It is perhaps in this comprehensive picture provided by psychoanalytic theory that we can see the basis for Freud's great influence on both our intellectual disciplines and our everyday lives. The value of the theory, then—and perhaps its greatest achievement—lies in Freud's full, meaningful view of man as a creature at once primitive and sophisticated, impulsive and rational, selfish and sociable, regressive and creative, animal and human.

REFERENCES

Bailey, P. Sigmund Freud: Scientific period (1873–1897). In J. Wolpe, A. Salter, & L. J. Reyna (Eds.), *The conditioning therapies*. New York: Holt, Rinehart & Winston, 1966.

Baldwin, A. L. *Theories of child development*. New York: Wiley, 1967.

Bergin, A. E. The evaluation of therapeutic outcomes. In A. E. Bergin & S. L. Garfield (Eds.), *Handbook of psychotherapy and personality change*. New York: Wiley & Sons, 1971. (Pp. 217–270)

Carus, C. G. *Psyche: Zur Entwicklungsgeschichte der Seele*. Jena: Eugene Diederichs, 1846.

Eysenck, H. J. The effects of psychotherapy: An evaluation. *Journal of Consulting Psychology, 1952, 16,* 319–324.

Eysenck, H. J. The effects of psychotherapy. *International Journal of Psychiatry, 1965, 1,* 97–178.

Freud, S. *The standard edition of the complete psychological works* (J. Strachey, Ed.), London: Hogarth Press, 1953–1974.

Freud, S. Analysis of a phobia in a five-year-old-boy. In the *Standard Edition* (Vol. 10). London: Hogarth Press, 1955. (First German edition, 1920.)

Freud S. Beyond the pleasure principle. In the *Standard Edition*. (Vol. 18). London: Hogarth Press, 1955.(a) (First German edition 1920.)

Freud, S. Notes upon a case of obsessional neurosis. In the *Standard Edition*, London: Hogarth Press, 1955.(b) (First German edition, 1909b.)

MacKinnon, D., & Dukes, D.   Repression. In L. Post, (Ed.), *Psychology in the making*. New York: Knopf, 1962. (Pp. 662-744).

May, R.   *The Meaning of anxiety*. New York: Ronald Press, 1950.

Sarnoff, I.   *Testing Freudian concepts: An experimental social approach*. New York: Springer, 1971.

Schatzman, M.   Kingsley Hall: The politics of madness. *Contemporary Psychoanalysis*. 1971, 8 (1), 107-121.

Schophenhauer, A.   *Welt als Wille und Vorstellung*. Leipzig: F. A. Brockhaus, 1819.

Schultz, D.   *Theories of personality*. Monterey, Calif.: Brooks/Cole, 1976.

Von Hartmann, E.   *Philosophie des Unbewussten*. Leipzig. Haacke, 1968.

Wolman, B.   *Contemporary theories and systems in psychology*. New York: Harper, 1960.

3

Ego Psychology:

Erik H. Erikson and

Heinz Hartmann

Sigmund Freud died on September 23, 1939, at 20 Maresfield Gardens, London, leaving a legacy of theory and therapeutic techniques constituting one of the major forces of twentieth-century psychology. The psychoanalytic theory and the techniques which arise out of his work exist and remain widely influential to this day. There have, however, been many who have chosen to modify Freud's theory in a wide variety of ways. One of the major attempts—one that is seen by some as a direct progression from Freud and a mainstream of modern psychoanalysis—is focused on the ego.

Freud's thinking about the development, structure, and functions of the ego changed during several major phases of his career. The earliest period actually began as a pretheoretical period and reflected the impact of a classic conflict on Freud's own thinking. Throughout much of his early life Freud demonstrated appreciation of a basically humanistic tradition, involving the view that man is an active self-determiner of his own forms of behaviors. This basic view, reflected in Freud and Breuer's (1895)

Studies in Hysteria, soon gave way to a scientific-mechanistic turn in Freud's thinking and a resulting philosophical conflict. Freud put forth a major effort, centered in his "Project" of 1895, to formulate a mechanistic, neurophysiological approach to understanding human behavior. In this effort, he characterized the ego as a set of ideas based on a particular set of physiological structures which he referred to as neurons. The Project was, perhaps, the major failure of Freud's career. He was simply unable, as he later remarked, to automate the ego function totally and in that sense to make humans operate without a will.

The failure of the Project caused Freud to turn his attention, in the second major phase of his career, to a more psychological approach to understanding human nature. In this second period, which began with the publication of the *Interpretation of Dreams* (1900), Freud did little to develop the ego concept, concentrating his efforts on the importance of dreams, the unconscious motivational system of the id, and the concept of defense.

The third period of Freud's work began in the years surrounding 1923, the year in which he published the *Ego and the Id*. In that work, and in subsequent papers, Freud greatly expanded his discussions of the ego concept and established its central importance in the psychic structure. The ego was not seen as an autonomous structure at birth but as growing and developing out of the id. The ego energy was gained from the id, and the ego itself represented simply a modification of id structures and energies brought about through environmental contact. As the theory progressively developed over the next fifteen years, it became clear in Freud's writings that the ego might not be developing entirely out of the id but that the ego might have original energy. His growing tendency to attribute greater independence and original energy to the ego seemed to culminate in one of his last major works, *Analysis Terminable and Interminable* (1937). It appeared to some psychoanalysts, particularly Heinz Hartmann, Anna Freud, and David Rapaport, that Freud had significantly modified a major tenet of the theory. Specifically, the ego, which had earlier been viewed as functioning only on borrowed id energy, was now seen as having original autonomy.

The detailed and important modification of the ego concept in psychoanalysis was not undertaken by Freud but was left to the work of several major psychoanalytic theorists, who were responsible for the full development of ego psychology. We have chosen here to focus on two of these theorists. The first, Erik H. Erikson, is perhaps the more obvious of the two, in that his psychosocial developmental theory has been widely recognized as representing a major thrust in the 1970s and 1980s. The second theorist, Heinz Hartmann, is a more direct descendent of Freud. He is widely recognized within the field of psychoanalysis as a major theorist in the ego movement.

ERIK H. ERIKSON

Erik H. Erikson was born in Frankfurt, Germany, in 1902 and was raised by his mother and stepfather, a pediatrician who had treated him for a childhood disorder.

Erikson had no formal education beyond the high school gymnasium and spent a number of years traveling rather aimlessly through Europe.

In 1927 he joined the staff of a day nursery established in Vienna by Anna Freud for children whose parents were in training to become psychoanalysts. Erikson soon began to train in psychoanalysis. He completed this education in 1933 and moved with his wife and two sons to Copenhagen. He soon left there, however, for the United States, where he became the first child psychoanalyst in the New England area. His career since that time has included appointments to the Department of Neuropsychiatry at the Harvard Medical School, the Department of Psychiatry in the Institute of Human Relations at Yale School of Medicine, the Psychology Department at the University of California at Berkeley, the Austen Riggs Center in Stockbridge, Massachusetts, the Center for Advanced Studies of the Behavioral Sciences in Palo Alto, California, and at Harvard University.

Among his major publications are *Childhood and Society* (1950; revised 1963), *Insight and Responsibility* (1964), *Identity: Youth and Crisis* (1968), and *Gandhi's Truth* (1969).

STRUCTURAL PRINCIPLES: THE EGO

Erikson's clear structural focus has been on the ego as the major element of the personality. The ego, rather than the id, is seen as the basis for human development and functioning, and the ego is regarded as largely autonomous, not falling under the constant influence of the id. The ego is capable of trust, hope, love, and other positive strivings. Moreover, the ego tends to take a problem-oriented, problem-solving approach to life, seeking new and better solutions to both old and new problems. It is because of his emphasis on such an active positive ego that Erikson is known as an ego psychologist.

DEVELOPMENTAL PRINCIPLES AND MOTIVATIONAL DYNAMICS

The ego of Erikson's theory differs from that of Freud's not only in its qualities but also in its developmental process. Freud emphasized heavily the early years of life and focused on the physiological origins of the ego, supplemented by the developmental influence of the parents. Erikson, on the other hand, sees ego development as spanning the individual's entire life and views the broader social and cultural environment as important in influencing development. The person is seen as interacting with the social environment throughout life in such a way that there is a mutuality of influence between the person and the environment. The environment contributes to the development of personality, while the person affects the environment to cause the gradual social evolution that we have seen throughout history.

Epigenesis, Crisis, and Virtue

The life-long developmental process takes place in a series of eight stages. The staging process is based on what is called an *epigenetic principle* of maturation. This principle basically means that development is a function of a "ground plan" that is of genetic origin and universal among humans. The emergence of each successive stage represents a physiological readiness, and, as an important part of the ground plan, the society is structured to meet this readiness and help the individual realize the potentialities of that stage. As Erikson puts it, ". . . society, in principle, tends to be so constituted as to meet and invite this succession of potentialities for interaction and attempts to safeguard and encourage the proper rate and the proper sequence of their unfolding" (1963a, p. 270).

Each stage of life has associated with it a crisis, a basic virtue, and a ritual. Each crisis is a conflict, arising out of the interaction between physiological maturation and societal requirements. Each crisis has both positive and negative potentials. If the conflict is resolved effectively, the positive potential is realized and adds to ego development. In this case, one of eight basic virtues, which greatly influence the individual's later attitudes and further development, will emerge. If the conflict is resolved unsatisfactorily or is left unresolved, the negative potential is realized and ego development is harmed. In addition to basic virtues, there develop during the various stages a series of rituals (Erikson 1976). Each ritual represents a particular approach that the society typically takes in its interactions among individuals. The positive form of each ritual is termed a *ritualization,* and each ritualization that the individual learns better prepares him or her to become a mature, contributing member of the community. Each ritual also has a negative form, termed a *ritualism,* which, if substituted for the ritualization, could make the individual more rigid and less effective as a member of the community.

The Eight Stages

The first four stages of the Erikson developmental model occur during infancy and childhood and will be recognized as similar to Freud's oral, anal, phallic, and latency stages. The fifth stage is a transition point occurring during adolescence, and the remaining three stages take place in adulthood.

1. *Basic Trust vs. Mistrust: Hope, Infancy.* The elements of crisis and conflict in the first stage of life, as the heading suggests, are basic trust and basic mistrust. The virtue that can arise from the successful resolution of this first conflict is hope. The entire process takes place during infancy.

Infancy is basically an oral sensory stage in which much of the infant's focus is on the mouth region. A mother who is appropriately responsive to the infant's oral and other needs and who provides affection, love, and consistency is helping the child learn trust in the surrounding world. The mother who does not provide adequately, is inconsistent, or rejects the infant contributes to a developing sense of mistrust. The impact of the child's first significant psychosocial experience—that with the mother—on personality development is seen in the infant's potential development of a major virtue and an early ritualization. The basic virtue that arises out of the successful resolution of the trust-mistrust crisis is hope, a true and important virtue as the individual prepares to face the world. The ritualization of infancy is called the *numinous* ritualization, which means, according to Erikson, the infant's sense of the presence of the mother and of the mother's recognition of the child and of mutuality with the child. The positive form of the ritual, the ritualization, can continue into childhood and contribute to the sense of security and trust. The negative form, the numinous ritualism, is termed *idealism* and predisposes the individual to worshiping idolatrous heroes in adulthood.

2. *Autonomy vs. Shame and Doubt: Will Power, Early Childhood.* The second stage of life, early childhood, plays out the crisis of individual autonomy against the shame and doubt fostered by continued, forced dependence. Basically, parents should gradually allow the growing child more and more freedom, independence, and autonomy. If they do so, the basic virtue of will power (determination to exercise free choice and appropriate self-restraint) will be developed, and the ego will be strengthened. If the parents do not encourage a reasonable degree of independence, tending instead to overprotect their child and do everything for him or her, there may develop a sense of shame and self-doubt.

The ritual of early childhood is the *judicious* ritualization, which forms the basis for using courtroom trial procedures in adulthood to determine guilt or innocence. A corresponding negative ritualism is termed *legalism* and involves the achievement of satisfaction through humiliating or punishing others by applying law blindly and without compassion.

3. *Initiative vs. Guilt: Purpose, Age of Play.* This is a genital locomotor stage of development in which the child learns to begin to strike out on his or her own, setting and attempting to achieve goals. If parents appropriately encourage this new initiative, the virtue of *purpose,* meaning the courage to pursue important goals, develops. If, on the other hand, the child is made to feel guilty for taking initiatives, this purpose virtue is thwarted. The *dramatic* ritualization, in which the child learns to pretend and imitate, develops at this time. Its negative side is the ritualism of impersonation, in which the individual learns to "put on a front," hiding the true personality throughout life.

4. *Industry vs. Inferiority: Competence, School Years.* As the child enters the formal educational process, he or she may develop a sense of industry by receiving rewards for hard work and diligence. The basic virtue of *competence* develops to supplement the hope, will power, and purpose of earlier stages. The failure to reward industry and establish competence leads to feelings of inferiority. The positive form of the ritual which develops during this stage is the *formal* ritualization, in which the child learns how to perform tasks systematically and methodically. The perversion of this ritual is *formalism,* a ritualism which leads the individual to meaninglessly repeat unnecessary formalities.

5. *Identity vs. Identity Confusion: Fidelity, Adolescence.* The period of ado-

lescence bridges the gap between childhood and adulthood and is often a time of upheaval and confusion. The conflict of this stage is the *identity crisis,* which arises out of the need to form an integrated sense of personal identity, coupled with the fact that the adolescent is often very uncertain of who he or she is and what his or her role in society should be. This *identity confusion,* or role confusion, involves a deep sense of conflict, indecisiveness, loneliness, and anxiety. As a result, the adolescent's behavior may be confused and unpredictable. The positive resolution of the identity crisis entails an integration of the individual's self-knowledge gained from a variety of sources. The result of successful resolution is the emergence of fidelity, which involves the ability to understand and, basically to abide by the standards and mores of the society. Fidelity, Erikson has held, is essential to a clear sense of self-identity. The ritualization of adolescence is the development of a consistent set of ideas, termed an *ideology.* The corresponding ritualism is *totalism,* the belief that one knows what is absolutely and undeniably right.

6. *Intimacy vs. Isolation: Love, Young Adulthood.* The resolution of the identity crisis of adolescence allows the individual to seek deep, intimate relationships, including true love that does not focus exclusively on sexual activity. The virtue of young adulthood is *love,* which to Erikson is the universally dominant virtue. The failure to become committed to intimate relationships and, hence, develop love leads to isolation and later, potentially, to personality problems. The ritualization and ritualism of this stage are, respectively, affiliation and elitism. *Affiliation* involves mutual sharing with and enjoyment of others, while *elitism* causes one to form selective groups that exclude others.

7. *Generativity vs. Stagnation: Care, Middle Adulthood.* Developing between the ages of about 25 and 65, *generativity* entails concern for the next generation and the society in which that generation will grow up. If the adult accepts the responsibility of generativity, there develops a sense of *care,* a basic virtue which involves essentially the attitude that the well being of others is important. Rejection of the generativity challenge means that the individual cares only about himself or herself. This leads to stagnation and a sense of hopelessness and meaninglessness that constitute "middle-age crisis." The ritualization of this time period involves the adult in teaching societal values to the young and is termed *generational.* The distorted ritualism is *authoritism* and involves an inappropriate encroachment of authority.

8. *Ego Integrity vs. Despair: Wisdom, Maturity.* The final stage of life, maturity, involves reflection on the accomplishments of the previous years. A sense of *ego integrity* develops when the individual is satisfied with prior accomplishments, including those of job, marriage, family, and social relationships. Where ego integrity is achieved, the virtue of *wisdom* arises. Failure to achieve ego integrity, because one's life is viewed as a series of unrealized potentialities and unattained goals, leads to despair. The *integral* ritualization develops to represent achievement through wisdom. Its counterpart, the *sapientism* ritualism involves the pretense of wisdom in its absence.

EMPIRICAL APPROACHES

Erikson's theory has led directly to very little empirical research. We will focus here on one major and rather special type of empirical contribution that Erikson has made, then briefly note other research that is relevant to his approach.

Psychohistory

Psychohistory is the application of psychoanalysis to the study of historical individuals. Erikson (1975) has proposed a fairly elaborate methodology for conducting psychohistorical investigations. The methodology has been developed and polished through a number of investigations that Erikson has undertaken, including such figures as Hitler (1950, 1963), Luther (1958), Ghandi (1969), and Thomas Jefferson (1974).

Erikson's view of psychohistory is basically that this approach represents an extension of the kind of psychoanalysis one would undertake with a living patient. For the patient's case history and self-description, one must substitute the life history of the historical figure as it is known through the individual's writings and others about him or her. In addition, the psychohistorian is trying to determine not what causes a patient to develop a disorder but rather how the historical figure was able to change the course of the world. The person in question is seen as formulating a concept of society and social change that is based on his or her own internal conflicts and yet is so inviting to many people that it brings them together to produce a major force for social change.

Erikson has noted the need to take great care in conducting a psychohistorical study to assure that the analysis is as valid as possible. One must take into consideration that the interpretation will be influenced by one's professional training and experiential background and even by one's state of mind at the time the history is being interpreted. In addition, the psychohistorian must take into account a number of historical factors that may influence statements made by the historical figure in question. Possibly influencing such statements may be the person's age and, hence, stage of development, at the time, the world situation, and the way in which the statement fits into the individual's overall life history.

Erikson's careful, detailed approach has been applied by a number of others, but he was, in effect, the founder of psychohistory.

The Study of Play

Noting that the problems of small children often become apparent in their behavior at play, Erikson (1963) developed a standardized play situation in which he asked 150 boys and 150 girls to use toys in order to construct an interesting scene on a table. He found what seemed to be clear-cut sex differences in these ten-to-twelve-year-old children. Boys tended to construct tall buildings and active street scenes, while girls tended to make interiors of houses and generally tranquil scenes. Erikson found these sex differences intriguing and began to search for a psychoanalytic explanation for them. He concluded that sex differences in play arise from innate differences between the sexes that cannot be readily changed by experience. He did add, however, that the underlying physiology interacts to some degree with sociocultural factors to influence sex differences in behavior.

Research on the Identity Crisis

Erikson has emphasized the importance of adolescence and its identity crisis, and some investigators have attempted to test his hypotheses about identity and its role in development. A good example of research on identity crises is a 1970 study (Waterman, Beubl, and Waterman), which began with the assumption that success in resolving the identity crisis should relate positively to the levels of previously developed ego components, including basic trust, autonomy, initiative, and industry. The researchers had tape-recorded interviews scored by independent raters to determine whether or not earlier crises had been resolved. They also had scale measures of autonomy and trust. In summary, they found that subjects with high levels of ego identity showed the greatest amount of autonomy, but ego identity and basic trust were unrelated. A second phase of the study used scales to measure both the resolution of the first five psychosocial crises and ego identity. Results showed that ego identity was related positively to basic trust, autonomy, initiative, and industry. Overall, these results did provide some support for Erikson's hypothesis that successful resolution of the identity crisis is positively related to the successful resolution of earlier crises.

EVALUATION

Erikson is widely acknowledged as having made major contributions in providing a detailed psychosocial theory of development. Separate plaudits have also come for his discussion of identity and the concept of the identity crisis and also for the interesting observations of human nature which he has made and upon which his theory is based. In addition, as we have noted, Erikson must be credited with creating the discipline of psychohistory.

On the other side of the ledger, the most important criticism that one can make of Erikson's work is that it rests on minimal empirical foundations. Erikson's careful personal observations have seldom been supplemented with careful scientific study. While the developmental crises he has described are a matter of common observation and the stagewise process is one that many psychologists feel represents an accurate interpretation of human behavior, no theory is likely to exist indefinitely without empirical validation. Critics have also suggested that Erikson is too optimistic about human nature—as Freud was too pessimistic—and that he, like the social analysts, has done little but expand upon Freud's basic theory. While Erikson's approach does adopt a positive view of human nature, we must, in fairness, note that certain negative aspects are a central part of the theory. The crises and conflicts that are so crucial to the developmental process represent a focal point in the theory, and Erikson sees the anxiety associated with these conflicts as a source from which psychological strengths can develop.

Whatever one believes about the relative merits and demerits of Erikson's work, it is clear that he is one of the major personality theorists of the late twentieth century and a leader of modern psychoanalysis.

HEINZ HARTMANN

As we have noted, Erikson is not the only ego psychologist. In fact, it was not initially Erikson but Heinz Hartmann who provided the major early thrust toward the development of ego psychology. Moreover, where Erikson has focused primarily on the developmental process, Hartmann has taken on the task of revising virtually the whole of psychoanalytic theory.

Heinz Hartmann was born in Vienna in 1894. His family background included a father who was both a widely respected historian and a leader of the adult education movement for working class people in Germany. Hartmann's mother was an accomplished pianist and a sculptor of considerable talent.

. As the great ship of psychoanalytic theory, with Freud firmly at the helm, was about to enter the waters of its third phase, Hartmann received his medical degree at the University of Vienna in 1920. His university years had been educational and productive ones. Hartmann had an early interest in pharmacology and, as a student, worked under a widely renowned pharmacologist, Hans Mayer, the work resulting in two pregraduation publications on quinine metabolism. Not content with merely pursuing a university education during this time period, however, Hartmann served as a secretary to his father, who was then the Austrian ambassador to Germany. In this role, Hartmann had a close view of the world's political processes and met many of the leading politicians.

Before graduation from medical school, Hartmann's interest changed from pharmacology to psychiatry, and he spent most of the fourteen years following graduation at the Psychiatric and Neurological University Clinics in Vienna. During this period, Hartmann published an important book, *Die Grundlagen der Psychoanalyse* ("The Fundamentals of Psychoanalysis").

Hartmann left the University Clinics in 1934, when he accepted the signal honor of an invitation to complete his training analysis with Freud. Following his training with Freud, Hartmann became a training analyst at the Vienna Psychoanalytic Institute and later at the Paris Psychoanalytic Institute.

Although he had been for some time widely respected among psychoanalysts, it was not until his delivery of a series of lectures at the Vienna Institute in 1937 that Hartmann began to present the tenets of the new ego psychology formally. His lectures were organized and presented in writing for the first time in 1939 as a monograph, *Ego Psychology and the Problem of Adaptation*. That ego psychology did not gain widespread influence within psychoanalysis more rapidly than it did can be attributed in part to this important monograph's not being published in English until its translation in 1958 by David Rapaport. In 1941, Hartmann left Europe and came to New York, where he became a teacher and training analyst at the New York Psychoanalytic Institute. He was later appointed medical director of the Treatment Center of the New York Institute; he has also been president of the New York Psychoanalytic Society and the International Psycho-Analytical Association.

The interested student will find many of Hartmann's most important papers on ego psychology collected in his book, *Essays on Ego Psychology* (1964), and in the collection of papers published jointly by Hartmann, Kris, and Loewenstein, *Papers on Psychoanalytic Psychology* (1964). In addition, many of the papers appearing in the Festschrift for Hartmann, *Psychoanalysis, a General Psychology: Essays in Honor of Heinz Hartmann* (Loewenstein, Newman, Schur, and Solnit, 1966) will be of interest. It is perhaps appropriate to warn the potential reader that Hartmann's writings are often complex and difficult.

After obtaining his medical degree in 1920, Hartmann studied psychoanalysis in earnest. His studies began before Freud had entered the third stage of his writings, that is, before some of the most significant systematic aspects of his theory had developed. What Hartmann saw as he began to study psychoanalysis was a theory that was the raw product of Freud's clinical acumen and creative genius. The major ideas encompassed by the theory were innovative and far reaching, but the theory itself was, as Schafer (1970) has pointed out, in a state of disarray. Many of the basic concepts in the Freudian treatment were as yet ill-defined, and there were apparent contradictions in Freud's own statements across the early years of his writings. In addition, Hartmann came to disagree with some major propositions in Freudian theory, particularly those concerned with the development and functioning of the ego, the importance of that structure in the total personality, and the relationship of the individual to external reality. It was, then, along these lines that Hartmann set out to revise the Freudian formulation, although he did not do so significantly until Freud himself had indicated some agreement with Hartmann's basic propositions concerning ego development and functioning.

Freud's Anticipation of Ego Autonomy

The basic Freudian formulation of the origins of psychic structures suggests that the id, as the most primitive of the structural elements, contains all that is innate. Inheritance is basically in the form of instincts housed in the energy reservoir that is the id. The ego is seen as developing out of this energic morass in the form of a set of functions necessary for environmental contact and interaction; it is seen as initially formless and without power. In order to develop and survive, it must subject itself to the demands of the id and is an essentially impotent guide to reality, riding upon the towering waves of the id's impulsive energies. Freud, indeed, likened the ego to "a rider, [who], if he is not to be parted from his horse, is obliged to guide it where it wants to go. . ." (1923, p. 15). This formulation of the relationship between the ego and the id suggests a view of an individual in whom the hereditary, impulsive, irrational functions are more basic and more powerful than the reality functions. The individual, in his or her relationship to the reality of the external environment, is at the mercy of the primitive id.

Hartmann did not entirely agree with this view of the individual. The alternative possibility that each person's active adaptation to external reality was as much a part of his or her inherited biology as was the pleasure seeking of the id seemed a real possibility for the future of psychoanalysis. As evidence that Freud was also moving toward this position, Hartmann and others have cited particular passages from Freud's work. The earlier position that the ego has no hereditary aspect is in the *Ego and the Id* (1923). There, Freud states bluntly and without immediate qualification that "It is not possible to speak of direct inheritance in the ego" (p. 28). The major change in his theory first comes in *Analysis Terminable and Interminable* (1937), where Freud states that

> . . . we have no reason to dispute the existence and importance of primary congenital variations in the ego . . . when we speak of "archaic heritage" we are generally thinking only of the id and we apparently assume that no ego is yet in existence at the beginning of the individual's life. But we must not overlook the fact that id and ego are originally one, and it does not imply a mystical overevaluation of heredity if we think it credible that, even before the ego exists, its subsequent lines of development, tendencies and reactions are already determined. (p. 240)

This passage can be interpreted in various ways. Hartmann interpreted it as Freud's statement that the ego is possessed of hereditary characteristics and original energy, a view in direct contradiction to Freud's statement of 1923 cited above. An alternative is to suggest that Freud was speaking here only of a predisposition to develop an ego, since he noted that, "*even before the ego exists,* its subsequent lines of development, tendencies, and reactions are already determined" (authors' italics) (p. 240). Further, one might conclude that Freud still thinks here only of the ego developing out of the id, in that the "*id and ego are originally one*" (authors' italics) (p. 240). The position suggested by this interpretation would not be as substantially different from that of 1923 as would Hartmann's somewhat stronger interpretation of the same passage. It may also be the case from these passages, and others in Freud, that he did not consider the question of ego inheritance important.

We might pause to wonder just why, at the age of eighty, Freud would make statements which might well lead to major modifications of his earlier formulations. We cannot, of course, know in any definitive way what the reasoning behind Freud's statement was. It might be appropriate, however, to speculate that two major factors—or rather two people—influenced Freud's thinking at the time he was writing *Analysis Terminable and Interminable*. The first was Hartmann himself, who was continuing his training analysis with Freud during the years 1934 to 1936 and whom Freud liked and respected (Jones 1957). Hartmann may thus have planted the seeds of ego autonomy which germinated in Freud's 1937 paper, grew to significant stature in Hartmann's paper two years later, and reached maturity during the remainder of Hartmann's career. A second possible influence was Freud's daughter, Anna, who entered the Vienna Psychoanalytic Society at almost the same time as Hartmann. Her thinking was also ego oriented, and in 1936 she published a major book, *The Ego and the Mechanisms of Defense.*

Whatever the influences on Freud's 1937 paper, *Analysis Terminable and Interminable* was not his last work, and by the time of publication of his next major publication, *Moses and Monotheism* (1939), he appears to have dropped the idea of an autonomous ego. In fact, in the *Outline of Psychoanalysis,* published posthumously in 1940, Freud appears to have returned to the position that the id "contains everything that is inherited, that is present at birth, that is laid down in the constitution" (p. 145).

Psychic Structure in Ego Psychology: An Overview

Hartmann's ego psychology, which has also been termed *psychoanalytic developmental psychology,* maintains the basic psychic structure seen in Freudian theory. Psychological processes are grouped under the three major Freudian structures: the id, ego, and superego. The id remains a primitive reservoir of basic instinctual impulses or drives striving nonrationally for satisfaction. The basic process of the id thus remains the primary process, and the id functions on the basis of the pleasure principle. The id also significantly influences the development of the ego and superego, though its relationships with these structures come to involve not only conflict but also cooperation. The ego continues, as in Freudian theory, to fulfill part of its function by providing for the satisfaction of instinctual needs. The reality function of the ego, relating to the individual's contact and interaction with the external world, is considerably expanded and elaborated in Hartmann's treatment, and the ego comes to serve a variety of reality-related functions, including motility and perception. The latter includes both perception of the external world and perception of the self, the term which Hartmann introduces to refer to the individual's knowledge of his or her own characteristics. The ego also tests reality, serves as a protective barrier against powerful or potentially disturbing external and internal stimulation, and controls thinking, language, object comprehension, recall, the nature of the individual's character, and action. In addition, the ego is charged with the operation of defense mechanisms and serves an active synthetic function, which involves coordination and integration of the individual's overall personality functioning. The superego, as in Freud's work, houses a set of moral values, attitudes, and strictures which act as the individual's conscience. It also performs, in Hartmann's theory, such functions as self-criticism and contains the ego-ideal, the state of perfection towards which the ego tends to strive. While both superego and id remain major aspects of the psychic structure, the central focus of the theory remains the ego. We will thus begin with a consideration of the theory relating to the ego in an attempt to show how its functions come about.

ORIGIN AND DEVELOPMENT OF THE EGO

The ego of Hartmann's ego psychology differs from the Freudian ego, as we have seen, both in terms of its origin and in terms of its later functioning *vis à vis* reality.

The Undifferentiated Phase

Freud had proposed that the id exists at birth and the ego develops out of that id. Hartmann postulated, instead, that life begins with an undifferentiated phase, during which both the id and the ego are gradually formed out of the totality of the individual's psychological inheritance. During this phase, the infant has neither pure id nor pure ego functions. There is, rather, a predisposition to develop an ego and a set of physiological processes, termed the *primary autonomous apparatuses,* which are involved in the development of the ego functions out of the matrix of instinctual inheritance. The id is similarly predisposed and develops out of the same instinctual inheritance that yields the ego. The id does not, however, as Freud suggested, have initial, genetically based dominance over the ego, and the ego can be said to have *primary autonomy* from the id. By way of analogy, Freud's theory provides the sculptor with a single mass of clay (the id), and a small piece of that clay is used to mold a separate structure (the ego). Hartmann, by contrast, gives the sculptor a mass of clay that contains two intermixed colors, and the sculptor separates the colors, making two differently colored and shaped structures (the id and the ego).

The first significant id-ego relationship is thus that of differentiation. In the early course of this process, the nonrational primary drive components become separated out of the total hereditary matrix to function as the id. At the same time, the apparatuses of perception, motility, and other environmental contact mechanisms differentiate out of the totality of the undifferentiated phase as a correlated set of functions capable of meaningful, rational interactions with external reality. Collectively, these functions are the ego.

As differentiation proceeds, the instincts of the id influence ego development in several ways. First, there are conflicts between id and ego, as is also the case in Freudian theory, but Hartmann has proposed that this is not the only relationship between ego and id. The ego often actively seeks satisfaction of the instinctual drives, using its energy and ability to interact rationally with the environment to obtain appropriate need satisfiers. The ego may also "borrow" energy from the id to satisfy its own reality-oriented needs and, as development progresses, the ego's aims are sometimes substituted for the aims of the id. In more general terms, according to Hartmann, the primary drive functions and the reality functions of the individual interrelate in a fairly wide variety of ways, not merely in conflict with one another. Moreover, since the reality functions are equivalent to the drive functions in terms of energy, the orientation of the individual to external reality becomes an important determinant of the particular ways in which drive energy is used.

The importance of the ego reality functions becomes even better established when it is recognized that the third major set of factors seen as influencing early ego development are those involving the *external environment*. As physiological development progresses, and particularly as the primary apparatuses of the ego begin to differentiate and mature, the child begins to develop a sense of himself or herself as an object and an entity different from the varied objects in the surrounding world. To emphasize the importance of this early differentiation between the individual and his environment, Hartmann introduces the concept of *self* to denote the child's developing sense of personal identity. As the child develops the sense of self, he or she also begins to differentiate among objects in the external environment and to perceive and conceptualize the relationships of those objects to himself. The relationship of the self to the differentiated environment is centrally important to the individual's further psychological development. We will consider the self-environment relationship in more detail later.

The person's relationship to the environment involves him or her in one final important developmental process, ego development through *learning*. Although Hartmann has not been specific in detailing the nature of the learning process through which the ego develops, his treatment goes well beyond Freud's in clearly indicating the importance of learning. He noted, in particular, the important role served by the mother and other central figures in the child's social environment. The mother, for example, provides the major rewards and punishments that serve to control the child's ego-relevant learning. In particular, she can give or withhold love, and her selective application of love can be quite effective as a form of reward and punishment in shaping the child's behavior. The mother also controls other rewards, including attention and the child's access to such desirable external objects as candy and toys. As the child grows older and comes into more frequent contact with people other than the mother, she necessarily relinquishes some of her control over the reward-punishment process and, hence, over ego-relevant learning. The principal point, however, is that the ego develops in part through learning based on reinforcements most frequently delivered by social others in the environment. As an example, the five-year-old girl may pick up a dropped toy and return it to her two-year-old sister. Seeing this behavior, the mother hugs the five-year-old and tells her what a good girl she is. The child is thus reinforced for being helpful or kind, and repeated experiences of this sort may help her develop that aspect of her behavior and ego functions.

It becomes clear that ego development is seen as an interactive function of the biological forces of heredity and maturation and the environmental forces of learning. It must be emphasized that virtually no aspect of personality can be seen as developing through either maturation or learning alone. Both are necessary, and the actual formation of the ego and other aspects of personality almost invariably represents the interaction of the hereditary and environmental factors.

THE ENERGY AND AUTONOMY OF THE EGO

The dynamics of human personality in Hartmann's theory remain those of an energy model. As in Freudian theory, the individual is given a quantum of energy which is continuously maintained and replenished, and it is through the ebb and flow of this energy that the personality functions, both internally and in relation to the external world. Behavior represents the distribution and utilization of psychic energy. The relative potency of each of the three psychic structures as it affects behavior is a function of the amount of energy controlled by that structure.

Hartmann's concept of primary autonomy of the ego goes beyond the proposal of inherited ego apparatuses to suggest a genetic basis for ego dynamics in the form of hereditary ego energy. This energy comes from a primordial energy pool which is a part of the undifferentiated phase and which also, through differentiation, eventually yields id energy as well as the energy of the ego. In Hartmann's words:

> . . . Part of the mental energy—how much or how little we can hardly esti-mate—is not primarily drive energy but belongs from the very first to the ego, or to the inborn precursors of what will later be specific ego functions, and may be also to those apparatus that come gradually under the influence of the ego and in turn influence its development. (1955, p. 236)

We have, then, in Hartmann's concept of primary ego autonomy, a partially conscious, rational, reality function which has original independence from the primitive forces of the id in both form and energy.

The Neutralization of Energy

The primary autonomous state of the ego does not provide sufficient energy for the ego to function indefinitely, and, as a result, the ego must borrow from the pool of psychic energy in the id in order to function maximally. This need for the ego to utilize id energy introduces a complication, since the energy of the ego was considered by both Freud and Hartmann to be qualitatively different from that of the id. More specifically, the energy of the id is always to some degree bound up with sexual or aggressive drives. Such energy is thus not pure or neutral energy, but instinctually charged energy which is already directed toward the fulfillment of specific sexual or aggressive functions. The energy of the ego, on the other hand, is a relatively neutral energy which is not charged with sexual or aggressive instincts and awaits the direction of the ego.

The theory of energy *neutralization* suggests that in most instances of ego utilization of id energy it is necessary for the psychic energy to first be deinstinctualized or neutralized. The instinctual charge which characterizes the id energy must thus ordinarily be withdrawn or at least partially withdrawn before the ego can direct the energy for its own purposes. It should be emphasized that instinctual and neutral energy are not considered here to be two entirely different forms of energy but rather a single energy form which may take on or become charged with the directive properties of a particular instinctual drive. The situation would be somewhat analogous to that of taking two glasses of water, one clear and one red. Both glasses still basically contain water; the chemical purification of the red water, resulting in a disappearance of the color, would be analogous to neutralization. Freud and Hartmann differ somewhat on the question of just what is neutralized to obtain ego energy. Freud's own pronouncements on the subject were, in fact, largely ignored in the psychoanalytic literature prior to Hartmann's discussions of neutralization. Freud (1926) referred to sublimation as essentially a desexualization of libido. In this process the ego was said to obtain energy by withdrawing the instinctual charge from the sexual energy of the id. The desexualized libidinal energy was then available to the ego for direction.

Hartmann agreed with Freud's sublimation hypothesis but believed that it did not go far enough in explaining the sources of neutralized energy for ego use. Sex is, of course, only one of Freud's two major instinctual drives, the other being aggression. It was on the latter that Hartmann focused his extension of Freud's deinstinctualization hypothesis. Freud held that the arousal of aggressive drives (for example, by a frustrating or dangerous situation) can lead, in some instances, to direct aggression against the arousing object. In other cases, where direct aggression is not possible, the aggression might be displaced to a substitute object, as when the clerk frustrated at work during the day acts aggressively against his or her family in the evening. When these methods of reducing the tensions of the aggressive drives are not available, the individual may internalize the aggression, turning it inward against himself. It might be noted that other psychoanalysts, such as Klein and Lampl-de-Groot, have agreed with Hartmann concerning the deaggressivation hypothesis, and Menninger (1942) considered deaggressivation even more important than desexualization as a source of ego energy.

The importance of neutralization in the Hartmann theory can be seen in the central significance of the functions served by neutralized energy. While virtually any ego process can employ neutralized energy, three particular functions of such energy have been identified. First, Hartmann places heavy emphasis on the reality and environmental contact functions of the individual, thus requiring that the ego, which carries out these functions, have greater amounts of energy in order to increase its relative power in the psychic structural hierarchy. Neutralization provides much of this excess energy. A second function of neutralization is its role in directly withdrawing charged energy from the id. This energy withdrawal serves to defuse the powerful impulses of the id and is thus an essentially defensive process, since it blocks the expression of the dangerous id drives. Finally, neutralized energy is used by the ego to neutralize further id energy. The function is an important one because it points up the fact that the more powerful the ego becomes (that is, the more energy it gains), the more capable it becomes of withdrawing further energy from the id. In other words, the more fully developed and stronger the individual's environmental interactive process become, the less influence biological factors will have on behavior. It is not surprising, therefore, that the ego's ability to neutralize id energy is considered an indication of *ego strength*.

Change of Function

The neutralization function becomes involved in a process which goes beyond the accumulation of a generalized ego energy pool and involves a modification of certain behavior forms in what is termed a *change of function*. In broad terms, change of function occurs when a behavior form or attitude originating in a given realm of the individual's life appears and functions in a different area. Put otherwise, a particular behavior or attitude which originally served one function comes to serve another. The most common instance is behavior originally serving some id function which later, through change of function, comes to serve instead an ego process. For example, energy originally serving the aggressive drives of the id, which may lead to dangerous and destructive behavior, may be neutralized and later, under ego control, serve as the energy involved in appropriate assertive behavior.

The change of function process is largely responsible for the production of *ego interests*. The ego interests are basically strivings for what is considered useful; they are part of the ego system but tend to cluster around the person or self. In fact, the ego interests, as defined by Hartmann, most frequently include behaviors which are quite literally self-serving behaviors, such as strivings for social status, influence, success, wealth, and comfort. Hartmann traces many of these ego strivings to instinctual tendencies, noting that they become neutralized and independent in the service of the ego.

The ego interests ordinarily exist, according to Hartmann, neither in consciousness nor in the deeply unconscious but rather in the preconscious sector of the psyche. Located at this level, the ego interests are not a part of immediate awareness, but they can either be brought into awareness or used to control behavior without having an immediate awareness that they are functioning. It is this latter process that Hartmann emphasizes in defining what he terms *preconscious automatisms*. Earlier psychoanalysts, including Freud, had generally emphasized the flexibility of ego functions in contrast to the relatively fixed nature of the id instincts. Hartmann would agree that many ego functions are highly flexible and that these are superordinate, occur largely in consciousness, and control much of human behavior. He also postulated, however, that some ego-controlled behaviors become quite inflexible and automatic in nature and that such behaviors are both necessary and adaptive. These behaviors, including many ego interests, exist as highly practiced actions which become preconscious automatisms triggered off by appropriate environmental situations. Driving a car, riding a bicycle, and swimming are physical examples of such behaviors. Once fully learned, they require relatively little of the individual's conscious attention to details. Behaviors involved, for example, in buckling seat belts, inserting a key in the ignition, starting the car, shifting to the appropriate gear, braking for a stop sign, generally require little conscious attention by the experienced driver.

The preconscious automatisms of Hartmann's theory represent an accumulation of appropriate, useful, complex psychological reactions that can be cued off by environmental situations. The adaptive function of such automatisms lies in the fact that they require less attention cathexis (that is, little investment of energy for purposes of attention) and little conscious preoccupation with frequently needed behavior patterns. The result is that energy, including that devoted to the maintenance of attention, can be focused on less frequently encountered and often more important aspects of behavior. Hartmann has argued that it would, in fact, be virtually impossible for an individual to carry out all reality functions if the adaptive economy of the preconscious automatisms did not carry out many of the ego's complex functions.

Secondary Autonomy

When an ego interest or other behavior becomes relatively independent of its original drive energy, it is said to have a degree of *secondary autonomy*. The genetic or instinctual contiguity of behavior remains intact as the history of that behavior, but its energy is now taken from a new source. Specifically, of course, the current energy is supplied by the ego through the process of neutralization. The secondary autonomy construct is very similar to the concept of *functional autonomy,* postulated by Gordon Allport (1937, 1961). He defined functionally autonomous behaviors as those whose current energy source is independent of the developmental history of the motive.

Centrally important to Hartmann's conceptualization is the question of the degree of secondary autonomy. After a behavior form or attitude has achieved autonomy, the original id forces can continue to exert some degree of control over the derived ego interests. This means that the interest, even though it has undergone a change of function and achieved relative secondary autonomy, tends to regress toward id control. For example, the assertive behavior powered by the neutralized aggressive energy may tend to regress toward id control and again involve the individual in potentially destructive aggressive behavior. The classic Freudian polarization of id and ego—of irrational and rational—exerts here, as in Freudian theory, the constant push and pull which underlie intrapsychic conflict. The tendency toward regressive instinctualization must thus be continually counteracted by the forces of the ego. The extent to which the ego functions are able to resist regression and instinctualization constitutes the degree of *secondary autonomy* of the particular ego function involved. The degree to which the ego displays a generalized tendency to resist the regression of ego functions contributes, along with the ability to neutralize energy, to *ego strength.*

ADAPTATION

In formulating his concepts of primary and secondary ego autonomy, Hartmann proposed to make psychoanalysis a general psychology. Freud, of course, emphasized the understanding of psychopathological states and the treatment of such states within the psychoanalytic framework. The "normal personality," to the extent that it was dealt with, was defined by negation as a personality free from pathology. Hartmann felt that to make psychoanalysis a truly general psychology, which could explain normal as well as abnormal personality functions, it was essential to move away from the emphasis on psychopathology and to understand the individual's normal behaviors in relationship to the external environment. The principal result of Hartmann's thrust in this direction is the concept of *adaptation,* which is defined as a relationship between the human organism and its environment in which the organism comes to terms with the environment and "fits" into that environment. A distinction is made between a *state of adaptiveness* and the *process of adaptation.* The former refers to an existing condition of adaptation which is reasonably stable and can be expected to continue over some period of time. The process concept is that of a set of functions which serve to bring about the state of adaptiveness. The infant enters the world in a state of adaptiveness in which its biological functions are automatically adjusted to the average expectable environment. Although unusual and severe environments may cause immediate adaptation problems, the normal infant in the normal environment need not begin life with a struggle to adapt. As the infant grows and begins to interact with the environment, particularly the social environment, the state of adaptiveness is ordinarily somewhat disrupted by growing environmental demands for action and adaptation on the part of the individual.

Hartmann proposed, in agreement with some other theorists, that there are several identifiable forms of adaptation. *Autoplastic adaptation* involves the individual's adjusting his or her own behavior to the demands of the environment. Although this conformity to environmental demands is often the most effective way to cope with the environment, its use can be maladaptive and may lead to adaptation disturbances. Neurotic symptoms, for example, can be seen in many cases as abortive attempts to adapt to environmental demands. The principal alternative to autoplastic adaptation, proposed earlier by Freud, is *alloplastic adaptation,* in which the individual changes the environment rather than his or her own behavior in relation to the environment. Alloplastic adaptation has generally been seen as a more adaptive form of adjustment than autoplastic adaptation and is implicit in such concepts as coping with the environment and competence (White 1959). Hartmann emphasizes the adaptive nature of alloplastic adjustment but points out that even this form of adaptation can be pathological if used inappropriately. A third form of adaptation is one in which the individual actively seeks out a *new* environment that is more advantageous for his or her functioning and to which he or she can more readily adapt. The selection of a new environment implies a change in the subject-environment relationship, as opposed to a change in either the individual alone or the environment alone. In essence, the modification in this case occurs at the meeting of the individual and environment.

Reality and the Self

Adaptation, whatever its form, is an ego function and as such is served by a variety of ego mechanisms. Of major importance, though by no means accounting for all aspects of adaptation, is the reality principle. As in Freudian theory, this important principle defines a rational relationship of the individual and the external reality with which he or she must deal. Specifically, the reality principle states that expenditures of energy (that is, cathexes) must be withheld until such time as the appropriate environmental object or situation for the satisfaction of the particular existing drive is available. The immediate, but often maladaptive, satisfaction prescribed by the pleasure principle is relinquished in favor of a more realistic, if somewhat delayed, drive satisfier. In Hartmann's work this *delay of gratification* principle is supplemented by the addition of a second aspect of the reality principle involving a knowledge of reality which allows the individual to perceive reality accurately and to deal in a "realistic" way with the environment.

Involved in the reality principle but going well beyond it is the concept of the *inner world*, Hartmann's earlier term for what he later called the concept of *self*. The self provides the individual with a perception of his or her own characteristics and also controls such major functions as thinking, memory, and perception. The inner world is partially protected from the impact of the external world by the *stimulus barrier*. This barrier is essentially a perceptual-psychological screening mechanism which rejects particularly intense external stimulation and decreases the effective intensity of other incoming stimulation. The stimulus barrier protects the ego from the external world in the same way that the defense mechanisms protect it from the instinctual impulses of the id.

The stimulus barrier is central to a particular adaptation process in which the individual faced with a problem originating in the external environment is able to withdraw from external reality, deal with and solve the problem internally, then return to reality to carry out the problem solution. In other words, the individual stops and thinks. Hartmann maintained that thinking and intelligence, by which he meant reason, are particularly important factors in adaptation, and both occur within the self.

Adaptive processes that are based principally on thinking, perception, memory, and other positive ego functions are termed *progressive* adaptations, and most environmental adjustments are of these forms. There are instances, however, in which regressive behavior, such as the return to nonrational thought forms, can be adaptive. Artistic accomplishment is an example. This form of adjustment is called *regressive adaptation,* or regression in the service of the ego, and was first proposed by Kris (1936) and later adopted by Hartmann.

Conflict and the Conflict-Free Sphere

Adaptation takes place, in part, in the context of ongoing conflict. Freud had proposed, of course, that one of the most important and universal aspects of psychological functioning is the more or less continual existence of conflicts. These take place either as clashes among the three major psychic structures, that is, intrapsychic or structural conflicts, or conflicts beween the individual and the external world. Such conflicts, particularly when they are intrapsychic, are a part of normal functioning and also serve as the basis for some instances of psychopathology.

Hartmann extended and modified the Freudian approach in two important ways.

First, he proposed two distinct types of structural conflict, intersystemic and intrasystemic. The *intersystemic* conflicts are those originally proposed by Freud and involve clashes among the id, ego, and superego. Both the ego and superego are involved in attempts to block the expression of dangerous id impulses, while the id attempts to force these impulses through into consciousness and reality. *Intrasystemic* conflicts, by contrast, involve two opposing or incompatible tendencies within the same psychic structure. These conflicts may occur within the id, where instinctual drives, such as the tendencies toward elimination and retention in toilet training, may oppose each other. There may also be conflicts within the Superego, including conflicts between incompatible moral values, contradictions between conscious and unconscious morality, and conflicts between the ego ideal (the striving for perfection) and moral taboos. It will not be surprising, however, that Hartmann focused most of his interest in intrasystemic conflict on the ego. In his work he points out that there are many contrasts of functions in the ego. First, this major psychic structure must function to satisfy instinctual drives, but it also opposes such drives in some instances. For example, a teenager may experience an urge to start a fight in the face of verbal abuse. The urge reprsents the operation of an aggressive id impulse, the ego should function to satisfy the impulse, yet a fight may place the person in danger. The teenager is battling an intrasystemic conflict in the ego as to whether to satisfy the id impulse or to block it. The second contrast in ego functions is that of insight, a higher order thought process based in the ego, which conflicts with rationalization, also an ego function. Further, the ego is functionally independent of the other two psychic structures, but it must neverthe-less consider the demands of these structures, both in connection with intrapsychic functioning and in its relationship to reality. And despite its necessary and defen-sive opposition to both id and superego impulses, the ego must serve to integrate the functioning of all three psychic structures, bringing some degree of harmony to the whole. These intraego contradictions may be expected, Hartmann has claimed, to serve as the basis for intrasystemic conflicts within this structure. The distribu-tion and redistribution of psychic energy within the ego thus becomes nearly as important as the redistribution of energy across psychic structures. It must be pre-sumed that the greater the overall degree of ego strength, and hence the greater the availability of neutralized energy, the less severe will be the conflicts within the ego.

Hartmann's second, and far more important, modification of Freudian conflict theory is his introduction of the concept of a *conflict-free sphere of the ego*. In a striking and far-reaching departure from Freudian theory, Hartmann proposed that not all ego functions involve conflict. In fact, a substantial portion of major ego functions, including potentially all of those involved in interaction with reality, may be contained in the conflict-free sphere. Some of the major functions involved are perception, intention, language, recall, object comprehension, thinking, and the motor development of such functions as grasping, crawling, and walking. All of these and other processes may function without conflict, and those which do so are collectively labeled the conflict-free sphere. Hartmann has carefully noted, how-ever, that he is not speaking of a separate mental province but only of a set of processes. It seems clear, in fact, that *any given process may at one time be involved in conflict and at another be a part of the conflict-free sphere.* Adaptation to the environment involves both conflicted and conflict-free functions. The emphasis, in ego psychology, on the conflict-free sphere allows Hartmann to better explain and understand nonpathological behavior, moves psychoanalytic theory a giant step toward becoming a general psychology, and represents one of the major bridges between psychoanalysis and other personality theories.

ADDITIONAL THEORISTS

A number of major figures in the modern psychoanalytic movement have contributed substantially to the furtherance of ego psychology. We have mentioned Kris and Loewenstein, whose primary contributions came through their elaborations of Hartmann's ideas and their work with him in the full explication of his ego psychology. Their work does not seem to require further specific commentary here.

Rapaport (1951, 1958) brought together Hartmann's various hypotheses about ego functioning and added his own ideas as an extension of Hartmann's theory. Much of Rapaport's contribution revolves around the concept of delay of gratification. Hartmann had conceptualized delay as primarily involving the use of ego thought processes to abstain at least temporarily from the satisfaction of an id drive. Rapaport extended and amplified the delay concept to include the use of reasoning and thought processes to delay the satisfaction of both instinctual and environmental demands. In essence, Hartmann had given man the free will to delay gratification of instinctual impulses, and Rapaport extended this framework to assure that man can similarly delay gratifications demanded by the environment. Ego autonomy is thus extended to include autonomous functioning both in relation to the id and in relation to the environment. Rapaport noted, however, that the autonomy of the ego from external reality is always a relative autonomy in that the ego can never be completely free from some dependence on the environment.

Another ego theorist, Mahler (1968), has contributed to an understanding of ego development. In her theory Mahler borrows the term *symbiosis,* which is defined in biology as the bringing together of two dissimilar organisms for mutual advantage. Mahler's use focuses on symbiosis as the infant's delusion of a common boundary between himself or herself and the mother, although they are physically separate individuals. The symbiotic union with the mother and accompanying symbiotic gratification are essential to normal ego development. It is an early phase of life seen as developing in about the second month.

In other theoretical contributions which serve as major examples of the development of ego psychology, Jacobson (1964, 1971) has modified a number of Freudian and ego psychological concepts to formulate a theory of depression and has dealt with the phenomena of psychosis and borderline states. In addition, Kernberg (1971) and Kohut (1971) have dealt with disordered states lying between the traditional transference neuroses of the Freudian theory and the psychoses, and

Blanck and Blanck (1974) have detailed methods for the extension of ego analytic techniques to therapy with the more severe disorders.

TREATMENT

The modifications in psychoanalytic theory introduced by the ego psychologists have led to a gradual evolution of psychoanalytic techniques to reflect the increased theoretical importance of the ego. While the ego analyst can point to many specific ways in which ego theory has modified technique (see, for example, Loewenstein 1951, 1969; Kris 1956, 1951; Blanck and Blanck 1974), the major changes center around the analyst's role in the interpretation of the patient's thoughts and behaviors. Much of the analyst's effort is traditionally spent in interpreting the patient's verbalizations in terms of their deeper, underlying meanings. The patient's slip of the tongue, for example, in which he substitutes the name of his mother for that of his wife, may be interpreted in terms of an early relationship between the patient and his mother. Similarly, dreams are often seen as representations of important, unconscious psychological functioning and are interpreted accordingly. And much of the patient's day-to-day behavior is also subjected to interpretation as to its "real" meaning.

Ego psychology has led the psychoanalyst to modify his or her interpretations to include events at various levels of personality functioning. Under the tutelage of Hartmann and the ego psychologists, attempts are made to explore functioning at levels of the personality that lie between surface and depth and to establish an optimal distance from the surface of the personality for interpretation. The willingness of the ego analyst to interpret closer to the surface of personality functioning is reflected in dimensions of both consciousness and time. In terms of the dimension of conscious-unconscious functioning, the concept of optimal distance often leads the analyst to deal actively with the patient's conscious thoughts and behaviors as well as with the unconscious. In terms of time, the Freudian emphasis had been on the interpretation of events in the distant past of the patient, often in childhood. The ego analyst frequently deals with events in the present and recent past or in earlier adulthood, which might also have significantly influenced the patient's functioning.

One additional change in interpretation which should be noted is a change from the highly symbolic interpretations of the Freudian analyst to the considerably less symbolic understandings of modern ego analysis. For example, Loewenstein (1951) considers the case of a girl who comes to the analyst with the fear that she will be run over by a car. Earlier theory would suggest as a primary interpretation that the car is a symbol for a man and that the girl's fear is basically a fear of men or of sexual contact with men. The ego analyst may also provide this symbolic interpretation but is likely to be additionally interested in the more current motives and reasons for the patient's particular fear. Thus his or her interpretation will go beyond the "obvious" symbolism of the phobia to examine causes and effects closer to the surface of the patient's personality. Her own previous involvement in

Breuer, J., & Freud, S. *Studies in hysteria.* New York: Nervous and Mental Diseases—Publications, 1937. (Originally published, 1895.)

Erikson, E. H. *Childhood and society* (2nd ed.). New York: Norton, 1950. (Enlarged and revised, 1963.)

Erikson, E. H. *Young man Luther.* New York: Norton, 1958.

Erikson, E. H. *Ghandi's truth.* New York: Norton, 1969.

Erikson, E. H. *Dimensions of a new identity.* New York: Norton, 1974.

Erikson, E. H. *Life history and the historical moments.* New York: Norton, 1975.

Erikson, E. H. *Poise and reasons.* New York: Norton, 1976.

Freud, S. [Interpretation of dreams.] In A. A. Brill (trans.), *The basic writings of Sigmund Freud.* New York: Random House, 1938. (Originally published, 1900.)

Freud, S. [*Moses and monotheism*] (K. Jones, trans.). New York: Vintage Books, 1967. (Originally published, 1939.)

Freud, S. [Analysis terminable and interminable.] In J. Strachey (Ed. and trans.), *The Standard edition of the complete psychological works of Sigmund Freud* (Vol. 23). London: Hogarth Press, 1971. (Originally published, 1937.)

Freud, S. [The ego and the id.] In J. Strachey (Ed. and trans.), *The Standard edition of the complete psychological works of Sigmund Freud* (Vol. 19). London: Hogarth Press, 1971. (Originally published, 1923.)

Freud, S. [An outline of psychoanalysis.] In J. Strachey (Ed. and trans.), *The Standard edition of the complete psychological works of Sigmund Freud* (Vol. 23). London: Hogarth Press, 1971. (Originally published, 1940.)

Freud, S. [Psychoanalysis.] In J. Strachey (Ed. and trans.), *The Standard edition of the complete psychological works of Sigmund Freud* (Vol. 20). London: Hogarth Press, 1971. (Originally published, 1926.)

Hartmann, H. *Essays on ego psychology.* New York: International Universities Press, 1964.

Hartmann, H., Kris, E., & Loewenstein, R. M. Papers on psychoanalytic psychology. *Psychological Issues,* 1964, *14* (4, No. 2). (Monograph)

Jacobson, E. *The self and the object world.* New York: International Universities Press, 1964.

Jacobson, E. *Depression.* New York: International Universities Press, 1971.

Jones, E. *Sigmund Freud: Life and work* (Vol. 3). London: Hogarth Press, 1957.

Kernberg, O. F. Prognostic considerations regarding borderline personality organization. *Journal of the American Psychoanalytic Association,* 1971, *19,* 595–635.

Kohut, H. *The analysis of the self.* New York: International Universities Press, 1971.

Kris, E. The psychology of caricature. *International Journal of Psycho-Analysis,* 1936, *17,* 285–303.

Kris, E. Ego psychology and interpretation in psychoanalytic therapy. *Psychoanalytic Quarterly,* 1951, *20,* 15–30.

Kris, E. On some vicissitudes of insight in psychoanalysis. *International Journal of Psycho-Analysis,* 1956, *37,* 445–455.

an automobile accident or her fear that a loved one, who tends to drive recklessly, may be involved in an accident would be more carefully considered by the ego analyst than by a traditional Freudian.

RESEARCH CONTRIBUTIONS

Much of the research reviewed in our earlier discussions of Freudian theory is also relevant to ego psychology and, therefore, need not be again reviewed here. In general, any of the wide variety of research which has focused on the development of ego functions and the expression of ego processes is pertinent. In a broad sense, research in cognitive psychology of recent years is quite relevant to Hartmann's psychology of the ego as well.

As one specific example of research growing out of and contributing to ego theory, one might consider the work of Rene Spitz. This investigator and theorist was interested in the study of conditions necessary and sufficient for normal ego development and functioning. In the quest to understand such conditions his primary focus was on the mother-child relationship and its impact on ego development. He conducted studies of hospitalized infants and compared infants raised in private homes with those raised in nurseries and foundling homes (Spitz, 1945, 1946, 1950). Studying changes in developmental level through the use of successive behavior samples, he found that infants separated from the mother often showed symptoms of anaclitic depression, such as a dazed expression lacking in emotionality, inactivity, heightened autoerotic behavior, and a general appearance of sadness and apprehension. In its severest forms anaclitic depression was found to incapacitate the child greatly, creating a syndrome which Spitz referred to as "hospitalism."

Spitz interpreted his results from an essentially ego analytic viewpoint, noting that the autonomous ego apparatuses which are present at birth require for normal development the experience of intensive, ongoing mother-child interaction. The mother provides a base of emotional support for the child and serves, in fact, as an auxiliary, external ego for the infant. She adds to the child's own rudimentary stimulus barrier an additional protective barrier against strong environmental forces. She also serves a variety of other ego-relevant functions and is thus essential to early ego development.

EVALUATION

Both the contributions and the problems of Hartmann's ego psychology relate to the sweeping nature of the changes Hartmann made in psychoanalytic theory. Thus, Hartmann's major contribution, broadly conceived, lies in his having moved psychoanalytic theory toward a view of humanity as a far more rational, environmentally influenced being than Freud had seen. At the same time, the problematic aspects of Hartmann's work lie in a failure to integrate fully these sweeping changes with the core concepts of the psychoanalytic framework.

Major Contributions

One of Hartmann's major contributions to psychoanalytic theory was his organizing influence on its major concepts and factors. The extensive but relatively chaotic mass of information which Freud produced during the first twenty years of his development of the theory was organized under Hartmann's influence into a coherent and logical theory.

A second major contribution was Hartmann's modification of psychoanalytic theory to attribute increased importance to the rational and environmental forces shaping the personality. The nonrational, physiological forces of the id which, in the original Freudian theory, were seen so heavily to influence behavior are largely balanced in Hartmann's treatment by the powerful impact of rational ego functions. The explanatory power of the theory is considerably increased by permitting a logical, theoretical account of the influence of conscious, willful cognition and of the external environment on behavior. As Schafer (1970) has pointed out, the Hartmann version of psychoanalytic theory is much more comprehensive in its treatment of behavior determination than the original Freudian formulation.

The application of Hartmann's concepts to the therapeutic setting has introduced important modifications in psychoanalytic technique. In particular, the analyst no longer feels compelled to focus almost exclusively on removing repressions and otherwise bringing unconscious memories into awareness. He or she may also deal with the patient's consciousness and with the cognitive elements which are now seen as contributing to neurotic phenomena.

Problems and Difficulties

Some criticisms of Hartmann have centered around the idea that he has moved psychoanalytic theory too far from the original Freudian concepts and thereby weakened the interpretive power of the theory, while countermanding criticisms have held that Hartmann's changes have not taken the theory far enough from its original form. Criticisms of the first type note that Freud had made considerable progress toward a better understanding of human behavior through introduction of the concepts of sexual and aggressive instincts and their associated energy; Hartmann has reduced the influence of these instinctual forces through his concepts of neutralization and secondary autonomy and thereby reversed the progress begun by Freud's insights. Another modification that has been described as "going too far" is Hartmann's emphasis on environmental influences. Again, Freud's insights into biological determinism can be seen as considerable and Hartmann's balancing of biology with environment thereby inappropriate and regressive.

Clearly representing the opposite side of a biased theoretical coin are those criticisms which are based on Hartmann's perceived failure to move far enough from

the original psychoanalytic doctrine. One such criticism points to his failure to move beyond the instinct and energy concepts of Freudian theory. It is clearly true that Hartmann made extensive use of the psychic energy concept and that he maintained the hypothesis that sexual and aggressive instincts play an important part in personality functioning. While he certainly deemphasized the importance of the instincts, it is clear that a further reduction in the importance of this concept or its abolition would permit even greater environmental influence on behavior than is currently true of the theory. On the other hand, removal of the instinct and energy concepts from the theory would make it difficult to argue that the orientation is still psychoanalytic in nature. Perhaps a more reasonable criticism of Hartmann is that he has failed to integrate fully the basically biological concepts of instinct and energy with the more psychological and environmental concepts that he introduced into the psychoanalytic framework. This, in fact, remains a task for future theorists.

Other criticisms have focused on the structure and functions of the ego in Hartmann's work. First there is a question of whether the term denotes an actual structure or entity or whether it is a construct referring to a set of related functions. A second ambiguity concerns the unity of the ego. At many points in his writings Hartmann emphasized that the ego functions as an integrated, reasonable, harmonious unit. Its functions complement each other, with primary autonomy and neutralization conjointly providing a pool of energy which is used in a coordinated way to serve the various ego functions. Hartmann has also spoken of intrasystemic conflict in the ego. Such conflict is seen as resulting from competition among the various ego functions for a limited pool of available energy. While the apparent theoretical contradiction might be resolved by introducing a concept of "cooperative competition," in which the ego functions compete in a healthy way to maintain and enhance personality functioning, such a conceptualization is not apparent in Hartmann's writings. The contradiction thus remains unresolved.

Overall, then, ego psychology represents both evolution and revolution in psychoanalytic theory. In its most progressive and useful aspects we see the Freudian theoretical framework evolving to become a more comprehensive, better organized theory capable of predicting and explaining an increased range of phenomena. At the same time, however, some aspects of ego theory represent a dramatic change—a true revolution—which brings at once progress and regress, new clarity and new confusion to the psychoanalytic perspective.

REFERENCES

Allport, G. W. *Pattern and growth in personality.* New York: Holt, Rinehart, Winston, 1937.

Allport, G. W. *Pattern and growth in personality.* New York: Holt, Rinehart, Winston, 1961.

Blanck, G., & Blanck, R. *Ego psychology: Theory and practice.* New York: Columbia University Press, 1974.

Loewenstein, R. M.   Ego development and psychoanalytic technique. *American Journal of Psychiatry*, 1951, *107*, 617–622.

Loewenstein, R. M.   Some thoughts on interpretation in the theory and practice of psychoanalysis. In A. Freud (Ed.), *The psychoanalytic study of the child* (Vol. 12). New York: International Universities Press, 1957.

Loewenstein, R. M.   Developments in the theory of transference in the last fifty years. *International Journal of Psycho-Analysis*, 1969, *50*, 583–588.

Loewenstein, R. M., Newman, L. M., Schur, M., & Solnit, A. J. (Eds.).   *Psychoanalysis—A general psychology: Essays in honor of Heinz Hartmann.* New York: International Universities Press, 1966.

Mahler, M. S.   *On human symbiosis and the vicissitudes of individuation.* New York: International Universities Press, 1968.

Menninger, K. A.   *Love against hate.* New York: Harcourt, Brace, 1942.

Rapaport, D.   *The autonomy of the ego.* Mass.: Austen Riggs Foundation, 1951.

Rapaport, D.   The theory of ego autonomy: A generalization. *Bulletin Menninger-Clinic*, 1958, *22*, 13–35.

Schafer, R.   An overview of Heniz Hartmann's contributions to psychoanalysis. *International Journal of Psycho-Analysis*, 1970, *51*, 425–446.

Spitz, R. A.   Hospitalism: An inquiry into the genesis of psychiatric conditions in early childhood. In A. Freud (Ed.), *The psychoanalytic study of the child* (Vol. 1). New York: International Universities Press, 1945.

Spitz, R. A.   Hospitalism: a follow-up report. In A. Freud (Ed.), *The psychoanalytic study of the child* (Vol. 2). New York: International Universities Press, 1946.

Spitz, R. A.   Anxiety in infancy: A study of its manifestations in the first year of life. *International Journal of Psychoanalysis*, 1950, *31*, 138–143.

Waterman, C., Buebel, M., & Waterman, A.   Relationship between resolution of the identity crisis and outcome of previous psychosocial crises. *Proceedings of the Annual Convention of the American Psychological Association*, 1970, *5*, 467–468.

White, R. W.   Motivation reconsidered: The concept of competence. *Psychological Review*, 1959, *66*, 297–333.

4

Analytical Psychology:

Carl Jung

Carl Gustav Jung was born in Kesswyl, Switzerland, in 1875. His psychological theory is to a great extent an interaction of opposing forces, and so was his life. His father and mother were strikingly different personalities, and their marriage was a difficult and divided one. Jung's loyalties were torn between the two. His mother was outgoing and worldly; his father was introverted and pious, a pastor in the Swiss Reformed Church. This unhappy marriage deeply affected Jung, and he notes often in his writings that the problems of children are automatically solved if one can deal with the problems of their parents.

In addition to his father, eight of his uncles were clergymen, so that the atmosphere of the Swiss Church dominated his early development. His father's life was, for the most part, ineffectual and filled with personal and religious doubts, which were communicated to Jung. Often he would turn to his father with questions on religion and life but seldom would he receive a satisfactory answer. It was not until much later, as an adult, that he was able to supply some answers of his own. In one of his later books (1954), he relates a revealing anecdote. As a boy he had to study his catechism diligently and recite it to his father. The book bored him. One day, while searching through it for something that would interest him, he came across a lesson on the Trinity which he could not understand but which nevertheless fascinated him deeply. In the weeks that followed, he waited with anticipation for the lesson on the Trinity. When that day finally came, his father said, "Let's skip over this one, I can't make heads or tails of it." Jung said that from that day on "religion bored me." It was not until much later when he had formulated his theory of symbols and their unconscious significance that he was able to supply an answer for his long deferred question.

Two experiences from Jung's school days show a striking relationship to elements in his later theoretical postulates. First, he became particularly bitter on one occasion when a school master accused him of cheating on an essay on which he had expended a great deal of effort. The master remained deaf to his protests. Suddenly he felt himself overcome with rage and anger, which threatened to get out of control. He was later frustrated by the thought that such feelings existed within himself and that it was possible to lose control over them (Jung 1963). Another incident involves an episode in his early years. When he was about twelve years old, he was knocked down as he was coming out of school and hit his head on the pavement. This blow started a series of fainting spells that exempted him from school, which bored him tremendously. One day he overheard his father speaking of the dim prospects for his son's future because of his poor health. Jung, startled by this, struggled against the attacks, which soon disappeared so that he could resume his education uninterrupted (Fordham 1953).

After his school days Jung's scientific interests began to develop. In 1895 he entered medical school at Basel University. After medical school he became an assistant in the Burgholzli Mental Hospital and the Psychiatric Clinic in Zurich, and thus embarked on a career in psychiatry. He collaborated with Eugen Bleuler and studied with Janet. In 1906 he began to correspond with Freud, and in the following year they met for the first time. For several years following their meeting, Jung was closely involved in the psychoanalytic movement, and from 1910 to 1914 he was the first president of the International Psychoanalytic Association. In 1909 Freud and Jung traveled to Clark University in Massachusetts to deliver a series of lectures. Freud for a time thought that Jung was to be his successor, but there was too fundamental a difference between the two men and their back-grounds for this to happen. Freud was mainly concerned with neurosis and its etiology, whereas Jung was also concerned with the psychotic trends (archaic elements) in otherwise normal persons. This led to basic differences in their respective views of the structure and dynamics of the human personality, particularly its unconscious aspects. Finally, in 1913 the two men terminated their relationship, or as Freud put it, "Jung caused me to withdraw my libido from him" (Jones 1963). In 1913 he gave up his instructorship in psychiatry at the University of Zurich in order to devote full time to private practice and writing. In 1944 a chair of medical psychology was founded especially for Jung at the University of Basel, but he was able to occupy it for only one year because of failing health. He continued to write and conduct research in Zurich until 1961, when he died at the age of eighty-five.

STRUCTURAL PRINCIPLES

The *psyche* or personality is a dynamically structured totality, involving integrative wholeness and, at the same time, the divisive polarity of its multifarious and complexly interacting subparts. It is both personal and impersonal, conscious and unconscious, internalized and externalized, constructive and destructive, public and private. It is an energy system, constantly ebbing and flowing, continually pulsating and changing, yet partially hereditary, highly structured, and consistent over time.

To Jung, individuals are of two basic types or *attitudes,* introverted and extroverted. Each of these can be further subdivided according to the dominance of one of four psychological *functions:* thinking, feeling, sensing, and intuiting. And, in addition, each subtype can be seen as operating at conscious or unconscious, or both, levels of the personality. Considerations of consciousness involve primarily the concepts of ego and persona. The unconscious subdivides into the personal unconscious, with its incorporated complexes, and the collective unconscious, containing primordial thought forms or achetypes. Finally, the dynamic interaction of conscious and unconscious over time produces the self, the fully integrated, fully functioning personality.

The Conscious Psyche

The essence of consciousness is the Jungian *ego.* It consists of all conscious aspects of functioning, including conscious thoughts, feelings, evaluations, sensations, perceptions, and active memories. The functions of the ego are both externally and internally oriented. Externally, it provides for the individual the perceptual structuring of reality that is necessary for interaction with the outside world. It is through the ego that the individual knows and deals with both the physical and the social environment. Internally, the ego structures the individual's perceptions of his or her own being, giving a sense of personal identity and temporal continuity.

In becoming socialized, the child must, through the ego, make many compromises between personal desires and the demands of society. As a result, during the process of ego development, a shell, the *persona,* forms around the ego. The persona is a social mask, a public personality, behind which the individual lives. It develops because of social pressures to represent the person in a way that is easily recognizable by and in conformity with the expectations of others. Says Jung (1963):

> *Society expects, and indeed must expect, every individual to play the part*
> *assigned to him as perfectly as possible, so that a man who is a parson . . .*
> *must at all times . . . play the role of parson in a flawless manner. Society*
> *demands this as a kind of surety; each must stand at his post, here a cobbler,*
> *here a poet. No man is expected to be both . . . that would be 'odd.' Such*
> *a man would be 'different' from other people, not quite reliable. In the*
> *academic world he would be a dilettante, in politics an 'unpredictable'*
> *quantity, in religion a 'free thinker'—in short, he would always be suspected*
> *of unreliability and incompetence, because society is persuaded that only*
> *the cobbler who is not a poet can supply workmanlike shoes. (p. 305)*

The persona is thus roughly analogous to the sociological concept, *roletaking* (see, for example, Clinard 1968). Although the persona is a response to societal pressures, it is also a response to personal needs. Through it, we relate to the world. It simplifies our contacts by indicating what we may expect from others.

In his book, *The Presentation of Self in Everyday Life,* Erving Goffman (1959) deals with the personal needs which are served by the development of an outward self presented to the public:

> *Regardless of the particular objective which the individual has in mind and*
> *of his motive for having that objective, it will be in his interests to control*
> *the conduct of the others especially their responsive treatment of him. This*
> *control is achieved largely by influencing the definition of the situation which*
> *the others come to formulate, and he can influence this definition by express-*
> *ing himself in such a way as to give them the kind of impression that will*
> *lead them to act voluntarily in accordance with his own plan. Thus, when the*
> *individual appears in the presence of others, there will usually be some*
> *reason for him to mobilize his activity so that it will convey an impression*
> *to others which it is in his interests to convey. (pp. 1–3)*

As both Goffman and Jung have pointed out, the danger involved in this social-psychological process is that the persona can become so rigid and pervasive that we might mistake it for the entirety of our personality and consequently deny the existence of those aspects of the personality which lie in the realm of the unconscious. For example, the individual who is viewed by others as a sociable, friendly, outgoing person may make this persona rigid and come to deny unconscious needs for privacy and quiet self-evaluation. This kind of denial, according to Jung, makes us vulnerable to psychological conflict when, during a crisis in life, elements of the unconscious force their way into consciousness.

The Personal Unconscious

At the near-conscious level of the personality, between the conscious ego and the deeper collective unconscious, lies an important twilight area which Jung called the *personal unconscious.* This region of the psyche consists of experiences that were once conscious but have been repressed or forgotten as well as experiences that were subliminal or below the threshold for awareness when they originally occurred. It is important to Jung's theory that the personal unconscious is unique to the individual. The personal unconscious is the storehouse of each person's past experiences, interactions with the world, and interpretations of environmental objects and concepts.

The material of the personal unconscious is usually accessible to consciousness, and, as a result, there is a constant interaction between the personal unconscious and the ego. Repressed or forgotten experiences may enter ego-consciousness, influence behavior or thought, and return to their unconscious state. Reciprocally, ego-experiences are often relegated to the storehouse of the personal unconscious to lie there until they are again needed in the conduct of conscious behavior.

The Complexes. The term complex, which has since been incorporated into psychoanalytic and Adlerian theories, originated in Jung's theory as the major component structure of the personal unconscious. As the individual interacts with the environment and gains a variety of experiences, he or she finds that experiential contacts with certain objects and concepts are repeated over and over again and are of central importance to life. As a result, the individual begins to gather a variety of relevant experiences around each of these core phenomena. Each collective organization of related thoughts, perceptions, emotions, and values is called a *feeling-toned complex*. A given individual may thus have a mother complex, a father complex, an achievement complex, a power complex, and many others. By way of example, the mother complex derives from many experiences with, thoughts about, and perceptions of the mother.

Each complex has constellating power, tends to be autonomous, and is capable of becoming conscious. The *constellating power* of a complex is its ability to attract, in magnetic fashion, a variety of supporting experiences, thus increasing its breadth and potency. Each complex, once formed, functions relatively autonomously and may act as a *splinter psyche,* a behavior determinant partially separated from and acting quite independently of the total personality. In its extreme form, complex autonomy may be responsible for the "splintering" of the personality in some forms of psychological maladjustment, particularly schizophrenia, in which Jung was strongly interested. Finally, although complexes operate primarily at an unconscious level, any of the associated components of a complex, or even the entire complex, may become conscious.

The Collective Unconscious

No doubt one of the most controversial of Jung's contributions to personality theory is the *collective unconscious,* also termed the *transpersonal* or *impersonal* unconscious. It includes all of a person's accumulated experiences from prehuman existence, providing that the experience has been repeated often enough to leave what Jung called *memory traces* in the cortex. It is identical in all humans, is universal, and its contents have never been at the level of awareness of consciousness. The collective unconscious is described as being so powerful and ubiquitous that any gross deviation from it, or its overdomination, can cause abnormalities in the psyche. For instance, child abandonment is a personality deviation, not because the law says so, but because it is against people's unconscious. Another example is mother love, which is not taught by imitation or example but is inherited from one's past through the collective unconscious.

The notion of the collective unconscious was a major source of disagreement between Freud and Jung. Freud maintained that the unconscious was composed of repressed material that was too threatening to the entire ego. Thus the elements of the unconscious were at one time conscious. Jung, on the other hand, noted that psychotic patients, whom he saw as controlled by the unconscious, displayed thoughts and behavior which were totally different from what he considered conscious processes. He concluded from these observations that the unconscious must contain a reservoir of thoughts and ideas which have an origin other than the repression of conscious material. As Jung (1954) observes:

> Neither Janet nor Freud had any specific psychiatric experience. If they had, they would have been struck by the fact that the unconscious displays contents that are utterly different from conscious ones, so strange indeed that we cannot understand them. (p. 493)

Furthermore, he noted that this "unconscious material" seemed to display certain thematic elements that were common to different people. Likewise, these thematic elements would be very similar to the content of dreams, ancient myths and rituals. It was on this basis that he postulated the common possession by all mankind of these thematic images, that is, the collective unconscious.

The collective unconscious may be viewed as composed of latent memory traces inherited from man's ancestral past. It is the residue of repeated experiences over many generations. Jung has been criticized for postulating the inheritance of ideas. This is a misconception of Jung's intended meaning. What is inherited is the predisposition to respond in a particular fashion, the potentiality to revive the experiences of past generations. This is not the inheritance of the idea, but rather of its potential to come into consciousness: "I do not by any means assert the inheritance of ideas, but only the possibility of such ideas" (Jung, 1956, p. 76). Again, quoting from Jung:

> Although our inheritance consists in physiological paths, it was nevertheless mental processes in our ancestors that trace these paths. If they come to consciousness again in the individual, they can do so only in the form of other mental processes; and although these processes can become conscious only through individual experience and consequently appear as individual acquisitions, they are nevertheless pre-existing traces which are merely "filled out" by the individual experience. Probably every "impressive" experience is just such a breakthrough into an old, previously unconscious river bed. (1954, p. 100)

The Archetypes. The collective unconscious is structurally composed of genetically transmitted universal thought forms. Each of these universal idea-potentialities is an *archetype*, a term used long before Jung and meaning a prototype from which copies can be produced. The archetypes function by producing images in consciousness of the archetypal forms existing in the unconscious. There are archetypal images corresponding to virtually all common human situations and abstract conceptions. Even the persona is based on an archetype. Other examples cited by Jung include archetypes of the mother, father, God, child, power, the hero, birth, death, and the demon. Each produces an imaginal predisposition to respond, an inherited picture of the generic characteristics of the object or concept that it represents. Perhaps the most frequently cited archetype is that of the mother, which provides for the infant a preconceived image of the universal characteristics of the mother figure. The importance of this archetype is that it will, in part, determine the child's perception of and reactions to his or her own mother.

Despite their universality and hereditary nature, the archetypes do not act in isolation, either from each other or from reality. Two or more archetypes may blend or fuse to form a new image, which may also predispose behavior. In addition, the archetypes must interact with reality through the ego and the personal unconscious. Archetypes may serve as the nuclei around which complexes are formed. It is thus important to note that a complex is often, in effect, an archetype that has been modified through personal experience. For example, the child's initial expectations concerning his or her mother are governed by the mother archetype. While the child's experiences with the actual mother will typically conform rather closely to the archetypal image, there will be some discrepancies. There will also be an elaboration and enrichment of mother-relevant experiences due to the unique interaction of *this* mother and *this* child. As a result, the mother archetype may serve as a core for the formation of the mother complex, which comprises a more personalized set of mother-relevant expectations.

Before leaving the collective unconscious, we stress again that what is inherited in Jung's archetypes is not knowledge, information, or personality characteristics but tendencies or predispositions. In Jung's words:

> It is not a question of a specifically racial heredity, but of a universally human characteristic. Nor is it a question of inherited ideas, but of a functional disposition to produce the same, or very similar, ideas. This disposition I later called archetype. (1956, p. 102)

Highly Evolved Archetypes

Jung proposed that not all archetypes are of equal importance in determining behavior. He has, therefore, devoted considerable time and space to discussions of three archetypes—the anima, the animus, and the shadow—which he felt are highly evolved and important behavior determinants.

Anima and Animus. Jung suggested that humans' widely recognized physiological bisexuality should be extended to the psychological level as well. He, therefore, postulated the *anima* as the feminine archetype in the male and the *animus* as the masculine archetype in the female. Each is based upon repeated ancestral experiences with members of the opposite sex.

The anima and animus serve two principal functions. First, they are responsible for the manifestation, in members of each sex, of certain characteristics usually associated with the opposite sex. The anima may, for example, influence the man at times to display tender affection or intuition. The animus may call out in the woman assertive or even domineering behavior or draw her towards a usually masculine profession. The second function of these archetypes is to permit each sex to understand and react appropriately to the opposite sex. Each archetype, therefore, produces an image corresponding to the generic characteristics of the opposite sex. The anima image in the unconscious of the man may then be projected upon a given woman, comparing her actual characteristics with those of the archetype, and, conversely, from a woman's unconscious comes the projection of the animus on a given man.

The Shadow. A third archetype, the *shadow,* is important not only in its own right but also because it provides a better understanding of some of the interrelationships of the personal and collective unconscious and the ego. The shadow, which draws elements from both the personal and collective unconscious, contains all of the primitive, uncontrolled, and instinctual parts of our personality that we try to deny exist within us. It is the set of impulsive, uncivilized desires and emotions which are unacceptable to society and are consequently respressed. The shadow also tends to be repressed because it is threatening to the conscious elements of the psyche. Jung suggested three reasons for the repression of the shadow. First, social demands are put upon the individual to conform to normatively accepted behavior.

Therefore, the more restrictive the society, the larger will be the shadow. Second, as the persona develops and is generally accepted as the entirety of the personality, emerging impulses from the shadow, which contains elements inconsistent with the ideal picture that the persona presents for others to see, threaten the integrity of the persona. And finally, since the shadow is an archetype, it acts in relation to such other archetypes as fear of the dark, which can affect the behavior of both children and adults. According to Jung, we must come to recognize the shadow as a part of our psyche; we should accept that latent within us are the drives of primitive man. If we do, when elements of the shadow surge into consciousness, we are not thrown into panic by such socially unacceptable thoughts and feelings.

The shadow also has aspects which are common to all humanity and, therefore, belong to the collective unconscious. It is the collectiveness of the shadow which is displayed in mob riots and collective disorders, when apparently well-meaning people behave in the most savage and destructive manner. Literature can provide us with many an illustration of the collective aspects of the shadow. In her short story, *The Lottery,* Shirley Jackson provides one such example. Here, a small town enacts an annual ritual of holding a town lottery in much the same spirit as a church social or a county fair. The citizens, well-mannered and harmless people, gather with anticipation and eagerness to see whose name will be drawn from the hat this year. The person whose name is drawn is placed in the center, and the entire town—men, women, children—proceeds to stone to death the winner of the lottery. On the following day, the citizens resume their customary activities until the time comes for the next lottery.

Attitudes and Functions

In describing the operation of the personality, Jung postulated in his early works two types, or attitudes, of personality, which he termed *introversion* and *extroversion*. These are undoubtedly Jung's best-known concepts. The introvert is interested in subjective experiences and feelings within the ego; the extrovert, on the other hand, is interested in people and in objects outside his or her own ego. Although both attitudes are present in each person, generally one is conscious and dominant, while the other is unconscious and subordinate.

Jung recognized, however, that the two-category typology of introversion-extroversion was not sufficient for the description of the complex variations that he observed in the human personality. As a result, he postulated that each of the two personality attitudes could be further classified in terms of the dominance relationships of four functions. He divided these into two pairs, contrasting *sensation* and *intuition* with *thinking* and *feeling*. Through sensation the individual is able to observe the environment closely, to classify and elaborate it, and to report it to others; sensation is the perceptual or reality function. Intuition organizes the world through impressions, which we cannot describe clearly but which nevertheless have some basis in reality; intuition is essentially perception through unconscious processes. The functions of thinking and feeling, on the other hand, elaborate and classify the experiences that are acquired by the psyche through the functions of sensation and intuition. Thinking takes these already acquired experiences and classifies them according to logical and discrete categories. The feeling function classifies already acquired information according to its pleasantness or unpleasantness and arranges it into a value structure. The feeling function must allow the emotions to play a full part, while the thinking function tries to suppress the emotions and view the environment from an exclusively factual perspective. Sensation and intuition are *irrational* functions, according to Jung, because they order experience in other than empirical or logical dimensions. Thinking and feeling, on the other hand, are considered *rational functions* since they arrange experience according to a logical or value-related mode of operation.

Like the attitudes, the functions are contrasted with one another and are never initially balanced in one person. Gradually, one function develops as the *superior function*, while the remaining functions are more or less undifferentiated and unconscious. The one function which is least differentiated is called the *inferior function*.

Jung postulated that under normal circumstances the dominant attitude and the superior function are determined by genetic factors, yet this constitutional predisposition can be thwarted by environmental circumstances. For example, if two "thinking" parents have a child who has the genetic potential to become an "intuitive" person, they may restrict development so that the child is forced to apprehend his or her environment in terms of logic and reason and fails to develop the intuitive function.

MOTIVATIONAL AND DEVELOPMENTAL PRINCIPLES

Like the Freudian person, the Jungian person is viewed as a complex energy system. Both physical (biological) and psychic energy derive from metabolic processes. Jung used the term *libido* to describe all vital energy, both physical and psychic, as well as to mean psychic energy alone. It is important to note that in neither usage does libido refer specifically to sexual energy but rather to a more general energy. The relationship of physical and psychic energy is, in Jungian theory, reciprocal; both make demands upon the general libidinal energy pool, resulting in a polarity of functions and a tendency toward balance.

Energic Principles

To explain the dynamics of personality, Jung postulated that the energy system which comprises man is a partially closed system that operates as though it were a fully closed system. The functioning of the system is governed by two principles drawn from physics. The *principle of equivalence* states that the personality system will neither gain nor lose energy. Recognizable as the first law of thermodynamics or the principle of energy conservation, equivalence thus means that energy which is lost by one component of the personality must reappear in another. For example, libidinal energy drained from the persona, thus weakening it, may appear in the shadow, strengthening the "uncivilized" side of the personality. Energy from the unconscious may enter the conscious psyche. In general, energy redistribution throughout the psyche is a constant, ongoing process. In fact, personality dynamics occur only through energy redistribution.

The second Jungian principle, that of *entropy,* is an application of the second law of thermodynamics or the principle of equilibrium. This principle states that energy redistribution throughout the system tends toward a state of balance or equilibrium. Ideally, then, all subsystems of the psyche would eventually control equal amounts of energy and hence be of equal strength—the system would be in total equilibrium. Although such an ideal state can never be permanently sustained, the operation of the entropy principle contributes significantly to the dynamics of the personality. Thus, if the shadow has become more powerful (energic) than the ego or the persona, there will be an entropic tendency for energy to be redistributed from the shadow to the weaker systems. If the ego becomes overvalued (invested with a large amount of energy), it may lose energy to a weaker anima. Similarly, the energy of the extroverted persona will tend to redistribute toward introversion, and the energy of the individual in whom the feeling function is superior will tend to be redistributed toward the other functions.

Since the equivalence and entropy principles operate perfectly only in a fully closed system, some deviations from these principles must be expected in the Jungian personality, which is a partially closed system. The psyche in such a system gains and loses energy, as, for example, when energy is expended through physical or mental work or gained through the metabolic processing of recently consumed food.

Development and Self-Actualization

Despite the operation of the entropy principle, in early life there tends to be considerable disharmony among the various systems of the personality, and the systems themselves are neither fully developed nor fully functioning. The potential for increasing harmony among the personality systems provides the principal basis for personality development in Jungian theory. Development tends to take place in a relatively continuous fashion, without the sharp breaks seen in Freud's developmental theory.

Jung postulated that the human individual is invested with an innate, archetypal striving for *unity,* for the achievement of an integrated, balanced, harmoniously interacting personality. In particular, he saw a need to integrate ego-consciousness, but this integration is not alone sufficient to guide the individual through life with the unconscious. The unity striving is embodied in the process of *self-actualization,* which involves the development of a new center to replace the ego. This new center he called the *self.* The self lies midway between the conscious and the unconscious and becomes the stellar center around which all of the other systems are constellated. It provides the system with balance and unity and is the ultimate goal toward which the personality is striving. This striving for psychic unity takes place in two phases. First, in the individuation process the primitive undifferentiated psychic elements strive to be complete, differentiated, and fully developed. Each system—ego, persona, psychic functions, and the others—strives to become differentiated from the primitive totality of the infant psyche and to become a highly developed, integrated system within itself. With the achievement of differentiation comes the second process, the transcendent function, through which the diverse, opposing elements of the system move forward into an integrated and balanced wholeness, with the self as the center of the system. When transcendence, and hence self-actualization and selfhood, is achieved, the psyche has reached its final state of development, the final goal toward which all of the hopes and aspirations of the ego, as well as the archetypal images of the collective unconscious, have been oriented. When is such unity achieved? Often, never. Selfhood is seldom reached before middle-age, since individuation and transcendence are complex, long-term processes, requiring broad experience and reasonably optimal environmental conditions.

Symbols and the Psyche. Throughout the processes of individuation and transcendent functioning, and deeply involved in the integration of conscious and unconscious, is the concept of *symbol*. Symbols supply individuals with the ability to apprehend their unconscious indirectly, particularly their collective unconscious. Most often symbols are the conscious expression of archetypal images and, therefore, provide the bridges between the conscious and the unconscious needed for the psyche to grow and mature. Another aspect of symbols is that they may provide representations of future goals, including those involved in self-actualization. It is through the use of symbols that individuals can strive toward integration, harmony, wholeness, and the related aspects of selfhood.

A major example of the use of symbols is seen in religion. In ancient times the archetypal images were expressed in the symbols of primitive religions as well as primitive rituals. Until the time of the Reformation, people in Western cultures used the symbols of Christianity as the mode of expression for these archetypal images. Yet, as Arnold Toynbee has said, symbols have life-spans, and the early symbols of Christianity became, with the passing of time, ritualized and finally rote experiences. Jung (1954) pointed out that with the development of numerous religions and the consequent final shattering of important Christian symbols, humanity was left in a perpetual state of restlessness, since the symbols so essential to psychic integration and self-actualization were gone. We are still in need, he noted, of new symbols that can act in the interest of psychic integration.

Causal and Teleological Motivations

In our consideration of substantive issues in personality theory, it was pointed out that some theorists, such as Freud, place principal motivational factors in the individual's past (causal motivation), while others stress a future-oriented, goal-striving approach (teleological motivation). Jung posited, at the outset, a *causal* motivation, involving primarily the inherited archetypes and the developed complexes, which structure behavior patterns and both activate and direct behavior. The individual is pushed in particular directions by these factors from his or her past. Jung also, however, postulated a teleological motivation, which includes, of course, the striving for unity and the related concepts of self-actualization, individuation, transcendent functioning, and selfhood.

Polarity and Dynamic Interaction

Throughout life, while the personality system strives for the dynamic unity of selfhood, the various subsystems of the psyche interact constantly through the transfer of psychic energy. Any two or more systems, attitudes, or functions may interact with one another in any of three ways: compensation, unification, or opposition. *Compensation* most often occurs between the systems of the psyche when the systems and materials of the unconscious compensate for those of the consciousness. The ego may be compensated by the personal unconscious or by the anima or animus. The person who is consciously extroverted will be unconsciously introverted, and the individual who is consciously dominated by intuition and sensation will unconsciously emphasize feeling and thinking.

Before dealing with unification and opposition, we must consider briefly the polarities that exist in Jungian theory. While many personality theories deal with polarities, that is, opposites, in the personality, Jung stressed the concept to the extent of suggesting that virtually the entire personality consists of polar tendencies. Perhaps most obvious is the opposition of extroversion and introversion, the polar extremes of an attitudinal continuum. Other polarities include the opposition of superior and inferior functions, of conscious and unconscious, of personal unconscious and collective unconscious, of persona and ego, of causality and teleology, and of physical energy and psychic energy.

The most direct expression of the polar tendencies in personality is, of course, *opposition.* The various opposites which comprise the personality are in constant struggle with each other. Such conflict is seen not as a negative quality but as a necessity of life. The opposition of polar tendencies is essential to the progression of life.

The systems of the personality are not, however, relegated to eternal conflict since they can, in the third type of interaction, unite. When two systems or functions unite, the polar tendencies that characterize them have not necessarily been resolved; union is possible because polarities have the power to attract as well as repel each other. The *unification* of polarities constitutes the mode of operation of the transcendent function discussed earlier. It is through the uniting of opposites that integration and selfhood are attained.

THE THEORY IN EMPIRICAL CONTEXT

Jung's theory, while deeply couched in the language of clinical psychology and psychiatry, was by no means developed entirely on the basis of the clinical observation of patients. In fact, throughout his career, Jung was an active researcher, always striving for an objective description of the unconscious phenomena so important to his theory. His research ranged from the study of reaction time to the analysis of dreams and from investigations of physiology to those of mythology.

Early Research

Jung's first research, conducted while he was still a medical student at the University of Basel, was a case study of a young girl who exhibited periodic trance states as well as a variety of psychological problems apparent even in a waking state. This study was the basis of his medical thesis and was later published in 1902.

In 1900, after receiving his medical degree, Jung worked with the noted European psychiatrist, Eugen Bleuler, at the Burgholzli Mental Hospital in Zurich. There he conducted studies of the etiology of schizophrenia, then called dementia praecox, examining microscopically the brain tissue of deceased patients. The research was notably unsuccessful in discovering any anatomical basis for the disorder, and Jung soon turned to other techniques.

The Word Association Technique

Sir Francis Galton, the eminent nineteenth-century genius who, among his many accomplishments, invented mental tests and the correlation coefficient, developed the word association technique as one possible measure of differences in intelligence. In a word association test the examiner presents a list of words, one at a time, to a subject who responds with the first word that comes to mind. The examiner records the response and the subject's reaction time. The technique was unsuccessful as a measure of intelligence but has since been widely applied in other areas of psychology.

Jung used the word association technique to study unconscious phenomena and introduced to the test important modifications, which have since become as widely used as the basic technique itself. After each long reaction time Jung asked his subjects the reason for the hesitation. Generally, the patient did not know the reason and was not even aware of having hesitated. It then became apparent that unconscious emotions played an important part in the hesitation phenomenon. Jung also introduced the technique of measuring physiological responses during the word association test. He recorded respiration, pulse rate, and the electrical conductivity of the skin, a measure of the activity of the autonomic nervous system. Prolonged reaction times were shown to be accompanied by changes in the physiological measure, supporting the hypothesis that unconscious phenomena were operating.

Jung postulated that a stimulus word which was followed by a hesitation and accompanying physiological changes had stimulated what he called a *complex* in the personal unconscious. He reasoned that association should provide a method for the determination and study of the complexes of his patients. When a particular complex was uncovered through word association, Jung could then discuss the complex with his patient, bringing the unconscious materials into consciousness where they could be handled more readily in therapy.

Dream Analysis

Jung came to view the dream as an inroad to the creative activity of the collective unconscious and was most interested in the collective images which appeared in the dreams of his patients. Although he recognized the value of Freud's methods of dream analysis, Jung did not entirely agree with them. Where Freud generally analyzed a single dream, dissecting it in detail through free association, Jung preferred to deal with a number of consecutive dreams. He treated each dream individually but only in the context of the series of dreams. As Jung pointed out, the series as a whole serves to fill in gaps and correct errors which might otherwise occur in the interpretation of a single dream.

Of particular importance for Jungian theory is the support found through dream analysis for the existence of archetypes. Much of the relevant evidence came about through Jung's studies of alchemy. This ancient philosophy-science is perhaps best known for the then notorious attempts of certain of its advocates to transmute base metals into gold. There was also, however, a branch of alchemy that was largely philosophical and attempted to deal with such basic issues as good and evil and the transmutation of the base aspects of life into noble aspects. It was this latter alchemy in which Jung was interested. He found it to be resplendent with symbols and discussions of opposites and, in many ways, to have anticipated his own theoretical positions. In interrelating alchemy and dreams, Jung was able to show that often the objects appearing in the dream are precise duplicates of the symbols of the medieval alchemists, even though the patient knows nothing of alchemy and has never experienced the dream objects in a waking state. Jung took the exact concurrence of dream objects and alchemical symbols as evidence for the existence of archetypes.

Studies in Comparative Mythology and Religion

It may at first seem strange that a well-trained scientist and widely renowned psychiatrist, whose early work involved such relatively exacting techniques as microscopic tissue analysis, reaction time, and psychophysiology, should have sought empirical support for his theory in mythology and religion. Jung, however, was scientifically open minded and was interested in obtaining any information which bore upon his concepts. As a result, he searched deeply in the areas of mythology and religion as well as in alchemy and the occult. His investigations took him into Christianity, Hinduism, Confucianism, Taoism, and Yoga as well as into studies of trance states and other psychical phenomena and the mythology of ancient peoples.

Jung's primary interest in such seemingly unscientific phenomena stemmed from his desire to investigate his concept of archetypes. Where it is difficult or impossible to provide actual evidence for the existence of archetypes in individual patients, Jung reasoned that the discovery of the archetypal imagery of his patients in the symbolism of religions and myths would provide such evidence. Therefore, just as he had found the symbols of the alchemists replicated precisely in the dreams of his patients, he sought to find the themes of major religions and the symbolism of mythology in the archetypal images brought out in therapy.

His studies of religion brought him many pieces of evidence from aspects of specific religions. He concluded, for example, that Christ is a symbol of the self, exemplifying the archetype of the self, and that the Christian Mass symbolizes the life and suffering of Christ and the transformation of God to the form of Humanity. More generally, and more importantly, he concluded not that any one religion or god-figure is more valid than any other, but that there is a universal god-archetype, an image of some unseen and unknown supreme being. The individual is likely to utilize this image at times of extreme emotion—fear, anger, joy—and religions may be developed on the basis of the god-archetype. Jung found evidence for the unconscious existence in his patients' use of symbols derived from religion. Since his patients ordinarily had no possible way of learning of these symbols, he concluded that they were representative of unconscious archetypes (Jung and Kerenye 1949).

Investigations of Attitudes and Functions

Most broadly influential of all Jung's concepts have been his attitudes of extroversion and introversion and, to a lesser extent, the four functions. Early investigations of the attitudes concentrated on their association with such variables as sex, age, maladjustment, and occupation. As an example, the sex variable was studied by Marston (1926), who reported 16 percent more extroversion in boys than in girls. Downey (1926) found 52.6 percent of women and only 42 percent of men to be extroverted. Heidbreder (1930) reported that the ratio of extroverted men to extroverted women was 1:07. Such demographic studies provided a mass of data—often collected under poorly controlled conditions—on the Jungian attitudes but little information concerning the validity of the theory.

More relevant are data obtained using two similar inventories, the Gray-Wheelwright Psychological Type Questionnaire (Gray and Wheelwright 1946; Gray 1947, 1948, and 1949) and the Myers-Briggs Type Indicator (Myers 1962). Both instruments provide subscales measuring Extroversion-Introversion (E-I), Sensation-Intuition (S-N), and Thinking-Feeling (T-F). The Myers-Briggs also measures Judging-Perceiving (J-P). Studies with the Gray-Wheelwright questionnaire have tended to concentrate on such variables as age and sex, but the operation of the attitudinal typology in marriage has also been investigated. The Myers-Briggs studies have investigated the dichotomous nature of the attitudes and related both attitudes and functions to a variety of ability, information, personality, and adjustment variables, demonstrating the breadth and importance of the Jungian concepts.

Perhaps most supportive of the importance of the introversion-extroversion concept are the factor analytic studies of Eysenck (see Chapter 13), who has developed several personality inventories to measure extroversion-introversion. Briefly, Eysenck, a prolific and precise researcher, has conducted numerous investigations, using both experimental and test variables, to determine empirically the basic dimensions of personality. These studies have demonstrated to his satisfaction that extroversion is one of only three major dimensions of personality that hold up repeatedly across numerous studies and large numbers of variables. If Eysenck's conclusions are valid, Jung had certainly hit upon a major differentiating dimension in postulating his attitudinal types.

EVALUATION

Jung's theory has been criticized on a number of fairly specific points, including his concept of the collective unconscious, the derivation of the theory itself, the lack of adequate developmental concepts, and a general tendency toward reification. We will consider here each of these points in turn.

Most controversial and widely criticized of all Jungian concepts is the collective unconscious and its incorporated archetypes. Critics (see, Glover 1950; Munroe 1955) have generally raised three major points: (1) it is difficult to believe that ideas, knowledge, personality characteristics, and the like can be transmitted genetically; (2) archetypes are not amenable to scientific investigation, and, as a result, there is and can be no evidence for their existence; and (3) behavior attributed to archetypes can be fully accounted for in terms of other concepts. The first two points have already been answered in part. As was pointed out above, Jung quite specifically did not postulate the direct inheritance of information or memories but of predispositions. While not conclusively demonstrated, the inheritance of tendencies or predispositions is much more consonant with current genetic theory and research than is the inheritance of memories or knowledge. It is only in relatively recent years that we have come to recognize that heredity is largely or entirely controlled by the sequence of bases in the DNA molecule, and, although significant strides have been made, we have but pricked a tiny peephole through which to view the mysteries of the complex biochemistry of heredity. In addition, recent investigations have shown that RNA, a substance closely related to DNA, is capable of storing information biochemically (see Eigen 1966). Who is to say definitively, then, that the complex predispositions of the collective unconscious—or even memories—cannot be genetically transmitted? The second point concerning archetypes, that they are not amenable to empirical study, is certainly a more valid one, for it is notoriously difficult for science to deal with concepts which are so far removed from directly observable empirical operation. We would suggest that the recent advances in genetics may eventually open the way to directly relevant investigations, using DNA-RNA models as a base from which to operate. Such studies are, however, probably quite far in the future.

The third point, that concepts other than archetype provide equally feasible explanations of relevant behaviors, is difficult to refute. A variety of alternatives can be offered. One critic (Glover 1950) has proposed that experience, particularly early experience, may be readily invoked to account for the aspects of behavior and personality covered in Jung's theory by the archetypes. Likewise, Munroe (1955):

> *The archetypes seem to me to be mainly personifications of significant persons and forces experienced by the infant in his initial efforts to relate himself to his world, and of the process of relationship. (p. 573)*

A second area of criticism (for example, Munroe 1955) goes to the very roots of the Jungian system. It holds that the theory is a reductionistic, philosophical approach, which deals primarily with universals and has little or no empirical base. It has been pointed out that, for example, the phenomena of opposites and the components of the shadow archetype, while common experiences of many people, cannot be given the status of philosophical laws or universals. They were derived by Jung on the basis of logical or intellectual generalization, without being directly observed or shown to be universal. Jung, however, had few qualms about the weak empirical base or broad generalizations of his theory.

If Jung's theory is a logical-philosophical treatment, it is well to note that its basic logic has not gone entirely without criticism. In discussing the logic of Jung's *Psychology of the Unconscious,* Murphy has pointed out that:

> Its method—it is no more than a friendly exaggeration to say this—is to argue that because A is somewhat like B, and B can, under certain circumstances, share something with C, and C has been known on occasion to have been suspected of being related to D, the conclusion in full-fledged logical form is that A = D. (1947, p. 424)

A third criticism has been that Jung's theory is lacking in developmental concepts. The personality tends to consist largely of derivations from inherited forms, and its development is not specified. Even the goal of whatever developmental process is present is inherited—the self is based on an archetype. The Freudian school, which is largely responsible for this criticism, points to Freud's detailed psychoanalytic treatment of the developmental process. While Jung has not set forth a specifically developmental theory, he does utilize some developmental constructs. The persona, the public personality, develops its characteristics through social interaction and adaptation. The personal unconscious and its complexes are likewise partially developmental in nature. In addition, he assumes that the learning process is basic to personality development and that without it the elements of the psyche would remain primitive and undifferentiated. Yet he fails to elaborate on how this learning takes place, leaving that determination to the experimental psychologist.

A final criticism is that Jung's theory lends itself too readily to a reification of its concepts. Not only are the major constructs of the theory universals, they are also relatively static and mechanistic. The systems of the personality interact, but they nevertheless tend to remain quite stable. Critics thus hold that Jung was little interested in the dynamics of the personality, in how systems change and are modified over time. It must be agreed that Jung's treatment of system interactions in terms of physical principles tends to be mechanistic rather than dynamic. On the other hand, the process of self-actualization, with its subsidiary individuation and transcendent function processes, is certainly dynamic, in that it involves widespread changes in the relationships among systems and, consequently, in the personality itself.

Heuristic Values of Jungian Theory

We have already noted some of the research fostered by Jung's concepts of attitude and function. In addition, Jung has inspired a number of theorists to extend, modify, and elaborate upon various aspects of his theory. Examples include Wickes (1948), Goldbrunner (1956), Progoff (1953, 1956), G. Adler (1948), and Read (1945). The theory has also been used as a basis for interpreting projective tests, including the Rorschach (Mindess 1955) and thematic tests (Spiegelman 1955; Strauss 1954). In addition, it has influenced the historian Arnold Toynbee (1956) and has had a highly significant impact on modern religious thought (Strunk 1956). A further indication of Jung's influence is that the *Journal of Analytical Psychology* is specifically devoted to the furtherance of Jungian psychology.

In addition to these direct heuristic influences of Jung's thought, his theory may have had more subtle but more broadly influential impact in other areas of psychology. Jung's conceptualization of teleological motivation—the goal-directed striving to attain integrative selfhood through self-actualization—was certainly among the earliest systematic formulations of both the self as central to the personality and of teleological motivation as an aspect of human behavior. These ideas have been incorporated as basic and central to theories of the phenomenological-humanistic school, exemplified by Carl Rogers and Abraham Maslow (Chapter 7).

Despite the heuristic influences, and the possible influences noted above, it would be a gross exaggeration to say that Jungian theory has been widely accepted in psychology. Quite the contrary. Aside from the relatively small circle of individuals who identify themselves specifically as analytical psychologists, the field has generally rejected Jungian theory as too metaphysical, too dependent on universals, and not amenable to empirical verification. Indications of this rejection are seen in the small amount of space allotted to Jung's theory in most histories of psychology and psychiatry, in the paucity of articles in publications (other than the *Journal of Analytical Psychology*) devoted to discussions of Jung's concepts, and in the fact that the theory has had few critics outside of Freudian psychoanalysts (probably an indication of lack of interest).

In the context of some serious criticism and general lack of acceptance, we must, in order to appreciate Jung's contribution, consider its robust unique qualities. Jung began and continued his writings as a willing outcast from the mainstreams of both psychology and psychiatry. On the one side was the giant Freud, the founder of psychoanalysis, vigorously—and successfully—defending his theoretical fort against all onslaughts, including that perpetrated by Jung. On the other side was the established German experimental and physiological psychology and the growing American behavioristic tradition. E.L. Thorndike's *Animal Intelligence* appeared in 1898, while Jung was still a medical student at Zurich. In 1902, as Jung published his medical thesis, Robert M. Yerkes took over the comparative psychology laboratory at Harvard; one year later J.B. Watson completed his thesis on the psychological and neurological maturation of the white rat; and in 1904 B.F. Skinner was born. Thus, as Jung began his career, the objectivistic orientation of behaviorism began its. And in 1913, two years before Jung published *The Theory of Psychoanalysis,* Watson exploded behaviorism into full bloom with his article in *Psychological Review,* "Psychology as the Behaviorist Views It."

Fully aware—perhaps painfully so—of his almost heretical position outside the doctrines of both Freudian psychoanalysis and Watsonian behaviorism, Jung persisted. He determined to develop his own lines of thought, refusing to yield to the blows or sanctions of his critics. The result was a creative masterpiece, as striking and original as any work of art, a set of concepts and postulates constituting what is probably one of the most unique theories of personality extant, a theory yet to be fully explored, a theory which still has much to offer psychology. Perhaps Jung's greatest contribution was that he dared—and that he was able—to deviate from the *Zeitgeist* to offer a refreshingly different approach to a psychology of personality.

REFERENCES

Adler, G. *Studies in analytical psychology.* New York: Norton, 1948.

Clinard, M. B. *Sociology of deviant behavior* (3rd ed.). New York: Holt, Rinehart, & Winston, 1968.

Downey, J. How the psychologist reacts to the distinction "extraversion-introversion" with observations concerning lateralization of function. *Journal of Abnormal and Social Psychology,* 1926, *20,* 407–415.

Eigen, M. Chemical means of information storage and readout in biological sciences. *Neuro-sciences research symposium summaries.* Cambridge, Mass.: M.I.T. Press, 1966.

Fordham, F. *An introduction to Jung's psychology.* Baltimore: Penguin Books, 1953.

Fordham, M. S. M. *The life of childhood.* London: Routledge and Kegan Paul, 1947.

Glover, E. *Freud or Jung.* London: George Allen & Unwin, 1950.

Goffman, E. *The presentation of self in everyday life.* New York: Doubleday, 1959.

Goldbrunner, J. *Individuation: A study of the depth psychology of Carl Gustave Jung.* New York: Pantheon, 1956.

Gray, H. Jung's psychological types and changes with age. *Journal of Clinical Psychology,* 1947, *3* (No. 3), 273–277.

Gray, H. Jung's psychological types in men and women. *Stanford Medical Bulletin,* 1948, *6,* 29–36.

Gray, H. Psychological types in married people. *Journal of Social Psychology,* 1949, *29,* 189–200.

Gray, H., & Wheelwright, J. B. Jung's psychological types—their frequency of occurrence. *Journal of Genetic Psychology,* 1946, *34,* 3–17.

Heidbreder, E. Self ratings and preferences. *Journal of Abnormal and Social Psychology,* 1930, *25,* 62–74.

Jones, E. *The life and work of Sigmund Freud.* New York: Anchor Books, 1963.

Jung, C. G. [Concerning the archetypes, with special reference to the anima concept.] In *Collected Works,* (Vol. 9). Princeton: Princeton Press, 1959. (First German edition, 1954.)

Jung, C. G. *Two essays on analytical psychology.* New York: World Publishing, 1956.

Jung, C. G. *[Memories, dreams, reflections]* (A. Jaffe, Ed. and R. & C. Winston, trans.). New York: Pantheon, 1963.

Jung, C. G. [The archetypes and the collective unconscious.] In R. F. C. Hull (trans.), *The collected works of C. G. Jung* (Vol. 9). New York: Princeton University Press, 1975.

Jung, C. G. [The development of personality.] In R. F. C. Hull (trans.), *The collected works of C. G. Jung* (Vol. 17). New York: Princeton University Press, 1975.

Jung, C. G. [The structure and dynamics of the psyche.] In R. F. C. Hull (trans.), *The collected works of C. G. Jung* (Vol. 8). Princeton, N.J.: Princeton University Press, 1975.

Jung, C. G. [Symbols of transformation.] In R. F. C. Hull (trans.), *The collected works of C. G. Jung* (Vol. 5). New York: Princeton University Press, 1976.

Jung, C. G. [Two essays on analytic psychology.] In R. F. C. Hull (trans.), *The collected works of C. G. Jung* (Vol. 7). New York: Princeton University Press, 1975.

Jung, C. G., & Kerenyi, C. *Essays on a science of mythology.* New York: Pantheon Press, 1949.

Marston, L. R. The emotions of young children: An experimental study of introversion and extroversion. *University of Iowa Study of Child Welfare,* 1925, *3* (No. 3).

Munroe, R. *Schools of psychoanalytic thought.* New York: Holt, Rinehart, & Winston, 1955.

Murphy, G. *Personality: A biosocial approach to origins and structure.* New York: Harper, 1947.

Myers, I. B. Inferences as to the dichotomous nature of Jung's types, from the shape of regressions of dependent variables from Myers-Briggs type indicator scores. *American Psychologist,* 1962, *17,* 364.

Progoff, I. *Jung's psychology and its social meaning.* New York: Julian Press, 1953.

Progoff, I. *The death and rebirth of psychology: An integrative evaluation of Freud, Adler, Jung, and Rank and the impact of their culminating insights on modern man.* New York: Julian Press, 1956.

Read, H. E. *Education through art.* New York: Pantheon Books, 1945.

Spiegelman, M. Jungian theory and the analysis of thematic tests. *Journal of Projective Techniques,* 1955, 19, 253-263.

Strauss, F. H. Interpretation of thematic test material: A Jungian approach. *Bulletin of the British Psychological Society,* 1954, *23,* 12-13.

Strunk, O., Jr. Psychology, religion, and C. G. Jung: A review of periodical literature. *Journal of Bible & Religion,* 1956, *24,* 106-113.

Toynbee, A. The value of C. G. Jung's work for historians. *Journal of Analytical Psychology,* 1956, *1,* 193-194.

Wickes, F. G. *The inner world of childhood.* New York: The New American Library, 1948.

Social Analytic Theory:

Alfred Adler, Karen Horney, Erich Fromm, and Harry Stack Sullivan

We have studied the development of the "orthodox" Freudian psychoanalytic theory and its modern extension, ego psychology, and have seen the massive impact of Freud's creative genius on twentieth-century psychology and psychiatry. Despite the widespread influence of both the man and the theory, there have been many who began within the psychoanalytic movement yet came to disagree with various aspects of the Freudian position. A number of these "deviants" split off from mainstream psychoanalysis to develop their own theoretical positions and, in some cases, gain their own groups of followers. Some of these theorists took up a particular point originally made by Freud and built it into a separate theory, others focused on what they saw as weaknesses in psychoanalytic theory and developed sets of hypotheses to fill these theoretical gaps. And still others went further to develop full-fledged theories that went well beyond basic Freudian theory to become essentially original theories in their own rights. The number of splinter theories, constituting the varied schools of psychoanalysis, is large, attesting to the tremendous heuristic power of the original Freudian theory. Major examples include the theories of Reich, Rank, Ferenczi, and Stekel. Reich (1972), best known for his emphasis on the potency of the orgasm and his "orgone" therapy, broke with Freud principally over the death instinct concept. Rank (1929) took Freud's concept of the birth trauma and developed an entire theory focusing on the role of this important experience and on the influence of the mother on the child. Ferenczi (1952) and Stekel (1949) both attempted to develop variations in the technique of psychoanalytic therapy.

While we cannot discuss in detail here the many theories which grew out of basic psychoanalysis, we will be concerned with a group of theorists who broke with Freud primarily because they disagreed with his emphasis on biological, rather than social, factors in personality development and functioning. To many, Freud's emphasis on the importance of the instincts as causes of behavior represented something of the ultimate in biological determinism. Critics of this aspect of Freudian theory have often held that Freud originally neglected the role of the society in shaping human behavior, while putting far too much emphasis on biological bases. The criticism is not entirely accurate, since Freud did include the superego as a major part of his personality model, in that way suggesting that social factors have some importance in behavior. The emphasis in orthodox psychoanalysis was clearly on biology rather than culture, however, and those who attributed greater importance to social factors were thus forced to develop their own points of view.

The full need to develop social theories of behavior did not arise entirely within the psychoanalytic movement. Paralleling Freud's work, McDougall (1908) developed an instinct theory of social behavior. Basically, he held that most human behavior is determined by inherited instincts and emotions associated with these instincts. Included among them are such things as curiosity, self-abasement, gregariousness, and self-assertion. The reaction against McDougall's initially influential theory was profound. On the one hand, Watson and the behaviorists held that many of the behaviors McDougall attributed to instincts, were, in fact, learned, while, on the other hand, anthropologists, such as Boas, showed evidence of cross-cultural variability in patterns of behavior. The result was a growing antiinstinct movement, which culminated in an insightful overview by Bernard (1924) of theory and in evidence pointing clearly away from the biological emphasis on instinct and toward the sociocultural emphasis on learning as a determinant of personality. More generally, the period around the turn of the century saw rapid developments in both cultural anthropology and sociology, as well as in psychology, and these related social science disciplines came to have an increasing impact on the thinking of theorists in psychology and psychiatry. It was inevitable, as Freud probably realized even in the early days of psychoanalysis, that sociocultural theory would find its way into the tightly woven fabric of the psychoanalytic movement. The task of actually bringing a more thoroughly social perspective to psychoanalysis was left predominately to the work of Alfred Adler, Eric Fromm, Karen Horney, Harry Stack Sullivan, Eric Berne, and recently, Robert Carson. All of their theories are at least partially psychoanalytic in origin, yet all have given biology a back seat, emphasizing instead the importance of social and cultural factors in both the development of human personality and the expression of specific behaviors.

By way of a somewhat more focused introduction to these important viewpoints, we should consider briefly the major emphases shared by the social analytic theories as a group. First, we have said that all six theories deemphasize the role of biological factors in the determination of human behavior. Munroe (1955), for this reason, called the neoanalytic theories *nonlibido* approaches. The term recognizes quite specifically that these theories give only a minor role to the centrally important sexual and aggressive drives of Freudian theory. The second shared emphasis is the interjection into the psychoanalytic approach of sociocultural factors. To amplify somewhat on this point, the neoanalysts as a group believe that both society and person are important determinants of behavior. The internal biological and psychological functioning of the individual thus continues to have some importance, but these factors are balanced by the influence of external, social factors. In addition, the person-society interaction is bidirectional, the person influences and changes the society while society shapes and modifies the behavior of the individual. Both society and person are thus flexible and able to be modified in the view of these theorists.

Additional similarities among the neoanalysts revolve around their shared views concerning the relative importance of conscious and unconscious factors and the need for a "self" construct. As compared with Freud, the neoanalytic theorists tend to deemphasize the importance of unconscious motives, although they never entirely deny the influence of such factors on behavior. They replace much of the Freudian emphasis on the unconscious with an awareness of self. Whether the self begins as an innate potential, as in Fromm or Adler, or whether it is a learned result of early life experiences, as in Sullivan, the concept represents for these theorists the unique individuality of the person as an entity. The presence of the self means that the individual will never entirely succumb to pressures of conformity of the society and will remain capable of creatively modifying the world around him or her in order to fulfill his or her own needs.

A final common quality of the social analytic theorists is their continued, if partial, reliance on important aspects of Freudian doctrine. While the theorists themselves would prefer to emphasize their differences with Freud—and we will focus on these differences here—any careful reading of their works makes it clear that the neoanalysts rely heavily on Freud. Their theories represent, for the most part, additions to and modifications of psychoanalytic theory, not the development of totally new theoretical systems. To put it otherwise, none of these theories could stand entirely on its own without some reference back to psychoanalytic doctrine, and probably none of them would have been developed had the Freudian theory not been available to provide a foundation on which to build.

While we give somewhat greater emphasis to the theories of Horney and Sullivan, we will begin our considerations with the work of Alfred Adler, who is the earliest of the social analysts to develop his own theory.

ALFRED ADLER

Biographical Sketch

Alfred Adler was born in Vienna in 1870, where he lived until the Nazi threat drove him to the United States in 1935. He received a degree in medicine from the University of Vienna in 1895, and, following a period of interest in ophthalmology and a brief stint as a general practitioner, he found his true interest in the study and practice of psychiatry. In 1902 his professional interests and activities brought him into contact with Sigmund Freud, who soon came to refer to him flatteringly as "The Eagle" (Der Adler). Adler, became one of the original members of the Vienna Psychoanalytic Society, serving, at various times, as its secretary and, in 1911, as president.

Inferiority and Its Compensations

In a 1907 book Adler brought into psychoanalysis the concept of defect and its compensation. It was already widely recognized in medicine that when an organ is defective, the individual may tend to compensate for the defect biologically. Injury to one lung, arm, eye, or kidney may cause the other to develop a hypertrophy of function, such that it is "better" than it originally was, hence compensating for the loss of function in the injured or otherwise defective organ. Freud had extended the compensation concept to describe the individual reaction to states of incomplete organic or inadequate sexual development. Adler wanted to further extend compensation to the area of social behavior and proposed that human beings tend to compensate for a variety of social inadequacies in their developmental backgrounds.

While his views initially seemed acceptable to most psychoanalysts, Adler continued to develop the social aspects of his theory and, increasingly, to reject the biological and sexual aspects of Freud's theory. In 1911 he requested that the Vienna group headed by Freud allow him to present a series of seminars regarding the nature and role of compensation in personality development and expression. Following his presentations, it was apparent to all that his views had deviated considerably from those of Freud, and the group of nearly forty physicians voted to ask Adler to withdraw. He did so, taking nine followers with him to continue outside the mainstream of psychoanalysis the development of a theory of individual psychology.

Inferiority

Extending the medical concept of organ defect, Adler proposed that human beings are, by both biological and psychological nature, frail and weak. Biologically and psychologically inadequate to cope with its surroundings, the young child develops feelings of *inferiority*, and these become central, causal factors in nearly all aspects of the personality development to follow.

The pervasive feelings of inferiority extend in particular into the realm of social and psychological functioning. More specifically, Adler postulated that every individual feels imperfect and inadequate in a variety of areas and that these feelings of inferiority are continuing and progressive. The child who has not learned to read, for example, may feel inferior to an older sibling. The child may strive to overcome this particular feeling of inferiority only to develop later the feeling that he or she is inferior to the older sibling or to others in the ability to interact socially with peers. Again, if the child's inferiority in this area is overcome, he or she will develop new inferiority feelings which will cause additional strivings. It is thus through progressive feelings of inferiority and the compensation that accompanies them that the personality develops, and *it is in the concept of inferiority and its compensation that we see the basic motivation behind virtually all human behavior.*

The Superiority Striving

The striving to compensate for inferiority is also a striving for *superiority,* by which Adler meant self-perfection. This striving is a purposive or teleological motive system, which involves an attempt to attain a higher state of being and functioning. Under the force of the superiority motive, the person is constantly attempting to become psychologically better by fulfilling his or her potential through interaction with the social environment. It should be clearly noted that *the superiority striving is not so much a striving to be superior to others as it is a striving to be superior to one's own earlier state of functioning.* Just as feelings of inferiority originate in the biological inferiority felt by the infant organism, so the superiority striving originates as an innate drive toward perfection.

Fictional Finalism

A teleological motive, like the superiority striving, is one which involves the attempt to move toward one or more goals. The goals may be relatively simple, concrete, obvious ones, as in the case in which the child does homework in order to receive a piece of candy or a word of praise, or the goals may be more complex, ambiguous, and long term. It is these latter goals in which Adler was interested.

Adler developed the conceptualization that human behavior can be understood only in terms of *finalism,* that is only by knowing the final goals toward which the individual is striving and which are thus guiding and directing his or her behavior. In developing his theory of goal striving, Adler adopted from the philosopher, Vaihinger, the interesting conception that the important goals are totally *fictional* ideals toward which the person strives. They have no actual substance, and, more important, the individual has no way of testing their validity. The goal is simply a given, a belief or an ideal that the person holds and on the basis of which he acts. Consider the goals stated or implied by such notions as "Work hard and you can accomplish nearly anything," or "If at first you don't succeed, try, try again," or "It isn't what you know but who you know that counts," or "Honesty is the best policy." A given individual may adopt any one or more of these goals to guide

These developments occur naturally, unless the flow of energy is blocked in so[
way.

In explicating the growth principle, Horney denied the validity of both [
Freudian pleasure principle and the death instinct. The pleasure principle is [
placed, in her writings, by two guiding principles, *the need for security or safe[
and the *need for satisfaction.* The former, which is quite similar to Maslow's ne[
for safety, involves both physical and psychological security and is the paramou[
guide to human behavior. The individual will, Horney believed, abandon all oth[
pursuits in order to preserve a threatened safety. The satisfaction needs, which [
both physiological (the needs for food, water, sex, for example) and psychologi[
(such as the needs for money and possessions), are important but will always be su[
ordinated to the need for safety. The death instincts postulated by Freud simply [
not exist.

The implementation of the growth principle involves a desire for inner *unity,* f[
a sense of integration or internal consistency. As a result, the individual m[
develop an idealized self, an image of the "perfect me," which provides a false sen[
of the integration and consistency so important to the unity striving. Difficul[
arises when the striving to attain the ideal self so dominates the *real self*—the actu[
or realistic characteristics of the person—that the individual becomes unrealistic [
his or her goal-directed behaviors. Under these circumstances the real self may b[
come lost, and the unrealistic behaviors directed at the preservation and attainme[
of the idealized image are termed *neurotic* behaviors.

Culture and Neurosis

Of central importance in Horney's theory is the influence of the culture on th[
development and functioning of both the normal and the deviant personality[
Individuals are largely a product of the social order. The mores and customs of th[
society become the rules governing the behavior of each individual and the guidir[
principles around which the personality must be structured. As a result, the pa[
ticular culture within which a given person develops will largely determine th[
personality characteristics which dominate his or her behavior. In addition, it is cu[
tural norms that define normality and abnormality, and the individual who deviate[
markedly from the norms of his own society will be considered abnormal. It is o[
this point of *normative cultural specificity* that Horney makes her major break wit[
Freud. Those cultures which create emotional isolation, tension, competition, ir[
security, and feelings of helplessness are, according to Horney, the most dangerou[
cultures. And the culture of the Western world in the twentieth century seems fa[
in the lead in the possession of these qualities.

Parental Influence and Basic Anxiety

The principal agents of the society in early life are, of course, the parents, and the[
exert a significant and lasting influence on the personality of the individual. The[
are first of all instrumental to the process of self-realization. The basic necessities o[

certain aspects of behavior, yet all are essentially untestable by the individual and, hence, fictional.

The Style of Life

Each person develops a complex pattern of interrelated behaviors which are used in a variety of situations to strive for superiority and compensate for inferiority. This configuration of personal characteristics and typical behaviors is termed the *style of life.* It is such a complex collection of personal characteristics that it sets the person apart from all others and thus determines what is unique about that person. The postulate that no two styles are ever exactly alike and, therefore, that each person is a psychologically unique individual is important because it makes Adler the first psychoanalytic theorist to emphasize the idiographic, or morphogenic, quality of the person as entity. Freud emphasized the universal application of his constructs and principles to all humans, systematically neglecting to focus on the idiographic qualities of the unique person. Other theorists outside the psychoanalytic school, most notably Gordon Allport, would later join Adler in emphasizing the impor- tance of the unique qualities of the individual.

There are many possible styles of life for a person, each representing an individ- ual's uniquely successful pattern of superiority-striving behaviors. The optimistic life style may lead to a very different set of behaviors from the pessimistic style. The extroverted style may lead the person to seek satisfactions through social contact, while an introverted life style may be equally productive but through relatively nonsocial means. Similarly, the artistic individual may emphasize the sub- jective or intuitive approach to problem solving and goal attainment, while the scientifically oriented person may achieve goals through the use of careful logic and reason.

While each life style develops in order to compensate for inferiority and provides a basis for the striving toward superiority, it is integrated by the *creative self.* In essense, the creative self is the individual's perception and understanding of his or her own being and is responsible for interpreting the experiences of inferiority and creating the style of life that will be used in compensating for these feelings. *The creative self is at once the original soil from which the style of life grows and the final fruit that it bears.*

Social Interest

Both those behaviors involved in the compensation for inferiority feelings and those engaged in for the sake of superiority or self-perfection could be potentially socially destructive in nature. Their harmfulness would be particularly possible if a purely selfish orientation were adopted, if the person were striving for self-perfection and inferiority compensation without special regard for the needs of others. Although Adler initially did little to discourage the interpretation that such selfish, socially destructive behavior may be the rule, he later (1939) mellowed and postulated that [ ]havior need not be selfish and socially destructive, therefore, but can be guided by social norms and mores, such that the individual's goals are not attained at the expense of social others. While this could imply a "life-and-let-live" concept of social interest, Adler went a step further to suggest that people also actively engage in behaviors that will be directly helpful to others around them and to society more generally. The ultimate expression of social interest involves an integrated satisfaction of the needs of the individual and, simultaneously, of society. The person thus interacts with the society in such a way that the striving for self-perfection is furthered and the society is also made more perfect. Like the striving for superiority, social interest has *innate,* biological, roots.

Birth Order and Personality

Although genetic factors did play a significant role in Adler's theory, he nevertheless emphasized the role of certain social factors. Of particular interest is his emphasis on birth order and the child's consequent position in the family as a major social determinant of later personality and behavior patterns. The "only" child, he postulated, tends to dominate the parents during the early formative years of childhood and develops habits that are based essentially on rewards received for this dominant behavior. The first-born child in a multiple-child family initially has much the experience of the only child, but the birth of a second child may divert the parents' affections, causing the older child to feel insecure and perhaps hateful. The second-born child may undergo the experience of initially dominating not only the parent but also the older sibling, and may thus become an ambitious, striving individual, who will be better adjusted than the first born. The youngest child has an even further expanded range of potential dominance and often becomes the continuing baby of the family. This child is basically spoiled and has a strong tendency to become a neurotic adult.

While Adler was not one to engage in laboratory research, others have carried out extensive research on the birth order question. Results over the years have not been consistent and are, to date, inconclusive. Very early work, summarized by Jones (1931), largely failed to support Adler's hypothesis, while more elaborate work carried out in the 1950s (Schachter 1959) was much more supportive. A burgeoning research literature that has followed Schachter's work has, however, yielded mixed results, and one reviewer (Schooler 1972) concluded that there are few consistent results in the literature on birth order. There is thus little current support for the Adlerian hypotheses concerning birth order effects.

KAREN HORNEY: THE GROWTH PRINCIPLE

Karen Horney was born September 16, 1885, in Hamburg, Germany. Her father, Berndt Danielson, was a Norwegian sea captain, and her mother was of Dutch descent. While attending medical school, Karen met and married Oscar Horney, a Berlin attorney. They had three daughters and were later divorced.

Horney received her M.D. degree from the University of Berlin in 1913 and took further psychiatric training during the years of World War I. In this same period she was analyzed by Karl Abraham and Hans Sachs. In 1919 she began her private practice in psychoanalysis, which she continued for the next fifteen years, despite increasing dissatisfaction with certain Freudian formulations. She came to the United States in 1932 at the invitation of Franz Alexander and assisted him at the Psychoanalytic Institute of Chicago. After two years she moved to New York City and began work with the New York Psychoanalytic Institute. At this time her first major theoretical works were published: *The Neurotic Personality of Our Time* (1937) and *New Ways in Psychoanalysis* (1939). These works signaled her modification and later rejection of Freudian libido theory. She broke completely with traditional psychoanalysis in 1941, when she was disqualified as a training analyst and instructor in a highly controversial vote. Horney and her followers immediately resigned and formed the Association for the Advancement of Psychoanalysis and the American Institute of Psychoanalysis.

An important aspect of Karen Horney's contribution that must not be ignored is that she was not only an M.D., a psychoanalyst, a training analyst (the pinnacle of the psychoanalytic profession), and a major theorist in her own right but also a woman. At a time when women had great difficulty in receiving training and entering the professions, Horney not only entered psychiatry but became one of its major theoreticians and leaders as well. She established her own school of thought, and her impact is still strongly felt as Horneyan analysts practice in the United States and other major countries. In accomplishing what she did, Karen Horney both made a major contribution to psychology and psychiatry and demonstrated to other women that such accomplishments were possible, even in the face of the great barriers placed in her path by a male-dominated society.

The Growth Principle

Karen Horney was, above all else, an optimist. Her whole theoretical structure, from personality dynamics to psychotherapy, rests upon one basic principle: There is an innate human capacity for growth, with humans always striving for, yet never achieving, the fullest realization of their potentialities. According to Horney (1945), "man can change and go on changing as long as he lives" (p. 19). The cessation of this striving represents either illness or death itself. She believes that:

> inherent in man are evolutionary constructive forces, which urge him to realize his given potentialities. This belief does not mean that man is essentially good, which would presuppose a given knowledge of what is good or bad. It means that man, by his very nature and of his own accord, strive toward self-realization, and that his set of values evolves from such strivin (1950, p. 15)

This *growth principle* is conceptualized as a flux of vital force. Human ene flows in such a way as to enable the individual to expand as fully as possible thus to allow himself or herself to experience and enjoy as much of life as pos

this process are a home full of warmth, understanding, and mutual respect. These allow the child to grow and develop unimpeded. Other factors which are conducive to growth are ". . . such parental attitudes as having real interest in a child, real respect for it, giving it real warmth and such qualities as reliability and sincerity" (Horney 1939, p. 86).

For Horney the basic wrong is a lack of love and understanding from the parents because this stifles the child's ability to adapt to and confront the world. It limits the child's ability to change and to incorporate new experiences, in short, the capacity for growth. Inadequate parental love occurs as a consequence of the parents' own neuroses, which, in turn, limit their ability to give. This limitation can occur in varying degrees and is the source of neurosis. For Horney *neurosis includes all disturbed or disordered behavior patterns, regardless of their degree of severity.* She gives many examples of these possible disturbances in the home: parents may exert so much pressure on the child that his or her initiative dies, preventing the child from realizing that he or she is "an individual with his own rights and his own responsibilities" (Horney 1942, p. 44), *or* the child may never be allowed to develop self-confidence, *or* the parents may make direct assaults upon the child by using, for example, sarcasm, *or* the parents may prefer other siblings, and so on.

The neurotic atmosphere produces in the child what Horney termed *basic anxiety,* a "terrible feeling of being isolated and helpless in a potentially hostile world" (1945, p. 39). Such anxiety is composed of feelings of helplessness, hostility, and isolation and is a severe threat to any sense of security that the child may possess. The reaction of the individual to the anxiety-arousing situation may be to form what Horney called the *basic attitude.* This attitude does not necessarily have to develop into a neurosis, but it is "the nutritive soil out of which a definite neurosis may develop at any time" (Horney 1937, p. 89).

Neurotic Trends

In order to cope with basic anxiety, the individual develops *neurotic trends.* Horney noted characteristics common to all neurotic trends. First, their essential elements are unconscious. Second, the neurotic trends are compulsive; they must find a release for their intense energy. Third, they are pursued indiscriminately. Fourth, any frustration of them may lead to a more severe anxiety reaction. Here, the use of the neuroses as a defense against anxiety is very clear. Finally, the trends can, and do, generalize and pervade the individual's entire personality structure and behavior. They come to dominate the individual's feelings, actions, thoughts, attitudes— in short, the whole *modus vivendi.*

In several publications, Horney has undertaken to detail specific neurotic trends which serve as coping devices or needs employed in the reduction of anxiety. In her first book (1937), she postulates four principal coping devices: affection, submissiveness, power, and withdrawal. She later extended the list to include ten *neurotic needs* (Horney 1942). As one example, the neurotic need for affection and approval consists of an indiscriminate need to please others and to be liked and approved of by others. The remaining neurotic needs are: the neurotic need to restrict one's life within narrow borders, the neurotic need for power; the need to exploit others, the need for social recognition; the neurotic need for perfection; the need for independence; the neurotic need for a "partner" who will take over one's life; the ambition for personal achievement; and the need for personal admiration.

Horney (1945) later grouped these trends into three main classes: moving toward people, moving against people, and moving away from people.

> When moving toward *people he (the person) accepts his own helplessness, and in spite of his estrangement and fears tries to win the affection of others and to lean on them. Only in this way can he feel safe with them. If there are dissenting parties in the family (as one example) he will attach himself to the most powerful person or group. By complying with them, he gains a feeling of belonging and support which makes him feel less weak and less isolated.*
>
> When he moves against *people he accepts and takes for granted the hostility around him, and determines consciously or unconsciously to fight. He implicitly distrusts the feelings and intentions of others toward himself. He rebels in whatever ways are open to him. He wants to be the stronger and defeat them, partly for his own protection, partly for revenge.*
>
> When he moves away *from people he wants neither to belong nor to fight but keeps apart. He feels he has not much in common with them. They do not understand him anyhow. (Horney 1945, pp. 42–43)*

These three directional trends of the neurotic personality roughly describe a typology consisting of dependent or compliant, aggressive, and detached personality types. The *compliant* neurotic finds security (that is, safety) only in a dependent, seemingly selfless, devotion to others. That individual craves approval, affection, and intense love or friendship and, therefore, attempts to achieve domination through weakness. The compliant neurotic's motto is love conquers all. The *aggressive* neurotic feels that the world is hostile and persecutory and must be dealt with. That individual is described as demanding, exploitative, hostile, and often ruthless. The *detached* neurotic is secure only in isolation from others and is independent, self-sufficient, asocial, even withdrawn. His or her job, at which the detached neurotic is the ultimate, compulsive perfectionist, may substitute for virtually all genuine human relationships. He or she is the accountant in an isolated office, the artist in an inaccessible cove, the research scientist in an off-limits laboratory, the isolated individualist in any walk of life.

The neurotic trends do not actually resolve the anxiety problem, since they provide only a false basis for the individual's security and, in the long run, increase dependency upon others. This dependency, in turn, builds up more anxiety and insecurity. In addition, "the individual is easily subject to anxiety as soon as they (the coping devices) fail to operate. They make him rigid, all the more so since further protective means often have to be built up to allay new anxieties" (Horney 1939, p. 277).

Conflict Resolution

There are several ways in which the individual tries to resolve neurotic conflicts and maintain a sense of unity. All of these are unconscious and all ultimately fail to resolve the individual's difficulties. The first method consists of repressing certain aspects of the personality and bringing their opposites to the fore. A second method is to become more detached from the world. The individual puts such distance between himself or herself and others that the conflicts can be ignored. A third method used to resolve conflicts is called *externalization*. This is the tendency to experience internal processes as though they occurred outside oneself and to hold the perceived external factors responsible for one's difficulties and failures. It means abandoning the self altogether. The fourth solution is to use the idealized image of the self as a neurotic mechanism. The attempt to achieve the perfection represented by the ideal self may become a central obsession, requiring the devotion of all the neurotic's energies to its attainment. This striving for perfection is the result of conflict between the real self and the ideal self and is *the major basis for the development of neurosis.*

The Vicious Circle

The development and operation of the neurotic syndrome is best summarized by Horney's concept of the vicious circle. Basic to the various neurotic trends or safety devices is the polarity between helplessness and hostility. The individual, feeling the competitive hostility of the cultural environment, develops a sense of helplessness, anxiety, and repressed hostility. As a result, he or she experiences an excessive need for reassuring affection and adopts neurotic techniques for obtaining affection and reducing anxiety. The neurotic techniques are, however, unsuccessful and, indeed, may alienate individuals around the neurotic. Coupled with the neurotic's oversensitivity to, and anticipation of, rejection, the alienation of others produces signs of rejection for the neurotic. The signs induce a feeling of rejection, which evokes hostility and anxiety. The hostility is repressed, and the vicious circle begins again.

ERICH FROMM

When Freud published his first major book, *The Interpretation of Dreams,* in 1900, Erich Fromm was born, literally at the turn of the century. After receiving his Ph.D. degree from the University of Heidelberg in 1922, Fromm trained in psychoanalysis at the Berlin Psychoanalytic Institute, coming to the United States in 1933, where he taught at the Chicago Psychoanalytic Institute and subsequently became a private practitioner in New York City. After teaching at other universities in the United States, he moved to Mexico, joining the faculty of the National University and becoming director of the Mexico Psychoanalytic Institute.

Despite his psychoanalytic training and experience, Fromm's writings are more clearly identifiable as those of a social philosopher than of a psychoanalyst. Perhaps more accurately, they represent a blending of the concepts of Sigmund Freud with those of Karl Marx, with the stronger emphasis clearly on Marx.

The theoretical hallmark of Fromm's work is his concern with both the individual and the society, as well as with their interaction. He has taken the basic position that there is an ideal set of social conditions and, indeed, an ideal society, as well as an optimal orientation that an individual might take toward the society and his or her interaction with it. Because these ideals have not been achieved, however, individuals are basically lonely, isolated creatures. Each one strives to obtain freedom, but with freedom comes an isolation that necessitates a continuing attempt to escape the freedom that has been achieved. The details of Fromm's theory grow out of these concepts of person and society, and his theory is an attempt to answer such questions as how people have become isolated, how each person might productively overcome this isolation, and how both the individual and the society can maximally profit from their ongoing interaction.

Individual and Societal Needs

All human beings, according to Fromm (1955), have five basic needs: relatedness, transcendence, rootedness, sense of identity, and frame of reference. Every human being experiences, and must attempt to satisfy, these essential needs. The need for relatedness is essentially a need to establish a positive and ongoing relationship with others. This need arises from the fact that humans, unlike other animals, have lost their close relationship with nature and, as a result, feel lonely and isolated. Establishing relatedness to other people can at least partially overcome the sense of isolation. However, although dominance and submission are both forms of relatedness, the most effective form is *productive love*. Such love, which may take the forms of maternal, paternal, erotic, brotherly, or self-love, occurs when the individual bases the relationship on mutual respect, understanding, and caring. The second need, that for *transcendence,* refers to the requirement that human beings go beyond their basic biological nature as animals. Transcendence, then, involves a realization of capacity and potentiality, leading to creative productivity for the individual. *Rootedness* involves the need to have continuing and meaningful relationships with both the surrounding environment and the past. It is basically a need to feel that one belongs. The need for a *sense of identity* reflects the individual's desire to know who he or she is and to understand clearly his or her role in society. Finally, the need for a *frame of reference* is a need to make perceptual order out of what would otherwise be a world of chaos.

Just as the individual has needs, so also does society. The specific needs will vary from one society to another, but in all cases the needs must be satisfied by training the individual citizen toward social need satisfaction. For example, if the society develops an assembly line technology for use in industrial settings, individuals must be taught not only to work on the assembly line but also to value that type of work.

If a society develops a system of individual possession of material goods, citizens must be taught to be honest and not steal these goods. The training of the individual to fulfill the needs of the society begins in early childhood. Very often, however, the demands that the society places on the individual are contradictory to that individual's very nature, and the satisfaction of the society's needs makes it impossible for the individual to satisfy his or her own needs. The society that is incapable of adequately satisfying the needs of the individual is an inadequate or "sick" society, and Fromm (1955) has indicted both communistic and capitalistic societies on these grounds.

The problems created by immediate societal demands are amplified by the very condition of being human. Fromm (1947) has maintained that every person is caught up in the *human situation* of being unique among the animal kingdom in the ability to experience discontentment, unhappiness, and boredom. Fromm has described the difficulty of the human situation as involving historical and existential dichotomies. To say that humans are faced with dichotomies is to say that there are certain difficulties that make the life of the individual less than ideal. *Historical dichotomies* are those difficulties that occurred as a result of the history of the society. Major examples include the facts that although most people would prefer a continuing state of peace, there is a world history of recurrent war, and although equality is widely touted as a virtue, discrimination of many kinds continues to exist. In addition, wealth is unevenly distributed across the population, abundant technology can seemingly not be used exclusively for the welfare of individuals, and the real benefits of technology and science are provided for only a small proportion of the population. *Existential dichotomies* are insoluble contradictions that are not merely accidents of history. For example, while all humans would like to be healthy and free from the occurrence of accidental injury, both poor health and accidents are common. Similarly, there are many situations in which human control would be desirable but over which control cannot be established. And while immortality would seem highly desirable to the average person, each is aware that the day of death will arrive. In the face of all these and other dichotomies, the individual human being must make his or her way in the world, satisfying needs and achieving whatever degree of harmony and happiness is possible under the adverse circumstances of the human situation.

Personal Traits and Orientations

The fulfillment of both individual and societal needs is a function of the nature of the interaction between the person and the social group. This interaction is determined, at least in part, by the individual's personality structure and consequent orientation toward the environment.

Fromm, in developing his concept of orientation, borrowed the concept of character from Freud and another psychoanalytic theorist, Abraham. Fromm has used this concept to emphasize the role of society in developing character and the role of character in interacting with society. Character traits are seen in Fromm's theory as central traits, organized and patterned at the core of the personality. The individual's character tends to be stable and consistent over time and is essentially a personality type which determines the person's behavioral habits.

The character types are expressed as one or more of several distinct orientations. The most effective orientation that one can take toward the world is the *productive orientation,* in which one engages in activity that is not compulsive or driven but rather is directed toward the realization of one's potentialities (Fromm 1947). The productively oriented person displays both reproductive comprehension and generative comprehension. The former refers to an objective, accurate perception of reality, while generative comprehension involves an internal processing of incoming information, which allows one to go beyond the relatively simple objective impressions gained from the external environment. The truly productive personality continually displays both of these characteristics. If the productive orientation is not adequately adopted by the individual, he or she must substitute for it one or more of several other personality types which are *nonproductive orientations.* The *receptive orientation* is seen in the individual who remains overly dependent on others (Fromm and Maccoby 1970). The *exploitative orientation* involves taking advantage of others in order to attain success in life. The *hoarding orientation* is basically acquisitive in nature, gaining and holding possessions, which may be either material goods or people. The *marketing orientation* focuses on both people, including oneself, and goods as commodities. A person with this orientation is basically a salesperson, who is, in part, his or her own product. Fromm has allowed for the possibility of other character orientations being identified and has, in fact, spoken of some additional ones himself (Fromm 1964). In addition, according to Fromm, a given individual is not ordinarily expected to display one orientation exclusively. Rather, there is some mixing of character types in a given individual, and no one is completely nonproductive.

Perfect Individuals and Perfect Societies. It is clear that the more productively oriented a person is, the more perfect and effective that individual will be. The ultimate possibility in Fromm's theory would be that of the totally productive individual, one who has attained the ideal personality and behavioral state possible. There is similarly the possibility of a perfect society, defined in general, as one in which all people would have full and equal opportunities to achieve all human potentials. Feelings of isolation and loneliness would be nonexistent, there would be no need to escape from freedom, and most or all people would be able to develop productive orientations (Fromm 1968). Fromm has called this ideal society Humanistic Communitarian Socialism.

SULLIVAN'S INTERPERSONAL THEORY

Harry Stack Sullivan was born February 21, 1892, on a farm near Norwich, New York, and died at the pinnacle of his career on January 14, 1949, in Paris, France. He was raised as a lonely, isolated child and became, perhaps as a result, an intensive reader on many and varied topics. One of the most important developments in Sullivan's career came in 1922 when he went to St. Elizabeth's Hospital in Washington, D.C., where he met and was greatly influenced by a major figure in American psychiatry, William Alanson White. A year later Sullivan began his association with the Sheppard and Enoch Pratt Hospital and the University of Maryland Medical School, where he began his study and treatment of schizophrenic patients. Sullivan later went to New York City to study and treat obsessive patients and, in 1933, returned to become president of the William Alanson White Foundation and director of the training branch of that foundation, The Washington School of Psychiatry. A new journal, *Psychiatry,* was founded in 1938 to promote Sullivan's developing theory of interpersonal behavior. By this time, Sullivan was widely recognized as a major leader in American psychiatry and served in various capacities with the United Nations, the U.S. government, and international psychiatric groups.

Sullivan's record of publication is unusual among major personality theorists. While he published numerous articles in various journals, only one book, *Conceptions of Modern Psychiatry,* appeared during his lifetime. Even this book was originally a series of lectures given in 1939, subsequently published in *Psychiatry* in 1940, and only later compiled as a single book in 1947. Several additional books have since been compiled from Sullivan's writings and recorded lectures.

THE FOCUS OF AN INTERPERSONAL THEORY

In the late 1920s and early 1930s Sullivan began to think seriously in the direction of an interpersonal theory of abnormal behavior. Psychoanalysis was then firmly established as the major theoretical beacon guiding psychiatric thought throughout the world. Sullivan was impressed with many aspects of Freud's thinking and credited Freud for believing and persuading so many others that a scientific understanding of abnormal behavior was possible. On more specific issues, Sullivan accepted Freud's emphasis on the importance of psychic energy as a basis for understanding the dynamics of human personality, agreed that anxiety was a particularly important concept in explaining abnormal behavior, and was influenced by Freud's concepts of unconscious motivation and the operation of defenses. At the same time Sullivan rejected other aspects of the Freudian formulation. He felt that biological influences, while present, were not nearly as important as Freud had made them. He did not subscribe to the libido theory, and he denied that the stages of development are based primarily on physiological maturational processes, although he did accept the importance of the early developmental years.

Sullivan's other objections to psychoanalytic theory not withstanding, his primary concern was Freud's failure to consider the influence of interpersonal interaction on personality development and functioning. Freud had emphasized the importance of intrapsychic functioning and held that an understanding of abnormal behavior could come only through a careful analysis of the internal functioning of the person. Sullivan adopted the alternative view that the individual's internal functioning consists of a series of private experiences that cannot be directly observed by another individual and, as such, are purely theoretical and not a legitimate basis for psychiatric evaluation. Personality functioning can, on the other hand, be directly observed when the person engages in interpersonal interactions, and it is this interpersonal behavior that constitutes the best basis for psychiatric study and for understanding abnormal behavior. It is worth noting that this point of view grows out of field theory, which originally came from physics and is seen most clearly in psychological theory in the work of Kurt Lewin (see Chapter 14). The emphasis is on the need to consider the context in which behavior occurs, and it was for this reason that Sullivan held firmly to the position that *personality does not exist apart from the social, interpersonal field in which the individual develops and functions.*

INTERPERSONAL NEED SATISFACTION

The basic thrust of Sullivanian theory is that the individual develops a personality in order to satisfy needs, primarily through interpersonal interactions. The individual has many needs, some biological, others induced by environmental conditions. Sullivan emphasized two primary kinds of needs, those for satisfaction and those for security. The *satisfaction needs* include the basic biological requirements for survival, such as needs for food, water, and sleep. The infant gradually learns to satisfy these needs through interactions with the mother and other humans. Out of these interactions, there develop interpersonal needs for affiliation with others, kindness, understanding, and warmth. Like the biological needs, these learned needs are satisfied through further interpersonal interactions. The *security needs* develop when the individual experiences anxiety, arising primarily from interpersonal interactions.

Dynamisms

The powerful satisfaction and security needs must be satisfied, and the mechanism for their satisfaction is the *dynamism*. Sullivan defined a dynamism as a continuing or recurring pattern of energy transformations, by which he means, in essence, a pattern of activity or behavior. For example, a person who repeatedly faces dangerous situations without fear might be said to have a courage dynamism, while one who is constantly seeking out the company of other people might be said to have a companionship dynamism. While Sullivan had emphasized the importance of dynamisms that are involved in interpersonal situations, his concept is otherwise quite similar to the concept of trait, as employed by Allport, Cattell, and other theorists, and to the concept of habit, as employed by Dollard and Miller and others.

Satisfaction of the Security Needs

Three dynamisms are especially significant in the personality because they have a primary role in the avoidance and reduction of anxiety, thus satisfying the security needs. The first and most important of these dynamisms is the *self-system*, an especially complex dynamism which is charged with the overall maintenance of security. The self-system develops through the person's early interactions, particularly with the mother, as the child learns various methods for avoiding and reducing anxiety in interpersonal situations. Later in life the self-system tends to become an isolated but important region of the personality and, because it rejects new experiences that are inconsistent with its structure at a given time, it may become a distorted, inaccurate representation of reality and thereby interfere with the individual's ability to interact effectively with others.

The other two important dynamisms, while also anxiety-reducing systems, are somewhat more specific and narrower in scope than the self-system. The *apathy* dynamism comes into use when the failure to satisfy biological needs causes frustration. In essence, the repeatedly frustrated infant learns to avoid the frustration by adopting an attitude of noninterest. The dynamism of *somnolent detachment* is seen in response not to frustration but to anxiety. It is the defense used by the infant when anxiety cannot otherwise be effectively reduced—falling asleep.

THE DEVELOPMENTAL PROCESS

Personality development is a process of ongoing and increasing interpersonal interaction. The thrust of development is toward the learning of progressively more complex interpersonal interaction mechanisms and patterns, which are utilized principally to fulfill the satisfaction and security needs.

Interaction takes place through certain zones of the body which enter into interpersonally significant contact with the social environment. The sensory intake functions of the retinal, auditory, and general tactile zones are apparent. The vestibulo-kinaesthetic region is concerned with feedback to the person concerning his or her orientation and the condition and movement of muscles and joints. Sullivan put somewhat greater emphasis on three other zones, the oral, genital, and anal, which are seen as being much more subject, in their dynamisms, to the influence of cultural training. The *oral* zone is the one most centrally involved in the development of the self-dynamism. The *genital* zone is subject to many culturally imposed limitations and is often the focus of considerable tension and anxiety generated through interpersonal interactions. Finally, the *anal* zone is often severely invaded by the society through the toilet-training process.

The Stages of Development

Sullivan followed Freud's example in believing that development is not a continuous process but rather is broken up into distinct steps or stages. Where Freud based the staging process on biological maturation, however, Sullivan focused instead on *the occurrence of interpersonally significant events.* The first stage of development is *infancy.* The developmental focus at this stage is on the interpersonal interaction between the infant and the mother, with the oral zone being the primary region of contact between the infant and the environment. The child's relationship with the mother is mediated by empathy, which is essentially a kind of emotional communion between the infant and the mother or other significant people. It is through empathy that the infant begins to learn about interpersonal processes and to perceive such feelings as warmth and anxiety in others. During infancy, the baby begins to develop the self-system, as well as the dynamisms of somnolent detachment and apathy.

Childhood is a stage of language acquisition and utilization. It begins with the onset of articulate speech and continues until the child shows an expressed need for interaction with peers. During childhood, many restraints on freedom are imposed, and the development of the self-system becomes an important focus of this stage. In addition, the individual learns that people will not always be kind, and that he or she has enemies as well as friends in the world. Sullivan terms this necessary but unfortunate development in the child's learning of interpersonal interaction the *malevolent transformation* of personality.

The next two developmental stages, *juvenile* and *preadolescent,* are seen as stages during which any early developmental problems can be potentially corrected. During the juvenile years, the child learns more and more complex social interaction patterns with peers and authority figures. The preadolescent years begin when the individual expresses a need for close relationships with peers of the same sex, which is basically a need to have a "best friend" to whom one can divulge the deepest of secrets. The next two stages, *early adolescence* and *late adolescence,* focus toward the development of heterosexual relationships. During early adolescence, the individual develops the lust dynamism, accompanying the biological changes of puberty. When the early adolescent has learned a behavior pattern which permits continuing gratification of sexual needs, late adolescence begins. This is a period in which earlier interpersonal interaction patterns are integrated, so that the individual has a fully developed repertoire of interrelated social skills. The late adolescent also learns in more detail about the responsibilities, as well as the advantages, of adulthood, and the self-system becomes more fully integrated and more effective in dealing with anxiety.

The final stage, *adulthood,* represents the culmination of the entire interpersonal developmental process that has gone before. Only now is the person fully human. Only now has the biological animal been completely transformed into a social animal, with all of the assets and liabilities that tranformation brings.

Experiential Modes

As the child passes through the stages of development, he or she also undergoes a highly significant chronological sequence of cognitive development. Sullivan's theory of cognitive development reflects his underlying assumption—and that of many other theorists—that behavior is determined by the individual's perception of reality and not necessarily by the reality itself. One major determinant of the accuracy of the individual's perceptions, and the one on which Sullivan chose to focus, is the cognitive ability to accurately grasp cause-effect relationships. He suggested, in effect, that internal cognitive-perceptual processes mediate our contact with the external world.

The cognitive ability necessary to achieve an accurate, or relatively accurate, perceptual interpretation of the environment develops gradually in a sequence of largely independent but partially overlapping modes of perceptual processing or experiencing. The earliest experiential mode, called the *prototaxic* mode, extends from birth until about three or four months of age. In this cognitive mode infants do not differentiate between themselves and their environment, but experience their contact with the environment as a continuous flow of undifferentiated events. The prototaxic mode may occur in later life in psychotic states.

The uninterrupted flow of prototaxic experience soon gives way to what is called the *parataxic* mode, which extends from the third or fourth month to about the third year of life. Then children begin to think in terms of cause-effect relationships, but their thinking is largely illogical or magical in nature. There is a tendency to draw cause-effect conclusions concerning events that occur at the same point in time and space but which may not, in fact, be related. For example, a child may finish the last bite of baby food, then accidentally drop the spoon on the floor. Immediately afterward the child receives a loving pat and kiss from the mother. On future occasions when finishing a meal the child may drop the spoon, even though the love reward was intended to reinforce only finishing the meal. Unlike prototaxic thinking, the parataxic mode is common in adults as well as in children. The adult who repeatedly, but unsuccessfully, kicks the television to stop the rolling picture after a single success, the individual who is superstitious, and the neurotic who always walks completely around the bed three times upon arising each morning are all exhibiting instances of parataxic thinking.

As cognitive development continues, children move into the all-important and, in the normal person, lifelong *syntaxic* mode. In this thought form cause-effect relationships are much more logically and accurately perceived, and individuals test and retest perceptions and consensually validate them by assuring that others are in agreement.

Personifications

While a child is developing increasingly more complex experiential modes which help in coping with the general environment, he or she is also developing sets of social expectations which can help to structure perceptions of the interpersonal sphere. Each set of expectations that is learned is initially specific to one individual or type of individual and is termed the *personification* of that type of person. A major example is the personification of the mother. During early life, infants typically undergo intense experiences with their mother and thereby begin to build up an idea or image of what she is like, a set of expectations concerning her future behavior, which is based on her past behavior. Typically, children will begin by developing separate personifications of the "good mother" and the "bad mother." The characteristics perceived as constituting the good mother might include warmth, tenderness, and satisfaction of biological needs. The bad mother is the anxious mother, who, through the process of empathy evokes anxiety in the infant. The good mother and bad mother images later join to form an overall mother personification.

The most important aspect of personifications is that they tend to generalize. Both the personifications of good or need-satisfying characteristics and those of bad or anxiety-evoking characteristics, once formed on the basis of contact with a single person, are applied to many similar people. The personification of the mother may, for example, be applied to a variety of adult women, such as teachers, aunts, and neighbors. The application of the personification comes when children enter into interpersonal interactions with people similar to the mother. If she is personified primarily as a kind, loving, tender, honest person, a child will expect to find these characteristics in other adult women who are perceived as similar to the mother. If, on the other hand, the mother is vindictive, rejecting, mean, and domineering, a child will expect to find these characteristics in similar adults. A child's expectations when entering into a new interpersonal relationship will, in part, determine the nature of his or her interactions with the new person and may well determine the course of development of the interpersonal relationship.

One particularly important personification is that of the *self*. The image of self incorporates *good me, bad me,* and *not me* personifications. All of these images arise from a child's perceptions of other people's evaluations of him or her. The *good me* includes positive, anxiety-reducing characteristics of the self, the *bad me* negative, anxiety-increasing characteristics, and the *not me* uncertainties arising from ambiguous emotional reactions to the child by others.

The Developmental Role of Anxiety

In Sullivan, as in Freud and many other theorists, anxiety is a centrally important determinant of the developmental process. In fact, Sullivan made this powerful emotion central to his understanding of the basis for many interpersonal relationships. Sullivan distinguished clearly between anxiety and fear. Anxiety is seen as arising when there is an interpersonal threat to the self-esteem of the individual, while fear arises from an external threat to survival or biological integrity. The effects of anxiety are not entirely negative. In fact, to an even greater extent than in Freudian theory, anxiety is seen as essential to the normal development of the personality. The personality basically develops in an effort to provide mechanisms for the reduction of tension arising from interpersonally generated anxiety. As has been noted, the self-system develops as a central anxiety-reducing dynamism in the personality.

PSYCHOTHERAPY

Sullivan's approach to psychotherapy provides a good example of the application of a social analytic theory to the treatment of psychological disorder. The approach is based on his theory of interpersonal dynamisms. He hypothesized that good mental health is largely a function of the quality of the individual's interpersonal relationships. Mental illness consequently involves the failure of adequate interpersonal relationships and a partial disintegration of the personality. Treatment must aim to bring the personality back into balance, to achieve a degree of reintegration, and thereby to improve the individual's interpersonal relationships (Sullivan 1954).

Therapy itself is seen not as a process of curing disease but rather as a means of educating the patient. The therapist, as in the Freudian approach, thus tries to help the patient gain insight into important unconscious factors affecting behavior. The goal is to return unconscious motivations to consciousness and, in that way, expand and strengthen the self-dynamism. The therapeutic situation is viewed as a two-person or dyadic interpersonal interaction, which Sullivan termed a *two-group*. The special, therapeutic two-group is one in which the therapist is an observer, who can understand and interpret the patient's behavior, as well as a participant in the two-group interaction. The actual Sullivanian therapy is conducted over a number of psychiatric interviews that progress through a series of steps, moving from the initial introduction of client and therapist to a final overview of plans, problems, and progress to the formal separation of client and therapist. The therapist is concerned with unconscious motivations and may use such psychoanalytic techniques as free association, transference, and dream analysis. There is also a strong emphasis on the patient's interpersonal relationships and the role that these play in the problem.

Social Psychological Treatment. Sullivan must be credited with an additional approach to treatment which has had widespread ramifications in psychology and psychiatry. It was his belief that individual psychotherapy was often not sufficient or was not the best approach to the problems of a given client. He believed instead that it should be helpful to create a psychotherapeutic environment, a climate in which the patient can feel accepted and can learn to grow and develop in his or her interpersonal skills and relationships. His idea led to the establishment of therapeutic communities on hospital wards and in halfway houses, which have been the conceptual forerunners of such approaches as Synanon for former drug addicts and Alcoholics Anonymous.

TRANSACTIONAL ANALYSIS: ERIC BERNE

Sullivan's theory has had a lasting impact in psychology and psychiatry, not only in providing an alternative method of psychotherapy but also in stimulating the development of further interpersonal theories. To demonstrate the nature of this latter heuristic influence, and because they are important positions in their own right, we will briefly discuss the post-Sullivanian interpersonal theories of Berne and Carson.

Eric Berne borrowed from Sullivan the basic concept that all important behaviors are interpersonal behaviors and that the personality develops through and functions in the context of interpersonal relationships. His popular theory, outlined in *Games People Play* (1964), provides not only an interpersonal theoretical basis for understanding personality functioning but also a method of therapy, transactional analysis, which has been brought into increasingly widespread use.

Ego States

Every person, in Berne's theory, is really several people. Each of these "people" is called an *ego state,* and there are three principal states, those of parent, child, and adult. When functioning in a parent ego state, the person displays behavior similar to that of his or her own parents, with a tendency to display a combination of dominant and nurturant attitudes toward others. The child state involves feelings of inferiority and helplessness. The adult state is essentially a coping state, in which the person feels confident and capable.

Transactions

Interactions between people are actually transactions between their ego states. Each person involved in the transaction assumes one of the three major ego states and behaves on the basis of that state. When one person behaves in a manner the other would expect, the response is said to be a *complementary* behavior, while an unexpected response pattern represents a *crossed* behavior. When, for example, a son complains of having a stomach ache and his mother responds by comforting him, she is responding to his child state with her parent state, a complementary response. If the response to the child's complaint, however, is that she doesn't know what to do for him and she feels worse than he does and doesn't know what to do about that either, she may be seen as responding from her child state, a crossed response.

Ulterior Transactions and Games. There is a third type of interaction, called an *ulterior transaction,* which involves a mixture of ego states. The same behavior either develops out of the combination of ego states or is directed toward a combination of ego states, or both. People involved in ulterior transactions are playing *games,* and it is this aspect of the theory for which Berne is best known. For example, in the game "See what you made me do," one person is able to blame his or her own mistake on another and possibly gain sympathy or an apology in the process. In another game, "Why don't you," "yes, but . . . ," one person appears in a child ego state asking another adult for advice. If the second person responds in the adult ego state, giving reasonable advice, the first person may repeatedly respond "yes, but . . . ." What has happened is that the person in the child ego state has addressed the other individual as a parent and, by rejecting each of the suggestions given by that person, has shown that the "parent" lacks knowledge and power.

In application, *transactional analysis* focuses on the nature of the transactions in which a given individual or group engages. Ego states are carefully analyzed in an effort to determine whether they are parent, child, or adult and under what circumstances each of these ego states seems to predominate in an individual. In the case of ulterior transactions, the occurrence of games can be analyzed, and it may be found that a particular individual repeatedly employs varied forms of the same game with different people. Once the individual understands his or her ego states and gameplaying behavior, he or she may be moved toward changing the behavior.

INTERACTION CONCEPTS: CARSON

A second post-Sullivanian theory is that of Robert Carson. In his book, *Interaction Concepts of Personality* (1969), he provides an integrative social psychological model of interpersonal interaction. Drawing from empirical research, as well as from Sullivan's theory and related theoretical perspectives, Carson proposed a multidimensional model for understanding interpersonal interaction.

A Typology of Interaction

Carson outlined a typology of interpersonal behavior in which most forms of behavior can be classified as either hostile or friendly and either dominant or submissive. The result is four major categories of behavior: hostile dominance (H-D), friendly dominance (F-D), hostile submission (H-S), and friendly submission (F-S). Each of these four types has two major subtypes associated with it: H-D behavior may be either aggressive or competitive; F-D may be managerial or responsible; H-S may be rebellious or self-effacing; and F-S may be cooperative or docile.

Interactions between persons vary in their effectiveness and accomplishments depending upon the types of behavior expressed and reciprocated. For example, competitive behavior by one person may be most successful if it elicits submissive behavior from the other. Similarly, managerial behavior by one person may be fulfilling for both if the response is cooperative behavior from the other.

Applying the behavior typology, it is possible to represent any given interaction or series of interactions between two people and to determine the relative gain or loss which the interaction represents for each person. By analyzing the interaction of one person with a number of others, it is also possible to determine what styles of interaction typically characterize that individual's behavior.

Interpersonal Power

Any interpersonal interaction carries with it the potential for one person to gain or exercise power over the other. Power or control can be achieved in three ways. First, it may be that only one type of behavior by Person A is rewarding to Person B. Person A can control B by selectively offering and withholding the essential behavior. In this situation A is said to have *fate control* over B. An alternative form of power occurs when the simple presence of Person A is very rewarding for B, perhaps because A is the only one who is friendly toward B. The result is that A has *contact control* over B. A final possibility is that A may selectively reward certain of B's behaviors and fail to reward others. Person B's behavior may become largely a function of the rewards administered and withheld by A, and A has achieved *behavior control* over B.

SOCIAL ANALYTIC THEORY IN AN EMPIRICAL CONTEXT

For the most part, the major social analytic theories were not cast in an empirical context and have influenced research primarily at the broad level of social psychological research as a field. That is, one can assert that many of the areas of study engaged in by social psychologists, as well as some sociological research, have been historically influenced by the sociocultural emphasis seen in the social analytic theories. Beyond this broad generality, we can give some examples of specific research areas stimulated by the social analytic theorists.

It has already been noted that Adler's theory has stimulated considerable research on birth order effects, although the findings have been somewhat contradictory and, in recent years, controversial. A second influence of Adler has been research concerned with inferiority feelings. Most of this research, however, has not directly tested Adler's hypotheses. In another area, life style has been investigated, though primarily through case studies and theoretical attempts to extend and further develop the concept (Ansbacher 1967).

Sullivan's approach to research consisted of the systematic application of the case study method. He viewed the therapist as a participant-observer, who collected data on the individual client but also contributed to that data through his involvement in the interpersonal situation. Despite his clear recognition that the therapist might thereby bias the data, Sullivan did not attempt to utilize other research methods in order to test his theory.

Carson has drawn much more heavily from empirical evidence than had the earlier social theorists. His presentation and review of empirical evidence as a partial basis for his theory is interesting and instructive (Carson 1969)

EVALUATION

The outstanding contribution of the social analytic theorists was clearly their emphasis on the influence of sociocultural variables in the development of personality. Freud had, as the neoanalysts themselves noted, largely neglected the role of social variables in personality functioning. Adler, Horney, Fromm, Sullivan, and more recent interpersonal theorists have quite systematically incorporated into basically psychoanalytic frameworks a variety of social concepts. Adler described the innate social nature of man. Horney dealt in particular with the family and its influence on individual development. Fromm focused on the nature of the society as it shapes the individual personality. And Sullivan concentrated on dyadic interpersonal relationships.

Although they made a very real contribution to the field, the social analytic theorists have often been criticized on a number of points. They have been faulted by some critics for stating social theories which continue to have too many biological concepts and by others for moving much too far away from the original biological concepts of Freud.

A more telling criticism is the suggestion that the neoanalytic theories are not really very original. Each theorist relied heavily on other theorists, primarily Freud and, in Fromm's case, Marx, adding only a few concepts to already developed theoretical systems. While it is probably true that the social analytic theories would not have been developed had not Freud's psychoanalytic theory preceded them as a stimulus, it must also be clear that each of the social analysts added some considerable richness of social concepts to the original psychoanalytic formulation. Although these theories were not as original as they might have been, neither were they simple rewordings of the Freudian approach.

One can also question the origins of the social analytic theories. First, it should be noted that these were theories developed without the benefit of any substantial empirical base. Although each theorist observed individual patients during therapy and based at least some theoretical conclusions on these observations, there was little that could be called systematic research carried out by the theorists. Their own theories were subjected to the empirical scrutiny only of the case study. A second critical point concerning the origins of the social analytic theories is that they were based primarily on observations of disturbed populations. This would not be a criticism if it were not for the fact that the theorists saw their approaches as general theories of human behavior, applying to normal as well as to abnormal populations.

Each of the social analytic theories has received some legitimate and important criticisms. It is essential to note that each has also withstood the test of time and that these theorists, individually and as a group, have made a very real and lasting contribution to the understanding of human behavior.

REFERENCES

Adler, A. *Social interest.* New York: Putnam, 1939.

Ansbacher, H. L. Life style: A historical & systematic review. *Journal of Individual Psychology*, 1967, *23*, 191-212.

Bernard, L. L. *Instinct: A study in social psychology.* New York: Holt, 1924.

Berne, E. *Games people play: The psychology of human relationships.* New York: Grove Press, 1964.

Carson, R. C. *Interaction concepts of personality.* Chicago: Aldine, 1969.

Ferenczi, S. *Further contributions to the theory and technique of psycho-analysis.* New York: Basic Books, 1952.

Fromm, E. *Man for himself.* New York: Holt, 1947.

Fromm, E. *The sane society.* New York: Holt, Rinehart, & Winston, 1955.

Fromm, E. *The heart of man: Its genius for good & evil.* New York: Harper & Row, 1964.

Fromm, E. Values, psychology & human existence. In D. E. Hamachek (Ed.). *Human dynamics in psychology and education: Selected readings.* Boston: Allyn & Bacon, 1968.

Fromm, E., & Maccoby, M. *Social character in a mexican village: A sociopsychoanalytic study.* Englewood Cliffs, N.J.: Prentice-Hall, 1970.

Horney, K. *The neurotic personality of our time.* New York: Norton, 1937.

Horney, K. *New ways in psychoanalysis.* New York: Norton, 1939.

Horney, K. *Self-analysis.* New York: Norton, 1942.

Horney, K. *Our inner conflicts: A constructive theory of neurosis.* New York: Norton, 1945.

Horney, K. *Neurosis and human growth.* New York: Norton, 1950.

Jones, H. E. Order of birth in relation to the development of the child. In C. Murchison (Ed.), *Handbook of child psychology,* Worcester, Mass.: Clark University Press, 1931.

McDougall, W. *Introduction to social psychology.* London: Methuen, 1908.

Munroe, R. L. *Schools of psychoanalytic thought.* New York: Holt, Rinehart, & Winston, 1955.

Rank, O. *The trauma of birth.* New York: Harcourt & Brace, 1929.

Reich, W. *Character analyses.* Berlin: Orgone Institute Press, 1933.

Reich, W. *Character analysis: New translation.* New York: Farrar, Straus, and Giroux, 1972.

Schachter, S. *The psychology of affiliation: Experimental studies of the sources of gregariousness.* Stanford: Stanford University Press, 1959.

Schooler, S. Birth order effects: Not here, not now! *Psychological Bulletin,* 1972, *78,* 161-175.

Steckel, W. Autobiography. *American Journal of Psychotherapy,* 1949, *3,* 37-46.

Sullivan, H. S. *The psychiatric interview.* New York: Norton, 1954.

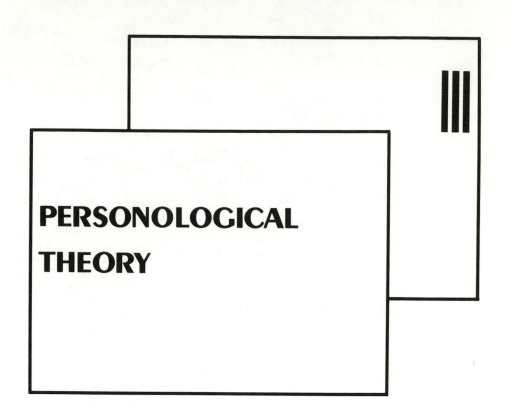

PERSONOLOGICAL
THEORY

6

The Psychology of the Individual:
Gordon Allport

All personality theories are developed, at least in part, in an attempt to understand the behavior of the individual, yet many of these theories seem virtually to ignore the unique human qualities of that individual, choosing instead to treat each person as simply representative of a species. Similarly, many theories of personality have attempted to be general theories, dealing with both "normal" and "deviant" people. Close examination of most personality theories reveals that the theorist was, however, initially and primarily interested in abnormal population, with the theory, therefore, being developed primarily on the basis of observations of psychologically disturbed people. Gordon Allport attempted to overcome both of these difficulties, which he saw in personality theory, and, in the process, provided an explicit, detailed trait theory representing an attempt to understand the functioning of the unique, normal person.

BIOGRAPHICAL ROOTS OF THE THEORY

Gordon Willard Allport was born in Montezuma, Indiana, November 11, 1896, and died in Cambridge, Massachusetts, on October 9, 1967. He was the youngest of four sons, all of whom achieved professional distinction. One brother, Floyd, was a noted psychologist in his own right, although the collaboration between him and Gordon was largely limited to the Ascendancy-Submission Scales of 1939. His father, a physician, was a hospital administrator and also operated a pharmaceutical distribution enterprise. His mother became a Christian Scientist during his early teens. It would be hard to imagine a more fertile seed bed for eclecticism than we have here.

Allport received his A.B. in philosophy and economics (with honors) from Harvard in 1919. During 1919–20 he served as instructor in sociology and English at Roberts College in Istanbul, did graduate work in psychology at the universities of Berlin, Hamburg, and Cambridge, and visited briefly in Vienna with Sigmund Freud. He reports that in the presence of Freud he found himself literally tongue-tied. He then returned to Harvard for further graduate study in psychology. He earned his M.A. in 1921 and his Ph.D. in 1922. He remained at Harvard as an instructor in social ethics until 1926. From 1926 to 1930 he was an assistant professor in psychology at Dartmouth College. In 1930 he returned to Harvard and was identified with that university until his death. In 1942 he was made full professor and chairman of the psychology department. He has been president of the American Psychological Association and has received many professional honors in the United States, Great Britain, and the European continent.

Allport's major publications include *Personality: A Psychological Interpretation* (1937), *The Use of Personal Documents in Psychological Science* (1942), *The Nature of Prejudice* (1954), *Becoming: Basic Considerations for a Psychology of Personality* (1955), and *Pattern and Growth in Personality* (1961). His theory of personality was formally propounded in the first of these works and is seen in each of the others. Among his better-known pupils were A. L. Baldwin, J. S. Bruner, H. Cantril, G. Lindzey, D. C. McGranahan, and M. B. Smith.

GENERAL CHARACTERISTICS OF THE THEORY

Consider the following brief psychology quiz and the responses indicated as correct by the parentheses:

T (F) The motivation behind most adult human behavior is *un*conscious.

T (F) One's behavior at any given moment is determined primarily by past experiences.

T (F) So-called normal and abnormal behavior are but arbitrary zones on a continuum.

T (F) The methodology of the physical sciences provides a useful model for psychological research and theory.

T   (F)   The term *personality* refers to a cluster of consistent behavior patterns rather than to any actual neurophysiological structure or condition.

T   (F)   The term *trait* refers to a particular pattern of behavior that is sufficiently predictable and common to be useful in describing personality types.

T   (F)   All normal human behavior seeks, directly or indirectly, to achieve or maintain pleasure, certainty, or peace, or to reduce or avoid pain, uncertainty, or tension, with the minimum expenditure of effort.

T   (F)   In general, the interpretability of psychological research findings increases with the number of cases observed.

T   (F)   The fundamental characteristics of the normal human personality are essentially determined by the age of seven.

T   (F)   Most guilt feelings in an adult can be traced, directly or indirectly, to violations of the injunctions of authority figures in his or her childhood.

Each of the foregoing propositions, which would be answered true by many theorists, is indicated as false for Allport. Indeed, his theory is, in many respects, deviant from the mainstream of psychological theory. In the remainder of this chapter we will encounter the specific position statements that suggested this hypothetical true-false overview of his theory of personality.

The Domain of the Theory

We might suppose that one holding a theoretical position as iconoclastic as that suggested by this hypothetical quiz would be in perpetual conflict with the majority of his profession. Allport was not. It was not so much that his position as "Harvard psychologist" put him beyond theoretical criticism; rather, he chose not to compete with those he regarded as behavioristic, deterministic, mechanistic, or reactivistic, these being listed in increasing order of distance from his position. Without meaning to be patronizing, Allport conceded the adequacy of each and all of these theoretical positions to handle all of the behavioral phenomena within the domain he allotted them. He limited this domain to the behavior of animals, infants, and grossly disturbed adults. He claimed for his own theory the domain of conscious, normal, adult, human behavior. He wrote:

> Some theories . . . are based largely upon the behavior of sick and anxious people or upon the antics of captive and desperate rats. Fewer theories have derived from the study of healthy human beings, those who strive not so much to preserve life as to make it worth living. (1955, p. 18)

STRUCTURAL PRINCIPLES

Allport was the first to admit that his theory was not rigorously systematic, and this chapter will not attempt to find more order in it than he did. As Allport puts it, "We need ideas before we can apply rigor" (1957, p. 21).

Definition of Personality

All of Allport's fundamental "ideas" are implicitly embodied in his definition of personality: "Personality is the dynamic organization within the individual of those psychophysical systems that determine his characteristic behavior and thought" (1961, p. 28). This definition of personality is probably the most thoughtful ever propounded and is deservedly acclaimed on this account, since Allport studied some fifty other definitions before developing his own.

Although Allport disclaimed any formal structure for his theory, its essential thematic coherence can be seen and, indeed, its conceptual burden can be reproduced by considering his interpretations of the substantive terms in this definition. The expression *dynamic organization* reflects the thrust of his book, *Becoming* (1955). In that book he wrote, quote "Personality is less a finished product than a transitive process" (p. 19). Dynamic organization refers not only to the present state of affairs inside a person but to how it got to be that way and how and why it is changing, becoming something else, something better. The expressions *psychophysical systems* and *within the individual* bespeak Allport's conviction that personality *actually* exists in physiological and neural systems. The term *determines* means that "Personality *is* something and *does* something . . . It is what lies *behind* specific acts and within the individual" (Allport 1937b, p. 48).

If one term in this definition characterizes it more than any other, it is the word *unique*. Allport wrote, "The first fact that strikes us is the uniqueness of both the process and the product. Each person is an idiom unto himself, an apparent violation of the syntax of the species" (1955, p. 19). In addition, he said, " . . . all of the animals in the world are psychologically less distinct from one another than one man is from other men" (1955, p. 23). Allport means, quite literally, that every single normal adult personality is different in some significant way from every other, to say nothing of the differences between adults and children or normals and abnormals. The implications of this distinction are discouraging. How can we understand something that is literally unique? If, somehow, we could come to understand one personality—whether our own or another's—there would remain N - 1 yet to be understood, where N is the population of the earth. Allport would have said that there is nothing to understand about personality but its uniqueness and nothing to do about it but to understand it.

Traits and Personal Dispositions

Allport's unit of personality is the trait. He went to some lengths to explain wherein his trait concept differs from the ancient concepts of humor and faculty, from the more recent concepts of need (Murray), instinct (Freud), and sentiment (McDougall), and from temperament, habit, and attitude. For Allport, a trait is:

> . . . *a generalized and focalized neuropsychic system (peculiar to the individual), with the capacity to render many stimuli functionally equivalent, and to*

initiate and guide consistent (equivalent) forms of adaptive and expressive behavior. (1937b, p. 295)

A trait . . . has more than nominal existence; it is independent of the observer, it is really there . . . there are bona fide mental structures in each personality that account for the consistency of behavior. (1937b, p. 289)

This definition is even more explicit than his definition of personality. In it he attributes to a trait the capacity to initiate behavior as well as to guide it and asserts unequivocally the neurophysiological reality of a trait. His parenthetical expression, "peculiar to the individual," extends the attribute of uniqueness beyond the individual personality as a whole to its constituent elements, traits. In one of his infrequent ventures in normative research, Allport sought to determine how many traits the "typical" person had. He asked some Harvard students how many descriptive terms they felt they would need to characterize a classmate they might select. Compared to the elegance of his conceptual definition, this "operational" definition seems crude. Be that as it may, he found that his Harvard students possessed from three to ten traits, with a mean of 7.2. Taking Allport literally, there are about 7.2 X N distinct traits in humans (where N is, again, the population of the earth).

In all fairness to Allport, this is taking him too literally. When we think of traits, we think of labels applied to predictable or characteristic behavior patterns, usually in others rather than in ourselves. The labels *honesty, charity,* and *loyalty* come readily to mind. And yet the briefest reflection will tell us that all of our "honest" acquaintances are not, and could not possibly be, identical in their "honesty;" we apply the lable of *charitable* indiscriminately to people who are forgiving and those who are generous, and to different or even competing causes; and "loyalty" is manifested in a different way toward each cause and in each test. It is apparent that the generality commonly ascribed to traits is due more to lexical expediency than to any genuine belief that certain behavior patterns are identical across sizable groups of individuals. Allport actually explored the lexical capacity of the English language for describing traits. With Odbert, a graduate assistant, he combed an unabridged dictionary for potential trait-labels (Allport and Odbert 1936). They found nearly eighteen thousand. Whether you take Allport at face value or not, having once read him it is difficult thereafter to regard the typical twelve to sixteen "trait" personality inventory as either specific or exhaustive.

Common Traits

Thus far we have pointed out Allport's position that every trait is unique to a given individual and never replicated in another. What, then, can he mean by the term *common* or *nomothetic trait?* Is there not here an inconsistency in the theory? Allport defines common traits as "Those aspects of personality in respect to which most people within a given culture can be profitably compared (1961, p. 340).

There is, of course, no real contradiction here. Some traits of the individual are unique. Others are very similar (but still not identical) to those of many individuals and are thus, in that sense, common. The nomothetic traits are the result of similarities in the environment, including social factors which influence the development of different individuals. It is as a result of the existence of common traits that we are able to compare individuals in terms of their personality structures. Personality assessment techniques thus measure the common components of unique traits.

Since the presence of traits must be assessed through the observation of behavior and since any given individual exhibits a vast array of behaviors, it is necessary to establish criteria for determining the existence of a trait. Allport (1961) denoted two types of criteria, *behavioral* and *statistical*. There are three behavioral criteria. The first criterion is the *frequency* with which the individual displays a given pattern of behavior. The second is the *range* of situations across which the same general mode of behavior is seen. (It should be recalled here that a trait is a *broad* determining tendency, and the inference of its existence thus necessitates the occurrence of the relevant behavior pattern across a wide range of situations. The third criterion is the *intensity* with which the trait-relevant behavior occurs. The greater the intensity, the more likely it is that the behavior represents the operation of a trait. The statistical criterion for existence of a trait is *reliability*. If various observers rate the presence of a trait, it is essential that they be in agreement, thus establishing interobserver reliability. If a test is used, it is essential that a given individual obtain approximately the same score upon repeated testing, thus providing test-retest, or repeat, reliability. The actual determination of test reliability is, of course, ordinarily not carried out on a single individual but on groups of individuals, permitting the use of correlational techniques to determine the reliability coefficients (of various types) for a given test. Examples of common traits, based on these criteria, include neuroticism, ascendance-submission, manifest anxiety, and extroversion-introversion.

Personal Dispositions

A personal disposition is defined as:

> . . . *a generalized neuropsychic structure (peculiar to the individual), with the capacity to render many stimuli functionally equivalent, and to initiate and guide consistent (equivalent) forms of adaptive and stylistic behavior. (Allport 1961, p. 373)*

Note how similar this definition is to Allport's 1937 definition of *trait* (see p. 142). By 1961, however, Allport was ready to state clearly that a unique trait or personal disposition results not from unique elements but from a patterning of basic elements. He coined the term *morphogenic trait* as synonomous with personal disposition (p.d.). The term *morphogenic*, borrowed from biology, refers to a patterning of elements, such as nucleic acids, to form unique wholes.

The major difference between common traits and personal dispositions lies in the postulate that the latter are unique to one person and, as such, cannot usually be labeled with single words, whereas common traits are at least partially comparable among individuals and can often be described with one-word labels, such as neuroticism or extroversion. It was Allport's contention that accurately assessed p.d.'s provide a true description of the personality structure, while common traits are categories into which aspects of a particular individual's personality are forced. The common traits are approximations; the personal dispositions are realities.

Classification Systems

Allport (1961) had undertaken to subclassify personal dispositions on two dimensions. In the first scheme, p.d.'s are viewed in terms of their *depth* in the personality. *Genotypical* dispositions are those which are most basic and fundamental to the personality. They are deep, long-term, higher-level p.d.'s, the ultimate broad bases upon which the personality is erected. The second category, *phenotypical* dispositions, represent current, important consistencies in behavior. Finally, there are *pseudo* dispositions, which are erroneous inferences reflecting a superficial analysis of the personality. We may, for example, classify a person who often smiles, laughs, and jokes with others as "happy," only to discover later that once out of sight of others this individual feels and acts insecure, worthless, and sad. Our superficial analysis was thus incorrect, and happiness was, in this case, a pseudo disposition.

The second classification scheme subdivides p.d.'s along a continuum of importance or centrality in controlling behavior. In this system the *cardinal* disposition is an all-pervasive, outstanding determining tendency. Nearly early behavior of the individual can be traced to his or her cardinal p.d. Each *central* p.d. is highly characteristic of the individual and forms a consistent aspect of his or her personality functioning. And *secondary* p.d.'s are not as general, consistent, or obvious as central and cardinal dispositions and are less influential in determining behavior. Thus, the person with extroversion as a cardinal p.d. might have friendliness, verbal aggressiveness, and achievement motivation as central dispositions and perhaps kindness and thoughtfulness as less consistent secondary dispositions.

Habits, Attitudes, Types, and Motives

Allport (1961) further clarified his concept of trait by differentiating it from habits, attitudes, types, and motives. A habit is, like a trait, a determining tendency, but it is much narrower than a trait. Brushing the teeth, for example is a habit; personal cleanliness is a trait. An attitude is a determining tendency which usually has a specific object and a value dimension. One has an attitude toward a college education, which may place a high value on education. A type is a determining tendency that is broader than a trait. It does not represent a "real" characteristic of an individual, however, but rather a conceptualization imposed on the person by the observer. The use of the type concept tends to obscure the individuality of the person. Finally, a motive is a driving force, which activates and may also direct behavior. Allport maintained that some p.d.'s are primarily energizers and can be called *motivational dispositions,* while others primarily direct behavior and can be called *stylistic dispositions.*

The Proprium

For Allport, traits are the substance of personality but not its mechanism. Even when he speaks of them as dispositions, they serve more to describe how one behaves than why. It is in his account of the "why" of behavior that Allport's theory differs from other theorists.

The burden of Allport's writings is that humans are more than towers of programmed meat, mindlessly reacting to external stimuli. It stands to reason that we cannot all be forever *re*acting to one another; someone must initiate each transaction with an internally originated *act* before others have anything to *re*act to. It is actions rather than reactions that comprise the domain of Allport's theory. He insisted that within this domain we do more than relive, in thinly disguised displacements, our childhood resentments toward weaning and toilet training. Our motives look to the future rather than the past. Somewhere along the line each of us creates an ideal self for himself or herself and thereafter not only accepts but also creates opportunities to *become* more like this ideal. In addition, the individual has an image of what he or she is like, a motion picture of himself, ever-changing, yet with certain themes remaining constant.

In explicating somewhat similar positions, many theorists have used the terms self and ego. These venerated terms have been defined in a variety of ways to describe the self-as-object and the self-as-process (see Chapter 7), to define the self-as-doer, -as-knower, -as-known. It is because of the confusion introduced by the varied definitions of self and ego that Allport had substituted the term *proprium.*

The proprium is "a temporary neutral term for central interlocking operations of personality" (Allport 1955, p. 54), and it "includes all aspects of personality that make for inward unity" (p. 40). It is "the self-as-known—that which is experienced as warm and central, as of importance" (Allport and Ross, 1967, p. 440). In certain ways it is, perhaps, the most elaborate ego or self-construct in all personality theory. As the representative of all major self and ego processes, the proprium has seven major aspects or functions (Allport 1961):

1. *Bodily self* or coenesthesis is the sense of self as apart from the environment. It involves the recognition of the body as a unit, a bodily me, through the perception of sensations constantly flowing from internal organs, muscles, joints, and the like.

2. *Self-identity* is the individual's sense of unity, entity, and continuity. It is the recognition that "I am me," that there is a person called John, and I am that person, apart from all other persons and all other objects. The thoughts which were uniquely mine yesterday are remembered as mine today, and I can project for tomorrow and tomorrow those private goals and thoughts, those feelings and tasks which are mine alone.

3. *Self-esteem,* also termed ego-enhancement, involves self-satisfaction, self-love, pride. It includes the tendency and desire to seek self-autonomy and to value the self, to see oneself as positive rather than negative.

4. *Self-extension* or ego-extension is essentially the sense of possession, the concept of "mine." In a sense, objects in the environment are incorporated into the self, resulting in such conceptualizations as *my* father, *my* home, *my* money.

5. *Self-image* is the person's picture of himself or herself, essentially an evaluative perception of one's own characteristics.

6. *Self as rational coper* is essentially the Freudian ego, responsible for reality contact and the realistic solution of problems relating to the environment, the society (superego), and the impulses of the individual (id).

7. *Propriate Striving* refers to the tendency of the individual to hold long-range purposes and goals, to have a sense of intentionality or directedness. Propriate striving is thus an energic construct, motivation to *become* more like one's ideal self. Allport cites Maslow's distinction between deficit motives and growth motives and specifies that propriate striving refers to growth motives and the achievement of long-range goals.

Intentions

How does propriate striving operate psychologically to further the process of becoming? The answer lies in the concept of *intention,* which is implied by and is inseparably interlocked with propriate striving. The intention construct incorporates the individual's goals, ambitions, desires, and plans. It is not just what he or she *wants* to do, but what he or she is *trying* to do. It is Allport's position that the present behavior of the individual is in substantial part a function of what that individual is trying to do and intends to do now and in the future. Allport maintained also that intentions in the normal person are ordinarily conscious, and if conflicts exist among the various intentions of a given individual, these conflicts are also usually conscious. Exceptions do occur, particularly in the neurotic, who is often not fully aware of his goals and, consequently, misinterprets his intentions.

The concepts of intention and propriate striving are, of course, purposive and motivational and place Allport squarely in the teleological camp. There is, however, one major difference between Allport's teleology and that of many other theorists. For Rogers, Maslow, and others who postulate self-actualization and similar motive systems, the future-oriented motivation of the individual is said to be an *inherited* characteristic of the human species and is carried out in large part without specific awareness. In Allport's propriate striving, the emphasis—despite the neurophysiological referent—is heavily on culturally-based *learning* and conscious awareness and endeavor.

ORIGIN AND DEVELOPMENT

The elaborate, multifaceted, all-important proprium is by no means present at birth. In fact, no aspect of the proprium has even begun to develop when the child is born. Consonant with the viewpoints of many other theorists, and with considerable evidence on his side, Allport held that the child at birth is an undifferentiated totality with no recognition of being an entity, a self, apart from the environment.

The infant is, however, equipped with the "raw materials" from which the proprium is to develop. For Allport, these are of three basic types. The first two, *physique* and *temperament,* are closely related. Physique refers to body build or body type, while temperament is the basic emotional nature or characteristic mood tendency of the individual. Theoretical arguments for the inheritance of both physique and temperament have been presented in various forms by individuals from the ancient Greeks to such relatively recent theorists as Kretschmer (1925) and Sheldon (Sheldon and Stevens 1942). The basic theoretical argument holds simply that internal biochemicals, such as humors and hormones, genetically inherited, regulate both physical growth and temperament. As a result, the two should be correlated, and we should be able to infer one from the other.

Allport did not accept theories like Sheldon's *in toto.* He agreed that both physique and temperament are at least partially hereditary and that the two are closely related but argued that the relationship may be due to environmental factors rather than to heredity. For example, the ectomorph, a person of thin, frail physique is said by Sheldon to have a temperament which includes introversive, secretive tendencies. Allport suggested that the frail ectomorph may have been repeatedly beaten in fights, left out of sports, and generally not respected by his peers. The introversive tendencies may develop as a result of these learning experiences rather than be inherited as Sheldon suggests.

The third raw material of the infant is *intelligence,* classed as hereditary because it is, in some way, related to the central nervous system. Intelligence certainly has its effects on personality development; at the extremes, the genius and the idiot will develop very different personalities. Allport said, however, that the interaction of personality and intelligence is a two-way street. Thus, intelligence, as measured and utilized in solving problems, is partially a function of motivation, and, in addition, is patterned by personality. That is, it is unique to the individual and closely interrelated with his or her traits, dispositions, and interests.

Principles of Learning

Many theorists, the neo-Freudians, for example, have been criticized for postulating a learned basis for personality but failing to specify the principles of learning involved. Others, the learning theorists, for example, have been taken to task for basing all aspects of personality development, including those which are obviously complex, on a few simplistic learning principles. Allport escaped both criticisms by carefully discussing a number of learning principles and taking a refreshingly eclectic viewpoint as the basis for his discussion of development.

He terms *quasi-mechanical* those learning principles which are usually associated with drive or S-R theories. *Classical conditioning* is basically the substitution of one stimulus for another through a pairing of the two stimuli. The child who is burned withdraws his hand and also quickly learns to avoid flames. The initial withdrawal is an unconditioned, that is, innate, reflex; the subsequent avoidance, triggered by the *sight* of the flame is conditioned. Another major principle, *rein-*

forcement, holds that actions which are rewarded tend to be repeated. Thus, the child whose crying is rewarded by a bottle of milk will learn to cry. Later the child learns that reaching for the bottle produces reinforcement more promptly, and reaching is learned. Both conditioning and reinforcement, and related phenomena, are valid and important principles for the satisfaction of drives, particularly early in life. According to Allport, these quasi-mechanical principles are hard pressed to explain the substitution of new or novel responses for previously learned responses and the learning of complex behaviors.

As the child grows older, such principles as cognitive learning, insight, and participation must, therefore, be invoked. *Cognitive learning,* also called organizational learning, involves the development of attitudes or learning sets which directly affect the learning process. The child with an early negative attitude toward mathematics may never be able to learn that subject adequately, while the child with a positive attitude may have no difficulty. *Insight* is best described as an "ah-ha" variety of learning, in which a "mental structure" seems to be gradually formed and the problem suddenly solved. An example is the sudden solution of a complex puzzle or mathematical equation over which one has slaved for hours. The *participation,* or biographical, learning principle shows that the individual's involvement in the task, including the individual's intent to learn, is an important factor in learning. At the highest level of participation, the individual is *ego-involved* in the task, meaning that he or she finds the task important and is interested in the learning involved.

Two additional principles of importance to Allport are *identification* and *subsidiation.* The former, so central to Freudian personality development, involves essentially the imitation of an ideal. Children, for example, identify with their parents or with a hero, taking on characteristics of these individuals. Subsidiation refers to the active, organizing property of cognition so important to Gestalt psychology. It involves the tendency to strive for completion, to move toward closure, and it is, Allport believed, also an important principle in some types of learning.

The Evolution of Self

The seven aspects or components of the proprium discussed earlier (p. 146) do not appear all at once or develop simultaneously, but they occur in a roughly chronological sequence from birth through adulthood.

Beginning with only physique, temperament, and intelligence, the child quickly begins to develop the proprium. First to develop is the bodily self, which arises from the constant flow of internal organic sensations and from experiences with the environment which demonstrate the child's own physical boundaries.

Somewhat later comes language and, with it, the development of self-identity and the child's learning his or her name. Between the ages of two and four the child develops self-esteem. Between four and six the child becomes egocentric and develops the extension of self and the culture-bound self-image. Between the ages of six and twelve, identification is a critical form of learning, and the self-as-rational-coper develops. Finally, the searching for life goals that we see in the adolescent brings the development of propriate striving.

MOTIVATIONAL DYNAMICS

A topic of central interest in Allport's theory is his treatment of what makes the human organism "go," what motivates the individual to forego quiescence and engage in activities. While the motivational principles which Allport invoked depend somewhat upon the individual's developmental level, his or her personality functioning (such as normal vs. neurotic), and other factors, one principle is of central importance: motivation is *contemporaneous.* It takes place in the present, not in the past or future, of the individual. This idea may seem bland enough, until we note that it implies the invalidity of the concept of "secondary drives," which is ordinarily postulated by learning theorists (see Chapter 11). Briefly, the secondary drive doctrine holds that certain present motives are learned through past reinforcement and, therefore, that present motivational energy is rooted in the past. In addition, the strength of the secondary reinforcer must be maintained through continued applications of some primary reinforcer.

To fully understand Allport's objection to past-rooted motivation, we must consider motivation as comprising two factors, *historical* and *energic.* The former refers to the development of a motive, the latter to the operation of that motive at a given time. Allport agreed that motives may be learned, may have a history, and thus, in this sense, may be rooted in the past. The energies or dynamics of a motive, however, are always completely in the present. A motive can have its history, but not its energy, in the past. In an Allport example, a man may like to fish because his father took him fishing and also satisfied many of his primary drives as a child. The "fishing motive" may indeed be learned in this manner, but the felt desire to go fishing *today,* the energy of the fishing motive, is not the energy of the primary drives of childhood. The motive is learned historically but energized contemporaneously.

Motivation in Infancy

Allport agreed with drive theorists that much of the motivation of the infant and young child is a quasi-mechanical, drive-reduction motivation. The child's principal concern in life is to see that his or her own basic needs are satisfied. The child must eat and drink to reduce hunger and thirst drives, have wet diapers changed to eliminate discomfort, play to satisfy an activity drive, and sleep to reduce fatigue. Any delay in the gratification of these impulses is frustrating and cannot be tolerated. The child has no conscience, no appreciation for the feelings of others, and certainly no altruistic motives. At the age of two or three, the child can often be described as a self-centered, impulsive, pleasure-seeking holy terror.

Many theorists hold that adult motivation is a direct, continuous derivative of the quasi-mechanical drives of the infant. The psychological hedonism of the Cyreniac and Epicurean philosophers of ancient Greece and later of Jeremy Bentham and others underlies much of the tension-reduction position of more recent vintage. This school holds that the overpowering motive from infancy through adulthood is to seek pleasure and avoid pain or displeasure. The learned motives of the adult are based on the primary motives of the infant, and all are hedonistic in nature. Other related theorists, such as Freud and McDougall, base virtually all human motivation on inherited instincts, which govern behavior throughout life. Still others postulate needs, which may or may not be inherited but which are said to be extremely widespread, as the basis for all motivation. A final group postulates that drives underlie motivation. The secondary drives of the adult are learned on the basis of the primary, biological drives of the infant.

Functional Autonomy

In postulating what is by far the most controversial construct in his theory, Allport disagreed with all these theorists. He proposed that many motives of the adult are not continuous with those of the infant but rather are *functionally autonomous,* involving different tensions than those from which the adult motives develop.

> *The principle of functional autonomy holds (1) that. . . . motives are contemporary, that whatever drives must drive now; that the "go" of a motive is not bound functionally to its historical origins or to early goals but to present goals only; (2) that the character of motives alters so radically from infancy to maturity that we may speak of adult motives as* supplanting *the motives of infancy; (3) that the maturity of a personality is measured by the degree of functional autonomy its motives have achieved. (1940, p. 454)*
>
> Functional autonomy, then, refers to any acquired system of motivation in which the tensions involved are not of the same kind as the antecedent tensions from which the acquired system developed. *(Allport 1961, p. 229)*

To further clarify the concept, it can be noted that functionally autonomous motives show, as was implied above, historical continuity, but functional or dynamic discontinuity. This means that a present motive may have been acquired on the basis of past learning and may even have been dependent in its original development on primary drives, but dynamically the motive is no longer dependent on the original tensions. It has become an end in itself.

Functional autonomy takes many forms in a variety of motivational systems. Consider some examples given by Allport. A man becomes a sailor because he is starving and can find no other job. Sailing reduces his hunger drive, and he learns to love the sea. Later, as a wealthy banker, he experiences a strong craving to return to the sea. Surely the hunger drive is no longer serving to reinforce the secondary "sailing drive." Rather, the desire has acquired functional autonomy. The highly skilled cabinetmaker (now a rarity) learned to maintain high standards out of the necessity for competing with others. His reputation now established, shoddier work would suffice, but he continues to do the best possible job. The maintenance of high standards, once a means to an end, has become an end in itself.

Varieties of Functional Autonomy

Functional autonomy varies in type. There are, first of all, two basic types of autonomous motivation. One is *perseverative autonomy,* which is seen in both animals and men, and which Allport believes is probably based on relatively simple neurological principles. It involves simple behaviors that persist even when reinforcement is withdrawn and that, in humans, are not of central importance to the individual. Examples include drug and tobacco addictions, circular, repetitive behavior in children, such as repeatedly throwing down a toy for no apparent reason, perseveration on trivial incompleted tasks, and the insistence of normal children and adults on maintaining certain familiar routines.

Far more important than perseveration is *propriate functional autonomy.* Propriate motives are always acquired, are more central to the organization of the personality, and are of greater importance to the individual. Interests, for example, have propriate functional autonomy. Interests are essentially acquired organizing and motivating systems which are no longer dependent on the original bases for learning. The individual who originally begins collecting coins because of their possible later monetary value or because it is "the thing to do" in his or her group may continue to collect them because of a passionate, absorbing interest. The individual no longer has any intention of either selling the collection or impressing the group; the interest has become a functionally autonomous, propriate motive. To Allport, interests are not merely isolated motivators but interact to form the complex *life style* of the individual. They act to organize an individual's personality and to guide and systematize significant and broad aspects of that person's behavior.

The Mature Personality

From the foregoing discussion of Allport's theory and particularly his concept of functional autonomy, it is apparent that his overbearing interest is in the normal, adult personality. It should come as no surprise, then, to learn that he has considered at some length just what it is that constitutes maturity. Allport (1961) proposed six criteria of maturity: (1) extension of self, meaning that the mature person is a participant in significant areas of human endeavor; (2) warm relationship to others; (3) emotional security and self-acceptance; (4) realistic perceptions, thoughts, and actions; (5) self-objectification, meaning that the mature person has accurate self-insight; and (6) a unifying philosophy of life or sense of directedness.

THE THEORY IN EMPIRICAL CONTEXT

Allport's concern with the development of a theory aimed at a better understanding of the personality of the unique, normal individual has been accompanied by an intense interest in personality research. From a research viewpoint he has dealt discursively or empirically with a wide variety of topics, including preferred methods of personality research, expressive behavior, traits, personal values, ascendance-submission, international cooperation, perception, and the phenomena of rumor and prejudice. No attempt is made here to discuss all, or even most, of Allport's research. Rather, we have selected as representative those topics which are most closely related to the theory or have been continuing concerns in Allport's writings, or both.

Idiographic and Nomothetic Researcn

As has been noted, the most general postulate in Allport's theory concerns the unique individuality of the person. He maintained not only that each person is a unique, never-replicated entity but also that each trait, each personal disposition, even each behavior is a unique occurrence in the universe. It will not seem inconsistent, then, that Allport consistently stressed the importance of research concerned with the intensive study of the individual, research aimed at the discovery of the unique characteristics which comprise *this* personality. He termed this type of research *idiographic* or *morphogenic* and contrasted it with the more common but, from his viewpoint, less desirable form of research which he termed *nomothetic* or *dimensional*. The latter involved groups rather than individuals and searched for generalities and universal laws rather than unique characteristics. The distinction and the case for the superiority of idiographic knowledge is clearly stated by Allport.

> *To many students of psychology it has become apparent that nomothetic abstractions have led to oversimplified versions of human motivation. Few are satisfied with schemes of four wishes, nine factors, eighteen instincts, or twenty-one needs. As seen in case documents, personal causation is a far more intricate matter.* What for the nomothetist is hard to contemplate is the very real possibility that no two lives are alike in their motivational processes. *To assume that causation is identified from case to case is to overlook the point that Lewin has emphasized, namely that* lawful determinism *need not be based upon frequency of occurrence in multitudes of cases, but may apply to one-time happenings (to the single life). If each personality harbors laws peculiar to itself; if the course of causation is personal instead of universal, then only the idiographic study of a case will discover such laws. (emphasis added) (1942, p. 57)*

The idiographic position, while broadly influential in psychology, is not without its critics and interpreters. O'Connell (1958), for example, has questioned whether idiographic knowledge is scientific knowledge. Science, he argued, deals with organized knowledge of observable realities, constructing systematic principles on the basis of objective observation. Idiographic knowledge is not objective or systematic but rather subjective and practical, more closely approximating common sense than science. In addition, according to O'Connell, there is no evidence that the behavior of the specific individual is more accurately predicted by the study of his or her unique personality than by the application of principles based on nomothetic data.

Perhaps the question of the scientific feasibility and value of the idiographic approach can best be resolved by distinguishing between strong and weak or "naive" and "sophisticated" forms of idiography. The strong form of the idiographic argument holds that the individual is completely unique, the components of his or her personality never being directly comparable with those of other individuals. The weak or sophisticated version argues that the individual is unique in the sense that each person's personality represents a unique combination or patterning of variables, the pattern being unique, but the component variables being amenable to comparison with those of other personalities. Eysenck (1952), in criticizing idiography, has implied a similar distinction, seeming to attribute to Allport the naive form of the argument: "To Allport, it appears to be some mystical quality, something *sui generis,* something 'afar from the sphere of our sorrow'" (Eysenck 1952, p. 19), while *"To the scientist, the unique individual is simply the point of intersection of a number of quantitative variables"* (p. 19). Allport (1962) later clearly endorsed the patterning principle of uniqueness.

Allport and others have developed a number of morphogenic research methods, each focusing on a single individual at a time. One such method, advocated by Allport, is the use of direct questions. That is, if you want to know something about an individual, simply ask the person. Others include matching of one aspect of the person's behavior with another, such as matching of handwriting with voice quality, personal structure analysis (Baldwin 1942), which involves an intensive analysis of such personal documents as letters, and a personal questionnaire method (Shapiro 1961), where the psychologist devises a specific questionnaire for a particular patient.

Expressive Behavior

Allport distinguished two components of human behavior which he terms *coping behavior* and *expressive behavior.* The former is the *what* of behavior, the immediate task, the adaptive aspect of behavior. It is present, Allport maintained, in every act, from a simple blinking of the eye to removing a speck of dust to such complex coping behaviors as repairing a lock or calling a doctor. More important for Allport's work has been the second component, expressive behavior. This aspect is the *how* of behavior, the style or manner in which the act is carried out. It is succinctly defined as *"one's manner of performing adaptive acts"* (Allport 1961, p. 462). Like coping, expressive behavior is present in every act; but it is not purposive or specifically motivated, it does not reflect immediate needs but rather deeper aspects of personality, and it is spontaneously emitted rather than elicited. Further, expressive behavior does not seek to alter the environment, is typically unconscious, and is much more difficult to control than is coping behavior. Common examples of behavior heavily laden with the expressive component include style of handwriting, conversational gesturing, personal mannerisms and the artistic style of the composer, sculptor, painter, or cabinetmaker. It is thus the expressive component which *individualizes* the coping act. The same act of coping performed by numerous individuals is never performed in precisely the same manner by any two individuals, due to the operation of the expressive component.

Expressive Consistency

If expressive behavior is the overt manifestation of the interacting personality characteristics that form the consistent personality of a person, we should be able to demonstrate that the behavior itself shows certain consistencies. In fact, greater consistency should prevail when expressive behavior is dominant than when coping is the major determinant. To illustrate this point, Allport (1961) suggested the following demonstration experiment: Label four lines on a sheet of paper a, b, c, and d. On the first three lines sign your name as you would normally sign it. On line d try to make an exact copy of line c. You will probably find, as Allport did, that lines a and b resemble each other far more than lines c and d do. Why? The first three lines are relatively spontaneous, and instructions for writing them are identical, permitting the dominance of the expressive component. Line d, however, involves conscious effort ("make an exact copy of line c"), and coping behavior is dominant.

More formal attempts to study expressive consistency have been reported by Allport and Philip E. Vernon in their book, *Studies in Expressive Movement* (1933) and by Estes (1938). As one example, Allport and Vernon studied expressive consistency in the forms of behavior of four subjects who were undergoing intensive case history analyses. It was found that: (a) judges were able to match personality descriptions with samples of handwriting and with kymographic curves of writing pressure; (b) various measures employed were all congruent with subjective impressions of the personalities of the subjects; and (c) insofar as the personality is organized, expressive movement is self-consistent. In other studies, a wide variety of expressive behaviors have been investigated by Allport and others. Examples include handwriting, facial expression, gesture, posture, gait, and speech fluency.

Letters From Jenny

As one approach to morphogenesis, Allport (1942) early advocated the study of such personal documents as letters and diaries as an inroad to the personality. In 1965 he published 172 *Letters from Jenny,* the raw material for a thorough clinical and quantitative study of a single personality. For the clinical aspect of the study, thirty-nine judges read the series of letters and listed adjectives to describe the central characteristics of Jenny's personality. The judges compiled a total of

198 adjectives (essentially trait names), many of which were synonomous. It was found that nearly all trait names listed fell into eight clusters, each describing a general trait of Jenny's personality. Separate statistical analyses (factor analyses) and clinical analyses of data from the letters showed a high degree of agreement, supporting Allport's view that such consistencies should be found within an individual personality.

The Study of Values: A Semimorphogenic Method

A value may be seen as ". . . a belief upon which a man acts by preference" (Allport 1961, p. 454). The German philosopher Eduard Spranger (1922) held that values are a major aspect of human functioning and argued cogently for the existence of six major value types: theoretic, economic, esthetic, social, political, and religious. Theoretic values are closely related to a seeking for truth, economic values to usefulness, esthetic to harmony, social to altruism, political to power, and religious to unity. Individuals are expected to differ in the relative emphasis that they place on each of these values.

Allport believed that Spranger's values could be treated as common traits and with this in mind set out to develop an instrument to measure their existence in individuals. The result was the Study of Values (Allport and Vernon 1931; Allport, Vernon, and Lindzey 1960), a test attempting to measure each of the six values independently. The instrument consists of forty-five forced-choice items, in each of which the subject is given a choice among two or more alternatives. Each value is paired an equal number of times with each of the other five values. Scores for a given subject on the six values are plotted on a profile, showing the relative importance of each value to the individual. Numerous studies have been done, some standardizing the test, others using it to examine the differential functioning of groups and individuals. Since Allport emphasized idiographic methods, and the Study of Values appears to be a nomothetic method (based on the use of groups of subjects), we must ask whether this test is consistent with Allport's own views. Allport (1961) argued that the test is semimorphogenic, since, for a given individual, we are interested primarily in his or her individual profile of values. It is thus the relative importance of each value for the individual that is emphasized. Nevertheless, the six value dimensions are being imposed on the individual, and the test is standardized on groups. We must thus conclude that despite his pioneering efforts in morphogenesis, Allport was, in part, caught up in the dimensional *Zeitgeist* which he sought to change.

EVALUATION

While Allport has been one of the most respected and influential of all psychologists, his theory has by no means gone without criticism. Of the various criticisms offered, no doubt the greatest fly in Allport's theoretical ointment has been functional autonomy.

Shortly after early treatments of this construct (Allport 1937a, 1937b), Bertocci (1940), working from a hormic orientation, pointed out several serious inadequacies in the formulation. In particular, he noted that no criteria were offered for determining whether or not a given behavior can become functionally autonomous. Allport's formulation, he held, implied that any frequently repeated behavior will become functionally autonomous, a postulate at variance with other apsects of Allport's theory and with empirical observations. In addition, if all repetitious behaviors become autonomous, the individual should soon develop seriously conflicting motive systems which would likely shatter the personality.

A second critique, this time from the viewpoint of learning theory, was provided by McClelland (1942). He argued, in effect, that functional autonomy is an unnecessary construct, since the behaviors which it explains can be otherwise accounted for. Specifically, McClelland held that, ". . . functional independence of an instrumental act is a special case of extinction which is delayed longer than the observer expects because there are unusual factors present in the situation which invalidate the normal expectation" (1942, p. 282). The delayed extinction which is seen as accounting for seemingly autonomous behaviors may come about through any number of factors, all consistent with learning theory. Despite efforts on Allport's part to answer McClelland's critique (Allport 1955, 1961), the major critical points have withstood the test of time. Moreover, even an improved formulation of the functional autonomy hypotheses has been strongly and effectively criticized (Kaul 1959; Seward 1963).

Most other substantive criticisms of Allport's work are relatively minor, based largely on the theoretical biases of critics and directly or indirectly related to functional autonomy. If we summarize Allport's treatment as largely a theory of the unique, normal, consciously motivated, adult human being, we have the basis for virtually all of these criticisms, for nearly every word of this summary has been disputed by critics. Individuals are not, it has been argued, as unique as Allport claims but share more important commonalities than he admits. Moreover, some critics believe that Allport never fully adopted the patterning hypothesis to explain uniqueness. Similarly, Allport's emphasis on conscious motivation runs counter to the psychoanalytic viewpoint and has been heavily criticized from that quarter. Some would also question whether adults are motivated differently than children and whether human beings operate on different motivational principles than do other animals.

A final criticism of Allport's early work was that, despite his position as a prominent social psychologist, he virtually ignored the influence of social and cultural variables on personality development and functioning. In his later writings Allport partially corrected this deficiency by bringing cultural concepts and social factors more specifically into the theory. Unfortunately, he never did fully integrate this treatment of sociocultural determinants with the remainder of the theory.

Turning to the positive, we must consider the man as well as his theory. We must remember that the theory was but one aspect of a virtually lifelong attempt to modify a *Zeitgeist*. The *Zeitgeist* of the psychology around him was, to Allport, not a noble and shining spirit, but the evergrowing spectre of a young science swallowed up by nomothesis. The individual was rapidly becoming lost in a vast forest of unconscious motives, factor analytic dimensions, and primary drives. It was thus in a fervent attempt to put the individual back on the psychological map that Allport formulated many of his ideas and ideals.

The greatest overall value of Allport's approach is, then, its unorthodoxy, making the very points of criticism the points of greatest praise. The dual emphases on the importance of conscious motivation and the uniqueness of the individual were refreshing theoretical positions in a psychology caught up in the unconscious and the nomothetic. The related stress on morphogenic research, though somewhat dampened by Allport's own tendency to do dimensional studies, has done much to modify the thinking of psychologists about appropriate research emphasis. A further point of value has been the postulation that motivation is primarily a phenomenon of the present and future, rather than of the past. Here, Allport is in general agreement with the phenomenological-humanistic school, though teleological motivation is less central to Allport's theory than to those of Rogers, Maslow, and others.

Somewhat different contributions come from Allport's treatments of the concepts of self, ego, and trait. At the turn of the twentieth century, self and ego were among the most popular of psychological concepts. They appeared in—indeed, seemed indispensable to—the writings of such scholars as James, Baldwin, McDougall, Titchener, and Hall. With the rise of behaviorism, however, these concepts fell into disrepute and were largely dropped from the mainstream of psychology. Even Freud's ego concept did not long survive without severe criticism, much of which came from within the psychoanalytic school. It was the ego psychologists, led by Heinz Hartmann (Chapter 3), the psychological phenomenologists, most notably Carl Rogers (Chapter 7), and Gordon Allport who revitalized and substantially restructured the self and the ego.

The concept of trait has a somewhat different history than do self and ego. Traits have been hypothesized, discussed, and used by philosophers and psychologists from the time of the ancient Greeks. Allport's contribution is that he was the first to present a formal and detailed theoretical treatment of the trait construct. An early article (Allport 1931) and Allport's major book (1937b) brought the concept of trait to the fore in psychology and fostered a wave of discussion, research, and criticism which has not yet entirely subsided. Critics have argued that there is always a danger of reifying traits (Carr and Kingsbury 1938), that traits are merely descriptive, not explanatory (Skinner 1953), and that recent evidence suggests a more appropriate emphasis on situational rather than stable (trait) characteristics (Hung 1965; Miller 1963, 1973). The recent controversy concerning the relative roles of traits and situations in determining behavior is reviewed in Chapter 12.

REFERENCES

Allport, G. W.   The functional autonomy of motives. *American Journal of Psychology*, 1937, *5*, 141-156.

Allport, G. W. *Personality: A psychological interpretation.* New York: Holt, Rinehart & Winston, 1937.

Allport, G. W. Motivation in personality: Reply to Mr. Bertocci. *Psychological Review,* 1940, *47,* 533–554.

Allport, G. W. *The use of personal documents in psychological science.* New York: Social Science Research Council, 1942.

Allport, G. W. *The nature of prejudice.* Cambridge, Mass.: Addison-Wesley, 1954.

Allport, G. W. *Becoming: Basic considerations for a psychology of personality.* New Haven, Conn.: Yale University Press, 1955.

Allport, G. W. European and American theories of personality. In H. P. David & H. von Bracken (Eds.), *Perspectives in personality theory.* New York: Basic Books, 1957.

Allport, G. W. *Pattern and growth in personality.* New York: Holt, Rinehart & Winston, 1961.

Allport, G. W., & Odbert, H. S. Trait-names: A psycho-lexical study. *Psychological Monographs,* 1936, *47,* (1, Whole No. 211).

Allport, G., & Ross, J. Personal religious orientation and prejudice. *Journal of Personality and Social Psychology,* 1967, *5,* 432–443.

Allport, G. W., & Vernon, P. E. A test for personal values. *Journal of Abnormal and Social Psychology,* 1931, *26,* 231–248.

Allport, G. W., & Vernon, P. E. *Studies in expressive movement.* New York: Macmillan, 1933.

Allport, G. W., Vernon, P. E., & Lindzey, G. *A study of values* (3rd ed.). Boston: Houghton Mifflin, 1960.

Baldwin, A. L. Personal structure analysis: A statistical method for investigating the single personality. *Journal of Abnormal and Social Psychology,* 1942, *37,* 163–183.

Bertocci, P. A. Critique of Gordon W. Allport's theory of motivation. *Psychological Review,* 1940, *47,* 501–532.

Carr, H. A., & Kingsbury, F. A. The concept of ability. *Psychological Review,* 1938, *45,* 354–377.

Estes, S. G. Judging personality from expressive behavior. *Journal of Abnormal and Social Psychology,* 1938, *33,* 217–236.

Eysenck, H. J. *The scientific study of personality.* New York: Macmillan, 1952.

Hunt, J. McV. Traditional personality theory in the light of recent evidence. *American Scientist,* 1965, *53,* 80–96.

Kaul, J. How autonomous is functional autonomy? *Journal of Educational Psychology,* 1959, *16,* 481–491.

Kretschmer, E. *Physique and character.* London: Routledge and Kegan Paul, 1925.

McClelland, D. C. Functional autonomy of motives as an extinction phenomenon. *Psychological Review,* 1942, *49,* 272–283.

Miller, D. R. The study of social relationships: Situation, identity, and social interaction. In S. Koch (Ed.), *Psychology: A study of a science. The process areas, the person, and some applied fields: Their place in psychology and the social sciences* (Vol. 5). New York: McGraw-Hill, 1963.

O'Connell, D. C. Idiographic knowledge. *Journal of General Psychology*, 1958, *59*, 21-33.

Seward, J. P. The structure of functional autonomy. *American Psychologist*, 1963, *18*, 703-710.

Shapiro, M. B. The single case in fundamental clinical psychological research. *British Journal of Medical Psychology*, 1961, *34*, 255-262.

Sheldon, W. H., & Stevens, S. S. *The varieties of temperament: A psychology of constitutional differences.* New York: Harper & Row, 1942.

Skinner, B. F. *Science and human behavior.* New York: Macmillan, 1953.

Spranger, E. *Lebensformen; geisteswissenschaftliche psychologie und ethik der personlicheit. 3., verbesserte Aufl.* Halle (saale)M: Niemeyer, 1922.

Wolfe, J. B. Effectiveness of token rewards for chimpanzees. *Comparative Psychological Monographs*, 1936, *12* (5, Whole No. 60).

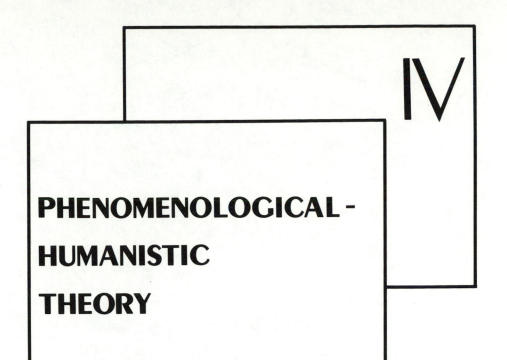

PHENOMENOLOGICAL -
HUMANISTIC
THEORY

IV

Phenomenological – Humanistic Theory:

Carl Rogers and Abraham Maslow

7

Current theories, such as that of Carl Rogers, in which self-concept is a central construct, represent an integration of elements of wholism, organismic theory, phenomenology, and self-theory.

Phenomenology, in its most general form, constitutes an attempt to designate and understand the distinction and the relationship of reality and individual perception. The originator of phenomenology, Edmund Husserl, was a student of both Stumpf and Brentano. He took as his point of departure Brentano's distinction between observable reality and the individual's perception of that reality. The interaction between the individual and his environment involves, in Husserl's view, a series of experiences, each of which is seen as a phenomenon that must be perceived interpretively by the individual. Such interpretation is often influenced by a variety of factors, including the expectations, perceptual sets, needs, and desires of the perceiver, which may produce a distortion of reality. Experience is, therefore, most valid and of greatest worth to the individual who is open to an experience when distorting factors are minimal or absent. In Rogers's theory such openness to experience is regarded as an important aspect of personality development and functioning.

Self-theory, of course, is not unique to Rogers. In fact, it represents the most recent in a centuries-old series of attempts to designate a center for the coordination of personality and psychological activity. In various theoretical formulations these centers have served such functions as to organize, integrate, control, or guide behavior as well as to provide the basis for the unique qualities of the individual. Various versions of soul theory, a precursor of self-theory, were stated by such ancient Greek philosophers as Democritus, Plato, and Aristotle. Soul theory was seen in the seventeenth century in the works of Leibnitz and Descartes and in the eighteenth century in the works of Berkley and Wolff. Other constructs employed as personality integrators have included the will, the mind, and the ego.

The use of the term *self,* or *self-concept,* as a formal theoretical construct is relatively recent. With the advent of behaviorism and the stress on scientific principles in psychology, the terms *will, mind,* and *soul* were virtually abandoned. The term *self* came into use partially to fill the gap left by the rejection of these terms and partially as the result of a reaction against the rather mechanistic principles of scientific psychology. In the early nineteenth century the French philosopher Maine De Biran formulated a concept of self as the representative of the individual and the integrator of personality. His writings substantially anticipated major aspects of modern self-theory. More influential were the writings of William James (1890), who proposed the concept of the *empirical me,* or self, as consisting of four aspects: the material self, the ego, the social self, and the spiritual self.

THE SELF IN MODERN THEORY

In some early philosophical and psychological theories, the term self or its counterpart tended to designate a "little man" or homunculus lodged in the soul, mind, or psyche that regulated behavior and personality. Such is not the case in current self theories. The self-concept is utilized as a highly developed theoretical construct. It is usually given a careful and scientifically sound verbal definition and often one or more operational definitions. The construct has received particularly thorough treatment in Rogerian theory, where it has been operationally defined and subjected to fairly rigorous empirical investigation.

As Hall and Lindzey (1957) have pointed out, the term *self* has been given two distinctly different meanings in modern theories. The *self-as-object* definition characterizes the self as an entity or object in the experiential field. It is an individual's view or perception of himself or herself, that individual's analysis and synthesis of his or her own individuality. The *self-as-process* definition, on the other hand, views the self as a group of psychological processes, often serving to organize and integrate the personality as well as to mediate interaction with the external environment. Processes such as thought, perception, attention, and memory may be included. The reader will note that the latter definition is quite similar to the

Freudian ego. We should point out that there is also a third definition, which we might call an *object-process* definition, in which the self includes both the self-perceiver function and the process function.

CARL ROGERS

Carl Ransom Rogers was born in Oak Park, Illinois, on January 8, 1902, the middle child in a conservative Protestant family. He attended the University of Wisconsin, where he majored first in agriculture and later in history. Following graduation he married Helen Elliott in 1924 and attended the Union Theological Seminary from 1924 to 1926. Subsequently, he transferred to Teachers College of Columbia University, with its heavily Thorndikean orientation, where he received an M.A. degree in 1928 and a Ph.D. in clinical and educational psychology in 1931. At Columbia, Rogers was exposed to the philosophy of John Dewey, taught there by William H. Kilpatrick, and had his first clinical experience with what he describes as the common-sense approach of Leta Hollingworth. From 1927 to 1928 he held a fellowship at the Institute for Child Guidance, where he encountered the Freudian orientation of David Levy and Lawson Lowrey. From 1928 to 1930 he served as a clinical psychologist in the Child Study Department at the Society for the Prevention of Cruelty to Children in Rochester. He remained with the society as director of the Child Study Department (later the Rochester Guidance Center) until 1940. During this time he learned of the theories of Otto Rank, which were to be important to him. His thinking has also been greatly influenced, he has noted, by colleagues, graduate students, teachers, and, most of all, his continuing clinical experience.

In 1940 Rogers joined the Psychology Department at Ohio State University. That year was an important one to him because it was also when he presented the first formal statement of his newly developing theory in the form of a paper presented to the Minnesota chapter of Psi Chi. Rogers became professor of clinical psychology at Ohio State University in 1945, was later professor of psychology at the University of Chicago, and in 1957 became professor of psychology and psychiatry at the University of Wisconsin. Since 1964 he has been at the Center for Studies of the Person in La Jolla, California. A widely respected innovator in psychotherapy research, as well as a major theorist, Rogers has been frequently honored by his profession. He has been president of the American Psychological Association (APA) and recipient of the APA Distinguished Scientific Contribution Award and Distinguished Professional Contributional Award.

MAJOR CONCEPTS AND CONSTRUCTS

Rogers's theory of personality is a result—almost a side-effect—of his continuing attempt to study, both theoretically and empirically, a method of psychotherapy called nondirective or client-centered therapy. Briefly, the method involves the therapist's entering into a highly personalized, one-to-one relationship with the client. The therapist is accepting of the client's feelings, empathic, and honest and expresses unconditional positive regard towards the client. Unconditional positive regard means accepting and valuing the client as a person, rather than the therapist's trying to impose his or her own values upon the client.

Rogers's theory of personality has grown out of his theory and method of therapy and has been continually subject to modification in the face of new data and experiences. We shall first present and define some major constructs in the theory and then discuss the development and functioning of personality as represented in some of Rogers's writings (1959, 1963, 1964, 1967, 1970).

Prefacing a presentation of his theories, Rogers (1959) lists and defines forty constructs which enter into the theory. We have elected to define six of these major constructs, some of which subsume or imply other constructs, plus one not listed by Rogers in his set of definitions.

1. *Organism.* This is the sum total of the person, including all that is psychological, as well as all that is physical.

2. *Experience.* Rogers (1959) defined experience as all that is going on in and around the organism at a given moment that is potentially available to awareness. It thus includes the psychological representations of such physiological drives as hunger and the momentary influence of memory and past experience as well as the impact of external stimuli on the sense organs.

3. *Self or Self-Concept.* These two terms are synonymous. Rogers (1959) defines self as the:

   . . . organized, consistent conceptual gestalt composed of perceptions of the characteristics of the "I" or "me" and the perceptions of the relationships of the "I" or "me" to others and to various aspects of life, together with the values attached to these perceptions. (1959, p. 200)

   The self, then, is basically a self-as-object, viewing itself as an object in the experiential field. At any given moment it is an entity, but over time it is a fluid, dynamic process. An important characteristic of the self is that it is always available to awareness, although it is not necessarily in awareness at a given moment.

4. *Actualizing Tendency.* In order to behave, to engage in activity, an organism must be motivated. Rogers postulated as the motivator of behavior the actualizing tendency, an *innate* tendency of the organism to realize capacities, to maintain and enhance itself. "It involves development towards the differentiation of organs and of functions, expansion in terms of growth, expansion of effectiveness through the use of tools, expansion and enhancement through reproduction" (Rogers 1959, p. 196).

5. *Symbolization.* This construct is synonymous with awareness and consciousness. Thus, an experience which has been symbolized in awareness is one that has come to be perceived consciously.

6. *Positive Regard* includes experiences of perceived sympathy, acceptance, liking, respect, warmth, and the like. The individual is said to have a *need* for positive regard from others, that is, a need to be socially accepted or liked. When the person learns to achieve a feeling of positive regard independently of others, he is said to be fulfilling a need for self-regard.

7. *Conditions of Worth.* In the process of developing self-regard, the individual introjects a number of values that he has learned from others (namely, parents). These values may then come to serve as the criteria for evaluating a given experience in terms of whether or not it is worthy of self-regard. Values which serve the criterion function are called conditions of worth.

AN OVERVIEW OF THE THEORY

An overview of Rogerian theory suggests that it may, like other theories, be viewed in terms of structural principles, motivational dynamics, and developmental processes. Basically, the structure of personality consists of the organism and the self, both terms in Rogers's set of definitions. As the totality of the person, the organism is of central concern in Rogerian theory, and it is through the continuing maintenance and enhancement of the organism that optimal psychological development and adjustment occur. The self, one major subpart of the total organism, is somewhat separately maintained and enhanced and, as we will see, the enhancement of organism and the enhancement of self may come into conflict. The motivational dynamics of the Rogerian theory involve the process of actualization, which is basically a motive to enhance the organism, and that of self-actualization, a motive to actualize the self. These motive systems, together with their structural counterparts, may operate in harmony or in conflict. Development depends heavily upon the actualization process and moves the person from the infant state of undifferentiated totality through a process of psychological differentiation and, eventually, integration.

Given this brief overview, we will take a basically developmental approach to understanding Rogerian theory, dealing first with the development of personality and its various constructs and then with the functioning of the adult personality.

ORIGINS AND DEVELOPMENT

Personality development, for Rogers, is a continuing, life-long process. He is careful, however, to specify the characteristics of the infant and to detail the developmental process. Two aspects of the infant are of primary importance in Rogerian theory. The first of these might be referred to as the mode of experiencing, which characterizes the infant. In the phenomenological viewpoint, experience involves perception, and perception can be biased or distorted by such factors as values and expectations. The infant has not yet acquired a self-concept or the biasing values associated with it and, therefore, is open to experience and is said to have an exclusively *internal frame of reference.*

The second important characteristic of the infant is his motivational system. Rogers (1959, 1963) postulated that a single motive, the *actualization tendency,* provides the impetus for all behavior. This tendency exhibits several specific characteristics: (1) It is *innate*. Every individual is born with the inherent motive to actualize. It is important to note, however, that learning can influence the specific ways in which the tendency is implemented in a given individual; (2) It is *directional*. The individual strives to realize only *positive* capacities, that is, those which maintain and enhance the organism. Capacities for self-abasement or self-destruction are not fulfilled through actualization; (3) It drives the organism toward *autonomy*. The individual strives to internalize control, to become relatively independent of the external environment; (4) It strives for *growth* and *differentiation*. The infant eneters the world as a weak, dependent, undifferentiated totality. It exhibits little or no differentiation of psychological functions, and, of particular importance, no self-concept. Actualization strives to attain the differentiation which will provide, among other things, the self; and (5) It is the only motivation in the Rogerian system. As such, it subsumes the tension-reduction drives common to Freud, Dollard and Miller, and others, as well as any specific motives postulated by other theorists. Each of these drives and motives is seen as merely a contributor to, and a part of, the actualization tendency. The importance of the actualization tendency in Rogerian theory was underscored by Rogers's statement in 1974 that the actualization hypothesis is the most basic postulate in the theory of client-centered therapy (Rogers and Wood 1974).

In order to implement the actualizing tendency, the infant organism must evaluate each experience which it undergoes as to whether or not that experience produces satisfaction. The construct which carries out this evaluative function is the *organismic valuing process*. As each experience is perceived, this process values it positively or negatively, with the actualizing tendency as the criterion. An experience which serves to maintain and enhance the organism, and hence to further the actualizing tendency, is valued positively; one which does not serve maintenance or enhancement is valued negatively. Thus, for example, the infant will value the presentation of food positively when hungry but negatively or neutrally when satiated. An important adjunct of the organismic valuing process is that *all experiences, whether positive or negative, are accurately symbolized in awareness.* There is no distortion or denial of reality so long as the organismic valuing process is the only determinant of experiential evaluation. The organismic valuing process thus provides the theoretical mechanism of the infant's complete openness to experience.

The Development of Self. The individual cannot, of course, long remain an infant, and, in Rogerian theory, the developing child cannot long remain an organism without self-awareness. The self-concept develops as a function of the tendency towards differentiation which is one aspect of the organismic actualizing tendency. In the course of normal ongoing interaction with the internal and external environment, certain experiences become differentiated as representing a feeling of "selfness," a realization by the child that he is something apart from the total environment. Rogers summarizes the initial development of self as follows:

> . . . *a portion of the individual's* experience *becomes differentiated and* symbolized *in an* awareness *of being,* awareness *of functioning. Such awareness may be described as* self-experience. *[emphasis in original] (Rogers 1959, p. 223)*

Through continued interaction with the environment, and, therefore, continued accumulation of self-related experiences, the initial self-experience becomes elaborated into, in Rogers's words, that "consistent, conceptual gestalt," the self-concept. It is basically the individual's perception of his or her own being, his or her own selfness, and, therefore, is primarily a self-as-object.

Accompanying the differentiation of experience to form the self-concept, Rogers has postulated the differentiation of the actualizing tendency, such that a portion of that tendency is diverted for the actualization of the self. The total actualizing tendency thus becomes subdivided into an organismic actualizing tendency and a self-actualizing tendency. The former continues to symbolize each experience in awareness and to motivate the individual to realize capacities. The self-actualizing tendency, on the other hand, strives to maintain and enhance the self, rather than the total organism. In addition, it motivates the individual to maintain the *consistency* of self-concept. In order to accomplish these goals, the self-actualizing tendency develops its own screening system for the evaluation of experience, a system which may or may not lead to the accurate symbolization of experiences in awareness.

The Regard Needs. The basis for the perceptual screening mechanism of the self-actualizing tendency lies in the regard needs. Following the development of the self-concept, the individual exhibits a need to be accepted and valued by other persons. This *need for positive regard* is postulated to be a universal need, although Rogers (1959, 1963) expressed uncertainty as to whether it is inherited or learned. In either case the need for positive regard is an extremely powerful need, which can be even more potent than the organismic valuing process in the screening of experience. With repeated experiences of frustration and satiation of the positive regard need through interpersonal interactions, the individual develops a learned ability to experience and satisfy the regard need independently of others. When this occurs, the individual has learned a *need for self-regard,* together with the ability to satiate that need without reference to social others.

Positive regard and self-regard may become selective with respect to experience. That is, the individual may come to evaluate experiences, not in terms of their contribution to the organismic actualizing tendency (that is, through the organismic valuing process) but in terms of their furtherance of self-regard. When such a situation occurs, the individual is said to have developed *conditions of worth.* Putting it otherwise,

> When self-experience *is avoided (or sought) solely because it is less (or more)* *worthy of self-regard, the individual is said to have acquired a* condition of worth. *(Rogers 1959, p. 224)*

Elaborating on conditions of worth, Rogers (1964) pointed out that in the course of experiencing, the child learns that what is organismically satisfying may be negatively valued by significant others, such as the parents. Thus, for example, the child may find that eating when and only when hungry is organismically satiating. Eventually, however, the child's parents will discourage this organismic behavior in favor of eating only at regularly scheduled meal times and may even punish the child for eating "between meals." As a result of such clashes of the organismic valuing process with the values of significant social others, two important developments take place. First, the child may begin to distrust the organismic valuing process, the operation of which may bring about rejection or punishment by others. Second, the child learns that only by conforming to the values of others can he or she experience the satisfaction of the developing need for positive regard. As a consequence of these considerations, the child tends to introject, and subsequently experience as his or her own, the values presented by others. Such inculcated values serve as the basis for conditions of worth.

If conditions of worth normally develop as a function of the selective perception and discrimination of self-experiences which accompany the needs for self- and positive regard, it is of interest to consider the situation in which conditions of worth will not develop. Such a situation exists when the individual perceives that no self-experience is seen by another as more or less worthy of positive regard. In other words, the individual perceives that he or she is positively valued by social others, unconditionally and without respect to specific behaviors.

THE FUNCTIONING PERSONALITY

In the course of normal development two dynamic systems emerge, the organism and the self, which comprise the major subparts of the functioning personality. Each system is postulated to consist of a central structure, a motivational component, and a screening process that evaluates experiences. The organismic system, or simply the organism, is, structurally, the total individual. The motivational component of the organism is the actualizing tendency, the goal of which is the realization of organismic capacities, the maintenance and enhancement of the organism. The mechanism which evaluates experience in the service of the actualizing tendency is the organismic valuing process.

The self-system has as its central structure the self or self-concept, which develops out of experiences of being and functioning and comprises the individual's self image. Once developed, the self is not, of course, a rigid, unchanging image. Rather it is a dynamic, fluid gestalt, modifying itself as the individual continues to undergo internal and external experiences. We will see, however, that under certain conditions the self can fail to relate adequately to experience and can thereby become relatively inflexible. The motivational component of the self-system is the self-actualizing tendency. This tendency develops as a differentiated portion of the overall organismic actualizing tendency and strives to maintain the consistency of and to enhance the self. The screening mechanism consists of the conditions of worth, which develop as a function of the regard needs and must be defended in order to maintain the consistency of the self.

A primary function of the adult Rogerian personality is to continue the interaction with the experiential field which was begun during development. Such interaction consists principally of the ongoing evaluation and symbolization (or nonsymbolization) of the experiential field by the organism and the self. The field impinges upon the individual as a series of discrete experiences in a manner somewhat similar to the discrete mental elements or ideas of the empiricists. As a given experience reaches the individual, it must be first received, then evaluated, and finally stored. In general, an experience may be received and interpreted either consciously or subconsciously. The former process is termed *perception*, the latter *subception*. Both processes have been shown, experimentally, to operate, and both are accepted in Rogerian theory. Rogers (1959) implied that each experience, upon being received by the individual, is evaluated by both the organismic valuing process and the conditions of worth. The former evaluates the experience as positive or negative with respect to actualization and would, if it were the only screening process, symbolize all experiences accurately in awareness. The conditions of worth, however, must defend the self-regard need in order to maintain self-consistency and are often more powerful than the organismic valuing process. As a result, self-experiences that are at variance with the conditions of worth may be either denied to awareness or symbolized in a distorted form. In the latter case, distortion serves to make the perceived experience congruent with the conditions of worth and hence to maintain the consistency of the self-concept. Two important consequences of the operation of conditions of worth are that: (1) experiences which are congruent with the organismic actualizing tendency may not be accurately symbolized in awareness and may not, therefore, further actualization; and (2) experiences which are congruent with the actualizing tendency may be symbolized and given a positive evaluation in terms of their enhancement of the self-concept. The result is an incongruence between self and experience, which may be of major significance to the individual.

To see how these processes operate, consider the example of the teenager whose self-concept is that he is a "tough guy," an image at least partially confirmed by some previous success in fights. On one occasion he becomes involved in a fight with a much smaller boy, who beats him badly. The organismic valuing process, acting alone, would accept this experience as accurately reflecting the fact that he is not as "tough" as he thought. However, self-actualization and the conditions of worth are likely to step in and distort the perception of what has taken place. Thus, our teenager may conclude that he lost the fight because he tripped and fell, because he was not feeling very well that day, or because he didn't want to hurt the other guy too much. The result is that the self-concept is now inaccurate. It still holds that the teenager is a tough guy, failing to take into account the relevant information from the lost fight. There is thus an incongruence between self and experience.

PSYCHOPATHOLOGY

The potential for psychopathology lies in the ongoing conflict between organismic and self-systems. As the self and its incorporated conditions of worth develop and function, the individual moves further and further from the adjustive safety of his or her organismic experiencing and more and more towards the hostile world of self-regard. He or she comes to experience the need to regard the self positively and to maintain the consistency of that evaluation. In the course of this effort to maintain regard and consistency, the conditions of worth form a defensive system. With this system in operation, all experiences that are incongruent with the conditions of worth, and hence with the existing self-concept, are defended against. Defense consists of either *denying* an experience to awareness or symbolizing it in a *distorted* form, such that it is perceived as congruent.

If we assume that experiences which are denied or distorted are stored *subconsciously* in an accurate form, we have the basis for Rogerian psychopathology, an *incongruence between self and experience*. That is, the subconsciously (and accurately) stored experiences of the individual are not congruent with the consciously symbolized self-concept. The result is that the person is no longer a unified whole. Perception and behavior are governed sometimes by the self and sometimes by the organism, and the personality is divided and functions less adequately and under greater tension.

> *This, as we see it, is the basic estrangement in man. He has not been true to himself, his own natural organismic valuing of experience, but for the sake of preserving the positive regard of others has now come to falsify some of the values he experiences and to perceive them only in terms based upon their value to others. Yet this has not been a conscious choice, but a natural—and tragic—development in infancy. (Rogers 1959, p. 226)*

Rogers (1963) has since revised his view that the rift between self and experience is a natural (inherent?) and necessary part of man's development. He now believes that the incongruence is the result of social learning. The individual, beginning in infancy, is reinforced or rewarded for behaviors which are at variance with the organismic actualizing tendency. The child thus introjects the values of the society and learns to behave in terms of the static, rigid concepts that characterize these values. As a result, he or she loses confidence in the flexible, spontaneous, nonconscious organismic valuing process which often conflicts with the values of the society. Rogers's view is in agreement with the philosopher of science, Lancelot Whyte (Rogers 1959), who suggested that social learning, upon which the incongruence of self and experience is based, is a relatively culture-specific phenomenon. The rigid constructs which are so detrimental to the functioning of the individual are particularly dominant in Western cultures, which have tended to develop such constructs as an integral aspect of language, thought, and philosophy.

Defensive Behavior

As a result of the incongruence between self and experience, there arises a corresponding incongruence in the individual's behavior. Specifically, those behaviors that maintain and enhance the self are symbolized accurately in awareness, while those that do not are denied or distorted to awareness. The individual thus begins to deny and distort his own behaviors if they are inconsistent with his self-concept. Although Rogers (1959) has not been entirely clear on this point, the incongruence of experience and behavior with the self-concept is apparently a phenomenon that tends to propagate itself. The greater the number of experiences that are denied or distorted due to conditions of worth—and the greater the incongruence between self and experience—the more likely a given experience is to be defended against, and the more rapidly the incongruence develops. Any experience which is at all incongruent with the self-structure is viewed as a threat, such that the symbolization of that experience produces a state of *anxiety*.

The defensive behaviors that distort and deny experience to consciousness include such classical defense mechanisms as projection, rationalization, fantasy, compulsions, and phobias. We would classify the individual characterized by the extreme forms of these defenses as neurotic. According to Rogers, however, defensive behaviors may also include such manifestations as paranoid and catatonic behaviors, which are usually included in the psychotic category. He, therefore, believes that *defensive behavior* is a more fundamental category than neurosis.

Disorganized Behavior

The second fundamental category in the Rogerian system is *disorganized behavior,* which corresponds closely to reactive psychosis. The prepsychotic individual has a high degree of incongruence between self and experience. The acute disorganization of behavior occurs when a sudden or very obvious experience breaks through the defensive system and demonstrates consciously to the individual the self-experience incongruence. The result of the precipitating experience is a state of anxiety and a disintegration of the consistent gestalt of the self-concept. Disorganized behavior, regulated at times by the remnants of the self-concept and at times by the previously denied and distorted experiences, follows.

A THEORY OF INTERPERSONAL RELATIONSHIPS

Rogers (1959, 1973) has extended his theory to deal specifically with the area of interpersonal relationships. In his view effective interpersonal relationships are helpful, if not essential, in maintaining a high degree of congruence between self and experience and in helping the person to actualize and grow psychologically.

Rogers (1973) has theorized that psychotherapy is more effective when both the therapist and the client can learn to trust their own feelings as well as those of each other. This mutual trust allows each to be more accepting, to be more flexible and creative, and to be less defensive and anxious. In short, a good interpersonal relationship leads toward greater actualization. Rogers suggested that this theory of interpersonal relationships applies not only to the interaction of therapist and client but to a wide variety of other interactions; included would be the relationships of teacher and student, husband and wife, and parent and child. Each of these relationships can be enhanced by the trust, openness, and acceptance described in the Rogers model.

CLIENT-CENTERED THEORY AND THERAPY

While our emphasis here has been on his theory of personality, Carl Rogers's own emphasis over the years has been instead on the theory and practice of client-centered psychotherapy. Rogers has emphasized that his client-centered approach is not intended to be viewed as a technique of psychotherapy or as a theoretical dogma specifying ways of doing therapy but rather as an attitude and an approach to "being with persons" in the specialized interpersonal relationship that is psychotherapy. The basic tenet of the client-centered approach is the actualization postulate, which states that man has the inherent capacity and tendency to develop and realize all capabilities and, thereby, to enhance the organism. As a result of this underlying principle, the client-centered therapist trusts the client to have a substantial amount of responsibility for the process and success of the therapy. This is, in part, why Rogerian treatment has sometimes been terms *nondirective therapy,* since it is often the client and not the therapist who controls the flow of the therapeutic process.

The goal of client-centered therapy is to provide a safe therapeutic climate in which the person can learn to reduce the incongruence between self and experience by learning to trust more in the experience itself. The therapist tries to help the client achieve this goal by establishing a therapeutic atmosphere in which the client is completely sincere or genuine (Rogers 1975; Rogers and Wood 1974), expressses unconditional positive regard or, as Rogers later called it, *caring,* and shows accurate empathic understanding. The latter concept means that the therapist must be able to experience what the client is experiencing and empathically understand the innermost private feelings and concerns of the client. If the therapist successfully adopts the three important attitudes, the client comes to trust the therapist and is able to express his or her feelings and thoughts more openly, thereby learning to accept experiences that were previously denied or distorted. In this way, the therapeutic process helps the client to move toward greater self-experience congruence, resulting in greater openness for further experiencing and moving toward actualization or psychological growth.

The Encounter Group

While the Rogerian approach to psychotherapy developed specifically as a set of principles concerned with individual psychotherapy, Rogers has, in more recent years, turned some of his attention to encounter groups and the conduct of group psychotherapy. Noting the rapid development of encounter group approaches, Rogers (1970) formulated a set of ideas and principles to be considered by therapists who are engaged in leading encounter groups. Not surprisingly, the Rogerian approach to group therapy follows directly from his approach to individual therapy. In the group it is important for the therapist to be accepting of the attitudes and feelings of the group members, to be genuine and open with the group, and to maintain a high degree of empathic understanding with regard to the group and each of its members. According to Rogers, the group is largely responsible for its own development and progress, and the therapist merely facilitates this progress. The details of Rogers's views on encounter groups are available in his book *Carl Rogers on Encounter Groups* (1970).

EDUCATING THE WHOLE PERSON

Rogers (1974a, 1974b, 1974c) applied his theory to personality not only to psychotherapy but also to the educational process. He became concerned about the results of an educational system which focuses exclusively on cognitive education, giving the person only a body of factual knowledge. A better approach to education, he suggested, would be to work toward the development of persons who are flexible, adaptive and open to change, and who are learning how to learn. He argued that it should be possible to move toward this kind of more humanistic educational system by introducing techniques aimed at the achievement of self-directed change in the system. Ultimately, the student would learn from the teacher about feelings as well as ideas and would thus develop much more fully as a total person than the student who is exposed only to cognitive education.

A pilot project to introduce and test some of Rogers's ideas concerning education was begun by Rogers and his colleagues at the Western Behavioral Sciences Institute in the late 1960s. The project was conducted in conjunction with the Immaculate Heart Community, which operates several high schools and a number of elementary schools within a few hours of Los Angeles. Encounter groups involving teachers, students, parents, and administrators were used to move toward greater openness and more effective interpersonal relationships within the school system. A careful study of the effectiveness of this educational approach was undertaken, comparing encounter group participants with a matched control group not involved in the encounters. Results showed both some positive and some negative effects, but Rogers concluded that the major project goal of initiating self-directed change in the system was achieved.

THE THEORY IN EMPIRICAL CONTEXT

At least as significant as his contributions as a theoretician have been Carl Rogers's pioneering investigations in psychotherapy and counseling. As an early investigator in this difficult area for research, Rogers has been instrumental in developing a variety of measures and techniques which have permitted for the first time the systematic study of variables entering into the practice of psychotherapy.

A vast majority of the studies reported by Rogers and his associates have been directed toward the exploration of therapeutic variables and the formulation and empirical evaluation of a theory of therapy. In this research context, the personality theory has taken a decidedly secondary role. Nevertheless, a substantial number of investigations have served to test, directly or indirectly, important aspects of the theory and thus to provide an empirical basis for the modifications and extensions which have characterized Rogers's theoretical efforts. We will concentrate here on studies most relevant to the theory of personality, considering these, as they must be considered, in the context of research programs in therapy.

Early Studies of Psychotherapy

The initial studies reported by the Rogers group were of two basic types. The first were purely *descriptive* studies of the therapeutic relationship. In these reports Rogers and his colleagues (Rogers 1942, 1948, 1951; Muench and Rogers 1946; Rogers and Wallen 1946; Snyder and others 1947) studied therapeutic interviews and described the therapeutic relationship and changes in the client which took place over the course of therapy. These qualitative studies included both case studies, involving an intensive examination of one individual, and group studies, in which variables of interest were examined in a number of clients.

The second method utilized in early studies was that of *content analysis,* which consists of the development of a set of categories under which the client's recorded statements can be classified. Following the pioneering study of Porter (1943), Snyder (1945) undertook a content analysis of nearly ten thousand client responses in forty-eight interviews. He classified and analyzed clients and found a definite tendency for clients' feelings to change from negative to positive with reference to both self and counselor over the course of therapy. Other early studies using content analysis included those of Raimy (1948) Lipkin (1948), and Seeman (1949), all essentially confirming Snyder's (1945) results.

Studies of Self-Regard and Self-Acceptance

The Rogerian concept of self-regard developed, as did the entire personality theory, largely out of studies of client behavior in therapy. Of the studies discussed here, some were conducted before and some after the formulation of the self-regard construct.

Q-technique Investigations. Q-technique is a research method which permits the evaluation and comparison of an individual's conscious perceptions of both the individual and others. The method was developed by Stephenson (1953) as a means of formally testing psychological theories. The subject in a Q-technique study is given a set of statements, each on a separate card, and asked to sort them into a series of stacks representing a continuum from those statements least characteristic of him or her to those that are most characteristic. The technique is not limited to self-description, and subjects may make as many sortings as the investigator wishes. The subject may, for example, he asked to sort the cards once to describe himself or herself, once to describe the ideal person, and one time to describe the therapist. Or the client may sort the cards on several different occasions, such as once before, once during, and once after the completion of psychotherapy. Applying correlational and factor analytic techniques, each sorting may be compared statistically with each other sorting, and comparisons may be stated for each subject or averaged across all subjects in a study.

In one study, Butler and Haigh (1954) randomly selected one hundred self-referent statements from therapy protocols and used these as a Q-sort set. Two groups of subjects were used. The experimental group consisted of individuals who had expressed interest in counseling. Each subject in this group was tested three times: before counseling, immediately after the completion of counseling, and on a follow-up six months to one year after counseling. On each occasion, subjects sorted the cards once to describe themselves and again to describe the ideal person. A control group consisting of persons not seeking counseling was tested at the same intervals as the experimental group. An additional control measure was provided by requiring half of the experimental group to wait sixty days before beginning counseling and to have these subjects sort the cards at the beginning and end of the sixty-day period.

Before counseling, control subjects showed a mean self-ideal correlation of .58, while experimentals had a zero correlation. After counseling, experimentals had a mean correlation of .34, a significant increase over the precounseling correlation of zero, and at follow-up the correlation had decreased only slightly to .31. Control subjects showed no change in self-ideal correlation over the same period, and those clients who waited sixty days before counseling showed no change over the precounseling period. Thus, Butler and Haigh demonstrated that: (1) clients are less satisfied with themselves (hold themselves in lower regard) before therapy than nonclients; (2) therapy increases the self-ideal correlation, while there is no change in controls; and (3) the correlation tends to hold up over the follow-up period.

Results of the Butler and Haigh (1954) study have been supported by a number of other investigations (see, for example, Dymond 1953, 1954; Rudikoff 1954; G. M. Smith 1959; B. Smith 1962. A study involving schizophrenic subjects was, however, not supportive (Kiesler, Mathieu and Klein 1967). The Q-sort measure in this study was a self-expert congruence measure in which each subject's self-sort was correlated with a standard sort representing the ideal person as judged by clinical psychologists. Both the self-expert measure and a second Q-adjustment measure failed to show change over therapy or to show differential change for control and therapy groups.

Acceptance of Self and Others. Rogers has postulated that positive regard and self-regard are related to regard for and acceptance of others. As one aspect of this postulate, he has specifically hypothesized that the more self-accepting a person is, the more accepting he or she will be of others.

A number of investigations have been undertaken to test this hypothesis. In early studies, Sheerer (1949) and Stock (1949) obtained correlations, respectively, of .51 and .66 between self- and other-acceptance, supporting the Rogerian hypothesis. Suinn (1961) required eighty-two male high school seniors to sort four adjective Q-sort decks, one each to describe themselves, their fathers, and male teachers, and one containing adjectives common to all three. Each deck was sorted twice, once to describe the "real" self, father, or teacher and once to describe the "ideal." An acceptance score was then determined for each as the intercorrelation of real and ideal sorts. Thus, self-acceptance was defined as the correlation between the real-self and ideal-self sorts, and so on. The acceptance scores were then intercorrelated with each other, and it was found that self-acceptance correlated .32 with father-acceptance and .25 with teacher-acceptance. Both correlations were statistically significant, supporting Rogers's hypothesis. A number of other studies (Berger 1952; Omwake 1954; Phillips 1951) have been similarly supportive with correlations generally ranging from .25 to .74, although one study (Zelen 1954) did not support the hypothesis.

The Problem of Self-Experience Incongruence

As was noted above, Rogers's important hypotheses concerning the effects of congruence and incongruence of self and experience have been difficult, if not impossible, to investigate. The principal reason for the problem is that phenomenal experience, since it is defined in terms of personal, internal perceptions, has defied operational definition. A few studies do, however, relate to the question. We will take up one major example here.

Chodorkoff (1954) undertook to test the hypothesis that when there is incongruence between self and experience, further incongruent experiences will be perceived as threatening and their symbolization in awareness defended against. To test this hypothesis, he predicted that the degree of congruence between self and experience is inversely related to degree of defensiveness. *Experience* was operationally defined in terms of a Q-sort describing the client and performed by a clinical psychologist familiar with both the client and his biographical and test data; *self* was defined as a Q-sort performed by the subject; and *defensiveness* was defined as perceptual defensiveness and expressed as the difference in recognition times between neutral and threatening words presented tachistoscopically. Self-experience congruence was then defined as the correlation between the self-sort and the clinician-sort, and the congruence-defensiveness hypothesis was tested by relating this correlation to perceptual defensiveness. The relationship was significant, thus supporting the hypothesis.

Research with Schizophrenics

Rogers (1967) and his associates have reported on a large-scale, long-term, intensive study of schizophrenics in a client-centered therapy situation. Included in the study were three groups of sixteen subjects each, comprising chronic schizophrenics, acute schizophrenics, and normals. Schizophrenia was defined in terms of clinical diagnosis. Half of the subjects in each group (including normals) were randomly assigned to a therapy condition, the other half to a nontherapy control condition. For the therapy condition, each of eight therapists saw three clients, one of each type. All subjects were given sampling interviews at three-month intervals, and all were tested with a number of standardized tests, such as the MMPI, TAT, and Rorschach. In addition, both therapists and clients were rated on a number of variables, using rating scales developed by the Rogers group.

In lieu of attempting any complete discussion of the findings of the study—a brief treatment could never do justice—we will consider partial results obtained with one scale, the Experiencing (EXP) Scale. This scale was developed as a measure of a subject's degree of self-awareness and relates to the goal of client-centered therapy, increased spontaneity and self-awareness. In terms of the theory of personality, increased experiencing would be indicative of decreased defensiveness, with a consequent symbolization of a larger proportion of experience and increased congruence between self and experience. The EXP Scale is a 7-point rating scale, with each point carefully described as to its meaning.

Results showed that there was no significant difference between the EXP level in early interviews and in late sessions. In more detailed analyses of trend over therapy, it was found that modal EXP (overall level of EXP) generally showed no significant change. Peak EXP (the highest achieved), however, showed a significant quadratic trend over the first thirty interviews and a linear trend over the total course of therapy. This means that over the first thirty sessions there was an initial decrease in EXP level (up to interviews eleven to fifteen), followed by an increase. Over the entire course of therapy, however, there was a consistent (linear) tendency for EXP level to increase (significant at the .10 level).

Additional Scales

One methodological contribution which the Rogers group has made to the study of psychotherapy is the development of a number of scales specifically for use in the therapeutic situation. In addition to those already mentioned, a Process Scale for the measurement of change in patients over the course of therapy was proposed by Rogers (1958) and later developed (Rogers, Walker, and Rablen 1960). Seeman (1954) developed a measure of success in therapy, consisting of ten, 9-point rating scales. Other process scales for the measurement of change in psychotherapy have included a Personal Constructs Scale (Tomlinson 1967), a Problem Expression Scale (Van der Veen and Tomlinson 1967), and a Relationship Scale (Gendlin 1967).

EVALUATION

Rogerian theory has come under two major types of criticism. The first, expressed in the relatively early years of Rogers's work, was that the theory is based on a naive phenomenology. In this attack, the theory is said to be based on the related assumptions that personality is primarily or entirely conscious and that the individual is capable of truthfully and accurately relating his personality structure and dynamics in the form of conscious self-reports, such as the Q-sort. The stress on consciousness to the virtual exclusion of the unconscious would, indeed, be subject to serious criticism, since there is extensive evidence for the existence of unconscious determinants. This criticism may have been a valid one for Rogers's early theory. It certainly does not apply currently, however, since, as we have seen, there is a definite and specific unconscious component postulated in recent formulations.

The criticism that self-report verity is dubious is no doubt at least partially valid. As Combs and Soper (1957) have pointed out, the accuracy of self-report data is doubtful for a number of reasons, including the dubious level of the subject's awareness of his or her self-concept, the subject's willingness to cooperate, feelings of adequacy and freedom from threat in the situation, and a variety of response sets, such as the subject's desire to present a socially desirable picture of himself or herself. Studies of the validity of self-reports (such as Combs, Soper, and Courson 1963; Parker 1966) suggest that reliance on self-reports of personality characteristics or behaviors is a questionable practice. The self-report criticism, on the other hand, applies not only to Rogers but to many other theorists and researchers who have developed and used the wide variety of self-report measures currently available in psychology. Rogers might also respond to the criticism by pointing out that he has, in some studies, used measures based on observer ratings rather than self-reports. Thus, in these cases the criticism would not be applicable.

Clarity of Major Constructs

The second general type of criticism of the theory has been from the standpoint of its formal properties (namely, Krause 1964), particularly with respect to the clarity of usage of major constructs.

Perhaps the major construct with which Rogerian theory has difficulty is that of experience. While Rogers has given a clear initial definition of this construct, his use of the term in the theory and his treatment of how experience is evaluated are open to question. There are two major points. First, Rogers has not been entirely clear as to the process by which experiences are received. In general, as we have seen, an experience may be received and interpreted either consciously or subconsciously. The former process is termed *perception,* the latter *subception.* Both processes are known, experimentally, to operate. What is not clear are the circumstances under which each process operates. Rogers points out that "perception and awareness are synonymous" (1959, p. 199). If perception is synonymous with awareness and awareness is synonymous with consciousness, there is the direct implication that at least some experiences are initially received directly in consciousness. This situation would, however, appear to contradict in part the postulated operation of the screening process, governed by the conditions of worth. This process is said to be capable of distorting and denying the symbolization of experiences in consciousness. Distortion presents no problem since perceptual distortion, as a function of set, expectancy, and variety of personality factors, is a well-known phenomenon. The denial of some experiences to awareness, however, implies that the regulatory process takes place at a subconscious level. Thus, the experience is subceived as incongruent with the existing self-concept and hence denied to awareness. Rogers does not specify the conditions under which experiences are subceived as opposed to perceived.

The second question relates to the storage and use of past experience. The question actually has two parts: (1) is there provision in the theory for the storage of experience in general, and, if so, does past experience influence current functioning? and (2) are those incongruent experiences which are denied to awareness stored, and if so, how? The first question must be answered affirmatively but with a qualification. Although Rogers has provided for the existence of a memory or accumulation of past experience, he has also held, with other phenomenologists, that only *current* experience influences the perception and behavior of the individual. What effect then, if any, does past experience have on behavior? The answer is that the experiential field at a given moment may include memory traces which are currently active. In this way, memory or past experience may serve to influence the individual's interpretation of current phenomena being experienced in the phenomenal field. Rogers does not, however, specify the mechanism by which memories are selected for inclusion in the phenomenal field.

A more important consideration concerns the storage of experiences that are inconsistent with the self-concept. A major focus of Rogerian theory—one which is critical to the theory of psychopathology—is on the role of incongruence between self and experience, which develops as a result of the failure to symbolize all experiences accurately. Again it must be recalled that experience is thus a current phenomenon. Yet, as Krause (1964) has noted, the incongruence that comes to exist between self and experience is not a momentary phenomenon. Rather, it is an enduring condition which tends to grow, the degree of incongruence increasing as more and more experiences are denied and distorted. This accumulation of incongruence implies that at least part of the experience on which incongruence is based must be stored and, further, that the stored experiences must have a major influence on current perception. The implication is, then, that experience is used somewhat ambiguously by Rogers, such that it is not always certain whether a given reference is to current ongoing experience, stored past experience, or both.

We hasten to note that the discussion of the experience construct should not be taken more generally as an indictment of the structural properties of Rogerian theory. In fact, Rogers has made a valiant attempt at clarity in specifying his theoretical constructs and, with the exception of the experience construct and some ambiguities in the actualization construct, he has largely succeeded. The syntactic structure of the theory is also generally good.

ABRAHAM MASLOW

One of the major features of Rogerian theory is its emphasis on the uniquely human, teleological motivation which Rogers termed *actualization.* A second theorist who has emphasized such purposive motivation and who has also taken a more general humanistic orientation somewhat similar to that of Rogers is Abraham Maslow.

Maslow, a former president (1967–68) of the American Psychological Association, was born April 1, 1908, in Brooklyn, New York, and died June 8, 1970. He received his B.A., M.A., and Ph.D. degrees at the University of Wisconsin. Maslow served as president of the Division of Personality and Social Psychology and the Division of Esthetics of the American Psychological Association and was elected a Fellow of the New York Academy of Sciences, a Fellow of the Fund for Advancement of Education, and a Visiting Fellow at the Western Behavioral Sciences Institute at La Jolla, California.

THE THIRD FORCE

While Maslow has been a prime mover in the phenomenological-humanistic movement, his theory is not a theory of personality in that it does not postulate a specific personality structure. It is, rather, a theory that deals primarily with the forces which move the individual, the elements in the development and functioning of the personality which make the human person uniquely human. In short, Maslow's is a theory of *human motivation.*

Maslow (1968b) proposed that his theory, like that of Rogers, is representative of the most recent of three major forces current in psychology. The first of these forces is the *behavioristic* (positivistic, objectivistic) school, which has been patterned after the sciences that deal primarily with objects like physics, chemistry, and geology. The second force, the *Freudian* approach, refers to both Freud and followers of his concepts and general methods. The Freudian school, following the Darwinian tradition, treats man as a mere animal, capable of having no characteristics that are uniquely human.

Both the behavioristic and the Freudian traditions base human motivation primarily or exclusively in a set of deficiency needs. The *humanistic revolution,* Maslow's third force, while postulating a biological basis for human needs, emphasizes the importance of "higher" needs. In general, the higher needs are those which function not only to prevent illness but also to promote the progress and further development of the individual. They enhance as well as maintain, the functioning person.

THE NEED HIERARCHY

Maslow (1954a, 1964) viewed the need-motive system of human beings as comprising a hierarchical structure. The needs in the hierarchy are of two general types, basic or deficiency needs, and higher or metaneeds.

The Deficiency Needs

All *deficiency needs* are prepotent to the growth needs or metaneeds. That is, before the metaneeds can become dominant, all deficiency needs must be satisfied. In addition, needs within the deficiency sector of the hierarchy are arranged in order of decreasing prepotence, the lowest in the hierarchy being the most prepotent.

Physiological needs are the lowest and the most prepotent needs in the hierarchy. They give rise to the physiological or primary drives. These needs, include both general needs, such as hunger and thirst, and specific needs, including those for various vitamins, minerals, calcium, and the like. The prepotence of the physiological needs over other needs is demonstrated by the starving or extremely thirsty individual, whose behavior and consciousness are so dominated by the deprived need that the individual will engage in virtually no activity not directed at the satiation of the need.

Safety needs arise when the physiological needs are chronically satiated and tend to dominate behavior in any situation which the individual perceives as potentially dangerous. Common examples include feelings of fear in situations which might cause death or injury and the general preference for familiar over unfamiliar situations. Needs for *belongingness* and *love* are basically needs for social acceptance and interpersonal interaction. According to Maslow, many cases of psychopathology are due to the failure to satisfy these needs. *Esteem* needs include the need for *self-esteem,* which causes the individual to strive to attain a perception of himself or herself as a generally competent person, and the need for *other esteem,* which is basically a desire to have a good reputation.

Metaneeds, B-Values, and Self-Actualization

When all deficiency needs have been adequately satiated, the individual is then ready to be motivated by "higher" needs, referred to by Maslow as growth needs or *metaneeds.* The general goal of the *metamotivation* which accompanies the metaneed is the realization of capacities and consequent psychological growth of the individual, which is attained through the pursuit of ultimate values. Maslow (1954, 1955) referred to this general goal as *self-actualization.*

Like deficiency motivation, metamotivation is instinctoid and compensatory. The instinctoid character of the metamotives means that they are innate and a part of the physiological makeup of the person. As a result, the individual is compelled to satisfy these needs once they become active. In his later publications, Maslow (1967b, 1967c, 1970) did hold, however, that the reduction of deficiency needs is a necessary but not a sufficient condition for metamotivation. His position is that metamotivation requires as a precondition not only the satisfaction of the deficiency needs but also that the individual have established a set of values, which he or she then strives to meet.

Maslow designated these values *being-values* or *B-values*. These are seen as intrinsic (and hence instinctoid), ultimate values which are specific to the human species. They include truth, beauty, self-sufficiency, and fourteen others. The importance of these values to the metamotivated individual is that they serve as needs which the person strives to satisfy. In fact, the term B-value becomes synonomous with metaneeds, when it is recognized that the specific metaneeds are the B-values (Maslow 1962, 1967b).

THE ACHIEVEMENT OF SELF-ACTUALIZATION

Self-actualization, viewed as an end-state, can probably never be fully achieved. Rather it is an ongoing process, involving a continual striving to fulfill metaneeds or B-values and hence to achieve a higher level of personal growth. Nevertheless, Maslow found it helpful to consider the characteristics of the ideal self-actualized person. This *fully human* person is described as totally open to experience, nondefensive, spontaneous, and problem-oriented. He or she is autonomous from the environment and culture yet feels deep empathy with other humans.

Maslow used various terms to describe the fully metamotivated person: self-actualizing person (Maslow 1954b), alpsy (Maslow 1968), fully-evolved person (Maslow 1967b), and fully-human person (Maslow 1967a). In various publications, he has gone to considerable lengths to describe the characteristics of (Maslow 1967b) and behaviors leading to (Maslow 1968b) self-actualization.

The concept of self-actualization may become clearer when we consider the characteristics of the fully human person. Such a person is perhaps best described as totally open to experience, in the Rogerian sense of nondefensiveness. The person's behavior is spontaneous rather than artificial, and problem-centered rather than ego-centered. The fully human person is autonomous of, and at times almost psychotically detached from, the environment and culture but feels deep empathy with all people, is capable of intense, profound interpersonal relationships, and is generally accepting of both the positive and negative aspects of self and others. Finally, the fully human person tends to have a keener perception of reality than the average person, is more discriminating with respect to right and wrong, and tends to be more creative in a primary-process sense.

Transient Self-Actualization: The Peak Experience

The experience of actualization is not entirely restricted to the self-actualizing person. In fact, Maslow (1970) postulated that the average person undergoes, from time to time, moments of actualization, referred to as peak experiences. These are moments of extreme ecstasy, rapture, great happiness, bliss. They occur in many situations, which, according to Maslow's (1963) subjects, include natural childbirth, profound esthetic experiences, parental love, and perfect sexual experiences. In addition to the feeling of great ecstasy, the peak experience is characterized by an unusually vivid perception, without self-based interpretation, of a delimited object or idea, with a momentary loss of reality contact, temporal and spatial disorientation, and a loss of defensiveness and anxiety. Putting it otherwise, there is a transcendence of reality and self which, Maslow held, is not unlike that of the mystic experiences of some religions. In summarizing his study of the peak experience, Maslow (1963) concluded that the characteristics of the peak experience are, in essence, the B-values.

THE HEALTHY PERSON: AN OPTIMISTIC VIEW

Even a brief overview of Maslow's theory begins to make apparent his overriding interest in psychologically healthy people. As he has often pointed out, many of his predecessors and colleagues, including Freud and even Rogers, have spent most of their time studying psychologically disturbed, unhealthy people. They have often attempted to generalize from these emotional cripples to formulate a psychology of the normal person. This approach, Maslow argues, is inappropriate and unfortunate. A vast majority of people are normal and healthy, and a small minority are "supernormal" and may conform to his description of the fully human person. Thus, Maslow's theory, unlike most others, is directed toward the study and understanding of normal and fully human people and experiences. His view is among the most optimistic developed to date, and the need for such a view is underscored by the substantial impact it has had on psychology. While one can question the relative lack of detailed theoretical development and of empirical research that characterizes Maslow's theory, his influence continues to be felt in the field.

REFERENCES

Berger, E. M. The relation between expressed acceptance of self and expressed acceptance of others. *Journal of Abnormal and Social Psychology*, 1952, *47*, 778–782.

Butler, J. M., & Haigh, G. V.   Changes in the relation between self-concepts and ideal concepts consequent upon client-centered counseling. In C. R. Rogers & R. Dymonds (Eds.), *Psychotherapy and personality change: Co-ordinated studies in the client-centered approach.* Chicago: University of Chicago Press, 1954.

Chodorkoff, B.   Self-perception, perceptual defense, and adjustment. *Journal of Abnormal and Social Psychology,* 1954, *49,* 508-512.

Combs, A. W., & Soper, D. W.   The self, its derivate terms and research. *Journal of Individual Psychology,* 1957, *13,* 134-145.

Combs, A. W., Soper, D. W., & Courson, C. C.   The measurement of self-concept and self-report. *Educational and Psychological Measurement,* 1963, *23,* 493-500.

Dymond, R. F.   The relation of accuracy of perception of the spouse and marital happiness. *American Psychologist,* 1953, *8,* 344.

Dymond, R. F.   Adjustment changes over therapy from thematic apperception test ratings. In C. R. Rogers & R. F. Dymond (Eds.), *Psychotherapy and personality change: Co-ordinated studies in the client-centered approach.* Chicago: University of Chicago Press, 1954.

Gendlin, E. T.   A scale for rating the manner of relating. In C. R. Rogers, E. T. Gendlin, D. J. Kiesler, S. C. B. Traux (Eds.), *The therapeutic relationship and its impact: A study of psychotherapy with schizophrenics.* Madison: University of Wisconsin Press, 1967.

Hall, C. S., & Lindzey, G.   *Theories of personality.* New York: Wiley & Sons, 1957.

James, W.   *Principles of psychology* (2 vols.). New York: Holt, 1890.

Kiesler, D. J., Mathieu, P. L., & Klein, M. H.   A summary of the issues and conclusions. In C. R. Rogers, E. T. Gendlin, D. J. Kiesler, & Traux, C. B. (Eds.), *The therapeutic relationship and its impact: A study of psychotherapy with schizophrenics.* Madison, University of Wisconsin Press, 1967. (Pp. 295-311.)

Krause, M. S.   An analysis of Carl R. Rogers' theory of personality. *Genetic Psychological Monographs,* 1964, *69,* 49-99.

Leeper, R.   A motivational theory of emotion to replace "emotion as disorganized response." *Psychological Review,* 1948, *55,* 5-21.

Lipkin, S.   The client evaluates non-directive psychotherapy. *Journal of Consulting Psychology,* 1948, *12,* 137-146.

Maslow, A. H.   The instinctoid nature of basic needs. *Journal of Personality,* 1954, *22,* 326-347.

Maslow, A. H.   *Motivation and personality.* New York: Harper & Row, 1954.

Maslow, A. H.   Deficiency motivation and growth motivation. In M. R. Jones (Ed.), *Nebraska symposium on motivation.* Lincoln: University of Nebraska Press, 1955.

Maslow, A. H.   Notes on being—Psychology. *Journal of Humanistic Psychology,* 1962, *2,* 47-71.

Maslow, A. H.   Further notes on being—Psychology. *Journal of Humanistic Psychology,* 1963, *3,* 120-135.

Maslow, A. H. Criteria for judging needs to be instinctoid. In. M. R. Jones (Ed.), *Human motivation: A symposium*. Lincoln: University of Nebraska Press, 1965.

Maslow, A. H. Synanon and eupsychia. *Journal of Humanistic Psychology*, 1967, *7*, 28-35.

Maslow, A. H. A theory of metamotivation: The biological rooting of the value of life. *Journal of Humanistic Psychology*, 1967, *7*, 92-127.

Maslow, A. H. Self-actualization and beyond. In J. F. T. Bugental (Ed.), *Challenges of humanistic psychology*. New York: McGraw-Hill. 1967.

Maslow, A. H. A theory of metamotivation: The biological rooting of the value of life. *Psychology Today*, July 1968, pp. 38-39; 58-62.

Maslow, A. H. *Toward a psychology of being*. New York: D. Van Nostrand Company, 1968.

Maslow, A. H. *Motivation and personality* (2nd ed.). New York: Harper & Row, 1970.

Muench, G. A., & Rogers, C. R. Counseling of emotional blocking in an aviator. *Journal of Abnormal and Social Psychology*, 1946, *41*, 207-215.

Omwake, K. T. The relation between acceptance of self and acceptance of others shown by three personality inventories. *Journal of Consulting Psychology*, 1954, *18*, 443-446.

Parker, J. The relationship of self-report to inferred self-concept. *Educational and Psychological Measurement*, 1966, *26*, 691-700.

Phillips, E. L. Attitudes toward self and others: A brief questionnaire report. *Journal of Consulting Psychology*, 1951, *15*, 79-81.

Porter, E. H., Jr. The development and evaluation of a measure of counseling interview procedures (Part I). *Educational and Psychological Measurements*, 1943, *3*, 105-126.

Raimy, V. C. Self-reference in counseling interviews. *Journal of Consulting Psychology*, 1948, *12*, 153-163.

Rogers, C. R. The use of electrically recorded interviews in improving psychotherapeutic techniques. *American Journal of Orthopsychiatry*, 1942, *12*, 429-434.

Rogers, C. R. Research in psychotherapy: Round table. *American Journal of Orthopsychiatry*, 1948, *18*, 96-100.

Rogers, C. R. *Client-centered therapy: Its current practice, implications, and theory*. Boston: Houghton Mifflin, 1951.

Rogers, C. R. A process conception of psychotherapy. *American Psychologists*, 1958, *13*, 142-149.

Rogers, C. R. A theory of therapy, personality, and interpersonal relationships as developed in the client-centered framework. In S. Koch (Ed.), *Psychology: A study of a science: Formations of the person in the social context* (Vol. 3). New York: McGraw-Hill, 1959.

Rogers, C. R. The concept of the fully functioning person. *Psychotherapy: Theory, Research, & Practice*, 1963, *1*, 17-26.

Rogers, C. R. Toward a science of the person. In T. W. Wann (Ed.), *Behaviorism and phenomenology*. Chicago: University of Chicago Press, 1964.

Rogers, C. R.   *Carl Rogers on encounter groups.* New York: Harper & Row, 1970.

Rogers, C. R.   Some new challenges. *American Psychologist,* 1973, *28,* 379-387.

Rogers, C. R.   Can learning encompass both ideas and feelings? *Education,* 1974, *95,* 103-114.

Rogers, C. R.   Questions I would ask myself if I were a teacher. *Education,* 1974, *95,* 134-139.

Rogers, C. R.   The project at Immaculate Heart: An experiment in self-directed change. *Education,* 1974, *95,* 172-189.

Rogers, C. R., Gendlin, E. T., Kiesler, D. J., & Traux, C. B. (Eds.).   *The therapeutic relationship and its impact: A study of psychotherapy with schizophrenics.* Madison, Wisc.: University of Wisconsin Press, 1967.

Rogers, C. R., Walker, A., & Rablen, R.   Development of a scale to measure process changes in psychotherapy. *Journal of Clinical Psychology,* 1960, *16,* 79-85.

Rogers, C. R., & Wallen, J. L.   *Counseling with returned servicemen.* New York: McGraw-Hill, 1946.

Rogers, C. R., & Wood, J. K.   Client-centered theory: Carl R. Rogers. In A. Burton (Ed.), *Operational theories of personality.* New York: Bruner/Mazel, 1974.

Rudikoff, E. C.   A comparative study of the changes in the concepts of the self, the ordinary person, and the ideal in eight cases. In C. R. Rogers & R. F. Dymond, (Eds.), *Psychotherapy and personality change: Co-ordinated studies in the client-centered approach.* Chicago: University of Chicago Press, 1954.

Seeman, J.   A study of the process of non-directive therapy. *Journal of Consulting Psychology,* 1949, *13,* 157-168.

Seeman, J.   Counselor judgements of therapeutic process and outcome. In C. R. Rogers & R. F. Dymond (Eds.), *Psychotherapy and personality change: Co-ordinated studies in the client-centered approach.* Chicago: University of Chicago Press, 1954.

Sheerer, E. T.   An analysis of the relationship between acceptance of and respect for self and acceptance of and respect for others in ten counseling cases. *Journal of Consulting Psychology,* 1949, *13,* 169-175.

Smith, B.   Handbooks for new employees. *Personnel Management,* 1962, *44,* 101-107.

Smith, G. M.   Six measures of self-concept discrepancy and instability: Their interrelations, reliability and relations to other personality measures. *Journal of Consulting Psychology,* 1958, *22,* 101-112.

Stephenson, W.   *The study of behavior.* Chicago: University of Chicago Press, 1953.

Stock, D.   An investigation into the interrelations between self-concepts and feelings directed toward other persons and groups. *Journal of Consulting Psychology,* 1949, *13,* 176-180.

Suinn, R. M.   The relationship between self-acceptance and acceptance of others: A learning theory analysis. *Journal of Abnormal and Social Psychology,* 1961, *63,* 37-42.

Synder, W. U. An investigation of the nature of non-directive psychotherapy. *Journal of General Psychology*, 1945, *33*, 193–223.

Synder, W. U., et al. *Casebook of non-directive counseling.* Boston: Houghton-Mifflin, 1947.

Tomlinson, J. R. Situational and personality correlates of predictive accuracy. *Journal of Consulting Psychology*, 1967, *31*, 19–22.

Van der Veen, F., & Tomlinson, T. M. A scale for rating the manner of problem expression. In C. R. Rogers, E. T. Gendlin, D. J. Kiesler, & C. B. Traux (Eds.), *The therapeutic relationship and its impact: A study of psychotherapy with schizophrenics.* Madison: University of Wisconsin Press, 1967.

Zelen, S. L. The relationship of peer acceptance, acceptance of others and self-acceptance. *Proceedings of the Iowa Academy of Science*, 1954, *61*, 446–449.

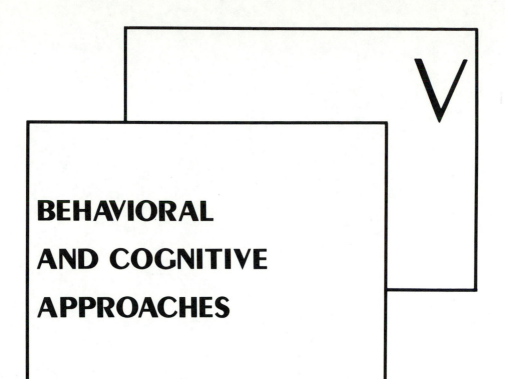

V

BEHAVIORAL
AND COGNITIVE
APPROACHES

Stimulus – Response Learning Theory:

John Dollard and

Neal Miller

8

The classic question of the relative extent to which personality development is influenced by nature and by nurture, by biology and environment, is, as we have seen, answered quite differently by different theorists. We have already been exposed to the relatively heavy biological emphasis of the Freudian formulation but have not yet studied the opposite extreme, the hypothesis that personality is entirely or almost entirely learned through contact with the external environment. The social analytic theorists, of course, do emphasize the role of the social environment, and both Allport and Rogers have recognized the important influence of environmental factors on personality development. Allport, in fact, even suggested several particular forms of learning that may influence personality development in specific ways. The task of formulating a set of theories that focuses primarily on learning processes and all but ignores the possible role of biological factors was left, however, to several individuals whom we might group loosely together and call the *learning theorists*.

The theories to be considered here are those of Dollard and

Miller, Skinner, Bandura, and Rotter. While formulating substantially different—indeed, in many ways, opposing—theories, these psychologists share the common conviction that *personality is learned*. They are also convinced that only a careful scientific approach to understanding behavior will produce the body of knowledge needed by psychologists.

The Origins

Learning theories of personality, are, as a group, an element of the overall movement in American psychology that is generally referred to as behaviorism. We will briefly consider some of the major early figures involved in this movement and their ideas to provide a perspective on the essentials of current theory.

In 1913 John Watson set ablaze what would become the towering inferno of behaviorism with his paper entitled *Psychology as a Behaviorist Views It*. The functional animal psychology in which Watson had received his training held that the basic approach to understanding behavior was to first observe the behavior and then to use the observational data to infer the consciousness of the animal and demonstrate how the conscious process influences the animal's behavior. Watson felt, however, that consciousness was an unnecessary element in the explanation of behavior and rejected it in favor of greater parsimony, which he saw as the hallmark of successful sciences. In Watson's view psychologists should study the simplest of behavioral phenomena by restricting their conclusions to those that could be based on externally observable behaviors. We may, for example, observe that a student who has studied fewer hours for an examination shuffles her feet and twists her hair more during the exam than her more studious counterpart. We need not necessarily invoke a concept of anxiety to explain the foot-shuffling and hair-twisting. Watson's emphasis on parsimony became also an emphasis on scientific method, and many psychologists were attracted by the promise of an approach which might, finally, provide a real understanding of behavior.

The mantle of leadership in behaviorism was eventually transferred from Watson to several other significant persons, including B. F. Skinner and Clark Hull. Skinner is the central figure of a separate chapter (see Chapter 9) and will not be discussed here.

Hull's approach is a theory of learning, which is intended to encompass all the major elements of the learning process in both animals and humans but is not intended to deal directly with such broader issues as human personality functioning. The theory was developed at the Institute of Human Relations at Yale, established several years after Hull had joined Yale's faculty. With the broad influence of his theory on the institute, some of the major psychologists of the mid-1900s developed their initial ideas and conducted their early research. Included among these were John Dollard and Neal Miller, two men who were perhaps uniquely equipped to apply Hullian theory to personality functioning. Their particular qualifications for this task included the fact that both had studied at the institute with Hull and were, therefore, thoroughly versed in Hullian theory; and both had also received earlier training in psychoanalytic theory.

John Dollard was born in 1900 in Menasha, Wisconsin. A man of varied interests spanning the behavioral sciences, Dollard received his B.A. degree from the University of Wisconsin in 1922 and later received the M.A. degree in 1930 and the Ph.D. in 1931 in sociology at the University of Chicago. He also trained in psychoanalysis at the Berlin Institute. He joined the Department of Anthropology at Yale University as an assistant professor in 1932, moved to a similar position in the Department of Sociology at the Institute of Human Relations at Yale in 1933, and in 1948 became a professor of psychology at Yale.

Neal E. Miller, born in 1909 in Milwaukee, Wisconsin, received his B.S. degree from the University of Washington in 1931 and his M.A. from Stanford University in 1932. His Ph.D. in psychology came from Yale in 1935. During the next year, he undertook postdoctoral study in psychoanalysis at the Vienna Institute of Psychoanalysis, returning in 1936 to the Yale Institute of Human Relations as an instructor. He stayed at Yale through the Hull years, with an absence during the war, moving through the ranks to professor of psychology. In 1966 he joined Rockefeller University as professor of psychology and head of the Laboratory of Physiological Psychology. Miller has received numerous high honors and is widely regarded as one of the foremost psychologists in this country and, indeed, in the world. In addition to serving as president of the American Psychological Association in 1959, he has been elected to membership in the National Academy of Science, an honor accorded to few, and has received the Presidential Medal of Science.

THE FUNDAMENTAL ELEMENTS OF LEARNING

Unlike many behaviorists, Dollard and Miller were both impressed with the ideas underlying psychoanalytic theory. They felt, however, that Freud's formulation was too complex and too vague on many points to be brought directly into the experimental laboratory for empirical testing. As a result, Dollard and Miller applied their knowledge of Hullian theory to a substantial reinterpretation of the basic psychoanalytic position and brought in elements of social anthropology to round out their theory. The reinterpretation begins with a basic point of difference between psychoanalytic and behavioral traditions—the origins of personality. Freudian theory rests, in large part, on the concept that most behavior can be traced to the operation of instincts or primary drives. The Dollard and Miller theory begins instead with the proposition that virtually all human behaviors (such simple reflexes as the eye blink would be exceptions) are learned. The theory thus deals with questions of just how behavior is learned, why one particular type of behavior may be learned rather than another, and how the complexity of human personality and psychopathology can be explained through parsimonious behavioral principles.

In general, the theory suggests that there are only four major factors involved in learning: drive, cue, response, and reinforcement. These factors combine in the formation of habits. While the learning process itself is somewhat complicated by the need to consider such functions as acquisition, extinction, spontaneous recovery, generalization, and discrimination, virtually the entire structure of the complex human personality is built on the basis of simple habits. The habits are learned stimulus-reponse (S-R) associations; therefore the theory is called an *S-R learning* approach. We will first consider the major elements of the learning process and then turn to the application of this process in some of the more complex issues in personality and psychopathology.

MOTIVATIONAL DYNAMICS

In the case of the Dollard-Miller theory, it is most straightforward to first examine the motivational dynamics of personality functioning, after which we will take up the question of structural principles.

The Stimulus as Drive

Any stimulus that is strong enough to activate behavior is a *drive,* and any stimulus can potentially become strong enough to energize behavior. Moreover, the more intense a stimulus becomes, the greater will be its driving function. For example, the faint sound of a hunter's gun miles away may be of little consequence for some-one's behavior, but the same gun fired two feet away is quite likely to have an intense activating effect on that person's behavior. The gun is an example of an external stimulus which can energize or drive behavior. Internal stimuli can also become strong enough to motivate behavior. In fact, certain internal conditions produce stimuli which commonly motivate behavior. These special stimuli are innate or *primary* drives in Dollard and Miller's theory; they include hunger, thirst, fatigue, extremes of temperature, sexual arousal, and pain.

We do not often observe extreme forms of the primary drives because society strives to achieve a chronic satiation of these drives and because of social inhibi-tions. We do, however, commonly observe the operation of powerful learned or *secondary* drives. These are strong stimuli that are not present as part of the innate physiological makeup of the individual but rather are learned through interaction wih the environment. Secondary drives are always based on primary drives. The secondary drive, fear, for example, is learned on the basis of the primary drive, pain. More specifically, internal responses that are associated with the internal stimuli of primary drives may become associated with originally neutral cues in the environment. If the association between the neutral cues and the internal responses becomes learned, the cues can then elicit the internal response and hence the asso-ciated internal stimuli, producing a drive condition.

In order to demonstrate that a drive is learned, it must fulfill two criteria: (1) it must occur as a response to cues that can be shown to have previous neutrality; and

(2) it must motivate behavior involved in new learning. An experimental example of the development and functioning of a secondary drive may be helpful. In a classic experiment, Miller and Bugelski (1948) placed rats in a white compartment where they received electrical shock and allowed them to escape to a black compartment where there was no shock. Once the rats had learned to escape from the white compartment, the shock was turned off, and they continued to run through the open door into the black compartment, demonstrating that they had learned to fear the white stimulus. To demonstrate that the fear was a drive and could serve to motivate new learning, Miller closed the door between the two compartments, and the rats had to learn to turn a wheel above the door in order to open it and thus escape. In the final phase of the experiment, the wheel no longer opened the door, and the rat had to learn a bar-pressing response, still with no further shocks. The experiment quite clearly demonstrated both that fear is learned and that it can serve as a drive. A more important conclusion is that the child who experiences pain when touching a hot stove is learning to associate fear with the stove cues, and that fear may motivate later behavior.

The Stimulus As Cue

Stimuli are not restricted to functioning as drives alone. Some stimuli are *cues*. While the drive serves to energize the behavior, it is the cue that directs the behavior, determining what particular response will be made, as well as when and under what circumstances the response will occur. Cues may be simple and absolute, as in the case of the raucous alarm buzzer signaling that another day has begun, or they may be complex patterns of stimuli, as when a specific configuration of musical notes cues the violinist to begin playing. A third possibility is that the cue may be a difference or change in stimulation.

The Response

The third component of the Dollard-Miller model is the behavior that occurs upon the presentation of an appropriate cue in the presence of a relevant drive. T' behavior is called the *response* of the individual. In order to become a respons' particular cue, the behavior must be expressed overtly. In the Miller fear ' ment, wheel-turning is an example of a response.

The occurrence of an initial overt response in a given learning situation mined, in large part, by the *initial hierarchy of responses* which exist b learning takes place. The initial hierarchy is simply the arrangement of order of probability of occurrence which exists before the cue is fir The learning experience which then occurs can rearrange this hierarc' ing certain responses in the hierarchy and not rewarding others. A n responses, called the *resultant hierarchy,* is produced in that w; Miller pointed out that prior to the first learning experience releva' set of cues, there may be an inherent or *innate hierarchy* that w learning experience has taken place, constitute the initial hierarchy. As an example, the preverbal infant faced with a meal of spinach may find it easier to throw the food on the floor than to verbalize that it is not wanted. If the dominant "throwing" response is blocked, the child's next response may be crying.

Reinforcement

It is in the concept of reinforcement that we see the hedonistic quality of the S-R theories. *A reinforcer is any object or event that serves to increase the probability or strength of the tendency for a response to be repeated.* In the Dollard-Miller theory, a reinforcer must reduce a drive in order to be rewarding; *drive reduction* is both the necessary and sufficient condition for reinforcement to occur in this theory. Reinforcement may involve the satiation of a deprivation-induced drive, as when food serves as a reinforcer for the hungry rat, or involve the reduction or termination of painful stimulation, as when the rat presses a bar to turn off a shock. Although both these examples involve primary drives, reinforcement can also come through the reduction of secondary drives. In general, reinforcing a response increases the probability of its future occurrence, failing to reinforce a learned response reduces its probability of future occurrence.

It may be noted that the drive-reduction model employed by Dollard and Miller is quite similar to the tension-reduction model of Freudian theory. Freud specified that instincts (drives) are either somatic conditions or psychological wishes that strive to be reduced or satisfied by obtaining some particular object from the environment. Recognition of this essential and basic similarity between the Freudian and Hullian models clarifies the rationale behind Dollard and Miller's attempt to reinterpret the Freudian model in terms of Hullian theory.

Despite the obvious commitment of the Dollard-Miller model to a strong drive reduction hypothesis, Miller has since gone on record as suggesting that drive reduction is probably not the final answer to the question of how learning occurs. In a more recent paper (Miller 1963) he has suggested that a number of possible alternatives to drive reduction deserve further exploration, and he has added to the hypotheses of others a proposal of his own for a viable alternative. He first noted that the level of activity or vigor of a response often dramatically increases after the first correct response has been made. For example, in the fear experiment, after the shock has been turned off and the door between black and white chambers closed, the rat may attempt a number of responses before finally rotating the wheel and escaping from the white chamber. Immediately thereafter the rat greatly increases the vigor of its activity, rotating the wheel furiously. Miller noted that this kind of observation may suggest the presence of an activating or "go" mechanism in the brain which is triggered by the sudden relief from pain (or fear). The go mechanism would serve to produce an increase in the level of activity in neural circuits that have been firing, and it may be this increase in neural activity, rather than a reduction in drive level, that reinforces the response.

STRUCTURAL PRINCIPLES

In this theory learning occurs in the form of connections or associations between stimuli and responses. The learned association is termed a *habit*. A habit is learned when a neutral cue is presented (usually repeatedly) in the presence of a relevant drive, and a response made by the individual leads to drive reduction and hence to reinforcement. An example of habit formation can be seen in the fear experiment. The initially neutral cue is the color of the box, the drive is shock-induced pain (or later fear), the response is running out of the white box into the black box (and later wheel-turning), and the reinforcement comes through the reduction of the pain or fear drive following the response. After a number of trials the rat learned the habit involving the connection between the white cue stimulus and the running response, which had been repeatedly reinforced by the reduction of the pain drive. Similarly, in the later phase of this experiment the wheel-turning response to the white cue stimulus was learned because it reduced the secondary fear drive.

The concept of habit, which pulls together the elements of the Dollard-Miller model, represents an integrated conceptualization of how learning takes place. Its importance however, goes far beyond this integration in that the habit concept is basic to the structure of the human personality. More specifically, the adult personality is seen as consisting of a complex structure of habits, relatively simple stimulus-response associations energized by drives and maintained by reinforcers. Most habits important to personality structure involve secondary drives, and many are relatively complex habits involving verbal stimuli. They are still habits, however, and, as a result, the Dollard-Miller analysis provides a strikingly simple, if mechanistic, basis for the structure of personality.

The Cue-Producing Response in Higher Mental Processes

It is difficult to talk about thought processes and, more generally, the higher mental processes in terms of simple S-R habits. As a result, Dollard and Miller introduced the concept of the *cue-producing response.* Distinguishing this response from the basic instrumental response, Dollard and Miller pointed out that the latter is a relatively simple response to a single cue or cue pattern and has some immediate effect on the environment. The wheel-turning response of the rat to the white box stimulus in the experiment discussed above is an example. The cue-producing response, by comparison, has as its principal function the production of a cue that will form part of the stimulus pattern eliciting a further response.

Basically, the cue-producing response, also known as a *mediating response,* is a labeling response. The label attached to a particular stimulus object associates that object with a particular class of objects that have specific responses previously associated with them. For example, labeling a particular situation as *pleasant* produces cues which cause the individual to respond in accordance with the idea of pleasantness. Thus, the person may tend to approach the pleasant situation rather than avoid it, may experience a positive effect, and may tend to relax the skeletal musculature. One result of the operation of cue-producing responses is to render various cues *functionally equivalent.* Three different situations, for example, an anticipated date with a member of the opposite sex, the receipt of a large sum of money, and a business success, may all be labeled *pleasant,* thereby leading to many of the same cues and associated responses being given to otherwise quite different stimulus situations.

The importance of the mediation concept in the Dollard-Miller model is considerable. It accounts not only for the functional equivalence of sometimes large masses of stimuli but also for such functions as reasoning, creative thought, and the control or partial control of emotional behavior. Reasoning occurs, in effect, when symbolic, cue-producing responses replace overt behaviors. Looking at a picture of a particular object may produce the verbal label *tree.* The individual can then think about other types of trees without actually having to see pictures of these trees. As another example, a college student may receive a call from his roommate asking where a particular book is located. The student may walk across the campus to point out to the roommate that the book is near the right end of the top shelf of the bookcase but will probably take the walk symbolically instead, by simply scanning his or her memory to recall where the book is located and then describing its location to the roommate. The roommate in turn uses the verbal labels *top shelf* and *right end* to think about the location of the book, and, translating this thought into action, finds it.

PERSONALITY ORIGINS AND DEVELOPMENT

The basic theory outlined above could, with some further elaborations, stand alone as a theory of learned behavior, explaining how human beings respond to the environment and how responses are learned and patterned. Since, however, the intention of the theorists was to deal more specifically with the phenomena of personality functioning, a number of considerations relevant to personality are essential.

The infant, in this theory, is an exceedingly simple creature, is capable of very little behavior, and, in fact, has only those capacities that are a necessary basis for later learning. Two of these innate elements are the *primary drives,* such as hunger, thirst and sex, and *innate response hierarchies,* which are basically sets of rank ordered responses to particular classes of stimuli. Both of these concepts have been discussed above. The third element is the *specific reflexes,* such as the eye blink, which require no learning. Beyond these minimal inherited elements, personality is developed through learning.

The Basic Learning Process

The process of personality development is straightforward. Beginning with only the primary drives, innate response hierarchies and reflexes, the infant starts to interact with the environment. Primary drives occur repeatedly and must in some way be satisfied. While some satisfaction may be provided with no action on the part of the child, as when the mother anticipates the infant's hunger and feeds it on schedule, instances arise when the infant's needs are not immediately met. The child may become hungry ahead of schedule, wet diapers may create discomfort, or fatigue may activate the powerful sleep drive when the child cannot readily go to sleep. On the basis of these and similar experiences, the child begins to engage in instrumental behavior. He or she may, for example, cry when hungry, wet, or tired and will later learn to respond to the stimuli associated with these conditions by using more selective and discriminated behaviors. Still later the child will learn verbal responses, such as asking for the bottle, in order to satisfy drives.

As the learning experience continues, the child will begin to learn significant social responses involved in interactions with parents, siblings, and, eventually, peers. The child will gradually correct initial errors in responding and learn more appropriate and more selective responses to various classes of cues. Throughout this learning process, the child will develop a series of increasingly complex secondary drives, such as fear, and associate these drives with a variety of cues and responses. In addition, he or she will modify many of the innate response hierarchies and create new initial and resultant hierarchies of response to a variety of cue classes to which the child is exposed. Through these basically simple learning processes, the personality is developed.

Helplessness and Conflict

Our discussion of the learning process should not be taken to imply that personality development is an entirely smooth, pleasant process. The infant is essentially helpless, and throughout early life the child is heavily dependent on parents and others around him or her for the satisfaction of primary and secondary drives, for the necessary attention to social and emotional development, and as a consequence, for personality development. Helplessness, however, can lead to severe conflict, since the child exists and functions largely at the mercy of others. Dollard and Miller have likened childhood to the adult experience with combat situations in wartime. The child is unfamiliar with the complexities of interacting with the environment and largely incapable of understanding either the physical or the emotional milieu in which he or she exists. As a result there are frequently experiences of extreme helplessness, fear, confusion, and fantasy. In Dollard and Miller's words, "Infancy, indeed, may be viewed as a period of transitory psychosis" (1950, p. 130).

Critical Training Situations

The helplessness and confusion of infancy and early childhood bring the child into many situations of severe conflict in which needs may go unsatisfied, frustration may be produced, and one traumatic experience may pile upon another. Dollard and Miller have identified four *critical training situations* which occur during early childhood. Each of these situations is seen as contributing significant early learning experiences relevant to the child's attitudes, later learning abilities and social skills, and also as potentially involving major *conflicts* for the child. These conflicts are largely unconscious and may serve as the basis for neurotic or other emotionally disturbed behavior in later life.

The first developmental stage or critical training experience is the *feeding situation*. This situation involves, of course, the periodic satisfaction of a major primary drive and also brings the child into close contact with the mother or some other person. The learning experience which the child undergoes in conjunction with feeding can lead to much positive and useful learning as a basis for the later development of desirable behaviors. For example, the child's initial social experiences in the feeding situation may be a partial basis for the development of sociability. Similarly, the child may experience love and begin to learn not only how to recognize that emotion in others but also how to experience it himself or herself. On the other hand, mishandling of the feeding situation by the parent can lead to difficulty. The child who is overfed when not hungry may be pushed toward a lack of adequate social development, since the food rewards are not presented in the presence of a relevant drive. Punishment for crying when hungry may lead to a severe hunger-anxiety conflict. The child who is not fed when hungry but rather allowed to cry for an extended period of time may learn to fear being alone, and this fear can become a powerful one if the experience is frequent. The fact that the conflicts involving these early feeding experiences occur before the infant is verbal means that they will be unlabeled. Since some form of verbal labeling is required for consciousness or awareness to continue, the conflicts of infancy will be unconscious and return in Freudian fashion to become involved in the development of abnormal behavior later in life.

The remaining three critical learning situations are cleanliness training, sex training, and anger-aggression training. *Cleanliness training* is required absolutely by the society and thus by the parents, yet is an exceedingly complex area of learning for the child. The child has earlier learned more or less complete freedom to urinate and defecate at will. With the coming of cleanliness training, it must learn to overcome this early tendency and form a complex association of the appropriate urethral responses with a very specific pattern of cues. Moreover, much of the cleanliness training experience must be undergone without the aid of many verbal cues, since the child is largely preverbal at this time. As with the early feeding situation, both important learning and important conflicts can occur in connection with cleanliness training. A particularly important element of the *sex training* situation is that the child, who has previously learned that reinforcements often come from his mother, turns to her expecting sexual rewards as well. The Freudian Oedipal drama is thus played out but with much of the maturational physiology of Freud replaced by learning in Dollard and Miller. Finally, the child must learn to experience and deal with *anger and aggression*. The fact that parents often resent and punish the child's periodic anger may lead to a fear of becoming angry and hence to an anger-anxiety conflict, which, like the feeding conflict described above, may become an unconscious basis for later behavior problems.

Throughout these critical training situations the conflicts which occur are *con-*

flicts between pairs of drives. In some cases the conflict is between primary drives, as in conflicts between hunger and pain in the feeding situation. In other cases the conflict occurs between one primary drive and one powerful learned drive, as in the case of sex-anxiety conflict, or between two learned drives, as in the case of anger-anxiety. The important point is that these learned conflicts, which are largely unconscious, can be the basis for later abnormal behavior.

Repression, the Unconscious, and Conflict

As we have seen, according to Dollard and Miller, the conflicts developed in the course of the critical learning situations are often unconscious. Like Freud, they hypothesized that unconscious ideas, experiences, and processes greatly influence human behavior, although they give less weight to the unconscious than Freud did.

Any behavior determinant is unconscious if it does not have an appropriate verbal label attached to it, since labels provide the cue-producing responses necessary for conscious thought processes. There are three major ways in which experiences may become unlabeled and hence unconscious. First, there are many experiences in early childhood that occur preverbally or when a child has only minimal verbal skills and which are, therefore, not adequately labeled. As was noted above, this is why the conflicts learned in the critical training situations are largely unconscious. Second, the failure to provide verbal labels also occurs later in life when certain kinds of skills, such as driving a car or playing tennis, are learned. Such skills are difficult to learn, in part because verbal labels for the finer details are often not provided. A third and more important source of unconscious materials occurs when an individual has a more or less complete set of verbal labels for an experience and "loses" these labels over a period of time. The process by which this loss takes place is termed *repression,* and it occurs most importantly in the presence of *anxiety.* To understand repression, it must be recalled that anxiety or fear is a learned drive and that the individual strives to reduce any drive. As a result, a person who feels anxious when thinking about a particular experience will strive to reduce the anxiety; when not thinking about the anxiety-arousing experience, the individual does not feel anxious. A response of *not thinking about* the event in question can, therefore, be considered drive reducing and reinforcing. Like any other response that leads to reinforcement, the not-thinking response will be learned through reinforced repetition. By way of example, thoughts of death may arouse anxiety and, therefore, be subject to mild repression, causing an individual to avoid planning adequately for this particular event. Similarly, the college student, anxious about examinations, may tend to selectively forget exam dates, while having no difficulty with other dates. More powerful repressions, often of conflicts, serve as the bases for neurosis.

The importance of consciousness should not be lost in a discussion of the unconscious. In fact, consciousness, defined as involving verbally labeled events and experiences, has been a central area of concern for Dollard and Miller. Cue-producing, including verbal, responses form the basis for rational thought and planning functions and are important in many areas of social training, such as training in the control and display of aggressive behavior learned largely through the exchange of verbal labels.

CONFLICT AND NEUROSIS

As in Freudian theory, the basic elements of neurosis in the Dollard-Miller model are anxiety and conflict. To Dollard and Miller neurosis involves a combination of misery, selective stupidity, and symptoms. These common terms are used in an effort to avoid being vague about the nature of neurosis. *Misery* refers to the prolonged and intense suffering the neurotic undergoes in day-to-day life. This misery arises from a variety of learned, neurotic habits and may take many forms, including phobic ideas, sleeplessness, sexual inhibitions, headaches, irritability, and restlessness. The underlying basis for the misery is conflict, usually a conflict between two or more powerful unconscious drives. The reference to *stupidity* means that the neurotic is unable to function effectively in those specific areas of life directly affected by the neurotic conflict. The appearance of stupidity is caused by the individual's strongly repressing the powerful conflicting drives, thus leaving these drives and the resulting conflict without labels. The result is that the higher mental processes, which depend on cue-producing responses, cannot function in the area of the neurotic conflict, thus making logical, rational behavior in this area difficult or impossible. The *symptoms* of the neurotic are learned responses that reduce anxiety. The symptoms, including a wide variety of compulsions, avoidance behaviors, phobias, rationalizations, and psychosomatic conditions, such as ulcers, do not resolve the basic conflict on which the neurosis rests. They provide only temporary relief from the conflict and resulting anxiety which the neurotic otherwise experiences.

A Model for Conflict

Freud had argued that neurosis is basically due to a severe conflict between the id and the ego. The clash between these two powerful forces of the personality is asssociated with very high levels of anxiety; symptoms, which are seen as overt expressions of repressed id impulses, can result from the conflict. While they did not invoke concepts of id and ego, Dollard and Miller agreed with Freud that conflict is a central element in both normal and neurotic behavior and serves as the basis for neurosis. They borrowed a basic idea from Lewin (1935) and used it to generate a model in which the development, expression, and resolution of conflict might be understood. The model is basically the work of Miller (1944) but was applied and extended in later work (Dollard and Miller 1950; Miller 1959). It assumes four basic types of conflict. In the *approach-approach* conflict the individual is faced with two positive or desirable goals and must decide between them.

The person deciding whether to buy a red or green car is an example. Miller has not, however, considered the approach-approach situation to be a true conflict. In the *approach-avoidance* conflict the same goal has both positive and negative qualities. An example is a woman deciding whether or not to marry a particular man who may seem to have both desirable and undesirable qualities in his makeup. In the third conflict, the *avoidance-avoidance* conflict, a person is faced with the necessity for approaching one of two goals, both of which are undesirable. A patient deciding between two operations, each of which has some potentially undesirable side effects, is an example. Finally, in *double approach-avoidance* conflict an individual must decide between two goals, each of which has both positive and negative qualities. A woman deciding between a handsome but stingy man and a less handsome but more generous man (or a man similarly deciding between two women) could be such a conflict.

The entire conflict model rests on four basic assumptions: (1) the tendency to approach a goal, termed a *gradient of approach,* grows stronger as the individual nears the goal; (2) the tendency to avoid a goal, termed the *gradient of avoidance,* grows stronger as the individual nears the goal; (3) the avoidance gradient is steeper than the approach gradient (that is, the strength of avoidance increases more rapidly as the individual gets closer to the goal); and (4) the strength of the drives underlying the approach and avoidance tendencies determines the strength of the tendencies. Thus, an increase in drive strength increases the height of both approach and avoidance gradients. Even without delving into the technical details of the Miller conflict model, it can be seen that this approach provides a relatively straightforward, testable basis for predicting the effect of conflict on the individual. The ability to predict and understand the effects of such conflicts is important because of role of conflict in neurosis.

Considerable research has been done to test the Miller model, and most empirical evidence is supportive. Such support has come both from animal studies (Brown 1942, 1948; Bugelski and Miller 1938; Kaufman and Miller 1949) and work with humans (Fracher and Blick 1973; Epstein and Smith 1967; Smith and Epstein 1967; Smith and Gehl 1974).

TREATMENT

Dollard and Miller outlined an approach to psychotherapy that is entirely consistent with their proposal that neurosis is basically a set of learned behaviors subject to the usual laws of learning. Just as neurosis involves a process of learning, psychotherapy involves a process of relearning. In detailing the suggested method of psychotherapy, Dollard and Miller again relied on the original psychoanalytic formulations, translating these into the language of learning theory and providing explanations of psychoanalytic treatment phenomena in learning theory terms. Basically, the psychotherapist is seen as a teacher. He or she strives to employ such learning processes as extinction, counterconditioning, and discrimination learning in order to remove repressions, improve the patient's ability to label important aspects of the environment, and more generally to return to the patient a larger proportion of his or her higher mental processes. Counterconditioning, for example, involves the substitution of a new, desirable response that is incompatible with an existing, undesirable response. Thus, the patient may be taught to relax (a relaxation response) and may then learn to substitute relaxation for anxiety.

THE THEORY IN EMPIRICAL CONTEXT

Miller has been involved in a variety of research over the course of his career. While much of this research has been relevant to the personality theory, we will necessarily be selective and note only some of the major empirical efforts that Miller has undertaken.

Drive Reduction

The drive reduction hypothesis, stated in the original Dollard-Miller theory and in Hullian theory, has been more or less constantly a focus of empirical study and has been surrounded by apparently contradictory findings concerning its efficacy. A study by Sheffield and Roby (1950) showed that a nonnutritive substance, saccharine, could serve as a reinforcement for the learning of a new response. Since an actual reduction of the hunger drive would require a nutritive substance, they concluded that drive reduction is not necessary for learning to occur. Miller then conducted a series of studies (Berkun, Kessen, and Miller 1952; Miller 1957; Miller and Kessen 1952) which demonstrated that feeding saccharine to a hungry laboratory animal reduced the animal's subsequent consumption of food. Moreover, Miller found that food taken by mouth is a stronger drive reducer than food injected directly into the stomach through a fistula. While Miller's results in these and other studies tend to support drive reduction, he has suggested that the hypothesis probably has less than a 50 percent chance of ultimately being correct (Miller 1959) and, therefore, has subsequently formulated the alternative go mechanism hypothesis discussed earlier.

Central Stimulation

Miller's concern with drive reduction led him to begin experiments involving brain stimulation and the role of the brain in motivation and learning. Miller's presidential address to the Division of Experimental Psychology of the American Psychological Association in 1953 reported initial work, published the next year (Delgado, Roberts and Miller 1954), showing that the stimulation of particular areas in the brain could lead to learning. Specifically, Miller and his colleagues stimulated the brains of experimental cats with minute electrical currents. On the basis of this stimulation, the cats learned to escape from one compartment to the other of a two-compartment box when the brain stimulation was given in the first compartment only. This and other results suggested that an emotional response resembling fear was being conditioned through brain stimulation and that the brain area being stimulated (the thalamus) was involved in the response. The same year that Miller's work was published, Olds and Milner (1954) reported that electrical stimulation in other parts of the brain would reinforce a bar pressing response in rats. The experimental situation was such that the rats were in no way deprived of food, water, or other substances but were able to self-administer electrical currents to the brain by depressing the experimental bar. Rats not only bar pressed to obtain the brain stimulation but did so at exceedingly high rates, later reported to be as high as seven thousand responses per hour (Olds 1958). Olds and Milner's study suggested that they had located primary reward centers in the brain.

The results of the brain stimulation studies of Olds, Miller, and others have been used to suggest that the drive reduction hypothesis may be inadequate. However, the cumulative results of the many brain stimulation studies done since the early ones do not definitively either support or refute the drive reduction hypothesis.

Conflict, Displacement, and Psychotherapy

The conflict model presented above has been subjected to a considerable amount of research, most of which has been supportive. Related to conflict in the Miller treatment is the concept of displacement, which involves, as in psychoanalytic theory, the substitution of a new object of a drive when the original object is no longer available. Miller has suggested that the displacement concept can be explained through learning theory in terms of stimulus generalization. Elaborating on this point, Miller (1944, 1959) developed a displacement model closely paralleling his conflict model. The first study done to test the displacement model (Miller and Bugelski 1948) clarifies Miller's view of displacement and provides a relevant experimental example. Before and after being forced to miss a desirable social activity, white boys at a summer camp completed questionnaires concerned with attitudes toward Japanese and Mexican people. It was found that the attitudes toward these minority groups were significantly more negative when the completion of questionnaires followed the frustration of missing the social activity. This response was interpreted as a displacement toward the minority groups of the hostility generated by the investigators in keeping the boys from the social activity. Additional studies have tested various assumptions of the model (Miller and Kraeling 1952; Murray and Miller 1952).

Learning of Visceral Responses

Psychosomatic symptoms range from the sweating palms of a college student during a difficult examination to the ulcers of the harried business executive and are basically physiological effects of psychological stress involving high states of drive.

Dollard and Miller (1950) proposed that these physiological effects are to some extent innate and to some extent classically conditioned responses to high drive. The restriction to classical conditioning considerably limits learning interpretations of psychosomatic disorders. As a result, Miller (1969, 1972) has since revised his theory of psychosomatic symptomatology to suggest that perhaps operant conditioning is significantly involved in the development of many psychosomatic symptoms. This theory is contrary to the earlier observations of Skinner (1938) and others that the visceral organs (like the heart and kidneys) cannot be operantly (instrumentally) conditioned because they are not under voluntary control. Miller (1969) conducted an interesting series of studies showing that it is possible to condition heart rate, blood pressure, kidney function, and other visceral processes operantly. Later research (Miller 1972), however, has been unsuccessful in replicating the early results. Research by many workers in the biofeedback field has shown that it is possible to produce some degree of self-control of certain visceral functions, but whether "true," direct operant conditioning of the involved organs is taking place is still open to question.

EVALUATION

It is clear that Dollard and Miller have developed a viable approach to personality which has some virtues among the personality theories but which has also been subjected to criticism. We will summarize here some of the major strengths and weaknesses of this theory, noting that some of these same points will apply to the learning theories discussed in the next two chapters.

Some Important Strengths

As the first theorists to provide a major application of learning principles to the understanding of human personality and psychotherapy, Dollard and Miller have frequently been lauded for their approach on several major points.

Clarity of Concepts. Some personality theories seem to become bogged down in a quagmire of vague constructs and unclear postulates. Dollard and Miller, on the other hand, have provided a clear, concise explication of their major theoretical constructs and postulates. Most concepts are lucidly and carefully defined in the theory, and even the relationships among constructs and postulates have been specified explicitly.

A Scientific Approach. The approach of learning theorists has generally been scientific. The empirical emphasis is apparent from the research activities of the theorists, particularly of Miller. Concepts developed in the theory, such as conflict and displacement, have been extensively researched in the experimental laboratory, both by the theorists and by others.

Personality Development and Change. Most personality theorists have dealt, in one way or another, with the development of personality from early infancy through adulthood, and some have dealt with the phenomenon of change in personality. Many treatments have been on the level of relatively broad, ambiguous theoretical constructs, however, and have failed to deal with the detailed nature of the process by which the human personality forms and changes. Examples can be seen in the neoanalytic theories of Adler, Horney, and Sullivan. These theorists rely on the assumption that the personality is largely a product of some social learning process, but all chose to leave the learning process vague and undetailed. Dollard and Miller provide a clear theoretical understanding of how personality development takes place through learning and through the development of habit structures and of how learning processes can also account for changes in the personality.

Difficulties and Criticisms

The Dollard and Miller treatment has been subjected to a number of criticisms over the years. As often happens, some of the major criticisms of the theory arise from precisely the same areas as its positive points. The strengths of the theory are also, from other viewpoints, its weaknesses.

Simplicity and Superficiality. The clear and straightforward use of a small number of concepts has connoted to some critics the formulation of an utterly simplistic theory, which deals in great detail with relatively minor instances of behavior and is too superficial to account for most human acts. This criticism actually has several aspects. First, the behaviors dealt with by the theory are too molecular. Such small units of behavior as stimuli, responses, and habits may be adequate for understanding animal behavior but are inadequate to the task of understanding complex human behavior. A second closely related point is that the research conducted by the theorists and their colleagues has focused on simple behaviors, often in animals, making extrapolation to complex human behavior difficult and dangerous. Third, the nature of the research conducted in connection with the approach has tended to tie the theory to a laboratory setting. It is difficult to study or predict behavior outside the tightly controlled experimental conditions of the laboratory. In particular, the theory has been taken to task for its failure to deal adequately with the appearance of novel responses which have no apparent S-R learning history.

Inadequacy of Structural and Organizational Concepts. Where is the personality in a learning theory of personality? The critical point has been made that the high degree of simplicity with which learning theory explains personality development and change is achieved at the expense of any real consideration of the structure and organization of the personality. While personality process is carefully detailed, personality content is not. The concept of habit does serve a structural function for Dollard and Miller, but it does not provide the clear specification of structure and organization of personality seen in such concepts as the id, ego, and superego of Freud, the personal and collective unconscious of Jung, or the self-concept and organism of Rogers.

Inadequacy of Biological Treatment. In the process of emphasizing the learned nature of behavior and personality, learning theory has perhaps paid too little attention to the biological organism. While primary drives and reflexes are a part of the Dollard and Miller theory, these minimal biological bases for behavior may not consitute an adequate treatment of physiological factors. While the learning theorist certainly can claim a vast array of research demonstrating the relevance of learning to the formation of personality and to the expression of a wide range of behaviors, the biologist has also been able to demonstrate the applicability of various physiological factors to the determination of specific behaviors. Particularly interesting is recent work in the field of behavior genetics, where an increasingly convincing collection of results suggests substantial contributions of genetic factors to both normal and abnormal personality functioning. The greatest volume of research has been concerned with schizophrenia, clearly pointing to a strong genetic factor in the etiology of, at least, many cases of schizophrenia. The relevant litera-ture is summarized by Slater and Cowie (1971) and others. Considerably less research has been done on possible genetic factors in "normal" personality traits. Examples include a study of identical and fraternal twins in which extroversion was found to be substantially influenced by genetic inheritance (Shields 1962) and a study demonstrating varied degrees of hereditary influence on several personality traits (Dworkin, Burke, and Maher 1976). A number of reviews of literature rele-vant to genetic influence on personality variables are available (Vandenberg 1969; Shields 1971).

REFERENCES

Berkun, M. M., Kessen, M. L., & Miller, N. E. Hunger reducing effects of food by stomach fistula vs. food by mouth measured by a consummatory response. *Journal of Comparative and Physiological Psychology*, 1952, *45*, 550-554.

Brown, J. S. The generalization of approach responses as a function of stimulus intensity and strength of motivation. *Journal of Comparative Psychology*, 1942, *33*, 209-226.

Brown J. S. Gradients of approach and avoidance responses and their relation to level of motivation. *Journal of Comparative and Physiological Psychology*, 1948, *41*, 450-465.

Bugleski, R., & Miller, M. E. A spatial gradient in the strength of avoidance re-sponses. *Journal of Experimental Psychology*, 1938, *23*, 494-505.

Chomsky, N. Review of Skinner's verbal behavior. *Language*, 1959, *35*, 26-58.

Chomsky, N. The case against B. F. Skinner, *New York Review of Books*, 1971 December, 18-24.

Delgado, J. M. R., Roberts, W., & Miller, N. E. Learning motivated by electrical stimulation of the brain. *American Journal of Physiology*, 1954, *179*, 587-593.

Dollard, J., & Miller, M. E. *Personality and psychotherapy: An analysis in terms of learning, thinking and culture.* New York: McGraw-Hill, 1950.

Dworkin, R. H., Burke, B. W., Maher, B. A., & Gottesman, I. A longitudinal study of the genetics of personality. *Journal of Personality and Social Psychology,* 1976, *34,* 510-518.

Epstein, S., & Smith, B. D. Modes and adequacy of resolution of three basic types of cognitive motor conflict. *Journal of Experimental Psychology,* 1967, *74,* 264-271.

Fracher, J. C., & Blick, K. A. Speed of motor conflict resolution as related to type of conflict and manifest anxiety. *Journal of Psychology,* 1973, *83,* 277-285.

Hull, C. L. *Principles of behavior.* New York: Appleton-Century-Crofts, 1943.

Kaufman, E. L., & Miller, N. E. Effect of number of reinforcements on strength of approach in an approach-avoidance conflict. *Journal of Comparative and Physiological Psychology,* 1949, *42,* 65-74.

Lewin, K. *A dynamic theory of personality: Selected papers.* New York: McGraw-Hill, 1935.

Miller, N. E. Experimental studies of conflict. In J. McV. Hunt (Ed.), *Personality and the behavior disorders* (Vol. 1). New York: Ronald Press, 1944. (Pp. 431-465.)

Miller, N. E. Experiments on motivation: Studies combining psychological, physiological and pharmacological techniques. *Science,* 1957, *126,* 1271-1278.

Miller, N. E. Liberalization of basic S-R concepts: Extensions to conflict behavior, motivation and social learning. In S. Koch (Ed.), *Psychology: A study of a science* (Vol. 2). New York: McGraw-Hill, 1959. (Pp 196-292.)

Miller, N. E. Some reflections on the law of effect produce a new alternative to drive reduction. In M. Jones (Ed.), *Nebraska Symposium on Motivation,* 1963, 65-112.

Miller, N. E. Learning of visceral and glandular responses. *Science,* 1969, *163,* 434-445.

Miller, N. E. *Comments at the symposium: Issues in bio-feedback and operant control of physiological processes.* Presented at the annual meeting of the Society for Psychophysiological Research, Boston, Nov. 9-12, 1972.

Miller, N. E., & Bugelski, R. Minor studies in aggression, II: The influence of frustrations imposed by the in-group on attitudes expressed toward the out-groups. *Journal of Psychology,* 1948, *25,* 437-442.

Miller, N. E., & Kessen, M. L. Reward effects of food vs. stomach fistula compared to those of food vs. mouth. *Journal of Comparative and Physiological Psychology.* 1952, *45,* 555-564.

Miller, N. E., & Kraeling, D. Displacement: Greater generalization of approach than avoidance in a generalized approach-avoidance conflict. *Journal of Experimental Psychology,* 1952, *43,* 217-221.

Miller, N. E., & Murray, E. J. Displacement and conflict; learnable drive as a basis for the steeper gradient of avoidance than of approach. *Journal of Experimental Psychology,* 1952, *43,* 227-231.

Murray, E. J. & Burkun, M. M. Displacement as a function of conflict. *Journal of Abnormal and Social Psychology*, 1955, *51*, 47–56.

Murray, E. J., & Miller, N. E. Displacement: Steeper gradient of generalization of avoidance than of approach with age of habit control. *Journal of Experimental Psychology*, 1952, *43*, 222–226.

Olds, J. Self-stimulation of the brain. *Science*, 1958, *127*, 315–324.

Olds, J., & Milner, P. Positive reinforcements produced by electrical stimulation of the septal area and other regions of the rat brain. *Journal of Comparative and Physiological Psychology*, 1954, *47*, 419–427.

Sheffield, F. D., & Roby, T. B. Reward value of a non-nutritive sweet taste. *Journal of Comparative and Physiological Psychology*, 1950-, *43*, 471–481.

Shields, J. *Monzygotic twins brought up apart and brought up together*. Glendon: Oxford University Press, 1962.

Shields, J. Heredity and psychological abnormality. In H. J. Eysenck (Ed.), *Handbook of Abnormal Psychology*. London: Pitman, 1971.

Skinner, B. F. *The behavior of organisms: An experimental analyses*. Englewood Cliffs, N.J.: Prentice-Hall, 1966. (First published, 1938.)

Slater, E., & Cowie, V. *The genetics of mental disorders*. London: Oxford University Press, 1971.

Smith, B. D., & Gehl, L. Multiple-exposure effects on resolutions of four basic conflict types. *Journal of Experimental Psychology*, 1974, *102*, 50–55.

Vandenberg, F. G. Human behavior genetics: Present status and suggestions for future research. *Merrill-Palmer Quarterly Behavior and Development*, 1969, *15*, 121–154.

A Behavioral Approach:

B. F. Skinner

9

Burrhus F. Skinner, without doubt one of the most influential psychologists in the world today, might be described as a reinforcement theorist. However, he himself has declined the application of the term *S-R* to his position and has, until recently, denied that it is a theory at all. We might, then, be more accurate in describing Skinner's position as a strongly behavioristic, reinforcement approach, which emphasizes the most direct possible study of behavior, minimizes the use of constructs, and relies upon operant, as opposed to classical, conditioning as the principal basis for the learning and modification of behavior. It might be well to add that although Skinner has used the terms *stimulus, response,* and *reinforcement* and emphasized the role of learning in the control of behavior, his position is substantially different from those of Hull and Dollard and Miller.

BIOGRAPHICAL SKETCH

Born in 1904, Skinner was raised in what he later described as a warm, stable home in Susquehanna, Pennsylvania. He entered Hamilton College with an interest in writing and was an English literature major, finding later that he was not cut out for a career as a writer. After spending some time in Greenwich Village in New York City and in Europe, Skinner decided to pursue graduate studies in psychology at Harvard University. There he took course work under E. G. Boring and Henry Murray, among others, receiving his Ph.D. degree in 1931 and remaining at Harvard to work with the biologist W. J. Crozier for five years beyond the doctorate. He embarked upon an academic career at the University of Minnesota in 1936 and in 1938 published his first and most important work, *The Behavior of Organisms*. In 1945 Skinner left Minnesota to become chairman of the Department of Psychology at Indiana University. In 1948 he returned to Harvard, where he has remained. It was in that same year that he published an important novel, *Walden II*, which described a utopian society based on the principles of Skinner's operant approach.

His reputation established, other important work followed, such as the publication of *Science and Human Behavior* (1953), the 1954 introduction of teaching machines based on the idea of programmed instruction which Skinner had begun to develop in the 1930s, and the subsequent publication of *Verbal Behavior* (1957), which contains an operant analysis of language. Many of Skinner's most important papers are contained in *Cumulative Record,* published in 1959 and expanded and revised in 1961 and 1972 editions. Two important books are *Contingencies of Reinforcement* (1969), which summarizes the Skinnerian position, and *Beyond Freedom and Dignity* (1971), which is a fascinating and controversial extension of his ideas on human behavior.

A BASICALLY DIFFERENT APPROACH

Most theoretical treatments that either constitute personality theories or can readily be applied to personality rely to some degree on an understanding of the "inner workings" of the person as a basis for explaining that person's behavior and defining his or her personality. Many constructs have been used to describe these inner workings in various theories. Such terms as id, ego, superego, self-concept, unconscious, anxiety, and trait are familiar constructs from psychodynamic, humanistic, and other theoretical orientations. Even such terms as habit, drive (in its usual usage), and cue-producing response are constructs and thus serve to provide inferences about structures and processes within the person that cannot be directly observed. To many theorists, such inferences have seemed essential. If we observe a person who is extremely irritable, is having great difficulty sleeping, finds it necessary to wash his hands at least once each hour, and is generally ineffective in conducting his life, it seems somehow essential to infer that this person is neurotic and is experiencing a high level of anxiety. Both neurosis and anxiety are constructs which carry with them further inferences about the person's inner state of functioning and additional forms of behavior.

Skinner has consistently denied the utility of employing such personality variables as neurosis and anxiety or, for that matter, terms such as *habit,* which appear in other learning theories. Such personality variables are simply verbal labels that have been unnecessarily applied to specific behavior patterns. The inferences that these constructs make concerning the unseen inner states of the person are not essential and, in fact, detract substantially from the conduct of a science of behavior. The focus of many psychologists on trying to understand the inner functioning of the person has actually diverted the field of human behavior (Skinner, 1975). In his approach to and understanding of behavior, Skinner has substituted for constructs and inferences a *functional analysis* of behavior. This approach focuses on determination of lawful cause-effect relationships. Such relationships can be determined by identifying and controlling antecedent effects, such as stimuli, and accurately observing the behavioral consequences. In such a functional analysis there is no need to infer inner states of functioning. The control of the environment affecting the individual and careful observation of the behavior the individual performs should be sufficient to explain the behavior. Thus, when faced with the individual described above as neurotic, the Skinnerian behaviorist would not need the term *neurosis* or its implications but would rather deal with each of the specific forms of behavior involved. For example, if the behavior of hourly hand washing was problematic for the person and needed to be changed, the behaviorist would not have to infer that the behavior was engaged in because it reduced anxiety. Rather, the behaviorist would attack the behavior directly in terms of its antecedents and consequences, leaving out the intervening constructs.

While Skinner has preferred to study specific, observable behavior in terms of its environmental antecedents and consequences, he has not denied the existence and influence of inner physiological processes. In Skinner's words:

> We know something about the chemical and electrical effects of the nervous system and the location of many of its functions, but the events that actually underlie a single instance of behavior—as a pigeon picks up a stick to build a nest, or a child a block to complete a tower, or a scientist a pen to write a paper—are still far out of reach. (Skinner 1975, p. 42)

While physiology may be important, the technological and scientific advances needed to understand it fully can be achieved only in the distant future. Meanwhile, the study of observable behavior and its environmental determinants is to be preferred.

ELEMENTS OF BEHAVIOR ANALYSIS

Respondent and Operant Behavior

Relevant to Skinner's functional analysis of behavior, two classes of responses can be identified. *Respondents* are those responses that are elicited by identifiable stimuli. Such responses may be either unlearned, as in the case of the reflex knee jerk to a blow, or learned, as in the case of a dog salivating to a tone which has previously been paired with meat. Whether learned or unlearned, respondent behaviors are elicited by a stimulus. The second class of responses is known as *operants*. An operant is a response that occurs without reference to a specific, known stimulus. Examples of operants not preceded by specific learning experiences include the occasional bar press by a rat or key peck by a pigeon in an experimental box when reinforcement has not been specifically associated with this response. Reinforcement may be used to increase or decrease the frequency of any given behavior. It can be seen, then, that respondents are elicited, while operants are emitted.

Based on the respondent-operant distinction, two major types of learning have been identified. The first is most appropriately ascribed to the original work of Pavlov (1927) and is usually termed Pavlovian, Type S, or *classical conditioning*. In this form of learning, a previously neutral stimulus is followed by a stimulus which "naturally" or through previous learning elicits a particular response. Repeated pairings of the neutral stimulus, called a *conditioned stimulus* (CS), with the eliciting stimulus, termed an *unconditioned stimulus* (UCS), is likely to result in learning. The Pavlovian dog learned to salivate to the sound of a bell or tone when that sound had repeatedly been followed by the presentation of meat, which naturally elicited the salivation. According to Skinner, a far more influential type of conditioning is *operant* conditioning, also termed *instrumental* or *type R* (for reinforcement) *conditioning*. In this form of learning, the animal or human emits a response without any particular stimulus being present. The response operates on the environment to change it. The probability that the response will be repeated is controlled by events that follow the response, and when such events increase the probability that the response will be repeated, we say that the events are reinforcers. Classic examples are the rat learning through reinforcement to press a bar or the pigeon learning to peck a key in the Skinner box. To take the pigeon training example, the Skinner box is an experimental chamber which typically has located on one wall a translucent disk behind which is found a red light. Just below the disk is a hopper fed by a magazine (dispenser) containing food pellets. While moving about the chamber, the pigeon may happen to peck the key (that is, it emits an operant key-pecking response). This operates the dispenser, giving the pigeon food, which may reinforce the response, thus increasing the frequency of pecking. We will consider shortly some of the complexities of the operant conditioning process.

Validity of the Respondent-Operant Distinction

While it has become traditional to distinguish between classical (respondent) and operant conditioning and to suggest that the two forms of learning are based on different laws or principles, the importance and validity of the distinction is now being seriously questioned. Clark Hull, whose work was referred to earlier, proposed what has been termed a one-factor reinforcement theory in which there is no critical distinction between classical and operant conditioning. This one-factor approach, for many years pushed aside, has recently been restated and extended by Terrace (1973). The basic argument is that the only differences between operant and classical conditioning lie in the method by which the response is initially elicited and the nature of the response as it is recorded. The actual principles of learning and reinforcement underlying the two types of conditioning are identical. This means that the only real difference between classical and operant conditioning is the experimental methodology used. It has been shown that during the course of operant conditioning there is often some evidence for classical conditioning, in that responses elicited by the reinforcer begin to occur in anticipation of the reinforcement. For example, the dog being conditioned to press a bar for food (operant conditioning) may also begin to salivate. Similarly, classical conditioning procedures are often accompanied by the operant conditioning of responses which become associated with the CS. If the operant-classical distinction is further blurred by additional research, this will in no way detract from the Skinnerian position and may, in fact, make the behavioral laws developed in operant research more generally applicable in the classical conditioning situation.

Drive

Skinner has not used the term *drive* in recent years, but his earlier discussion of drives (Skinner 1953) is instructive in understanding how his approach compares with those of others. In his approach a drive is not seen as a strong stimulus or as a physiological condition or, in fact, as any state of the organism at all. Rather, the word *drive* is used simply as a convenient way of labeling a particular set of operations which affect the rate at which organisms respond. Thus, the only meaning of the term "hunger drive" in Skinner's usage is that it distinctly describes a certain set of operations which affects the frequency of occurrence of a particular set of responses. Hunger has no status as an intervening variable or as a drive state, but refers, instead, to the operation of depriving an animal of food for a specified number of hours and reducing body weight to some particular proportion of previous or average weight.

In a similar way, Skinner has employed the term *emotion* only to label a set of responses. The individual who has wet palms, stutters, gulps, averts his eyes, and jumps upon hearing a slight noise may be said to be exhibiting the emotion of fear or anxiety. In the Skinnerian treatment the use of the emotional label is only as a descriptive term to specify the occurrence of these behaviors. An example of the study of emotion within the Skinnerian paradigm is the work on fighting in animals, which has shown, for example, that physical blows or electrical shock can cause animals to engage in indiscriminate fighting behavior, attacking innocent targets in their environment (Azrin, Hake, and Hutchinson 1965). The term *aggression* may be used in this context to label the specific types of behavior engaged in by the animals following delivery of the electrical shock. A further example is the conditioned emotional response (CER), originally studied by Estes and Skinner (1941). In the prototypical CER experiment an animal is taught to press a bar for food or water reinforcement and is then subjected to classically conditioned tone-shock pairing, so that the animal learns to respond to the tone with fear behaviors. The animal is then returned to bar pressing. When the bar-pressing response is well established again, the tone is sounded, frequently resulting in such behavior indicative of fear as crouching, freezing and response termination, or rate reduction. The tone has caused a conditioned emotional response to occur, but again the emphasis is on the operation involved in causing the CER.

REINFORCEMENT

Given the importance of the response and drive in the Skinnerian paradigm, we must still ask how a response is actually acquired or modified in the course of operant conditioning. The only remaining element of the model necessary to accomplish response *acquisition* is *reinforcement*. For Skinner, a reinforcer is any stimulus or event which, when it follows a specific response, increases the future probability of occurrence of that response. Thus, acquisition (that is, increase in probability of the response) occurs when that response is followed by reinforcement. In the pigeon experiment noted above, the animal acquires the key-pecking response when that response is followed by the presentation of an appropriate food or water reinforcer. In general, the *modification* of an existing response occurs in exactly the same way. In fact, what we have called acquisition is really a special case of response modification. *Extinction* is the reduction in probability of a learned response when the reinforcer is withheld.

Primary and Secondary Reinforcement

As in other approaches, a distinction is drawn between primary reinforcers, which are unlearned, and secondary reinforcers, which involve some previous learning. The *primary reinforcer* is, as usual, a stimulus which ordinarily has a direct and known relationship to some drive. Food or water, for example, can act as reinforcers for hungry (food-deprived) or thirsty (water-deprived) animals. If, however, we want to use a light to reinforce a bar-pressing response in water-deprived rats, it would be necessary that the light acquire reinforcing properties. The light can become an acquired reinforcer if the bar press made by a thirsty rat causes the light to come on, followed, a short time later, by the delivery of water from a water dispenser. The light then remains on for a short time after the water is delivered. The light is a *secondary* or *conditioned* reinforcer.

Applied to human personality, the principle of conditioned reinforcement takes on special significance, for it is through this principle that words (verbal stimuli), nonverbal human forms of behavior, and social types of behavior can become reinforcing. The child, who receives only primary reinforcers, such as food, water, and pain, throughout early childhood would acquire only a very limited repertoire of social behaviors, and only with great difficulty. On the other hand, with the availability of conditioned reinforcers in the form of verbal praise and punishment as well as social reinforcers, such as the smile of the adult, the child could acquire numerous behaviors and, hence, personality quite readily.

Positive and Negative Reinforcement

The pigeon pecking in the Skinner box or the child developing a personality may acquire and modify behavior through either of two types of reinforcers, termed *positive reinforcers* and *negative reinforcers.* The types are distinguishable by the specific effects which they have upon responses. An operant response increases in probability when a positive reinforcer is *present* following the response or when a negative reinforcer is *absent* or reduced following the response. Food and water for the pigeon and the mother's smile for the child are examples of positive reinforcers. If the food, water, or smile is applied after the pigeon's key pecking or the child's first clearly spoken word, the effect is to increase the probability of the response. An example of a negative reinforcer is the electric shock often used in aversive conditioning experiments. The Skinner box may be set up in such a way that the pigeon or rat will receive an electric shock until the key is pecked or the bar pressed, at which time the shock terminates. The shock will serve as a reinforcer and the key-peck or bar-press response will be learned with repeated trials. It is the removal of the shock, however, not its introduction, that reinforces the response.

Punishment is not the same as negative reinforcement. Whereas the removal of a negative reinforcer strengthens an escape or avoidance response, punishment is an unpleasant consequence of behavior designed to modify or stop the behavior. One way to clarify this difference further is to note that in negative reinforcement the aversive stimulus occurs *before* the response, while in punishment the aversive stimulus comes *after* the response. Thus, the behavior preceded by the negative reinforcer is likely to increase in frequency, while the behavior followed by punishment is likely to decrease in frequency. As an example of punishment, we may observe that a rat placed in an experimental chamber without specific prior learning experiences tends to move about, exploring the chamber rather than remaining in one place. We could introduce electric shock each time the rat moves, turning off the shock if it remains in one place. The shock is punishment for movement and should stop or significantly reduce the rat's movement behavior.

The distinctions among positive and negative reinforcement and punishment have important implications for the development of human behavior and, therefore, personality. The adult personality is assumed to be a collection of forms of behavior developed through varied *histories of reinforcement* during a person's earlier life. We may thus ask whether reward, negative reinforcement, and punishment in the person's reinforcement history carry different implications for the development of behavior. Skinner has suggested that the development and modification of social behaviors is best accomplished through the use of positive reinforcement. The reason for this is that the positive reinforcer produces learned behavior that is relatively free of negative consequences and often has associated with it positive respondent emotional behaviors, such as pleasure and joy. Punishment, on the other hand, has several problems associated with it: (1) behaviors suppressed by punishment may be replaced by others, since the punishment does not remove the cause of the undesirable behavior; (2) removal of punishment often leads to the recurrence of the suppressed behavior; (3) escape and avoidance behaviors caused by the punishment may themselves become problematic; (4) punishment may be a factor in the development of conditioned emotional responses, such as anxiety and hatred, and such physical, psychosomatic symptoms as asthma or ulceration; and (5) punishment is difficult to administer without also reinforcing the response. For example, a child who is frequently punished but seldom rewarded may find that the best means for gaining the reinforcing attention of parents is to engage in undesirable behaviors. Negative reinforcement treads a middle ground in this analysis. It is essentially similar to punishment in its effect when the response learned through negative reinforcement simply prevents the recurrence of a punishing stimulus, but the effects are more like those of positive reinforcement when the learned response continually serves to remove aversive stimuli.

Skinner (1971) has pointed out that on a broader social level there are various instances of the differential consequences of the various types of reinforcement. For example, criminal behavior is typically treated after it occurs and through the use of punishment by imprisonment. The punishment may temporarily suppress the criminal's behavior by inducing fear, but the removal of punishment by release from prison reduces the fear and may permit the criminal behavior to recur. Skinner has suggested that if criminal behavior must be treated, it would be better treated by rehabilitation involving positive reinforcement. The still better answer, bringing us closer to the idea of a utopian society, however, would be the prevention of crime through systematic, positive reinforcement of noncriminal, socially desirable behavior.

Results of some research suggest the possible need to reconsider the Skinnerian position on the relative ineffectiveness of punishment. Holz and Azrin (1963), for example, compared the traditional methods of reducing the frequency of operant responses. They concluded that punishment may actually be more effective than the other methods they employed. More generally, Azrin and Holz (1968) have concluded that punishment may be very effective under clearly specified circumstances, in which the punishing stimulus is intense, frequent, immediate, and inescapable. Extended periods of punishment must be avoided, and positive reinforcement must not accompany the punishing stimulus. Under these and additional specified conditions they believe that punishment may be as effective as or more effective than other methods for reducing responses. It should be emphasized, however, that a definite answer to the question of differential effects of the various types of reinforcers is not yet available.

Shaping

In operant conditioning the experimenter cannot reinforce a response until the subject emits that response. Thus, the Skinnerian experimenter might have to wait some time for the pigeon to emit the key-pecking response "accidentally," and, similarly, the parent might have to be extremely diligent in waiting for the child to make a correct response so that the reinforcing smile, verbal praise, or candy can be provided.

The problem of awaiting emitted behavior is solved in the operant paradigm by reinforcing a series of ordered behaviors which represent *successive approximations* to the desired behavior. The rat entering a Skinner box may initially be allowed to eat from the food hopper in order to learn its location and function. It may then be selectively reinforced for responses of turning toward the bar, approaching the bar more closely, and finally depressing it.

Shaping also applies to the development of human behaviors. Suppose the mother wants to each her young son to hug her when she picks him up. She can simply wait and be careful to reward the child each time he does hug her. A more rapid procedure, however, would be to initially reward the child for orienting his head and arms toward her as she picks him up, then for touching her shoulders or neck, then for getting at least one arm around her neck, and so on until the hug is accomplished.

Schedules of Reinforcement

In an operant conditioning experiment reinforcement can be given *continuously,* such that the pigeon or rat receives reinforcement each time it makes the response. While continuous reinforcement does occur in the development of human social behaviors, the more usual situation is one of noncontinuous or intermittent reinforcement, where the individual is not reinforced on every occurrence of the correct response. Ferster and Skinner (1957) identified two major bases for intermittent reinforcement. The first is the *ratio schedule,* in which the delivery of reinforcement depends simply upon the number of correct responses emitted by the subject. Instead of delivering a reinforcement for every response, the ratio schedule delivers reinforcement for every third, or fifth, or tenth response, or in some other ratio, depending upon the purpose of the experiment. There are two types of ratio schedule. The first is a *fixed ratio* (FR) schedule, in which reinforcement is consistently delivered in the same ratio of reinforcers to operant responses. A ratio of 1:3, for example, would mean that one reinforcement is delivered for every three responses made by the subject. A schedule designated *FR 20* would simply mean that one reinforcement is given for every twenty emitted responses. The second schedule is the *variable ratio* (VR) schedule, in which the experimenter randomly varies the ratio of reinforcements to responses. The random variation is around some mean (average) ratio and is usually set between certain definite limits. An experimenter might use a VR 120, in which the average number of responses preceding reinforcement would be 120, but the subjects might receive reinforcement after either 90, 100, 110, 120, 130, 140, or 150 responses. Animals on ratio schedules tend to respond at very high rates, often in what Skinnerians call "bursts", presumably because the higher rates of responding lead to more frequent reinforcements.

A second major type of schedule is the *interval schedule,* in which the reinforcement follows a response which occurs after a specified time period has passed. A *fixed interval* (FI) schedule is one in which the designated time lapse is constant from one period of the experiment to the next. The pigeon on an "FI 2" schedule is thus reinforced for the first response which occurs after each two minutes have passed. The typical FI response pattern is described as *scalloped,* referring to the rate of responding, which typically increases to its highest level just prior to the delivery of reinforcement, then drops to zero or near zero, and gradually increases again until the next reinforcement appears. This is, of course, quite different from the high rate burst responding of the ratio schedules. A *variable interval* (VI) schedule, in which a range of randomly varied interval lengths around some average length are used, tends to be characterized by stability rather than scalloping. The VI schedule is widely used, in part because learning on this schedule is extremely resistant to extinction.

While the basic combination of interval and ratio—fixed and variable—produce only four major kinds of schedules, more complex combinations of schedules, probably more closely approximating real life situations, can be used. Many such complications in scheduling have been examined experimentally and typical response patterns determined. Among the most widely used of these more complex schedule techniques is the *multiple* schedule, in which the subject is trained to respond differentially to several different reinforcement schedules. The pigeon thus learns that when a lighted disk is green, reinforcements will be delivered on a variable ratio schedule, while a red light indicates a fixed interval schedule.

Due to the greater complexities of reinforcement scheduling in humans, we can best control and understand human behavior by having knowledge of the history of reinforcement that the person has undergone relevant to particular responses. Most responses of adults will thus not be under the immediately obvious control of present reinforcers but rather will have been developed through particular reinforcement histories that the person has undergone.

Discrimination, Generalization, and Differentiation

Stimuli that differentially indicate situations in which particular behaviors will be reinforced or schedules on which a given behavior will be reinforced are termed *discriminative stimuli.* The child learns for example, that it is acceptable to shout and run when outside with other children but is not when in the house. Behavior thus discriminated by stimuli is said to be under stimulus control. *Stimulus generalization* occurs when a response is exhibited to some degree to a stimulus different from that originally associated with the learning situation. The pigeon that learns a key-pecking response to a red disk may also display that response if the disk coloration is changed to pink. A third phenomenon, *response differentiation,* refers to the use of operant procedures to modify the nature, particularly the intensity, of a given response. Shaping procedures may be used to determine the force with which the pigeon pecks the key or the voice intensity that characterizes normal verbal communication.

Superstitious Behavior

Reinforcement delivered to the key-pecking pigeon or the smiling child may reward not only the desired behavior but also any other responses which happen to occur simultaneously. These additional, accidental responses are said to be reinforced adventitiously and, if they are maintained by continued reinforcement, are termed *superstitious behaviors.* Such behaviors are important both because they often constitute control problems in experimental settings and because human societies reinforce many behaviors adventitiously and may thus unintentionally cause an individual or group to engage in unusual, useless, or even destructive behavior through this process. An example might be a man who wins money on a horse race after using a folded-over bill to place the bet. He may subsequently fold the bills with which he places bets, even though this action bears no causal relationship to winning.

AN OVERVIEW OF THE THEORY

With the basic elements of the Skinnerian approach in hand, we are now in a position to recast the theory as it applies to personality in terms of structural principles, motivational dynamics, and developmental processes.

Structural Principles

What little emphasis there is on structure in the Skinnerian approach focuses on the proposal that there are two major classes of behavior, respondent and operant, and two corresponding learning processes, classical conditioning and operant conditioning. The emphasis, of course, is on operant responses, which may be increased in probability through the application of reinforcement. Skinner has suggested, further, that structure includes the underlying biology of the organism, which is important but which we do not yet have the technology to understand.

Motivational Dynamics

By depriving an animal of food or a human of desired social praise, we may find that the subject will now show a tendency to increase the probability of responses that result in food or praise. The deprivation operation may be termed a *drive*. Similarly, we may use emotion as a motivational label for certain kinds of behavior, so long as it is clear that it is only a label for externally observable responses. While Skinner has preferred not to use even the labels, it should be noted that motivational operations are important in his theory. The rat is not likely, for example, to show an increase in bar pressing to obtain food if it has not been deprived of food.

Origins and Development

The real emphasis in the Skinnerian approach is on the development or acquisition, modification, and extinction of responses. Behaviors can be developed through either classical or operant conditioning, although the latter is considered more important. Any given response may be acquired, modified, and extinguished through the systematic application and withholding of reinforcements. Any acquired response has a reinforcement history, and we can ask whether primary or secondary reinforcers, or both, were involved in the development of the response; whether reinforcers have been positive or negative; and whether or not punishment has been involved. We can also determine whether or not generalization, differentiation, and discrimination have occurred. In addition, we can examine the schedules of reinforcement involved in the acquisition and modification of the behavior. The Skinnerian approach provides us with a detailed analysis of the developmental process and attempts to understand and control behavior largely through that knowledge.

APPLICATIONS TO HUMAN BEHAVIOR

We have seen a number of examples of human behavior that might be developed and modified by operant conditioning procedures. It may, however, be instructive to examine further the more detailed application of operant procedures to particular areas of human behavior relevant to personality, both to better understand the applicability of the Skinnerian theory to personality and to appreciate its ramifications in human behavior.

Social Behavior

Within the operant framework, social behavior is seen as simply any instance of behavior involving interaction among people. Having defined social behavior in this way, Skinner has not needed to develop a special theory to deal with this particular behavioral situation. Social behavior is like any other behavior. It consists of responses reinforced on particular schedules and subject to all the various phenomena of the operant position, including stimulus control, response differentiation, generalization, and extinction. An individual will typically learn during childhood and throughout life a wide variety of apparently complex social behaviors, ranging from relatively simple verbal and nonverbal responses used in communicating with another individual to complex patterns of both individual and group interaction. The precise nature of each of these social behaviors will depend upon the individual's history of reinforcement relevant to that behavior. For example, individuals who attend many parties, interact continually with a substantial number of people whom they describe as friends, and readily strike up conversations with people they do not know might be described by some theorists as having a trait of extraversion. Operant theory would simply suggest that these people have, in the past, been reinforced for interacting with other people in specific ways and particular kinds of situations.

The particular social behaviors in an individual's repertoire and the probability of occurrence of these behaviors will be a function, in part, of the schedules of reinforcement under which the behaviors are learned. Since this is the case, it is interesting to note that the selection of reinforcement schedules is not likely to be random. In fact, it appears that the reinforcement underlying most social behavior is intermittent, that the delivery of reinforcement is more a function of the number of occurrences of the response than of the passage of time (hence, a ratio schedule), and that the ratio of reinforcements to responses is not fixed but varies. Thus, a variable-ratio reinforcement schedule would appear to be predominant. It should be noted, however, that much human behavior is undoubtedly learned on more complex combinations of multiple schedules.

Research has confirmed the relevance of operant reinforcement procedures to the development of social behaviors. For example, Endler (1965) provided reinforcements to different groups of college students for either conforming to a response made by another (a confederate), deviating from that response, or remaining neutral. Subjects reinforced for conforming showed the most conforming responses; those reinforced for deviating showed the least conforming responses.

Awareness of Self

Rogers (1959), Allport (1937), and numerous other theorists have pointed to the individual's conceptualization of his or her own characteristics and, hence, self-awareness as a major aspect of personality functioning and an important determinant of behavior. Skinner has not denied the phenomenon of self-awareness, but, rather than attributing such awareness to introspective observation, he has suggested that the observed self-characteristics are *collateral products* of the individual's genetic and environmental history, with the emphasis on the environmental aspects of the person's history. Such collateral products are seen as facts which may be taken into account in discussing behavior but which have no independent explanatory power. That is, self-awareness is not considered a construct but rather a lable to describe the observations made.

The terminology used by the individual to describe self-observations must be, like other verbal labels, learned from others. However, the labels associated with internal states are often more difficult to teach and to learn than those associated with externally observable events. The parent or other social agent teaching the child to describe particular internal events must typically observe the situational context in which the child's feelings are taking place, infer from this context what the child should be feeling, and provide the child with a verbal label for those sensations. Thus, the social agent may observe a child who has just broken a favorite toy and is crying and may say to the child "that's too bad, you must feel very sad, very unhappy." With repeated experiences of various feelings, emotions and bodily states labeled by others, the child will begin to develop a verbal repertoire for describing these feelings and thus for obtaining some degree of self-awareness.

Self-awareness is often distorted, and Skinner (1975) has suggested two major reasons for this lack of accurate self-awareness. First, there is no real opportunity for the consensual validation of internal feelings in the descriptions of other persons. This is because the world within the person is a private world that does not impinge directly upon the senses of any outside observer and cannot be experienced by that observer exactly as it has been experienced by the person. The second difficulty is that the human nervous system is simply not designed to make available for verbal description the large complex of information that would be needed to accurately reflect the functioning of internal systems. Skinner sums up this point succinctly, "To put it crudely, introspection cannot be very relevant or comprehensive because the human organism does not have nerves going to the right places" (1975, p. 44).

It is possible to build on the Skinnerian approach to self-awareness in a variety of ways. Of particular interest is the theory that individuals' attitudes are determined by their self-perceptions (Bem 1967, 1972). Termed *attribution theory,* this currently important position in social psychology hypothesizes that individuals gain self-knowledge of emotions, attitudes, and internal states largely by inferring it from direct observations of either their own overt behavior or the situational context in which that behavior occurs, or from both. If the internal cues associated with particular behavioral observations and attitudes are weak or ambiguous, the individual has little advantage over the outside observer and is forced to rely upon external cues as a basis for inferring the internal states.

Having a Poem

A further illustration of the applicability of Skinner's theory to complex human behavior is seen in his discussion of how poetry is written (Skinner 1972). Surely poetry is often complex, frequently creative, always subjective. How can such an experience as writing a poem be accounted for in simple, behavioral terms? Skinner, controversial as always, has likened "having a poem" to having a baby. In both cases it is a set of interacting genetic and environmental factors that cause the individual to have the poem or the baby. The poet, in a sense, contributes no more to the process than the mother. The poem occurs to the poet as a function of that person's reinforcement history. Skinner's more general and important point is that many aspects of human behavior are commonly, but inappropriately, attributed to the operation of complex constructs. Thus, not only poetry but love, neurotic behavior, creativity, will, feelings, the conscious and unconscious mind, and other esoteric constructs are often misattributed. Both the poet and the neurotic are displaying behaviors controlled largely by the environment and in particular by their reinforcement histories.

TREATMENT: BEHAVIOR MODIFICATION AND CONTROL

The operant approach has been applied, from about the 1950s through the 1970s, in a variety of attempts to modify human behavior that is deviant by some specifiable definition. Operant therapy has come to be considered a part of a broader class of behavior therapy. As contrasted with traditional psychotherapies, such as Freudian and Rogerian, the behavior therapies deal directly and immediately with problem behaviors of the individual. Basically, the therapist identifies as specifically and narrowly as possible the nature of the deviant behavior, determines what events or objects will be effective reinforcers for the particular individual or group in question, then applies systematic reinforcement to gain control over and modify the behaviors.

Individual Therapy

Operant procedures have been applied in a number of ways to the modification of deviant behavior in individuals. One example is the treatment of a three-year-old autistic boy, who initially was severely deficient in both social and verbal behaviors, engaged in such self-destructive behavior as head-banging, did not eat properly, and frequently displayed tantrums (Wolf, Risley, and Mees 1964). The immediate behavior questioned was the boy's refusal to wear the glasses he needed for normal visual development. The therapist reinforced the boy initially with candy or fruit for picking up empty glass frames, then for holding the frames, then for carrying them with him, for putting them on, and finally for wearing them correctly for more extended periods of time. He quickly learned to wear the glasses up to twelve hours per day.

Token-Economy Programs

Patients in mental hospitals, particularly psychotic patients, are generally characterized by a lack of the social skills necessary to obtain social reinforcement outside the institution. The lack of these skills is, in a large part, what makes it impossible for the patient to live effectively outside the institution. The broad aim of token-economy programs is to help the patient develop social skills through the use of simple operant techniques.

A typical token-economy program has three basic elements. First, a set of particular patient behaviors or potential behaviors are identified, usually by the hospital staff, as desirable behaviors. Included might be such types of behavior as keeping a neat room or making the bed. The second element is the identification of the reinforcers, consisting of activities of objects which the patients consider desirable. Listening to records, attending movies or getting candy would be examples. The third element is the designation of an acquired reinforcer, such as poker chips, that can be given to patients when they perform the desired behavior and can later be exchanged for reinforcers. Following the early work of Ayllon and his colleagues (Ayllon and Azrin 1965), a number of investigators have reported the successful operation of token economies with a variety of patients, various systematic behavioral changes, and a number of different reinforcers.

Freedom and Dignity

Some have argued that Skinnerian procedures can establish such control over behavior that there is reason to be concerned about the possibility of attacking the freedom of the individual. Skinner (1971) has argued that freedom is an illusion. The basic illusion lies in the belief of individuals and societies that human beings are responsible for causing their own actions, that they are willful. In fact, such convictions constitute the attribution of a virtually magical quality to the causation of human behavior. The fact that a person decided to do X does not really indicate why that person did it. What was it that made the individual "decide"? Skinner's answer is that it was largely the person's reinforcement history which caused the decision.

Behaviorism has similarly been taken to task for reducing human dignity by insisting that environmental variables control human behavior. We like to believe, for example, that the work of a great "creative" artist is under that artist's willful control, while the behavioral position credits environmental stimuli in conjunction with the history of reinforcement.

Skinner's more general point is that the perceived attack by behavioral approaches on human freedom and dignity has contributed heavily to the virtual suppression of extensive scientific studies of behavior. In fact, however, *the goal of the behaviorist is not to reduce human dignity but to understand it and not to control behavior by changing people but by changing the world around them.*

Using this basic operant approach, Skinner (1972) has gone so far as to suggest that the technology of behavior control may be systematically applied in order to improve social conditions. The use of operant techniques, he argues, could accelerate the rate of cultural evolution and result in long-term social improvement. His ideas have certainly met with some support within the behavioral movement, but Nolan (1974) and others have also criticized them for being unlikely to lead to significant sociocultural progress.

EMPIRICAL APPROACHES

The substantial volume of research attributable to the Skinnerian approach is attested to by the establishment of journals devoted especially to publishing research from the operant camp. Included is the "voice" of American behaviorism, *The Journal of the Experimental Analysis of Behavior* (JEAB), and *The Journal of Applied Behavior Analysis.*

The approach to research espoused by Skinner is consistent with the proposal that psychology should be a science that engages in the functional analysis of the organism to determine the specific, directly observable conditions that control behavior. The basic aim of a Skinnerian science of behavior is to produce direct control over specific behaviors in individual subjects, thus establishing a cause-effect relationship that becomes the basis for scientific laws. Like any other science, a science of behavior must progress from the relatively simple to the more complex and thus determine on a continuing basis the extent to which the laws discovered at one stage or level of complexity are adequate for the next (Skinner 1953). As a result, operant behaviorism has studied both simple and complex behaviors in both animals and humans. It has progressed from the early determination of the effects of simple schedules of reinforcement to knowledge of more complex human social and psychopathological behaviors. Research has thus ranged from the animal laboratory to the mental hospital and from the training of pigeons as missile guidance devices to the modification of psychotic behavior in humans.

Scientific emphasis throughout this research has focused in particular on two of Skinner's major points. First, a truly scientific approach should be able to focus on the behavior of an individual subject, study that behavior intensively, and determine specifically the nature and extent of the various influences on the particular behavior under study. Much Skinnerian research focuses, therefore, on single subjects or small groups of subjects, as opposed to the relatively large-group studies done by the majority of psychologists. The second approach has been on the establishment of scientific control in the laboratory, such that extraneous or unknown factors do not influence the behavior of experimental subjects. As a result of this scientific dictum, most laboratory experiments have involved carefully selected animals, often bred to control for possible genetic factors. In addition, experimental subjects are typically run and housed in carefully isolated environments, such as the Skinner box discussed earlier, in order to eliminate unknown influences on behavior. If careful controls are established and there are still unknown factors apparently influencing behavior, these factors should not be ignored but studied, according to Skinner, as they may be important in establishing the scientific laws governing behavior.

Schedules of Reinforcement

We have already considered the influence of reinforcement schedules on behavior. It might be instructive, however, to consider here a specific example of the study of reinforcement schedules that typifies much of this research literature. One of

Skinner's colleagues, Charles Ferster, a major figure in the operant movement, conducted a study concerned with the establishment, through intermittent reinforcement, of a complex response in the chimpanzee (Ferster 1958). The experiment involved a single chimpanzee, deprived of food and reduced in body weight. The subject was placed in an experimental chamber with two keys which operated a food magazine. Initially either key operated the food magazine if the two keys were depressed alternatively. Once this response had been learned, the procedure was changed, such that depression of the right key operated the magazine only if preceded by one, and later two or three, presses of the left key. A fixed ratio schedule was then introduced and the ratio gradually increased until the animal was responding at a ratio of one reinforcement to thirty-three responses (FR 33). The experiment thus established the possibility of conditioning a complex response sequence.

Pigeon "Pilots"

An interesting demonstration of the effectiveness of reinforcement schedules in controlling behavior was the attempt, during and after World War II, to use trained pigeons as "mechanisms" to control missiles in flight (Skinner 1960). Skinner employed operant reinforcement schedules to train pigeons to track on a particular stimulus pattern displayed on a key. The pattern could be moved from one key to another in a row of keys, and the pigeon would peck wherever the pattern was located, thus steering the missile. The pattern could be moved from one key to another, and the pigeon would peck wherever the pattern was located.

Psychopharmacology

Psychopharamocologists have long been interested in determining the specific effects of experimental drugs on behavior, yet such determinations cannot be made unless the animal's behavior apart from drug influence can be precisely controlled. Operant techniques have, for this reason, become a major tool of the psychopharmacologist. The procedures, in general, are straightforward. The rat or other animal is placed in a Skinner box and trained operantly to produce a stable rate of bar-press responding. The drug to be tested is then given to the rat so that it will be in effect during the next session in the experimental chamber. The precise effects of the drug can be determined by noting the variation in performance between the drug session and the previous, stable nondrug performance of the animal.

Social Behavior

Some of the major concerns of those questioning the introduction of techniques aimed at the control of human behavior have been with the possibility of controlling social behaviors with such techniques. We have already seen some examples of such control, as in the Endler (1965) experiment dealing with the differential establishment of conforming versus deviant behavior in college students. A further example is seen in the study of cooperative behavior in children reported by Azrin and Lindsley (1956). The experiment demonstrates the power of operant conditioning procedures in quickly establishing or modifying human behavior. Ten teams of two children each were seated opposite one another at a table. Each child had a stylus, and the table in front of the child contained three holes. Jelly bean reinforcers were delivered initially on a continuous reinforcement schedule every time the two children on a team placed their styli in holes that were directly opposite each other's (although the children were not told this and had to discover it for themselves). When a stable response rate had been established, extinction was introduced, followed by a third period in which continuous reinforcement was again given to reestablish stable responding. This experimental procedure serves to demonstrate that the behavior can be acquired, maintained, extinguished, and then reestablished under the direct control of the reinforcers. Response in the Azrin-Lindsley study demonstrated that the cooperative, social behavior of the children could be brought under reinforcement control.

Behavior Therapy

Research concerned with the application of operant conditioning to therapeutic control of behavior has burgeoned in recent years. We have seen some examples of this in the work of Burgess (1967) and others. We will not examine other work in behavior therapy in detail, but a number of authors have provided reviews in this and related areas (see, for example, Honig 1966; Sherman 1973; Kanfer and Phillips 1970; Krasner 1971).

EVALUATION

Any great theoretical oak which stands so much taller than most of the others can well expect to be at once gentled by the soft breezes of virtuous admiration and buffeted by the winds of disparagement. Such has clearly been true of Skinnerian behaviorism. On the one hand, proponents and admirers extol its virtues as the most significant contribution thus far to twentieth-century psychology, while, on the other hand, critics caustically attack each point, from its basic tenets to its most minor methodologies.

Positive Points

Clarity of Terms. Like Dollard and Miller, Skinner has been clear and concise in his usage of terminology, lending to the approach an air of carefully honed precision.

Personality Process. Like Dollard and Miller, Skinner has provided the basis for a strikingly clear and detailed understanding of the formation of behavior (and by extension, personality) and its modification. Thus, the processes of development and change are better understood in terms of the Skinnerian approach than in terms of most other theories.

Behavior Control. Psychologists have long held as major goals the understanding and prediction of behavior. Skinner was among the first to emphasize, in addition, the need to control behavior, noting that the ability to control precisely implies the ability to produce positive development and positive change. The extensive work on the systematic application of reinforcement schedules in both animals and humans has demonstrated that a fairly high degree of behavior control is quite possible and, moreover, that the achievement of such control does not require an elaborate theoretical, constructual understanding of the underlying bases for the behavior.

Criticisms

Simplicity and Superficiality. It can be argued that the operant approach over-simplifies its concepts to an even greater degree than that of Dollard and Miller's and, hence, becomes an unacceptably superficial approach to the understanding of human behavior.

Structural and Organizational Inadequacy. Skinner provides little in the way of organizational concepts relevant or applicable to an understanding of human personality. An understanding of personality content has been sacrificed in favor of the process of behavior development and change.

Biological Organism. Skinner's insistence on remaining outside the physiological "box" of the organism has brought about the obvious criticism that he is ignoring an important determinant of behavior—biology. It must be noted, however, that Skinner (1975) has not denied the importance of genetic endowment and biological functioning. Rather, he has said that we are so far from a clear understanding of the biological basis for behavior that it is more desirable to stay outside the organism than to apply biological concepts inaccurately in attempts to understand behavior.

Behavior Control. We noted above the significant accomplishment of the operant approach in developing methods for the control of behavior. It has often been pointed out, however, that this ability carries with it serious social and ethical implications. Simply stated, if the ability to control human behavior precisely and systematically becomes highly developed, there is no automatic assurance that the methods will be applied only to the benefit of the individual and the society. Autocratic governments, dictators, unethical businesses or others might employ advanced operant techniques to establish substantial control over the behavior of individuals and groups to the detriment of the people involved. The issues have been quite thoroughly discussed (Rogers and Skinner 1956; Krasner 1962; Kanfer 1965; Goldiamond 1965), although the concerns have not been resolved.

Verbal Behavior and Thought Processes. Skinner has, for some time, been concerned with an understanding of verbal behavior and, in fact, wrote an entire book on that topic (Skinner 1957). He offered a straightforward operant analysis of verbal behavior. Speech sounds, he maintained, are emitted and then, if reinforced, tend to be repeated; words, sentence structures, and other aspects of language and thought are, therefore, basically learned and modified through reinforcement. This operant analysis of verbal behavior was immediately the subject of a sweeping critique by Chomsky (1959). Working from a substantial body of linguistic data, Chomsky argued that a language cannot be learned on the basis of the simple response-reinforcement sequences suggested by the Skinnerian system. Evidence indicates, in Chomsky's view, that the central nervous system of humans is structured such that it readily accepts and organizes a series of rules relevant to the construction of sentences. These rules then generate sentences as theorems, such that sentences never before specifically learned or utilized can be spoken readily. Partially as a result of Chomsky's critique, Skinner's theory of verbal behavior has had little influence.

Equipotentiality. The Skinnerian approach assumes that any clearly discriminable stimulus can readily become associated with any response in the presence of any reinforcer. This assumption may be untenable. Seligman's (1970) searching review of an impressive array of evidence leads to the conclusion that particular species are innately better equipped to make certain stimulus-response-reinforcement associations than to make others. Lenneberg (1967) has, for example, suggested that there may be an innate propensity for language acquisition, a point supporting the Chomsky (1959) argument against Skinner's treatment of verbal behavior. Perhaps more striking is evidence of the apparent specificity of response performances in laboratory rats and pigeons. In an avoidance conditioning setting, for example, rats very quickly learn a jumping response to avoid shock (Baum 1969). However, it is extremely difficult to teach the rat to press a bar to avoid shock (D'Amato and Fazzaro 1966), although the bar-pressing response is readily learned when food is the reinforcer. Similarly, it now appears that the association between the key-peck response, traditionally learned by pigeons in the Skinner box, and food as a reinforcer may be genetically influenced. Brown and Jenkins (1968) presented pigeons with a key that could be lighted. Whenever the key was lit, the pigeons received food in a hopper, whether, or not they pecked the key. Nevertheless, the pigeons began to key peck and continued the pecking response despite the fact that food was not contingent on the response. The investigators termed this process *autoshaping*. Of further relevance to the question of genetic influence on response-reinforcement specificity is work on shock avoidance in pigeons. Some investigators have attempted to train pigeons to key peck in order to avoid shock rather than obtain food. It has been found that this key-pecking avoidance response is extremely difficult to condition (Hoffman and Fleshler 1959; Rachlin and Hineline 1967). Applied to humans, such results may suggest that behavior modification therapists and others will have to select the stimulus-response-reinforcement pairings they use very carefully or they can expect great difficulty in modifying the behavior. It is apparent that Skinner's approach is, overall, a powerful and widely influential paradigm which has both strong pros and cons.

REFERENCES

Allport, G. W. *Personality: A psychological interpretation.* New York: Holt, Rinehart and Winston, 1937.

Ayllon, T., & Azrin, N. The measurement and reinforcement of behavior of psychotics. *Journal of the Experimental Analysis of Behavior,* 1965, *8,* 357–383.

Azrin, N. H., Hake, D. F., & Hutchinson, R. R. Elicitation of aggression by a physical ball. *Journal of the Experimental Analysis of Behavior,* 1965, *8,* 55–57.

Azrin, N. H., & Holz, W. C. Punishment. In W. K. Honig (Ed.), *Operant behavior: Areas of research and application.* Englewood Cliffs, N.J.: Prentice-Hall, 1966.

Azrin, N. H., & Lindsley, O. R. The reinforcement of cooperation between children. *Journal of Abnormal and Social Psychology,* 1956, *52,* 100–102.

Baum, M. Dissociation of respondent and operant processes in avoidance learning. *Journal of Comparative and Physiological Psychology,* 1969, *67,* 83–88.

Bem, D. J. Self-perception: An alternative interpretation of cognitive dissonance phenomena. *Psychological Review,* 1967, *74,* 183–200.

Bem. D. J. Self-perception theory. In L. Berkowitz (Ed.), *Advances in an experimental social psychology* (Vol. 6). New York: Academic Press, 1972.

Brown, P., & Jenkins, H. Autoshaping of the pigeon's key-peck. *Journal of the Experimental Analysis of Behavior,* 1968, *11,* 1–8.

Burgess, E. P. *The modification of depressive behaviors.* Paper presented at the annual meeting of the Association for the Advancement of Behavioral Therapies, San Francisco, September 1, 1967.

Chomsky, N. A review of B. F. Skinner's Verbal Behavior. *Language,* 1959, *35,* 26–58.

D'Amato, M. R., & Fazzaro, J. Discriminated lever-press of avoidance learning as a function of type and intensity of shock. *Journal of Comparative and Physiological Psychology,* 1966, *61,* 313–315.

Endler, N. S. The effects of verbal reinforcement on conformity and deviant behavior. *Journal of Social Psychology,* 1965, *66,* 147–154.

Estes, W. K., & Skinner, B. F. Some quantitative properties of anxiety. *Journal of Experimental Psychology,* 1941, *29,* 390–400.

Ferster, C. B. Intermittent reinforcement of a complex response in a chimpanzee. *Journal of the Experimental Analysis of Behavior,* 1958, *1,* 163–165.

Ferster, C. B., & Skinner, B. F. *Schedules of reinforcement.* New York: Appleton-Century-Crofts, 1957.

Goldiamond, I. Justified and unjustified alarm over behavioral control. In O. Nelton (Ed.), *Behavior disorders.* New York: Lippincott, 1965.

Hoffman, H. S., & Fleshler, M. Aversive control with the pigeon. *Journal of the Experimental Analysis of Behavior.* 1959, *2,* 213–218.

Holz, W. C., & Azrin, N. H. A comparison of several procedures for eliminating behavior. *Journal of Experimental Analysis of Behavior,* 1963, *6,* 399–406.

Honig, W. K. *Operant behavior: Areas of research and application.* Englewood Cliffs, N.J.: Prentice-Hall, 1966.

Kanfer, F. H. Issues and ethics in behavior manipulation. *Psychological Reports,* 1965, *16,* 187–196.

Kanfer, F. H., & Phillips, J. S. *Learning foundations of behavior therapy.* New York: Wiley & Sons, 1970.

Krasner, L. The therapist as a social reinforcement machine. In H. H. Strupp & L. Luborsky (Eds.), *Research in Psychotherapy* (Vol. 2). Baltimore, Maryland: French-Bray, 1962.

Krasner, L. The operant approach in behavior therapy. In A. E. Bergin & S. L. Bardfield (Eds.), *Handbook of Psychotherapy and Behavior Change.* New York: Wiley & Sons, 1971.

Lenneberg, E. *The biological foundations of language.* New York: Wiley, 1967.

Nolan, J. D. Freedom and dignity: A "functional" analysis. *American Psychologist,* 1974, *29,* 157–160.

Pavlov, I. P. *Conditioned reflexes.* London: Klanden Press, 1927.

Rachlin, H. C., & Hineline, P. N. Training and maintenance of key pecking in the pigeon by negative reinforcement. *Science,* 1967, *157,* 954–955.

Rogers, C. R. A theory of therapy, personality, and inter-personal relationships as developed in the client-center framework. In S. Koch (Ed.), *Psychology: A Study of Science* (Vol. 3). New York: McGraw-Hill, 1959. (Pp. 184-256.)

Rogers, C. R., & Skinner, B. F. Some issues concerning the control of human behavior. *Science,* 1956, *124,* 1057–1066.

Seligman, M. E. P. On the generality of the laws of learning. *Psychological Review,* 1970, *77,* 406–418.

Sherman, A. R. *Behavior modification: Theory and practice.* Monterey, California: Brooks/Cole, 1973.

Skinner, B. F. *Science and Human Behavior.* New York: Macmillan, 1953.

Skinner, B. F. *Verbal Behavior.* Englewood Cliffs, N.J.: Prentice-Hall, 1957.

Skinner, B. F. Pigeons in a pelican. *American Psychologist,* 1960, *15,* 28–37.

Skinner, B. F. *Contingencies of reinforcement: A theoretical approach.* Englewood Cliffs, N.J.: Prentice-Hall, 1969.

Skinner, B. F. *Beyond freedom and dignity.* New York: Knopf, 1971.

Skinner, B. F. *Cumulative record: A selection of papers* (3rd ed.). Englewood Cliffs, N.J.: Prentice-Hall, 1972.

Skinner, B. F. The steep and thorny way to a science behavior. *American Psychologist,* 1975, *1,* 42–49.

Terrace, H. S. Classical conditioning. In G. S. Reynolds, C. Catania, & B. Schard (Eds.), *Contemporary experimental psychology.* Chicago: Scott Foresman, 1973.

Wheeler, H. *Beyond the punitive society.* San Francisco: W. H. Freeman, 1973.

Wolf, M., Risley, T., & Mees, H. Application of operant conditioning procedures to the behavior problems of an autistic child. *Behavior Research and Therapy,* 1964, *1,* 305–312.

10

Cognitive Theory:

George Kelly

Many personality theories, as we have seen, propose a specific set of structural concepts that define the personality. Freud has his id, ego, and superego, Rogers his organism and self, and Dollard and Miller their habit construct. Moreover, many of these theories can be interpreted as suggesting that one basic aspect of personality functioning is motivational or dynamic in nature. In Freud, a basic function of the personality is to satisfy the powerful instincts; in Rogers personality and behavior are oriented toward actualization and self-actualization; and in Dollard and Miller habits are formed in order to assure drive reduction.

George Kelly begins his major work, the *Psychology of Personal Constructs,* by warning us "that the reader is likely to find missing most of the familiar landmarks of psychology books . . . there is no ego, no emotion, no motivation, no reinforcement, no drive, no unconscious, no need" (Kelly 1955, p. 10). What kind of strange theory, then, is Kelly's? Basically, it is a *cognitive* theory, meaning that its emphasis is on the way in which the individual perceives and interprets the environment and the way in which these perceptions and interpretations influence subsequent behavior. Kelly has not proposed a specific personality structure with concepts like ego and self but has hypothesized that behavior is determined by the particular ways in which the individual perceives or *construes* the environment. It becomes important, therefore, to understand the ways in which this process of construing takes place and how previously formed constructs or ways of understanding the environment influence later behavior.

Having drawn such a sharp line between Kelly and other theorists, we must, before going further, point out that there are some similarities between Kelly's approach and that of earlier theorists. For example, like Rogers and to a lesser extent Freud, Kelly had emphasized the importance of understanding the individual person. In addition, in his theory he opts for a holistic approach, not unlike that of Rogers or Freud, in which the emphasis is on understanding behavior in the context of the whole person. The real significance to the personality field of Kelly's theory lies, however, not in the extent to which he agrees with some other theorists but in the unique, innovative approach that he takes to the understanding of human behavior. It is specifically his emphasis on cognitive factors and the influence these have on behavior that makes his theory theory a unique and important alternative way of understanding human behavior.

BIOGRAPHICAL SKETCH

George Alexander Kelly was born in Perth, Kansas, the only child of a Presbyterian minister-turned-farmer and his wife. Kelly attended high school in Wichita and later obtained his bachelor's degree in education at the University of Edinburgh, after first attending college at Friends University and Parks College, where he had received a bachelor's degree in mathematics and physics in 1926, and the University of Kansas, where he obtained an M.A. degree in 1928. Kelly received his Ph.D. degree at the University of Iowa in 1931.

Kelly joined the faculty at the Fort Hays, Kansas State College and there developed a traveling psychological clinic for the state of Kansas. In 1945, after a stint as a naval psychologist, he joined the faculty at the University of Maryland, leaving after only one year to become professor and director of clinical psychology at Ohio State University. In 1965, Kelly went to Brandeis University, where he accepted the Riklis Chair of Behavioral Science. One year later, while working on a book to be composed of his earlier papers, Kelly died. The book was later completed under the editorship of Brendan Maher.

A PHILOSOPHY OF SCIENCE AND PERSON

Kelly's approach is unique among personality theories in its view of science and of the relationship of science to the individual person.

A Philosophy of Science: Constructive Alternativism

Seeing a term like *constructive alternativism,* the reader may immediately have the sinking feeling that Kelly's will be a rather obtuse, difficult-to-understand theory. Actually, however, constructive alternativism simply means that our current ways of understanding and interpreting events and reality are subject to change. There is no such thing as one absolutely correct way of viewing the universe or any aspect of it. No given religion or religious interpretation is necessarily right; no political viewpoint is definitively correct; and no one scientific theory represents absolute, unalterable fact. Indeed, "facts" and "truths" exist only in the beliefs of the individual. There is no such thing as an objective reality.

If there is no one right way of construing events, there must be a number of alternative ways of viewing them. As an example, consider the situation in which a company vice-president criticizes several subordinates after the company loses out in its bid to obtain a large contract. Some employees may interpret the criticism as meaning that their work actually is poor. Others may believe that the vice-president is venting frustration because of trouble with superiors. Still others may think that the vice-president is trying to motivate the employees toward greater success in future negotiations. Each of these employees viewed the same event, but each interprets or construes it in a quite different way. Moreover, the varied ways of interpreting the event may lead these employees to act in quite different ways toward the vice-president.

The Individual as Scientist

Science involves an attempt to predict, control, and understand events. In this effort, theories are generated, hypotheses about specific events derived, and empirical tests carried out. Einstein, Freud, Rogers, and Kelly, all scientists, have each provided an important theory with the basic aim of understanding some set of events.

Kelly argued that each and every individual is also a "scientist." By this he meant that we function like scientists in our approach to the world. Like the scientist, though with perhaps less lofty goals, each person wants to predict, control, and understand aspects of his or her environment. Thus, each person formulates many hypotheses about the world, tests these hypotheses, and, if necessary, revises them. The hypotheses that one forms are useful because they provide a reasonably consistent framework within which to interpret and construe events. The hypotheses also allow the individual to anticipate occurrences, and Kelly held that all behavior can best be understood as future-oriented and anticipatory. It is not the past or present but the *future* which determines behavior, and it is the hypotheses held by the individual that allow him or her to anticipate that future and behave accordingly.

The process of construing can be illustrated by considering the example of a young man who listens to a single speech by a politician whom he has never heard of before. Based on this one exposure, he may formulate the hypothesis that this politician is honest. If he now follows the politician's career, he may operate on the basis of this assumption. For example, he may tell friends about his favorable impression, vote for the politician, or even work to get him or her elected. The hypothesis is, however, subject to change. Should the young man begin to see evidence of possible dishonesty, he might partially or completely revise his view of the politician and anticipate dishonest, rather than honest, behavior. This modified anticipation of what will happen may substantially change the man's behavior. He may now vote against the politician or even work to get an opponent elected.

STRUCTURAL PROPERTIES: CONSTRUCTS

To the scientist or to the individual, the world is basically a hodgepodge of information and events, or in Kelly's words, an "undifferentiated homogeneity." To impose order on this perceptual chaos, scientists develop *constructs*, which are, as we have seen before, concepts used to explain the phenomena with which they deal. For example, the construct "anxiety" provides a way of understanding the behavior of the college student who, during an examination, fidgets, squirms, and chews his or her nails more than usually.

Just as the scientist forms constructs to help understand phenomena, the individual develops *personal constructs* in an effort to reduce the complexity of the world to a point where it becomes understandable. Personal constructs, then, are ways of construing or categorizing people and events in the experiential world of the individual. Categorizing politicians as honest or dishonest, as in our previous example, would be a case in point. Other categories or constructs might be fair-unfair, beautiful-ugly, and competent-incompetent.

The major function of constructs is to provide for the *anticipation* of events. Through the application of existing constructs, the individual can predict or anticipate and thereby control, or at least influence, events. Deciding, for example, that a person is honest (vs. dishonest) or a situation dangerous (vs. safe) helps one to anticipate what will happen next and vary one's behavior accordingly. Of course, the construct is most useful to the individual when it provides an accurate anticipation of events, but even if inaccurate, it will affect the way the person behaves in a situation. For example, the college student may categorize examinations as easy or difficult. If an upcoming math exam is categorized as easy, the student may study less and feel less anxious than if the exam is predicted to be difficult.

Characteristics of Constructs

All personal constructs have certain characteristics. First, they are *bipolar*. The bipolar nature of constructs suggests that we tend to categorize people and events at their extremes. We are likely to view the situation as dangerous or safe, as pleasant or unpleasant, and to view a person as honest or dishonest, tall or short. Such perceptions involve the establishment of similarities and contrasts in which a minimum of three elements, two similar to each other and one different from the other two, are involved. For example, sport parachuting and auto racing are dangerous, while tennis is safe.

Another set of construct characteristics is that they are *variable* and *changeable*. Constructs can vary from one person to another in that one individual may perceive a situation as dangerous, while another sees it as safe. Alternatively, two people might apply different constructs to the same situation. One person might construe the situation in terms of safety, while the second person might view the same situation in terms of excitement and label it exciting or dull. Constructs are also changeable. If a construct leads to an accurate anticipation of events, it is likely to remain consistent; but if predictions from the construct are inaccurate, it is likely to be modified, as in our example of the politician perceived as honest and later as dishonest.

A further characteristic of constructs is that they are related to each other in a *hierarchical* or ordinal fashion. That is, some constructs may be superordinate and others subordinate. For example, the construct sick-healthy may subsume other constructs. One may thus label as "sick" people who are diseased, injured, or psychologically disordered, while healthy people are disease-free, uninjured, and psychologically unimpaired.

Formal Properties of Constructs

In addition to their general characteristics, constructs have certain formal characteristics or properties. First, the construct has a *range of convenience,* meaning that it applies to certain kinds of events or people and not to others. For example, the construct honest vs. dishonest may be useful in characterizing a variety of kinds of people in many occupations and situations, but it is not very useful in deciding whether or not to enter a strange, darkened house. Here the dangerous-safe construct would be more helpful.

The construct also has a *focus of convenience.* The focus is both narrower and more person-specific than the range. For example, the focus of one person's dangerous-safe construct may be on the characterization of events as physically dangerous or safe, while another person may be more concerned with safety in social situations.

The final property of constructs is their *permeability.* A construct is permeable to the extent that it allows the addition of further elements. For example, the construct honest-dishonest may be used primarily to characterize politicians and advertisers. If the construct is reasonably permeable, it may allow the additional construing of newspaper articles as honest (that is, unbiased) or dishonest.

Functional Typology of Constructs

Although constructs share certain characteristics and formal properties, they also vary in some ways and can, therefore, be classified or typed in terms of their functions or properties. Constructs can thus be differentiated in terms of whether they are *core* constructs, central and basic to the individual's overall functioning, or *peripheral* and, hence, modifiable without changing the person's basic nature. On another dimension, constructs can be *comprehensive* or *incidental.* The former are broadly applicable, as in the case of the construct good-bad, while incidental constructs have relatively narrow use.

Constructs may also be typed as propositional, constellatory or preemptive. *Propositional* constructs are those that allow the individual flexibility in perceiving the environment. For example, if honesty is a propositional construct for a given person, viewing another individual as honest does not necessarily lead to the assumption that the person has certain other characteristics, such as sincerity, forthrightness, religiosity, or goodness. Conversely, a *constellatory* construct is one in which other characteristics follow from the initial classification. In this case, the person viewed as honest will be seen as having a certain set of characteristics that may be viewed as common to all honest people. Stereotyping involves constellatory constructs: Bankers are rich and work short hours, physicians are hard-working and money-hungry, and college professors are brilliant but absent minded are examples of constellatory thinking. Finally, a construct may be *preemptive* in that an event entering membership in this construct category is excluded from membership in other constructs. Once one has decided that a particular politician is dishonest, this may become the only relevant property of the politician. His or her stands on particular issues, appearance, and experience are ignored.

PERSONALITY DEVELOPMENT AND MOTIVATIONAL DYNAMICS

As we have seen, Kelly proposed that personality structure is a complex system of constructs that the person uses to anticipate the future and thus to control his or her behavior. If the construct system forms the structural basis for personality, how does the personality develop and what are its dynamics?

Personality Development

Development, of course, must consist of the formation of constructs and construct systems. Kelly had suggested, essentially, that constructs develop through repeated exposure to and interaction with the environment. New experiences add to and modify existing constructs or cause the development of new constructs. The overall goal of this developmental process is to maximize the individual's ability to anticipate, control, and understand the environment. Kelly spoke of development in relatively broad generalizations and was never very specific as to the exact nature of the developmental process.

Motivation

Kelly rejected traditional theories of motivation. Such theories typically hold either that the individual is driven, or pushed, by drives or motives or that the individual is pulled by goals or purposes. The theories of Freud and of Dollard and Miller exemplify the former approach, those of Rogers and Maslow the latter. According to Kelly, people are motivated to behave by the simple fact that they are alive. Being alive is virtually synonymous with being motivated, and such concepts as drive, instinct, and purpose are, therefore, not necessary.

THE FUNCTIONING PERSONALITY

Kelly suggested that the human personality functions on the basis of one fundamental postulate, supplemented by a number of corollaries.

Fundamental Postulate

The central assumption of Kelly's theory is that: "A person's processes are psychologically channeled by the ways in which he anticipates events" (1955, p. 46). The "ways" that the person anticipates events are his or her constructs, and Kelly's postulate means that these constructs channel or direct human thoughts and actions. For example, construing a dark house as dangerous may lead us to avoid it, while construing it as having exciting possibilities may lead us to enter it. A number of important corollaries supplement the basic postulate.

Individual Corollary. People differ in their constructs and, therefore, in their anticipations of events. One person may view a particular politician as honest, another as dishonest. Still another may not employ the honest-dishonest construct at all but may view the politician as progressive as opposed to traditional.

Commonality Corollary. Some constructions of experience are shared by two or more people. To the extent that there is such sharing, there is commonality. The "hawks" advocated fighting the Vietnam War to win, while the "doves" favored a quick and peaceful end to the war. People in each group had certain commonalities in their goals and perceptions. Similarly, political liberals share certain values which traditionally differ from those shared among political conservatives.

Organizational Corollary. This corollary formalizes the ordinal relationship among constructs that we have already examined.

Fragmentation Corollary. Despite the existence of organization in the construct system, there is also at times inconsistency among constructs. For example, an individual may generally construe a person who has the characteristics of being vindictive, sarcastic, and argumentative in terms of the supraordinate construct, "bad." Yet, we may find that this person loves someone whom he or she agrees has exactly those characteristics. The apparent contradiction occurs because the person in question is that individual's mother, and mother is a more important and, for that reason, governing construct.

Choice Corollary. Kelly recognized that we must often make choices between the opposing ends of our construct dimensions. Is a person good or bad, a situation dangerous or safe, a politician honest or dishonest, a college degree desirable or undesirable? Where choice is possible, the individual will opt for the construct pole that is more likely to increase his or her overall level of understanding of the event, person, or situation. If the right choice is made on this basis, the result will be an elaboration of the construct system which will allow the individual to construe events more accurately in the future.

Sociality Corollary. Effective social interaction requires that one person be able to anticipate accurately what another person will do in a situation and to adapt his or her own behavior accordingly. This necessity suggests, then, that each person must attempt to understand the ways in which other persons construe events in order to anticipate adequately their actions and reactions. In Kelly's words, "to the extent that one person construes the construction process of another, he may play a role in a social process involving the other person" (1955, p. 95).

Experience Corollary. Successive experiences with particular situations or events will tend to modify a person's construct system as it relates to those situations or events. Thus, the construct system is in a constant state of potential change, accounting for the flexibility of personality.

The C-P-C Cycle

What is the process by which constructs influence the individual's behavior? Kelly's answer is that the process is a recurrent, cyclical one, related particularly to the choice and experience corollaries, and termed the *circumspection-preemption control (C-P-C) cycle*. During circumspection, the individual is open minded and evaluates a variety of constructs as they may relate to the understanding of a particular event; during preemption, the large number of alternative ways of construing is reduced to a smaller number; and during control, a specific alternative is chosen and acted upon. For example, a college student about to graduate may entertain a variety of career alternatives, ranging from those that do not require a college degree but may yield high incomes to those requiring a bachelor's degree and into which he or she could enter immediately, to still others requiring graduate training. The wide variety of alternatives considered during the circumspection phase might be narrowed during preemption to only those requiring graduate training, and a specific career would be chosen and followed during the control phase. It should be noted, however, that the C-P-C cycle may be repeated as events are reexperienced or as situations change.

APPLICATIONS

Kelly's theory has been applied in an effort to understand the origins of psychopathology and to treat psychological disorder.

Psychopathology

In Kelly's words, "we may define a disorder as any personal construction which is used repeatedly in spite of consistent invalidation" (Kelly 1955, p. 831). This means that the disordered person holds certain constructs that are inaccurate or inappropriate and lead to unrealistic appraisals of reality. Nevertheless, these constructs are maintained and continue to be used over a period of time. A good example is the paranoid patient, who typically has a systematic delusion or false belief, usually involving a sense of persecution by someone or something. He or she may believe relatives, coworkers, neighbors, or the government are plotting against him or her. This belief is held tenaciously, despite repeated invalidations.

Psychological disorders involve anxiety and the continuing attempts to alleviate that anxiety. We have seen that anxiety is an important concept in many theories of psychopathology. For Kelly, anxiety is defined as the awareness that one's construct system is not adequate to anticipate the events with which one is confronted. An inadequate construct system means that the individual cannot predict or anticipate events and, therefore, cannot be prepared for the events or act appropriately when they occur. He or she, as a result, feels helpless and, therefore, anxious. The behaviors that we typically call "neurotic" represent the person's desperate attempts to find adequate ways of construing events or, alternatively, to adhere rigidly to old but invalid constructs and resulting anticipations.

Psychotherapy

The principal aim of psychotherapy is to help the client develop new and more adequate constructs and to modify the use of old constructs, permitting the patient to deal more effectively with the environment.

Therapy involves three major phases: role definition, acceptance, and working through problems. In the role definition phase, both therapist and client try to arrive at similar conceptualizations of their own and each other's roles in the therapeutic process. Next, the therapist must show the client a willingness and ability to understand the person's construct system. This attempt represents a form of acceptance of the client. It does not necessarily imply, however, the total acceptance of client behaviors and characteristics that is seen in Rogerian and other humanistic therapies. Finally, the therapist asks the client to engage in a *controlled elaboration* of his or her problems, thinking these problems through to their long-term outcomes. During this elaboration process, the therapist tries to help the client modify the usual construct applied to problems or even to develop new constructs, thus revising the overall constructs system. The therapist might, for example, suggest ways in which the job, which the client sees as meaningless, is actually an important one in society or suggest that the client reconsider certain positive characteristics of his or her father to help balance negative ones that appear central to the client's problem.

The therapist often also employs *fixed-role therapy.* In this technique, the client is first asked to elaborate on his or her constructs by writing a *self-characterization sketch,* a character sketch of another person written as though that person were a central character in a play. The therapist uses the sketch to write a *fixed-role script* for the client, who then acts out the role of the "fictional" character in the therapist's script. This permits the client to try out the new role in a relatively nonthreatening way. An example is provided by Kelly's case of an actual client,

Ronald Barrett. Ronald's self-characterization sketch suggested that he was compulsively bound by the belief that all problems must be solved through the use of logic and that feelings are unimportant. Kelly provided for the client a fixed-role script which focused on attending to the feelings of others and seeking answers in these feelings, rather than solely in fact and logic. Ronald rehearsed the role in Kelly's office, then began to play the role in his daily life, and, finally, in effect, modified his construct system and became the character in Kelly's script.

THE THEORY IN EMPIRICAL CONTEXT

Research associated with Kelly's theory has not been extensive, and most of the work that has been done has pertained not so much to the theory as to an inventory that Kelly developed, the Role Construct Repertory Test. This test, referred to as the RCRT or, more commonly, the REP Test, is basically a diagnostic inventory that provides a description of the individual's construct system and the use of that system to interact with the environment. The subject is presented with a list of role titles and definitions of important people, such as mother, father, boss, happy person, intelligent person, and spouse. The subject is asked to write, for each role, the name of a person who best fits that description for him or her. The subject is then asked to consider the figures he has listed in groups of three, in each case indicating how two of the three are similar and the third different. The end result is that the examiner can develop reasonable hypotheses about how the individual construes and interacts with a number of different people.

The test is available in several different forms, which can be used either in counseling individual clients or in conducting research. Unfortunately, the test does not have good traditional psychometric properties, and thus its reliability and validity are questionable.

Despite its psychometric problems, the REP test does follow quite clearly from Kelly's theory and has been used in some research. For example, Bieri (1955) conducted a study of cognitive complexity. It was hypothesized that subjects high in cognitive complexity (that is, those having numerous constructs in their construct systems) would see other people as having a wide variety of qualities, while a cognitively simple person would tend to see others as having only a small number of qualities. Bieri used the REP test to differentiate between cognitively simple and complex subjects and then had these subjects predict the behavior of others. The more complex subjects predicted behavior more accurately and also noted more readily the differences between themselves and others.

EVALUATION

Bruner (1956), in an early review of Kelly's theory, called it the greatest contribution to personality theory of the decade between 1945 and 1955. This would suggest, of course, that Kelly's theory has much to recommend it, and, indeed, it has made some substantive contributions. First, Kelly formulated an innovative theory, focusing on cognition, rather than emotions, and offering a viable alternative to most of the personality theories developed in earlier years. Second, the theory is largely a parsimonious one, offering a straightforward explanation of human behavior. Third, in most respects the theory is clearly stated, and many aspects of it can be tested through empirical research. In addition, Kelly has offered a significant challenge and provided a viable alternative to traditional theories of motivation. Whether or not one agrees with this approach to the elimination of elaborate motivational constructs, at least Kelly forces the reader to rethink traditional issues in the psychology of motivation.

In addition to the specific virtues of the theory, Kelly's approach has had a substantial amount of heuristic influence. Specifically, his ideas have formed the basis for a body of research in the area of cognitive style. Perhaps more important, however, has been the influence of the REP test, which has been the focus of a considerable amount of research and has been used by a number of investigators. This should not be taken to imply, however, that the theory itself has had much breadth of influence. In fact, quite the contrary is the case. Relatively few psychologists have become "Kellians," and most of the research attributable to Kelly's influence has dealt with the REP test rather than with his theory per se. While it must be recognized that Kelly's is a relatively new theory and has perhaps not yet had time to "catch on," it seems unlikely that the theory will ever have the widespread influence, of, for example, the Freudian or Rogerian approaches.

Problems and Difficulties

The major problems with Kelly's theory, together with its major emphases, are focused on his use of the personal construct as a central concept. The first problem is that the theory is too narrowly cognitive in nature. It focuses on rational, cognitive determinants of behavior to the virtual exclusion of the feelings, emotions, and irrational factors that may contribute to action. Behavior to him is governed basically by cognitive constructs not by human feelings, despite the fact that the approach is often referred to as a humanistic theory. We must then ask a number of more detailed questions about how constructs develop and function, questions which Kelly chose not to answer clearly. For example, what determines which constructs govern a given behavior? One may view a situation as both dangerous and interesting or a person as both dishonest and creative. Kelly's theory does not specify which of the multiple constructs will determine the behavior. How, exactly, do constructs develop? The nature of the learning or other process is not detailed. How do constructs change with experience? Bonarius (1965) has pointed out that this change process has never been explicit. Finally, why and how do constructs vary from one person to another? Why doesn't everyone apply the same basic constructs to a given event or person? Kelly was explicit in noting that there is individuality of constructs, but he was never entirely clear in describing how or why this person-to-person variation occurs.

It seems reasonable to conclude that Kelly's is a potentially useful, innovative theory, which has challenged much of the traditional thinking of personality theorists and shown psychologists that cognitions may play an important role in the determination of human behavior. The cognitive-humanistic emphasis in Kelly's theory has thus provided a stimulus for psychologists to revise their construct systems for understanding personality functioning and behavior determination. At the same time, the theory has not yet had widespread influence, perhaps because it is lacking in important details and because it fails to deal very thoroughly with emotional determinants of behavior or to integrate these with cognitive determinants. It may, nevertheless, have the long-term heuristic value of stimulating other theorists to develop approaches which take into account both cognitive and emotional determinants in an integrative framework which will provide a more complete understanding of the determinants of human behavior.

REFERENCES

Bieri, J. Cognitive complexity—simplicity and predictive behavior. *Journal of Abnormal and Social Psychology*, 1955, *51*, 263-268.

Bonarius, J. C. Research in the personal construct theory of George A. Kelly: Role construct repertory test and basic theory. In B. A. Maher (Ed.), *Progress in experimental personality research* (Vol. 2). New York: Academic Press, 1965.

Bruner, J. S. You are your constructs. *Contemporary Psychology*, 1956, *1*, 355-357.

Kelly, G. *The psychology of personal constructs*. New York: Norton, 1955.

11

Social Learning Theory:

Albert Bandura, Walter Mischel and Julian Rotter

In his theory of personality development, Freud assigned to the process of identification a major role in the shaping of the behavioral repertoire that constitutes the adult personality. By identification, Freud meant the process in which children observe the behavior of others, such as their parents, and copy certain elements of each of a number of different behaviors.

In addition to the work of Freud, there were a number of other early attempts to take imitative behavior into account. Watson (1925) treated imitation in the respondent conditioning model of Pavlov, suggesting that imitative responses are learned simply through the pairing of conditioned and unconditioned stimuli in a classical conditioning paradigm. Various other early theorists, such as Allport (1924), Humphrey (1921), and Holt (1931), also espoused respondent conditioning views of imitation. According to these viewpoints, an imitative response is no different from other classically learned responses. While not all early theorists based imitative learning on classical conditioning, most major approaches were in agreement in suggesting that imitative responses are learned on the basis of the same conditioning laws that apply to other responses.

As an alternative to the Pavlovian approach, Thorndike (1898) took an essentially instrumental or operant view of imitation, suggesting that an imitative response is learned only when it is followed by some reward. He suggested that animals and humans make many responses, including many essentially imitative responses. If the response is not followed by some rewards, it will tend not to be repeated or least not to increase in probability, while responses that are followed by reward will show a probability increment.

A more fully developed and influential position concerning imitation was that of Miller and Dollard (1941), who also argued that imitation falls within normal learning laws. They identified three different types of imitative behavior, but focused largely on *matched dependent* behavior. In the matched-dependent situation, an essentially inferior person, such as a child or unskilled individual, comes to rely on an older, more skilled, or otherwise superior person for aid in the discrimination of cues which guide the individual's behavior. The older person or model thus serves an essentially directive function, guiding the behavior of the child in such a way that the behavior terminates in the reward. Miller and Dollard used the example of two siblings seeking candy. The older child has learned that her father will give her a candy reward whenever she meets him at the door as he returns home. On those occasions when the younger child happens to follow her sibling to the door, she also receives the candy reward. In this situation the behavior of the model is simply serving as the discriminative stimulus or cue for the observer's running response, while hunger serves as a relevant drive state and candy is the reinforcer. Miller and Dollard (1941) reported a number of experiments supporting and extending this viewpoint. It is of interest to note, however, that after the early efforts in this research area these authors make little mention of imitation theory or experiments in their later theoretical work on personality. Thus, despite the strong background of Miller and Dollard in the social learning or imitative area, they did not choose to make this aspect of personality development a major focus of their theory.

The establishment of imitation learning, alternately referred to as identification or social learning, in a position of central importance as a determinate of personality development awaited the work of Albert Bandura and his colleagues and, in particular, Bandura's 1963 book with Richard Walters, *Social Learning and Personality Development*. Since the publication of this major work, considerable experimental and theoretical effort has been devoted by Bandura, Walters, and a growing community of investigators to the study of social learning through imitation.

BIOGRAPHICAL SKETCH

Albert Bandura received his baccalaureate degree from the University of British Columbia in 1949 and took up graduate work at the University of Iowa, where he completed his master's and doctoral degrees. Bandura completed a one-year postdoctoral clinical internship at the Wichita Guidance Center in 1953 and then joined the faculty of Stanford University, later becoming professor of psychology at Stanford. He was elected president of the American Psychological Association and served in that office in 1973.

Among Bandura's other major works are another book written with Richard Walters, *Adolescent Aggression* (1959), *Principles of Behavior Modification* (1969); *Social Learning Theory* (1977a); *Psychological Modeling* (1971); and *Aggression: A Social Learning Analysis.*

THE SOCIAL LEARNING VIEWPOINT

In his most recent work, Bandura (1977a) has taken up where he and other social learning theorists earlier left off with the development of a social learning conceptualization of human behavior. Bandura has pointed out that the relatively simple, mechanistic behavioral theories cannot adequately account for the acquisition of complex human behavior. Such theories tend to ignore important internal determinants of behavior and insist that learning occurs only when responses are actually performed and their consequences experienced.

The social learning view is that human behavior is the sole product of neither environmental stimuli nor inner forces. Rather, there is a continuous reciprocal interaction of personal and environmental factors. These determinants interact with one another to influence the complex resulting human behavior. In addition, Bandura has held that it is not actually necessary for people to perform responses in order to learn them. Rather, most learning through direct experience occurs *vicariously* when the individual observes the behavior of others and learns through this observational process. Trial and error is replaced, in this theory, by observation and instruction.

OBSERVATIONAL LEARNING

Observational learning can be said to occur whenever a novel, or simply new, form of behavior is acquired by observing the behavior of another person. Bandura and others have called this form of learning *social learning,* since it is always person-to-person learning and often involves the development of socially relevant behaviors. Although observational learning has often been described as imitation, Bandura has chosen to substitute the word *modeling,* since imitation implies a simple copying response. Modeling, he suggests, is much broader in its psychological effects than mere imitation, although both are forms of observational learning.

Theoretically, virtually any response can be learned through modeling. Included are such simple motor behaviors as striking a nail with a hammer and such complex social behaviors as those associated with anxiety, sex role differentiation, conformity and deviance, and aggression. In addition, abstract modeling is used to transmit such rule-governed behaviors as language and judgment. Various responses potentially acquired through modeling have been studied experimentally by Bandura and his colleagues. A typical experiment is one in which a child is asked to watch a live or video-taped model performing some behavior. The model performs a carefully detailed sequence of behaviors. The child is later placed in a situation where he or she could, but need not, repeat the behavior of the model. Modeling is demonstrated if the child closely approximates the behavioral sequence of the model. A partial description of a specific experiment will serve to exemplify the experimental paradigm. In the experiment in question, Bandura (1965) used thirty-three boys and thirty-three girls as experimental subjects and two adult males as models. Each child was brought into a waiting room to watch on television a five-minute film depicting a model using an adult-sized plastic Bobo doll. The model displayed four specific aggressive responses toward the doll. Following the film, the children were taken to an experimental room containing the doll and a variety of other toys and equipment. Results showed that the children did tend to reproduce the behaviors of the model rather than engage in other types of behavior.

FOUR BASIC PROCESSES

The results of the representative experiment described above—and of many other studies—support the basic assumption of social learning theory. The assumption is that observational learning occurs through the acquisition of predominantly cognitive representations of modeled behaviors rather than of specific responses. Modeling theory goes on to propose that the symbolic representations basic to modeling are formed through the operation of four essential processes.

Attentional Processes

The success with which observational learning takes place depends in part on the attention of the observer to the modeling cues involved in the situation. Bandura has pointed out that if the individual is exposed to cues to which he or she is attending only minimally, the individual clearly cannot be expected to learn from those cues. In addition to simply observing, the person must perceive the cue accurately and must select from the total available stimulus complex those cues that are most relevant to the behavior being modeled. The observer who does not accurately select or differentiate those essential features of the model's responses that define the behavior will fail to acquire a matching behavior. Thus, accurate discriminating observation is a requirement for observational learning.

It is clear that a full understanding of the modeling process requires study of those variables that serve to control attention. Bandura has identified some attentional control variables that are related to observer characteristics, others that relate to particular characteristics of the modeling cues, and an additional set determined by the incentive conditions relevant to the learning experience.

Retention

Attention and accurate cue discrimination would be of little use if the modeled behavior were not retained following the initial modeling experiences. While the necessity of *retention* seems, obvious, Bandura noted that this component has not been specified in earlier theories of imitation. Moreoever, any attempt to understand the processes involved in retention considerably complicates this aspect of the modeling process.

Bandura has suggested that one of the major factors involved in the retention of modeled behavior is the *symbolic coding* of modeling stimuli. Such coding involves the classification, organization, and incorporation of stimulus elements into previously learned representational memory systems. Two specific representational systems, an *imaginal* one and a *verbal* one, are proposed for observational learning. Modeling stimuli are encoded into sensory images and words, which function as coded, internalized cues that can be used at a later time to retrieve and reproduce the modeled behavior. The formation of images involves a process in which observers construct a conception of the activity that encompasses essential aspects from specific examples. Thus, for example, one child may carefully observe another riding a tricycle and, after one or more exposures, but with no verbal instruction, may be able to roughly approximate the riding behavior. This child is using imaginal coding to retain the riding behavior of the model.

While some forms of behavior are retained imaginally, a majority involve at least some verbal coding. Most social behaviors learned through modeling involve or are accompanied by verbalizations of the model or even direct verbal instructions, which are directly encoded verbally. Such verbal coding aids immensely in retention and, in fact, seems almost essential in the learning of more complex behaviors. The somewhat older child learning to ride a bicycle, for example, may have greater difficulty learning to ride merely by watching another person, than the young child did with a tricycle. While some direct observation will be helpful, verbal commentary and perhaps direct verbal instruction will probably be most helpful in learning the more complex bicycle riding technique. A number of empirical studies (for example, Bandura, Grusec, and Menlove 1966; Bandura and Jeffery 1973; Gerst 1971) have provided support for the hypothesized utility of symbolic representation in observational learning.

Motor Reproduction

A third element in the modeling process is the actual *motor reproduction* of a modeled response. Such motor reproduction does not automatically follow from careful attention to cues and retention of the modeled behavior. In fact, physical limitations or the presence of many small, hard-to-observe components in the response often prevent or at least delay response performance. For example, an avid baseball fan may repeatedly observe Hank Aaron hitting home runs but find it impossible to reproduce the modeled behavior. More generally, the individual formulates a conception of the motor action after watching the model and then may be able to achieve a rough approximation of the performance. The disparity between conception and execution indicates the amount and direction in which behavior must be altered to achieve the desired performance. The best results will probably be achieved through *corrective modeling* in which the model or teacher identifies various segments of a performance, models them, and provides feedback to the learner. A wide variety of skills, ranging from tennis and golf to dramatics and violin virtuosity, can be learned in this way.

Motivational and Reinforcement Processes

It is probable that a typical individual observationally learns a substantial number of responses which are never overtly performed or are performed only on rare occasions. This is because, according to modeling theory, the individual performs the response only when motivated to do so or only when reinforcement is given for the performance of the response. Alternatively, the presence of negative incentive conditions, such as the possibility that a given response will be punished, will tend to suppress the performance of that response directly.

Skinnerian theory and other reinforcement approaches have focused on reinforcements which come to the individual from the external environment, suggesting that it is these reinforcements which largely control human behavior. Social learning theory holds that human behavior is not controlled solely by external reinforcers. Much behavior is regulated by internalized, self-reinforcement processes. Self-evaluation is an ongoing process in which the individual observes his or her own behavior, sets particular performance standards, and engages in self-punishment or self-reward depending on the degree of agreement of behavior with self-imposed demands. Of course, external reinforcers still play a part in many instances of behavior expression, but internal self-evaluation and self-reinforcement are emphasized as the basis for the expression of behaviors previously learned through modeling.

The Role of Reinforcement. The careful distinction drawn by Bandura between the acquisition of modeled behavior and its performance should be emphasized. Responses are basically acquired through the operation of the sensory and cognitive processes involved in attention and retention. The performance of the behavior at some later point in time, however, is determined largely by the presence of reinforcement contingencies relevant to the behavior in question. The role of reinforcement is in this way quite different than in the Skinnerian or Hullian theories, where it is critical to the initial learning or modification of responses. In modeling theory reinforcement is not importantly involved in acquisition (although it may influence the acquisition process), but it is critical in the performance of the response.

TYPES AND EFFECTS OF EXPOSURE

The four-process model proposed by Bandura (1969) accounts theoretically for the basic determinants of social learning. The theory goes well beyond this basic model, however, to specify the effects of exposure to models, to propose that modeling may occur symbolically as well as more concretely, and to deal with the observational learning of more complex behaviors.

Effects of Modeling Exposure

We have already noted evidence that behavior can be learned through modeling and have cited Bandura's assumption that a wide variety of behaviors are subject to the modeling effect. To be somewhat more specific on this latter point, social learning theory proposes that the exposure to behavior models may have three distinguishable effects on the behavior of the observer (Bandura and Walters 1963; Bandura 1965; Bandura 1977): (1) *novel response acquisition,* in which the individual learns a new response by observing it in a model (The learning may take a variety of forms, including response patterns, judgmental standards, cognitive skills, and generative rules); (2) *inhibitory response modification,* in which such behavior-inhibiting responses as fear are strengthened or weakened by observing a model's behavior; and (3) *social facilitation* of existing responses. Novel response acquisition is exemplified by the experiment described above in which a child observes a model aggressing against a doll and then imitates that behavior when a similar doll is available. Bandura has suggested that this *modeling effect* usually involves the unique combination or recombination of response components already existing in the subject's behavioral repertoire or the elicitation of previously acquired responses by new stimuli. The modification of existing inhibitions can be seen in work with snake phobias (Bandura, Blanchard, and Ritter 1969), in which the intense fear or phobia of subjects was reduced through modeling techniques. The individual who observes an exciting tennis match and then decides to go out and play tennis for the first time in several years is demonstrating the elicitation through observation of a previously learned but dormant response.

Behavioral Consequences to the Model

To a substantial extent, the expression of modeled behavior is a function of the observed consequences to the model performing that behavior. If the model is obviously rewarded as a result of the behavior, the observer is considerably more likely to exhibit that behavior than if the model is punished (Bandura, Ross, and Ross 1963). In the study of observed aggressive responses toward the Bobo doll (Bandura, 1965), there were actually three groups of children. One group observed a condition in which the model who was hitting and generally aggressing against the doll was punished by an adult; a second group saw the model rewarded for his aggressive behavior; and a third group observed no reward or punishment to the model. The greatest tendency to reproduce the aggressive behavior sequence occurred in the rewarded model condition and the least in the punished model condition.

Symbolic Modeling

Social learning theory would have relatively limited implications if modeling depended entirely on the exhibition of behaviors by live models, such as parents and teachers. While such live figures are important sources of behaviors to be modeled, a substantial proportion of modeling is based not on live models but on *symbolic* ones. The latter include direct pictorial presentations, such as television and movies, written materials, such as books and school papers, and verbal presentations, such as direct verbal instruction relevant to a particular behavior. Bandura, Ross, and Ross (1963) conducted a study in which they exposed children to aggressive behavior in an adult model, or to a film of the model performing the behavior, or to an animated cartoon. There were no substantial differences among the three conditions in the amount of modeling behavior produced. The symbolic models were just as effective as the live model. A number of other studies have supported this basic observation.

Abstract Modeling

If we want children to learn a particular aspect of language, such as use of the passive voice, we may provide them with sentence examples, such as "The car was sold" or "The child was punished." We may then ask the child to make up some totally different sentences that use the passive voice. This teaching process is termed *abstract modeling*. A number of exemplary responses are modeled, and the observer must derive from these the common attributes and the rules for generating similar behavior. A variety of cognitive operations, information-processing strategies, and judgmental orientations, all involving abstract or rule-governed behavior, are learned in this way.

Creative Modeling

Creative behavior patterns can be developed through a modeling process. The model displays and the observer learns a new style of behavior, which is then more broadly applied by the observer to produce new innovations. For example, parents may teach their children a craft, such as macramé, and model creative uses of the craft. One of the children may later design individual, totally different, macramé creations. In addition, a particular observer may draw from the behavior of several different models, integrating elements of their behavior patterns into a new innovative pattern.

Complex Behavior

Many of the behaviors employed in modeling experiments have been simple behaviors, exemplified by the aggressive behavior of the model toward the Bobo doll. While this may cause some concern over the potential application of modeling theory to more complex behaviors, there is ample evidence in the modeling literature that considerably more complex behavior patterns are subject to observational learning. In one study, for example, several models displayed complex, diverse patterns for naive observers (Bandura, Ross, and Ross 1963). The later responses displayed by observers clearly indicated a modeling effect but were relatively novel responses formed by combinations of response elements copied from multiple models.

DETERMINANTS OF BEHAVIOR

While modeling is central to the development of many important behavior patterns, a better understanding of how behavior occurs is gained through an examination of several major determinants of behavior. These include certain antecedent determinants, consequent determinants, and cognitive factors. A detailed treatment of the roles of these various factors in behavior determination is provided by Bandura (1977a). We will give here only a brief overview.

Antecedents of Behavior

People behave in part as a function of the consequences that they anticipate their behavior will create. What the person anticipates or expects will happen is a function of previous experience with the stimuli present in a situation. What is learned is not, however, a set of stimulus-response connections but rather a set of expectancies, and the person does not respond simply to the stimuli but rather to an interpretation of the stimuli. The expectancies that thus so importantly influence behavior may be learned and influenced in a variety of ways. Direct experience can lead to *symbolic* expectancy learning. For example, one study showed that men became sexually aroused at the sight of women's boots when pictures of these boots had been systematically paired with pictures of sexually stimulating women (Rachman 1966). Some expectancy learning, on the other hand, is *vicarious*. For example, a person who has had no experience with people from another culture may adopt a set of attitudes and expectations modeled by others who are seen as knowledgeable about that culture. Emotional expectations and reactions (like the fear of bats) are often also learned vicariously by observing a model. Cognitions can further control anticipatory responses. For example, a person who has previously learned affective reactions to stimuli followed by painful events will quickly show a reduction of fear and avoidance behavior when informed verbally that the painful event will no longer occur.

A person who undergoes expectancy learning is learning a set of *contingency rules.* These rules specify, essentially, the circumstances under which certain behaviors should and should not be used. Driving through an intersection, for example, is appropriate when the light is green and inappropriate when it is red. More complex contingencies may characterize social behavior. The person may learn, for example, that aggressive behavior is appropriate when there is excessive and obvious provocation from a social equal, but it is inappropriate when the provocateur is significantly superior or inferior, when the provocation is minimal, or when the person is a member of the opposite sex. To operate effectively, contingency rules require the presence of predictive cues or stimuli (such as the red or green color of the light). One major source of such predictive cues is the behavior of other people. Thus, modeling by others often significantly influences immediate behavior. For example, students in a large classroom may begin to pack up their books when they see others preparing to leave, people in an auditorium may stand for an ovation at the end of a concert when they see others stand and may laugh when they hear others laugh, and the like.

Consequences of Behavior

Behavior is based in part on expectations, as we have seen, but it is also influenced by its consequences. It should be noted, however, that in social learning theory, response consequences influence behavior largely in antecedent fashion by creating expectations of similar future outcomes. Thus, it is the informative and incentive value of consequences that has the greatest influence on behavior.

Three major sources of reinforcement can be identified. *External reinforcement* is a response consequence coming from the outside environment. This is the type of reinforcement emphasized by Skinner as controlling most behavior. Bandura has noted that when desired reinforcements are available, they can serve in an antecedent way as incentives for the performance of behavior. *Vicarious reinforcement* may occur when a person observes another individual being rewarded or punished for a particular behavior. One form is in the differential responses to seeing a model rewarded or punished, as in the Bobo doll experiment discussed above. Vicarious punishment is centrally important in law enforcement in which exemplary punishment of others will deter a given individual from breaking the law. Despite the importance of external and vicarious forms of reinforcement, both of which originate outside the individual, most behavior is controlled by *self-reinforcement.* A lone golfer attempts a perfect drive, the author writes a paragraph, and the artist produces an original painting, all, in at least some cases, without specific external sources of reinforcement. Bandura defines self-reinforcement as "a process in which individuals enhance and maintain their own behavior by rewarding themselves with rewards that they control whenever they attain self-prescribed standards" (1977b, p. 130). The more general term, *self-regulation,* simply recognizes that both positive and negative self-reactions are possible. In administering self-regulated reinforcement the individual improves performance by making self-reward contingent upon achieving some self-determined standard of performance. Sometimes self-reinforcement may involve quite specific rewards, as when the woman promises herself that she will buy a new dress if she loses twenty pounds. More often, however, self-reward is a somewhat more subtle self-evaluative reaction or feeling. Clearly, the central role given to the self-evaluation and self-reinforcement process in social learning theory brings to that theory a shared perspective with phenomenological approaches, such as that of Carl Rogers. The individual is seen as having an evaluative self-concept, which can be either relatively positive or relatively negative. The self-concept, through the self-reinforcement process that it administers, has a centrally important role in determining behavior.

Cognitive Control

Bandura has postulated that external influences on behavior operate through the mediation of *cognitive* factors. Cognitive processes are involved in determining which of many external events will be observed and how the individual will receive and react to these events. Cognitions influence behavior in a number of ways. First, some motivation is cognitively based, in that actions may originate not from external stimulation in some cases but from internal cognitive activities. Thus, thoughts about the future consequences of an act may be motivating, and cognitively set goals may motivate behavior. More generally, through cognition "people function as active agents in their own self-motivation" (Bandura 1977b, p. 165).

Cognitions also play a number of other roles in determining behavior. They serve, as we have already seen, to provide representations of contingencies and through them guide behavior. For example, the aeronautical engineer will attempt to determine cognitively that a newly designed plane will fly, rather than construct the plane and then use a trial-and-error process.

RECIPROCAL DETERMINISM AND THE SELF-SYSTEM

The antecedents, consequences, and cognitive factors which determine behavior do not do so in an individual or independent fashion but rather through interaction. Specifically, Bandura (1977b, 1978), has hypothesized that behavior, internal personal factors, and environmental influences all function as interactive determinants of one another. He termed this complex process *triadic reciprocal interaction.* Triadic refers, of course, to the three factors, behavior, person, and environment, while reciprocal makes it clear that each of the three factors influences the others. A good example is television viewing behavior (Bandura 1978). The programs watched are determined by individual preference (a person variable), which may be modified by the content of the program on a given occasion (an environment variable). Further, what the person watched (the viewing behavior) will partly determine the nature of the future television environment. Finally, the viewing options provided by the environment influence viewer preference. The triadic reciprocal nature of the interaction is clear.

The idea that some internal self-system is centrally involved in the regulation of human behavior is alien to the behavioral approaches of Skinner and Dollard and Miller. However, recent years have seen an increasing emphasis on the central role of such self-regulatory processes in social learning theory.

Bandura (1977a, 1977b, 1978) has proposed that the individual does have a self-system that strongly influences behavior. This system is not a psychic agent, as in Rogerian theory, but rather a set of cognitive structures and of subfunctions of the perception, evaluation, and regulation of behavior. More specifically, Bandura has proposed that there is a process of self-observation of performance followed by a judgmental process leading to a self-response. The self-response, in turn, affects behavior and the environment, which provide feedback for modification of the self-regulatory system. Thus, there is again a reciprocal interaction.

The cognitive nature of self-regulation becomes somewhat clearer when one considers Bandura's (1977) concept of *self-efficacy*. We have already discussed the hypothesis that an individual behaves partially as a result of cognitive expectations. Among the most important of these expectations are *efficacy expectations,* which represent the extent to which the individual believes that he or she can achieve the desired outcome in a particular situation.

The efficacy expectations held by the individual collectively constitute the person's sense of self-efficacy and will significantly influence the person's choice of and persistence in coping behaviors. The greater the person's perceived self-efficacy in a given situation, the more likely the individual is to enter that situation and the more persistent will be the efforts made.

Self-efficacy develops through a special type of observational learning in which the person repeatedly observes the effects of his or her own actions in a particular situation in relationship to the outcome of the situation. In contrast to some other views that behavior is largely controlled by its immediate consequences, Bandura has suggested that the person amasses and synthesizes information about behavior-outcome relationships from sequences of events over a period of time. This process should provide a generalized sense of self-efficacy which will influence behavior in a wide variety of situations.

AN OVERVIEW OF SOCIAL LEARNING THEORY

While we have largely completed discussion of the basic tenets of Bandura's theory, we have not yet dealt specifically with the question of what structural, dynamic, and developmental principles comprise this viewpoint. In fact, the structural and motivational principles cannot be as clearly separated as can be done with some theories, due to the reciprocal interactive nature of the model. There are, however, some points of differentiation.

Structural Principles

Perhaps the major structure of the personality in Bandura's theory is the self-system. As we have seen, the self-system is cognitive in nature and constitutes a major regulatory influence, partially through the cognitive self-efficacy expectations held by the individual. Some other cognitions, not necessarily involved directly with the self-system, are also structural in nature. Response-outcome expectations are essentially structural cognitions which represent the individual's estimate that a particular behavior will produce a certain outcome in a given situation. More generally, the cognitive processes that provide for the representational guidance of behavior are essentially structural in nature.

Dynamic Principles

Social learning theory identifies two major classes of behavior motivators. First, there are biologically based motivators similar to those seen in other theories. Included are internal aversive stimulation arising from tissue deficits, as in hunger and thirst, and external sources of aversive stimulation, as when pain activates behavior. The second major source of motivation is cognition, which has dynamic as well as structural properties. Two major cognitive sources of motivation have been proposed. The person thus establishes outcome expectations which may be material (like consumption of food), sensory (pleasant stimulation, for example), or social (such as a positive or negative evaluation by others). The second cognitive source of motivation operates through the intervening influence of goal-setting and self-evaluative reactions. Self-motivation requires standards against which to evaluate performance. By making positive self-evaluation conditional on attaining a certain level of behavior, individuals create self-motivation to behave in such a way as to attain the self-imposed standards.

Origins and Development

The individual is born with only elementary reflexes and genetically influenced behavior potentialities. All actual behavior patterns must therefore be learned.

There are two major types of learning. The first is the more traditional learning through response consequences for reinforcement. The child, for example, smiles and is rewarded or plays in the street and is punished. This type of learning has two important consequences. First, it imparts information, and the child learns which behaviors are most appropriate in which situations. Second, it serves a motivational function by creating learned expectations that certain actions will bring about positive or negative consequences. Having learned to anticipate consequences, the individual is motivated to behave accordingly. The second form of learning is observational learning through modeling. We have seen that this form of learning is central to Bandura's theory. It is clearly emphasized over learning by reinforcement and is seen as accounting for most important social behavior.

SOME APPLICATIONS OF SOCIAL LEARNING THEORY

Bandura (1973, 1977a) has applied his social learning theory to the questions of how aggressive behavior originates, how it is elicited and maintained, and how it can be controlled and reduced. The particular importance of considering aggressive behavior lies in the need to reduce the overall level of societal violence.

Rejecting as inadequate a number of earlier theories of aggression, such as those of Freud and of Dollard and Miller, Bandura has hypothesized that aggression is lerned primarily through the modeling of aggressive behavior demonstrated by others. Family members, subcultures, and television can all be major sources of models for aggressive behavior. Once learned, and available in the individual's behavioral repertoire, aggressive behavior can be elicited by a variety of social conditions which provide incentives or reinforcements.

Bandura has proposed that aggressive behavior can be modified through the application of treatments based on social learning theory. Essentially, alternatives to aggressive behavior are modeled, and the learner then engages, with guidance, in the successful practice of the nonaggressive behaviors.

Psychotherapy

The application of social learning theory to psychotherapy is straightforward. Basically, a problem behavior is identified, a model demonstrates an alternative or desirable behavior, and the client, who observationally learns the modeled behavior, then attempts the behavior.

An example is provided by the application of modeling to adult phobic behaviors in which models are seen carrying out the threatening activities without experiencing any adverse consequences. Several variations on this basic approach have been used. Let us take the example of adults who have snake phobias. Here *graduated modeling* has been used. In this technique, a model may gradually approach, tentatively touch, and finally pick up a snake. There are several ways of presenting this modeling exposure. One is live modeling, in which the model simply gives a live demonstration; a second is symbolic modeling, in which the model is shown on film; and a third is participant modeling, in which the therapist models responses toward the snake, then gradually draws the individual into performing the behavior.

A number of studies have demonstrated the success of modeling techniques. It has been found, for example, that symbolic modeling used in treating snake phobia subjects is equally as effective as systematic desensitization, while live modeling is significantly better (Bandura, Blanchard, and Ritter 1969). More generally, modeling techniques have been successfully used in phobic children (Ritter 1968) and adults (Rimm and Mahoney 1969) and in the development of verbal behavior in mute psychotics (Sherman 1965). Recently, Bandura (1977b) has shown that different treatment methods alter expectations of personal efficacy and that behavioral changes correspond closely to the level of self-efficacy of the individual.

EMPIRICAL APPROACHES

Bandura and his colleagues have been actively involved for many years in a research program designed to test various aspects of social learning theory. We will briefly consider here some of the kinds of research done by the Bandura group in an effort to test various theoretical assumptions about the observational learning process.

Learning through Modeling and Observation

A basic tenet of the Bandura theory is that learning can take place through observation without response performance and without reinforcement. An early, exemplary study (Bandura, Ross, and Ross 1963) was done to test this assumption. Nursery school children observed a model enter a room and assault a doll in several novel ways. When the children were later placed in a room containing the doll and other toys, they performed more of the model's specific aggressive responses against the doll than did a control group of children who had seen the same model behaving nonaggressively toward the doll. The children had learned the aggressive responses by simply observing the model, without previously having performed the responses themselves and without having received prior reinforcements. A number of other studies are also supportive of the basic observational learning assumption (viz., Bandura 1971; Flanders 1968).

Even champanzees display observational learning. When these animals are raised in human families, they display a variety of modeled behaviors, such as opening cans with screwdrivers and striking the keys on a typewriter. They have even been shown to acquire observationally and later use a sign language (Gardner and Gardner 1969).

Performance through Incentives

Bandura has hypothesized that the primary role of reinforcement and incentives is in eliciting and maintaining the performance of behaviors previously acquired through observation. Bandura (1965) tested this hypothesis by exposing children to a model who was either rewarded for aggressive behavior, punished for it, or received no reward or punishment. Children who saw the model punished were less likely to perform the aggressive responses than those who had seen the model rewarded. When the child was offered an incentive for imitating the model's behavior, however, children in all three conditions performed the response well. This experiment demonstrates not only that incentive or reinforcement may elicit previously learned behavior but also that the consequences of behavior to the model (reward or punishment) can affect the likelihood that the response will be performed.

Symbolic Coding and Rehearsal

One of the important processes in observational learning is retention, and, according to Bandura, retention is aided by the use of symbols (that is, by symbolic coding) and by mental rehearsal. As an example, subjects in a recent study (Bandura, Jeffery, and Bachicha 1974) observed a model performing complex movement sequences. Subjects symbolically coded the modeled performance by either constructing sentences to describe the features of the modeled patterns (sentence coding condition), or assigning letters to the component movements (letter coding condition) or doing both (dual coding condition). The best later performances of the modeled responses were achieved by subjects in the dual coding condition. In addition, a previous study (Bandura and Jeffery 1973) had shown that subjects who employ no coding at all cannot reproduce any of the response patterns after a delay.

Rehearsal of the response is also useful. Half of the subjects in the Bandura, Jeffery, and Bachicha study rehearsed the memory codes, while the other half did not. Those engaging in rehearsal gave superior performances later.

Self-Evaluation Standards

Such complex concepts as standards for self-evaluation can be learned through modeling. In one study (Bandura and Kupers 1963), a model rewarded himself with candy for either excellent performances or poor performances. Children exposed to the model later rewarded themselves accordingly. Those who had seen rewards only for excellent performances modeled the high standards exhibited, while those who saw rewards for poor performances rewarded themselves for similar poor performances.

The Scope of Observational Learning

Studies have demonstrated that a wide variety of behaviors and concepts can be learned observationally. For example, feelings of helplessness can be learned through modeling. Various studies have shown that humans can learn to feel helpless by experiencing failure and that this learned helplessness can undermine subsequent performance (for example, Hiroto and Seligman 1975). In a recent study (Brown and Inouye 1978), subjects observed a model fail on an anagram task. Those who saw themselves as comparable in ability to the unsuccessful model and those given no comparative information persisted less on subsequent tasks than either subjects who saw the model as less competent than themselves or control subjects who did not observe a model. Thus, the subjects had learned to feel helpless by observing another person failing at a task.

Additional studies have shown that observational learning can be involved in the acquisition of such behaviors as altruism (Bryan and Test 1967), judgmental orientation and rules for behavior (Rosenthal and Zimmerman 1976), linguistic behavior (Bandura and Harris 1966), and delay of gratification (Bandura and Mischel 1965).

Modeling in Therapy

The modeling techniques noted above have been used successfully to treat behavior problems. In one study, Bandura and Menlove (1968) randomly assigned children with strong dog phobias to one of three experimental conditions. The children either observed a single model gradually approaching a cocker spaniel, saw multiple models playing with a wide variety of dogs, or saw movies unrelated to dogs (a control condition). Results showed that the modeling procedures were effective in reducing the phobia. The control children showed no change in their phobic behavior. A second study (Bandura, Grusec, and Menlove 1967) confirmed this result.

EVALUATION

Bandura's social learning theory shares with Skinner's and with Dollard and Miller's some of the same plaudits and criticisms. Because it is a theory which allows for cognitive variables and omits some of the major elements of other learning theories, it is also subject to several unique critical points.

Major Contributions of the Theory

Like the theories of Skinner and Dollard and Miller, Bandura's is marked by a considerable degree of conceptual clarity. He has outlined the basic elements of observational learning in a succinct, concise theory of modeling behavior. In addition, social learning theory, like other learning models, is basically scientific in its approach to the understanding of behavior, although it does not have the exclusive emphasis on externally observable behaviors that is seen in Skinner's approach. A final major similarity to other learning approaches is that Bandura has provided an admirably detailed account of the processes of behavior development and change.

In addition to these shared virtues, social learning theory incorporates complex cognitive processes, such as imagery and coding, thus making it perhaps more applicable to human behavior. Such considerations as planning, evaluation, and selection of alternative behaviors, and self-control of behaviors are readily understood in social learning terms. On a broader level, Bandura provides a carefully developed conceptual framework within which many of the contributions of empirical research can be integrated and understood. Moreover, the Bandura paradigm has been extended to the understanding of a wide variety of behaviors and situations.

Difficulties and Criticisms

Perhaps because it is a relatively new theoretical paradigm and because it incorporates at least to some degree much of the thinking of many learning-oriented psychologists, the Bandura approach has not encountered the volume of criticisms to which Skinner's theory has been subjected. Some difficulties must, however, be noted.

First, it can be argued that social learning theory is not an adequately parsimonious treatment of the behavioral phenomena with which it deals. Some support for the allegation of unnecessary complexity in the theory could be gained from an explanation of modeling phenomena in terms of some simple framework, such as that of operant conditioning. Such analyses have been done (for example, Gewirtz 1969; Gewirtz and Stingle 1968), and they suggest that observational learning is based on what can be termed *generalized imitation.* Gewirtz and Stingle (1968) have argued that imitative responses initially take place by chance, are reinforced by stimuli in the environment, and thus are learned operantly. When a number of imitative responses have been acquired and maintained on an intermittent reinforcement schedule, a generalized imitative response is likely to occur. That is, the fact that the individual has experienced reinforcement for multiple modeled behaviors means that modeling itself has been repeatedly rewarded and hence is likely to be engaged in more frequently. Moreover, since a generalized class of imitative responses has been repeatedly reinforced, it is not necessary for each and every new imitative behavior to be rewarded in order for it to be maintained. If Gewirtz and Stingle and others are correct, the "no-trial" observational learning to which Bandura subscribes may not necessarily occur at all. The observationally learned response becomes simply a specific instance of generalized modeling or imitation. There are, however, some important theoretical difficulties with the alternative proposed by Gewirtz and Stingle.

Does Imitative Learning Occur? It has been argued (Aronfreed 1968) that in some of Bandura's experiments, the children were merely displaying response tendencies already present in their behavioral repertoires and had learned nothing new. However, Bandura has ordinarily employed control groups of children who do not observe the model's behavior but are placed in the performance setting and tested. They do not show the new response.

COGNITIVE SOCIAL LEARNING THEORY: WALTER MISCHEL

Walter Mischel, who presents a somewhat different social learning theory than Bandura's, published a paper in 1968 which argued strongly that much data in the psychological literature show little consistency in individual behavior across situations. In particular, he concluded that traditionally measured personality dimensions do not predict behavior across situations at all well and that the situation is more important than traits in determining behavior. The paper was controversial, since it appeared to argue that personal dispositions or traits, which are so central to most major personality theories, actually have little influence on behavior and may not exist at all.

Bowers (1973), among others, argued that Mischel had gone too far away from a trait psychology, which looks for individual consistencies in behavior, and too far in the direction of situationism. He argues, instead, for a view which takes into consideration the interaction between traits and situations. That is, he holds that one needs to know the contribution to specific behaviors or responses not only of the person and of the specific situation but of the interaction of the two.

Mischel (1973) clarified and extended his position to adopt quite clearly an interactionist view, which argues for taking into account the person (that is, traits), the situation, and the interaction of these two in predicting behavior. Mischel (1973), Bowers (1973), and others have compiled a number of studies which tend to support the interactionist position. Basically, this position holds that if one measures both personality traits and situations in which behavior occurs, it will not be either of these factors alone but the interaction of two that contributes most heavily to the ability to predict the person's behavior in that situation. Thus, for example, Moos (1970) had observers rate psychiatric patients on a series of dimensions following the participation of the patients in each of six different situations. The relative influence of the individual person (patient), the situation, and the situation-by-person interaction can be assessed by determining the percentage of variance accounted for by each factor. For our purposes, percentage of variance is simply the statistician's way of saying amount of influence. In the Moos study the situation accounted for 3.08 percent of the variance, the person accounted for 9.93 percent of the variance, and the situation by person interaction accounted for 32.37 percent of the variance.

It is of interest to note that while interactionism is widely viewed as a relatively recent development in psychology, Raymond Cattell adopted basically an interactionist viewpoint many years ago. His specification equation (see p. 296) quite specifically takes into account the trait-situation interaction in predicting behavior.

Interactionism vs. Reciprocal Determinism

How does the interactionism of Mischel and his colleagues relate to the reciprocal determinism of Bandura's theory? Both positions clearly suggest that there is an ongoing interaction of person and environment, but Bandura (1978) has criticized the interactionist position for not including behavior itself in the interaction conception. His view, as we have seen, suggests that the interaction is not merely dyadic (that is, person and environment) but triadic (that is, person, environment, and behavior). All three factors reciprocally affect one another.

In accepting an interactionist view of behavior, Mischel (1973) noted the need for a set of person variables that are consistent with the social learning viewpoint. Such variables cannot be traits in the traditional sense of direct causal determinants of behavior. Rather, Mischel's variables focus on what the person *constructs* or builds with relevance to particular situations. The hypothesized variables can thus be seen as specifying those aspects of the individual's behavior that are determined by his or her long-term social learning history and its interaction with current, situational variables to determine specific behavioral output. For example, behavior is partially determined by the individual's *competencies* to generate or construct diverse behavior patterns under varied conditions. Such competencies reflect the extent to which the person is capable of the adaptive behavior required by a given situation. They tend to be stable and enduring over long periods of time. Mischel (1973) described four other person variables as well.

Given the social learning viewpoint that human functioning involves a person-situation interaction or, in Bandura's extended view, a person-environment-behavior interaction, it may be useful to reflect for a moment on just what differences would exist between the "new" social learning approaches and the "old" trait theories.

The differences are not as great as might appear at first glance. No trait theorist—Gordon Allport, Sigmund Freud, Carl Rogers, or others—would insist that behavior is determined entirely by broad determining tendencies inherited or learned over a long period of time. All agree that to some extent behavior is mediated by the individual's situation. It is now also apparent that the more recently stated positions of Mischel, Bandura, and others in no way denies the relevance of person variables to behavior determination and, in fact, gives these variables a major role. There is, however, an important difference in emphasis. Where the trait theorist tends to rely most heavily on broad determining tendencies and to expend relatively little effort in the search for situational cues that may affect behavior, the situational theorist tends to stress the role of the situation, giving person variables a relatively small role. Moreover, where the traditional trait theories attribute a strong causal role to traits, Mischel prefers to think of trait concepts simply as labels for observed behavior. The resolution of the situation-trait controversy, toward which both sides have moved, is that both traits and situations are important and interact to determine behavior.

JULIAN ROTTER'S SOCIAL LEARNING THEORY

A social learning theory does not necessarily have to be one which emphasizes the role of observational learning and details the process of personality development through modeling. The Rotter theory was first stated as an alternative to other approaches, including other learning theories, (Rotter 1954 and 1971) and has recently been updated and its applications considered (Rotter, Chance, and Phares 1972; Rotter and Hochreich 1975).

Basic Tenets

The central assumption of Rotter's theory is that the most important determinant of behavior, and, hence, the essential unit of study, is neither the person nor the environment but rather the interaction of the two. The environmental determinants that enter into the interaction are not all equally important. Only those aspects that are *meaningful* for the individual are to be seriously considered as behavior determinants. The personality component of the interaction is conceptualized as a set of *potentials to respond* to relatively specific types of social situations. These potentials are a function of the individual's behavioral history and, as such, are learned through the individual's experiences with the social environment.

A second central assumption is that behavior is *goal-directed*. The goal-direction principle is a motivational hypothesis which replaces the traditional drive reduction tenet of such theories as that of Dollard and Miller. Rotter defines reinforcement, in effect, as any behavior, act, or event which influences the person's movement toward a goal. Those events that facilitate progress toward the goal are positive reinforcers, while those that inhibit such progress are negative reinforcers.

BEHAVIOR DETERMINANTS

Rotter's theory is directed toward the prediction of relatively specific human behavior in relatively specific situations. The theoretical model designed to accomplish this prediction begins with three basic constructs, which enter into a prediction formula, and includes a fourth construct that is, at least implicitly, involved.

Behavior Potential

The *behavior potential* (BP) is the likelihood or potential that a specific behavior will appear in a given situation in relationship to a particular reinforcement or set of reinforcements. The behavior referred to is an observable or measurable response of the individual, including overt motor movement, verbal expression, cognition, and a variety of others. In a given situation any of a variety of behaviors might be possible. Each behavior has associated with it a behavior potential based on the past history of the individual. As an example, consider the situation in an examination setting. The reinforcements available are such things as good grades, parental praise, and status among fellow students, and the student may engage in any of a variety of possible behaviors, such as careful, long-term study, "cramming" before the exam, feigning illness to avoid the exam, or cheating. Each of these behaviors has a specific potential for a given individual in a particular situation.

Reinforcement Value

The second essential determinant, *reinforcement value* (RV), is the degree or extent to which the individual prefers to receive a given reinforcement. Each individual will differentially value particular kinds of reinforcement in specific situations, and these learned values will contribute to the determination of his behavior.

Expectancy

Like Mischel and Bandura, Rotter employs a concept of *expectancy* (E), defined as the individual's subjective probability that a specific behavior will lead to a particular reinforcement in a given situation. The expectancy concept proposes that the individual not only behaves but anticipates his own behavior and its consequences. This anticipation enters into the determination of the probability of occurrence of a given response. Some expectancies are quite specific to particular situations, while others apply to an entire class of somewhat varied situations and are thus termed generalized expectancies (GE). A student may hold a relatively specific expectancy of passing or failing a particular exam and a much more highly generalized expectancy of academic success or failure in all or most courses undertaken.

Two Generalized Expectancies. One major generalized expectancy on which Rotter has focused considerable attention is the dimension of *internal-external control* of behavior. People whose generalized expectancies lead them to anticipate that reinforcements are dependent upon their own behaviors are under internal control, while those who tend to attribute reinforcement contingencies to other people, to situations, or to chance are under external control. Considerable research has been undertaken to determine the differential characteristics of those who attribute their reinforcements to internal versus those who attribute reinforcements to external control (Rotter 1966). While much of the research has supported predictions made from the Rotter framework, other research has failed to support these predictions, and research using the Internal-External Control Scale continues in attempts to better understand the influence of this type of generalized expectancy on specific areas of human behavior (Rotter, Chance, and Phares 1972).

The second major generalized expectancy studied by Rotter is *interpersonal trust,* referring to the extent to which individuals tend to believe and feel that they can rely on others. Rotter (1967) has noted the extent to which the interpersonal trust expectancy can affect an individual's life. Since most reinforcements for adults are obtained through the behaviors of other persons and since individuals must frequently make judgments concerning the extent to which they can trust or rely on another individual to provide reinforcements, the interpersonal trust dimension enters into many activities in life. In fact, it can be argued that nearly every social interaction concerned with the reinforcement of one or more of the persons involved in the interaction is affected by the generalized interpersonal trust expectancies of those engaged in the interaction. Rotter (1967) has developed an Interpersonal Trust Scale designed to measure this expectancy.

The Psychological Situation

Rotter's emphasis in considering the situation as a fourth major factor in behavior determination has been similar to Mischel's. Rotter has pointed out that the situation, as it applies to behavior, is defined or can be defined both objectively and subjectively. The more objective definition of the situation in scientific terms is necessary in order to study the influence of the situation on behavior. At the same time, it must be recognized that the individual's reactions to the situation are based on the meaning that the person attributes to the situation through subjective interpretation.

A Prediction Formula

Rotter has specified the interrelationships among his four major variables in determining behavior in the form of a simple prediction formula: $BP_x, S_1R_a = f(E_x, R_aS_1 + RV_a, S_1)$. The meanings of BP, E, and RV are already known. The x refers to a specific behavior, S_1 to situation 1, R_a to reinforcement a. Thus, the formula reads: the potential occurrence of behavior x in situation 1 in relationship to reinforcement a is a function of the expectancy that reinforcement a will follow behavior x in situation 1 and the value of reinforcement a in situation 1. The formula thus indicates that if we can assess for a particular reinforcement in a particular situation the individual's expectancies and reinforcement values, we should be able to predict the potential for studying hard (behavior) for a specific exam (situation), in order to achieve a high grade (reinforcement). We must know the individual's expectancy that hard study will produce a high grade and the value the individual attaches to the particular reinforcement available.

Need Potential

Rotter has developed a second, parallel system of constructs to deal with more complex instances of behavior going beyond any one expectancy, reinforcement, or situation. The concept of *need potential* parallels that of behavior potential and refers to a functionally related group of behaviors leading to the satisfaction of one particular need.

As need potential parallels the behavior potential concept, so *freedom of movement* is the class of broader behavior-determining tendencies related to expectancy. Freedom of movement may be defined as the average level of the individual's expectancies that a particular class of behaviors will lead to the attainment of certain kinds of satisfiers. Freedom of movement refers to the individual's freedom to progress toward satisfaction of a need. The individual with considerable facility to progress toward the need has a high freedom of movement, reflecting expectancies that a number of types of behavior could lead to the desired goal.

The third component of the model is *need value,* which parallels the concept of reinforcement value. Basically, the need value is the extent to which the individual prefers one particular class of satisfiers over another.

Based on the need potential (NP), freedom of movement (FM), and need value (NV) concepts, Rotter proposed a second prediction formula: NP = f(FM + NV). The formula indicates that the probability or potential for the occurrence of a particular group of behaviors that are likely to satisfy some need depends upon the averaged expectancies that these behaviors will result in reinforcements (freedom of movement) and the value which the individual attaches to the class of reinforcers in question (need value).

The individual who attaches a high need value to a particular set of reinforcers and has a high freedom of movement for the attainment of those reinforcers should have little difficulty in dealing effectively with her environment to attain goals. Rotter has been particularly interested, however, in the case of the individual who has highly valued goals that cannot be readily obtained due to low freedom of movement. Such a situation is likely to involve expectations of failure and a resultant avoidance of particular situations in which the probability of failure seems high. The behaviors engaged in are likely to be those often referred to as defensive or psychopathological behaviors and treated in social learning theory as avoidance behaviors and irreal behaviors. Avoidance behaviors keep the person out of situations even when involvement might potentially lead to success, while irreal behaviors are fantasy goal-achievement attempts that have no chance of success at all.

Minimal Goal Level. One reason why an individual may have low freedom of movement is that he or she sets goals unrealistically high. Such behavior may be understood in terms of a concept of *minimal goal level,* which relates to the concepts of reinforcement value and need value. The minimal goal level for a particular behavior or class of behavior is the lowest level of reinforcement that is considered positive and below which reinforcement ceases or even becomes aversive. A good example is seen in the academic goal-setting of students. Some students establish a general minimal goal grade level of B, meaning that they will not be positively reinforced or "feel good" unless they achieve a grade of B or higher in any given course. Provided these students are generally capable of achieving the B grade, their minimal goal is realistic. Other students may set a minimal goal of an A, which may be unrealistic and may thus lead to repeated "failures." One specific result of setting a minimal goal level which is unrealistically high is thus repeated failure to attain the goal level. Broader effects may include the use of unrealistic behavior patterns in attempts to achieve goals, the development of high levels of anxiety on failing to achieve the goal, and even psychopathology.

SOCIAL LEARNING THEORY AND INTERACTIONISM: INCREASING FORCES

We have seen that the social learning and interactionist theories as a group are relatively recent developments in the personality field. The scope of influence of these theories has expanded rapidly in recent years, and many psychologists are turning to the social learning theorists and the interactionists in the ongoing search for the causes of human behavior. While these theories may eventually be incorporated in somewhat broader approaches that deal in more detail with the prediction of behavior and the factors involved in that prediction, it appears likely that the social learning and related interactionist views will continue to increase in their impact on psychology for many years to come.

REFERENCES

Allport, F. H. *Social psychology.* Boston: Houghton Mifflin, 1924.

Aronfreed, J. *Conduct and conscience: The socialization of internalized control over behavior.* New York: Academic Press, 1968.

Bandura, A. Social learning through imitation. In M. R. Jones (Ed.), *Nebraska symposium on motivation.* Lincoln: University of Nebraska Press, 1962.

Bandura, A. Behavioral modification through modeling procedures. In L. Krasner & L. P. Ullman (Eds.), *Research in behavior modification.* New York: Holt, 1965.

Bandura, A. Influence of model's reinforcement contingencies on the acquisition of imitative responses. *Journal of Personality and Social Psychology*, 1965, *1*, 589-595.

Bandura, A. *Principles of behavior modification.* New York: Holt, Rinehart, & Winston, 1969.

Bandura, A. (Ed.) *Psychological modeling: Conflicting theories.* Chicago: Aldine-Atherton, 1971.

Bandura, A. *Aggression: A social learning analysis.* Englewood Cliffs, N.J.: Prentice-Hall, 1973.

Bandura, A. *Social learning theory.* Englewood Cliffs, N.J.: Prentice-Hall, 1977.

Bandura, A. Self-efficacy: Toward a unifying theory of behavioral change. *Psychological Review*, 1977, *84*, 191-215.

Bandura, A. The self system in reciprocal determinism. *American Psychologist*, 1978, *33*, 344-358.

Bandura, A., Blanchard, E. B., & Ritter, B. The relative efficacy of desensitization and modeling approaches for inducing behavioral, affective, and attitudinal changes. *Journal of Personality and Social Psychology*, 1969, *13*, 173-199.

Bandura, A., Grusec, J. E., & Menlove, F. L. Observational learning as a function of symbolization and incentive set. *Child Development*, 1966, *37*, 499-506.

Bandura, A., Grusec, J. E., & Menlove, F. L. Vicarious extinction of avoidance behavior. *Journal of Personality and Social Psychology*, 1967, *5*, 16-23.

Bandura, A., & Harris, M. B. Modification of syntactic style. *Journal of Experimental Child Psychology*, 1966, *4*, 341-352.

Bandura, A., & Jeffery, R. W. Role of symbolic coding and rehearsal processes in observational learning. *Journal of Personality and Social Psychology*, 1973, *26*, 122-130.

Bandura, A., Jeffery, R. W., & Bachicha, D. L. Analysis of memory codes and cumulative rehearsal in observational learning. *Journal of Research in Personality*, 1974, *7*, 295-305.

Bandura, A., & Kupers, C. J. The transmission of patterns of self-reinforcement and the behavior of models in shaping children's moral judgements. *Journal of Abnormal and Social Psychology*, 1963, *67*, 274-281.

Bandura, A., & Menlove, F. L. Factors determining vicarious extinction of avoidance behavior through symbolic modeling. *Journal of Personality and Social Psychology*, 1968, *8*, 99-108.

Bandura, A., & Mischel, W. Modification of self-imposed delay of reward through exposure to live & symbolic models. *Journal of Personality and Social Psychology*, 1965, *2*, 698-705.

Bandura, A., Ross, D., & Ross, S. A. Imitation of film-mediated aggressive models. *Journal of Abnormal and Social Psychology*, 1963, *66*, 3-11.

Bandura, A., & Walters, R. H. *Adolescent aggression: A study of the influence of child-training practices and family interrelationships.* New York: Ronald Press, 1959.

Bandura, A., & Walters, R. H. *Social learning and personality development.* New York: Holt, Rinehart, & Winston, 1963.

Bowers, K. S. Situationism in psychology: An analysis and a critique. *Psychological Review*, 1973, *80*, 307-336.

Brown, I., & Inouye, D. K. Learned helplessness through modeling: The role of perceived similarity in competence. *Journal of Personality and Social Psychology*, 1978, *57*, 65-73.

Bryan, J., & Test, M. Models and helping naturalistic studies in aiding behavior. *Journal of Personality and Social Psychology*, 1967, *6*, 400-407.

Endler, N. S., Magnusson, D., Ekehammar, B., & Okada, M. The multi-dimensionality of state and trait anxiety. *Scandinavian Journal of Psychology*, 1976, *17*, 81-96.

Flanders, J. P. A review of research on imitative behavior. *Psychological Bulletin*, 1968, *69*, 316-337.

Gardner, R. A., & Gardner, B. T. Teaching sign language to a chimpanzee. *Science*, 1969, *165*, 664-672.

Gerst, M. S. Symbolic coding processes in observational learning. *Journal of Personality and Social Psychology*, 1971, *19*, 7-17.

Gewirtz, J. L. Potency of a social reinforcer as a function of satiation and recovery. *Developmental Psychology*, 1969, *1*, 2-13.

Gewirtz, J. L., & Stingle, K. G. The learning of generalized imitation as the basis for identification. *Psychological Review*, 1968, *75*, 374-397.

Hiroto, D. S., & Seligman, M. E. Generality of learned helplessness in man. *Journal of Personality and Social Psychology*, 1975, *31*, 311-327.

Holt, E. B. *Animal drive and the learning process.* New York: Holt, 1931.

Humphrey, G. Imitation and the conditioned reflex. *Pedagogical Seminary*, 1921, *28*, 1-21.

Miller, N. E., & Dollard, J. *Social learning and imitation.* New Haven, Conn.: Yale University Press, 1941.

Mischel, W. Cognition in delay of gratification. In R. L. Solso (Ed.), *Contempo-*

rary issues in cognitive psychology: The Loyola Symposium. Washington, D.C.: V. H. Winston and Sons, 1973.

Moos, R. H. Generality of questionnaire data: Ratings by psychiatric patients. *Journal of Clinical Psychology,* 1970, *26,* 234-236.

Rachman, S. Sexual fetishism: An experimental analogue. *Psychological Record,* 1966, *16,* 293-296.

Rimm, D. C. & Mahoney, M. J. *The application of reinforcement and modeling-guidance procedures in the treatment of snake phobic behavior.* Unpublished manuscript, Arizona State University, 1969.

Ritter, B. The group desensitization of children's snake phobias using vicarious and contact desensitization procedures. *Behavior Research and Therapy,* 1968, *6,* 1-6.

Rosenthal, T. L., & Zimmerman, B. J. Organization and stability of transfer in vicarious concept attainment. *Child Development,* 1976, *47,* 110-117.

Rotter, J. B. *Social learning and clinical psychology.* Englewood Cliffs, N.J.: Prentice-Hall, 1954.

Rotter, J. B. Generalized expectancies for internal versus external control of reinforcement. *Psychological Monographs,* 1966, *80* (1, Whole No. 609).

Rotter, J. B. Beliefs, social attitudes, and behavior: A social learning analysis. In R. Jesser & S. Feschbach (Eds.), *Cognition, personality and clinical psychology.* San Francisco: Jossey-Bass, 1967.

Rotter, J. B., Chance, J. E., & Phares, E. J. (Eds.). *Applications of a social learning theory of personality.* New York: Holt, Rinehart, & Winston, 1972.

Rotter, J. B., & Hochreich, D. J. *Personality.* Glenview, Ill.: Scott-Foresman, 1975.

Sherman, J. A. Use of reinforcement and imitation to reinstate verbal behavior in mute psychotics. *Journal of Abnormal Psychology,* 1965, *70,* 155-164.

Thorndike, E. L. Animal intelligence. *Psychological Monographs,* 1898, *2,* (Whole No. 8).

Watson, J. B. *Behaviorism.* New York: Norton, 1925.

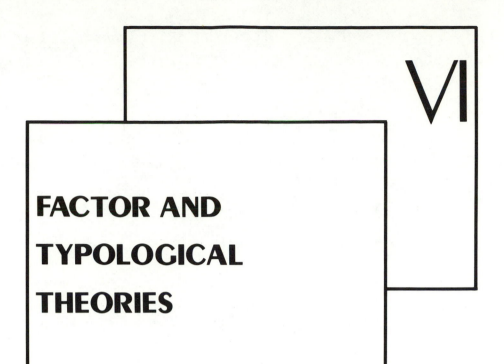

FACTOR AND TYPOLOGICAL THEORIES

12

Structure–Based Systems Theory:

Raymond Cattell

The history of Cattell's theory is the history of trait theory, of the fascination of psychologists and statisticians with numbers and quantification and of a specific quantitative method, factor analysis. The theory goes well beyond basic trait theory, however, to attempt an understanding of the growth and functioning of personality through the application of multivariate experimental methods and structured learning theory.

Trait theories of personality attribute to the individual a number of specific structures or characteristics that are called *traits*. The prototypical trait theory is surely that of Gordon Allport, whose approach, as we have seen, consists largely of defining the personality in terms of a number of behavior-determining tendencies. Many other psychologists have applied the trait concept in their attempts to understand personality, but none has done as much systematic work as Raymond Cattell. In this chapter we will look at Cattell's use of the trait concept as a way of understanding the determination of behavior. We will also see that he uses a number of other concepts to demonstrate the role of states and situations and of the learning process in the development and functioning of personality. The systematic and virtually all-inclusive nature of the theory will become clear as we examine Cattell's methodical integration of the various behavior determinants that he proposes.

CATTELL'S METHOD: FACTOR ANALYSIS

Cattell's work marks a break with traditional trait theory, for he was the first to apply statistical concepts and methods to the study of traits. His focus on quantification is related to a broader interest, extending far beyond the bounds of psychology, in reaching a level of precision in the prediction and understanding of phenomena which can perhaps be achieved only through quantification. Qualities must ultimately become quantities, and thus qualitative descriptions of the human personality must finally become quantitative descriptions. If we are to become more precise in our ability to understand and predict human behavior, we must seek quantitative methods for the study of human personality. One method which has been widely applied is factor analysis.

The basic factor analytic approach can be described with a brief example. Suppose an investigator wants to determine the interrelationships among fifty different personality variables, each represented by a score on a test or an item in a test. Rather than attempting to study all the interrelationships among these variables (over 1,200 correlations), the investigator can search for a smaller number of variables that characterize the overall set of fifty. The variables forming the smaller set are called *factors*.

Modern Factor Analysis

Modern factor analysis usually begins with a large set of psychological variables. These may be test scores, each indicating the performance of one particular subject on a personality variable, such as anxiety, or they may be a number of individual items, such as those found in typical personality inventories. In either case, the basic procedure is to obtain a large group of subjects and get from each subject a score on each variable. The next step is to determine the degree of relationship between each two variables in the total set. Thus, in a fifty-variable problem, the relationship between variable one and variable two, and that between one and three, one and four, and so on, must be determined as well as the relationship between vriables two and three, two and four, and so on. The measure of degree of relationship is the *correlation coefficient,* and the total set of correlations among all variables is the correlation matrix. The next step is to determine whether or not there are small groups of variables within the total correlation matrix which go together to form subsets or dimensions of the total set. This is done by factor analysis, and the factors that result are mathematical representations of the subsets of variables.

For example, a total set of fifty variables may be represented in the principal factor solution as a set of five or ten factors. Each factor or dimension will have one or more variables which are quite closely related to it and are said to "load" highly on the factor.

Unfortunately, the set of factors produced is not psychologically meaningful and must be further modified if the analyst is to learn anything about personality structure. The solution is generally to turn, or rotate, the factors into a specific mathematical relationship with one another. One of two basic types of rotation, orthogonal or oblique, is typically performed. Orthogonal rotation places the factors at right angles (90°) to each other. These are uncorrelated factors. Oblique rotation yields correlated (nonorthogonal) factors. Each type of rotation has certain advantages and disadvantages.

The final step in factor analysis is naming the factors. The mathematical procedures yield only a set of dimensions with an indication of the correlation or loading of each variable on each factor. They do not tell us directly that factor one is anxiety, factor two is extroversion, and so on. The naming process is one of the major points at which a significant amount of subjectivity is introduced into the factor analysis. Two analysts studying the same set of factors may well arrive at different names for each one and thus at different conclusions about the nature of the dimensions underlying the set of variables being investigated.

One last consideration is the possibility of obtaining *higher order* factors. If the original or first order factors are correlated (oblique), it is possible to obtain a smaller number of dimensions by intercorrelating the factors and analyzing this new correlational matrix. If we begin with fifty variables and obtain ten factors on the first factoring, we might reduce this total to four second-order factors. We could intercorrelate and again analyze these factors to obtain two third-order factors. Cattell has sometimes applied higher order factor analysis to his data to obtain the broader dimensions these factors represent.

In summary, factor analysis is a statistical method for summarizing and simplifying sets of variables, reducing a relatively large set of variables to a relatively small set of factors. The steps in carrying out a typical factor analysis are these: (1) obtaining scores from a large number of subjects on each of a number of variables; (2) intercorrelating all variables; (3) factor analyzing the correlation matrix; (4) rotating the factors to the desired solution; (5) interpreting and naming the factors; and (6) obtaining higher order factors.

Major Correlational Alternatives

So far, we have assumed that we have, for a given study, a large number of people providing scores on a number of different variables. All tests are intercorrelated on all persons to yield the correlation matrix. Cattell has called this most common use of correlation *R-technique* to differentiate it from several other uses.

The less common approaches include P-technique, Q-technique, and differential R-technique. In *P-technique*, we begin with a single person and obtain measures from that person on the same set of variables on several different occasions. For example, one person might take a battery of personality tests once each week for a year. We would then have fifty-two separate measures on this one individual on each of the variables involved in the personality tests. Correlations between variables would then be calculated across occasions. In this case, the correlations tell us how constant the person's behavior is over time. In the most basic application of Q-technique, we correlate one person with another, usually across a number of variables, to determine how similar the two people are. This approach is readily extended to intercorrelating a number of people in order to determine which person has the highest average correlation with all the other people. Such an individual might be said to be representative of a particular type that is more generally represented by the group as a whole. For example, the individual in a group of neurotics who showed the highest average correlation with other people in the group might be said to be the best example of a neurotic person. The final approach, differential R-technique, begins with an application of ordinary R-technique. In this case, however, all tests are given to the same group a second time, and the differences between the two occasions on all variables are intercorrelated and factor analyzed.

BIOGRAPHICAL SKETCH

Raymond B. Cattell was born in 1905 in Staffordshire, England. He attended King's College of the University of London and received a B.S. in chemistry, magna cum laude, in 1924 and a Ph.D. in psychology in 1929. He later received an honorary D.Sc. in 1937. Before completing his degree, he became a lecturer at University College, Exeter, England, where he remained until 1931. After spending the next five years (1932–1937) as a director of the city psychological clinic in Leicester, he came to the United States to spend a year as a research associate at Teacher's College, Columbia University. In 1938 he joined the faculty of Clark University as G. Stanley Hall Professor of Psychology and then later moved again to accept a position as lecturer in psychology at Harvard in 1941. He became in 1944 research professor of psychology and director of the Laboratory of Personality and Group Analysis at the University of Illinois. Following his retirement in 1973, Cattell became a visiting professor at the University of Hawaii, where he has remained.

Cattell's career focused on the application of factor analysis and other multivariate statistical techniques to the understanding of personality structure and functioning. Cattell's publications range from those oriented primarily toward a better understanding of personality structure, such as *The Scientific Analysis of Personality* (1965d) to contributions focusing more on the mathematical aspects of his research, such as *Higher Order Structures: Reticular vs. Hierarchical Formulae for Their Interpretation* (1965c). One of the most prolific of all personality theorists, Cattell has published over 30 books and 350 journal articles in the course of his career.

A SCIENCE OF PERSONALITY STUDY

Skinner (1953) has often emphasized the need for a scientific study of behavior, which he seeks in terms of a focus on externally observable behaviors. Cattell (1966b) has also emphasized the need for a scientific approach to personality, but his emphasis has been on the study of internal traits and states which can be made observable through the use of personality tests and other techniques. Cattell's views on the nature of science convey his attitude toward the development and empirical testing of personality theory.

The Scientific Spiral

Cattell has proposed that scientific progress is best achieved through the application of what he termed the *inductive-hypothetical-deductive* method (IHD). The scientist begins not by developing a specific hypothesis about some phenomenon but rather by making one or more experimental observations of the phenomenon in question. He or she then engages in a process of inductive reasoning that leads to the development of one and sometimes many hypotheses. The hypothesis in turn leads to a deduction about the results to be expected from experiments or observations. The actual experiment is then conducted, and from its results the process begins again. The optimal effect is an upward spiraling of scientific knowledge with the IHD spiral repeating itself in each stage of the process.

Three Approaches to Research

Cattell has described the three major approaches to research as bivariate, multivariate, and clinical. The *bivariate* method grew out of the early works of Wundt and Pavlov and follows the methods employed in the physical sciences. The Wundt-Pavlov tradition typically involves experiments in which one variable (the independent variable) is manipulated by an experimenter, and a second variable (the dependent variable) is observed or measured. This is, of course, the "textbook" method for conducting research and is said to establish cause-effect relationships. The *multivariate* method arises from the work of Galton and Pearson and focuses on the quantifiable observation of behavior in living, functioning human beings. In this approach, the variables are measured rather than manipulated. Thus, for example, the bivariate researcher might study anxiety by placing subjects under stress (the independent variable) and measuring the amount of anxiety (the dependent variable) created as a result of this manipulation. The multivariate experimentalist would ordinarily eliminate the manipulation and focus on a large array of variables which he or she has reason to believe might relate to anxiety. These variables would then be studied using advanced correlational techniques. The *clinical* method involves the observation of behavior in a clinical setting, as when a psychotherapist makes a case study of a patient. This method, which involves no quantifiable measurements of behavior, is implicitly multivariate, since the clinician is observing a number of variables in operation.

Cattell has used primarily the multivariate method, because for him the bivariate approach is too simplistic for the task of analyzing complex human behaviors. It tends to break the person up into small bits of behavior which are then studied out of the context of that person's total behavioral pattern. The result is that the bivariate experimentalist tends to focus on relatively small, trivial aspects of behavior and to provide, in some cases, fairly definitive answers to questions that never really needed to be asked. The multivariate approach, on the other hand, allows for the study of a large number of variables more representative of the functioning of the individual and can reveal patterns of relationships. Moreover, the precise nature of the variables to be studied need not be determined a priori, it can be determined experimentally through the factor analytic study of a large number of variables in a large number of individuals.

THE DATA BASE

Cattell's systematic approach to understanding human personality functioning begins by specifying the three major types of data that can be employed in determining the independent factors contributing to behavior determination.

Life record data (called *L-data*) are derived from actual records of the person's life history or direct observations of behavior in real situations. Life history data might come from records of the person's performance in a job setting or in school or from statements or ratings provided by individuals familiar with the person in question. Questionnaire, or *Q-data,* are derived from an individual's own statements about or ratings of his or her own behavior. A person may be asked to answer true or false to a number of self-relevant statements or to indicate the extent to which a particular behavior is characteristic of him. The self-ratings of Q-data have sometimes been considered objective or accurate representations of the individual's behavior and, therefore, personality. Cattell, however, has argued that, because the individual may choose to be self-deceptive or to deceive the experimenter, Q-data are better thought of as bits of behavior that may or may not be accurate self-appraisal. This weakness of Q-data makes objective test or T-data (also called *OT-data*) the best source of information for personality research. An objective test is basically a behavioral situation, often created by an experimenter, in which the individual is not aware of the relationship of his or her behavior and the personality assessment being conducted. As an example of the different data types, high school records (L-data) might show an individual to have a history of fights; he or she might answer yes to the Q-data item "I may hit someone who offends me"; and he or she may score high on a physiological (OT-data) index that is correlated with aggressiveness. Of course, the three different methods of assessment may not always agree that an individual is aggressive or has some other particular trait.

Cattell has systematically used all three major data sources in his search for the basic dimensions of human personality. Together, they allow him to assess the totality of the personality, which he calls the *personality sphere*, and to cross check his findings. Cattell has derived a set of factors for each type of data.

Factor Indexing System

Different investigators, working with the same or different sets of tests and items, may tend to assign different names to what are basically the same personality factors. In the long run this situation is bound to lead to confusion in the field and to retard progress. In order to avoid this problem and keep track of the important tests, variables, and factors isolated in multivariate personality research, Cattell has devised three listing or indexing systems. The T-system assigns each personality test a number. The Master Index (M.I.) system lists each of the separate variables that may appear within tests, since any one test may have several variables. The Universal Index (U.I.) system assigns numbers to the major personality factors. While the T-system and the M.I. system are not yet widely used, the U.I. system is gradually becoming standard for indexing factors. A survey of U.I. factors isolated by the Cattell group has been provided by Cattell and Warburton (1967).

Life Record Data

Cattell's search for basic dimensions began with L-data studies of the personality sphere. He began with well over four thousand terms, reduced these to forty-two variables, and had each variable rated by a large number of subjects. The ratings were factor analyzed to yield a total of twelve factors, which were expanded by later experiments based on L-data to fifteen factors.

Each of the fifteen factors, which Cattell saw as basic dimensions of personality, was assigned a letter of the alphabet and a name. Some of the factor names, such as *intelligence* (Factor B) and *superego strength* (Factor G), are fairly common. Most, however, are unique labels defined by Cattell. For example, the Premsia-Harria factor represents a dimension running from tender-minded to tough-minded, while Parmia-Threctia runs from venturesome to shy.

Questionnaire Data

One of the goals of Cattell's research was to locate factors that appear across two or all three of the major data sources. As a result, he conducted a number of studies to determine the factors deriving from Q-data as well as the extent to which these factors agreed with the L-data factors. Cattell began work on Q-data with a survey of the questionnaire literature and previous factor analyses. The survey turned up a large pool of potential questionnaire items to which he added items written specifically for his work. An initial factor analytic study involving 80 variables and 370 subjects yielded 15 factors in addition to a single general intelligence factor. Each factor appeared in Cattell's data simply because a particular subset of items clustered together to form that factor. Cattell went on to develop two parallel forms of a test, each consisting of 187 items measuring the 16 factors, with 10 to 13 items measuring each dimension. More recent factor analyses have added items and forms and have further refined the questionnaire, which Cattell called the *16-Personality Factor Questionnaire* (16-PF). It should be noted that more recent research suggests that there are perhaps eighteen primary factors, plus an additional seven factors that constitute the typical range of personality structure common to both normal and some abnormal behavior (Cattell and Delhees 1973). In addition, there appear to be some seven factors that appear only in connection with abnormal behavior (Cattell and Specht 1968). Some of the factors not appearing in the 16-PF have been included in other questionnaires developed by the Cattell group.

To determine the higher order factors in personality, Cattell and others have subjected the dimensions of the 16-PF to higher order factor analysis. One example is a study in which Cattell compiled 16-PF data on a widely varied sample of over sixteen hundred subjects. The higher order factor analysis yielded two major factors, anxiety, and exvia-invia (extroversion-introversion). Others have since been added.

Objective Test Data

To complete the study of data types, Cattell located and developed a series of behavioral situations as T-data sources. The tasks assess a variety of areas of functioning, including motor, verbal, emotional, and physiological responses. One example of such an objective test is letter cancellation, in which the subject is instructed to draw a line through each occurrence of the letter *E* or any other letter appearing in a mixed list, and to work as rapidly as possible. This test is related to (that is, correlated with) such factors as task-oriented realism and independence. Another example is a test of pulse rate under shock. Here, a pistol is fired and the heart rate recorded. This test relates to an abnormal assertive ego factor, a dimension on which the self-assured, decisive individual is high. Other tests include reading preference, hidden pictures, moral expediency, voice pitch, and salivation. In all, the Cattell group has compiled over four hundred such tasks.

The search for factors in T-data has led to a number of factor analytic studies and to the development of the Objective-Analytic (O-A) Battery. In a typical study, each subject receives a numerical score on each of a number of different T-data tasks, and the scores are intercorrelated and entered into a factor analysis. Results have supported the existence of twenty-one distinct T-data factors, numbered in the Universal Index coding system as U.I. 16 through U.I. 36. Twelve of the most often replicated T-data factors can now be routinely measured by using the O-A (objective analytic) Test Kit (Cattell and Scheier 1961). Each is a bipolar factor defined by a particular subset of objective tasks. U.I. 32, for example, is the exvia-invia factor and is essentially extroversion-introversion. At the introversion end of the dimension subjects display a tendency to pursue inwardly initiated themes of life and are relatively inattentive to externally imposed requirements. The exvia-invia factor is defined in terms of loadings on twenty-eight different objective tests from the Cattell battery. Among the more important of these defining tasks are *tower construction with blocks, bridge construction with blocks, altruism,* and *aesthetic judgment.*

Factor Matching

Do the factors derived from the three types of data correspond? Basically, L-data and Q-data appear to have quite close correspondence. Twelve of the sixteen factors measured by the 16-PF are very similar to factors derived from L-data. The relationships of T-data and the other data types are more complex. In most instances first order T-data factors bear some reasonable resemblance to second order Q-data factors (Cattell and Nichols 1972) and in four cases have been statistically shown to approach complete identity (Cattell, personal communication 1979). For example, both anxiety (U.I.-24) and exvia-invia (U.I.-32), primary factors in T-data, are second order factors in Q-data. Similarly, restraint (U.I.-17) is aligned with the Q-data factor, control.

STRUCTURAL PRINCIPLES: TRAITS

The factors derived from any one or all three of the data types are viewed as stable, behavior-determining tendencies of the personality or traits. Cattell has not been, strictly speaking, a "pure" trait theorist; he has not relied on the idea that behavior is totally determined by the existence of long-term, cross-situational traits. He is careful to incorporate situational and state factors as a part of his theory. His major organizing concept, however, has been that of trait, which he defines as a broad reaction-determining tendency. The trait concept deals with both the structural and dynamic or motivational aspects of personality functioning. The personality in Cattell's theory consists almost totally of traits, although behavior is determined by the interaction of traits and situational variables.

Trait Classifications

Cattell's traits can be classified in several ways, including (1) origin; (2) uniqueness; (3) level of functioning; (4) depth or importance in the personality. Classified in terms of *origin,* traits are divided into those that arise from hereditary influences (*constitutional traits*) and those that arise from environmental conditions (*environmental-mold traits*). On the *uniqueness* dimension, some traits are seen as specific to a single individual. Some unique traits are intrinsically unique, meaning that the trait is totally different from those found in other individuals. Other traits are only relatively unique, that is, elements of the trait may be found in other individuals, but the precise organization of these elements is found only in a single person. In contrast, common traits are behavior-determining tendencies found in many and sometimes all individuals. The basic similarity in the treatment of unique and common traits to Allport's theory (see Chapter 6) is evident.

Traits also vary in the level of functioning at which they occur. On this dimension, they can be divided into cognitive, motivational, and emotional. Those associated with cognition are *ability traits* that deal with goal-oriented instrumental behavior. Those relating to motivation, *dynamic traits,* are concerned with impelling the individual into action toward some goal; these are the driving forces of the personality. Finally, *temperament traits* are concerned with the expressive quality of the individual's behavior. They deal, for example, with the degree of emotional volatility and the quickness or speed of movement characterizing the person.

The most important dimension divides traits into source and surface traits. *Source traits* exist at a "deeper" level of the personality and represent sets of behaviors constituting unitary, independent personality characteristics. In origin, source traits may be constitutional or environmental mold traits. They may also be unique or common traits and may exist at the dynamic, ability, or temperament levels of functioning. *Surface traits* are sets of *apparently* interrelated behaviors which look superficially like traits but are not consistent over time. Surface trait behaviors do not have a unitary basis; in fact, they represent an interaction among the far more important source traits.

The Dynamic Source Traits: Heredity and Learning

Most theorists take heredity and learning into account as factors in personality and behavior, and many lean heavily toward one side or the other of the nature-nurture argument. Cattell is no exception, and his concept of *dynamic source traits* is his theoretical vehicle.

Basically, Cattell's theory states that behavior is determined by heredity, environment, and the interaction of hereditary and environmental factors. Some instances of behavior are more heavily determined by genetic influences, others are attributed primarily to environmental learning. The three major concepts are erg, sentiment, and attitude. An *erg* is a genetic trait which may importantly influence behavior. A *sentiment* is a learned trait that is perhaps less influential than the erg but nevertheless a substantial behavioral determinant. *Attitudes* are overt expressions of the influence of ergs and sentiments and represent the individual's interest in a particular course of action in a specific situation. Let us look at each in turn.

Attitudes. The statement "I want to satisfy my sexual needs" is an attitude statement. It indicates a specific interest in taking a particular course of action under some implied set of circumstances and with regard to some particular implied person or object. In the more general case, the attitude statement takes this form: "in these circumstances, I want so much to do this with that" (Cattell 1965d, p. 176). The number and importance of attitudes in the personality structure may potentially be of considerable interest. In fact, however, attitudes are so numerous that Cattell found it necessary to select for study particular sets of attitudes which may be logically related to ergs or sentiments. Although a given attitude may have a substantial influence on behavior, the real importance of attitudes derives from the fact that collectively they represent the operation of a relatively small number of important ergs and sentiments.

Ergs. Ergs are hereditary in origin, as we have said, and, therefore, in Cattell's system they are constitutional traits. Since they are also source as opposed to surface traits and dynamic as opposed to ability traits, ergs are constitutional, dynamic source traits.

As a genetic concept, the erg is related to the instinct and primary drive of other theories. William James and William McDougall, for example, saw instincts as genetic guides to human behavior, James specifying forty-four major instincts, McDougall, sixteen. Cattell, however, found nine to eleven ergs, depending upon the particular type of data studied. The major ergs in Cattell's system are sex, parental protectiveness, gregariousness, fear, curiosity, self-assertion, narcissism 1 (sensuality), appeal pugnacity, and constructiveness.

As their genetic origin implies, ergs are viewed as constant and continuing characteristics of the individual. They do vary substantially, however, in strength or intensity. Cattell (1965d) called the intensity of an erg its ergic tension, a concept similar to the idea of the impetus (intensity) of an instinct in Freudian theory or the strength of drive in learning theory. For example, an individual may be hungrier on one occasion than on another. In Cattell's system, *ergic tension* is a function of three major factors. The first is drive strength, the individual's excitation or tension level as determined by constitutional, historical, and physiological conditions. The second component, need strength, represents a condition of physiological deprivation relevant to the particular erg in question but not affected by current stimulation. The third component is current stimulation level. Thus, hunger intensity may be affected by the individual's hereditary hunger drive strength, the extent to which there has been physiological deprivation (need strength), and the availability of more or less desirable foods (current stimulation level).

Each erg is expressed and measured as a set of attitudes, all related by having the same ergic root or emotional goal, despite the diversity of sociocultural learning situations that might affect behavior. For example, "I want to satisfy my sexual needs" combines, in Cattell's work, with eight other specific attitude statements to represent the sex erg.

Sentiments. Just as ergs are constitutional source traits expressed as sets of attitudes, sentiments are environmental mold source traits, which are also motivational or dynamic in nature and expressed as sets of attitudes. Sentiments develop when the individual undergoes, over a period of time, a learning experience which simultaneously raises the strength of a number of related attitudes and gives the attitude set some structural unity. For example, the "home" sentiment would develop over time as the child continually experiences life with the family and learns many interrelated attitudes toward the family and the home. Like the home sentiment, most sentiments are social in nature and play major roles in determining an individual's behavior in relevant situations. Thus, the home sentiment influences behavior in family settings, as a patriotism sentiment would influence attitudes and behaviors toward one's country.

Sentiments are social in nature and usually represent sets of attitudes toward a particular social institution. The home sentiment represents a set of related attitudes toward home and family and plays a major role in determining an individual's behavior in situations defined as relevant to home life. A patriotism sentiment reflects a set of related attitudes toward one's country.

As ergs are related to primary drives, so are sentiments related to secondary drives. In learning theory, the secondary drive obtains its energy from a single primary drive which must periodically be present in order to maintain the secondary drive. The sentiment, however, borrows its energy not from a single erg but from several ergs and derives its form entirely from a cultural learning process. Once the sentiment has been developed, it may be quite constant over a long period of time, may change with further relevant learning experiences, or may disappear. Cattell's research has identified a number of specific sentiments which are found fairly consistently across different studies. These major sentiments relate to career, religion, mechanical construction, spouse-sweetheart, home, superego (social desirability), patriotism, and self-sentiment. The major ergs and sentiments can now be readily measured using the Motivational Analysis Test (MAT), which provides profiles potentially useful in clinical, occupational, and educational settings.

Self-Sentiment. The one sentiment which stands above the others in importance is the *self-sentiment*. The central significance of this particular sentiment pattern derives from the scope of its influence, which cuts across nearly all the individual's attitudes. Virtually every attitude the person expresses, even though it may be closely related to some other sentiment, will be expressed and evaluated partly as a function of the way it relates to the self.

The self-sentiment involves, in addition to a complex set of attitudes toward the self, an evaluative function and a preservation or consistency function. The individual thus perceives his or her own characteristics, evaluates these characteristics and their associated attitudes and behaviors, and strives to maintain the consistency of the self-sentiment as a central organizing concept.

The similarity of Cattell's self-sentiment to the self-concept of Rogerian theory and the ego of Freudian theory is apparent, but Cattell has not given his self construct the central role that the related constructs have in the Rogerian and Freudian treatments. In fact, Cattell suggests the existence of a control triumvariate, in which the self-sentiment measured by the MAT combines with the superego (Factor G) and the ego (Factor C) of the 16-PF to strongly influence much behavior.

Measuring Ergs and Sentiments

Specific ergs and sentiments were derived from factor analyses conducted by Cattell and his colleagues in a number of different studies over a period of time. Cattell's basic research strategy has been to identify a substantial number of attitudes, typically about sixty in a given study, and then to find several objective tests or questionnaire items to measure each one. The various tests are administered to a large number of subjects and the data factor analyzed to determine the ergs and sentiments represented by the attitudes. The result is a list of attitudes relating to each erg and sentiment identified. As an example, the first list below gives some of the major attitudes associated with the sex erg (Cattell 1947) and with the pugnacity of aggression erg (Sweeney 1961). The second list provides examples of two sentiments, the self-sentiment (Cattell and Cross 1952) and the sports and games sentiment (Cattell and Baggaley 1958) and their associated attitudes.

Two Ergs and Associated Attitudes

Sex Erg	*Pugnacity (Aggression) Erg*
I want to fall in love with a beautiful woman	I want to "get even" with other kids
I want to satisfy my sexual needs	I want the United States to beat its enemies
I like sexual attractiveness in a woman	I want to see monsters in science fiction
I like to see a good movie now and then	I (do not) want to show my father awe and respect
I would like a novel with love interest	I (do not) want the teachers to like me
I like to enjoy smoking and drinking	
I want to eat in more good restaurants	
I want to listen to music	
I want to travel and explore the world	

Note. Adapted from Sweeney in Cattell and Warburton 1967 (Tables 10.3 and 10.31, pp. 155, 176).

Two Sentiments and Associated Attitudes

Self-Sentiment	*Sports and Games Sentiment*
I want never to damage my self-respect	I like to watch and talk about athletic events
I want to keep good control of mental processes	I like to take an active part in sports and athletics

I want to maintain a good reputation	I enjoy hunting and fishing trips
I want (not) to have a sure place to turn for help	I do not like to make things with my hands.
I want (not) to sleep and rest	I like to get into a fight
I want never to be unemployed	I like to spend time playing cards
I do (not) want to see danger and disease reduced	

Note. Adapted from Cattell and Warburton 1967. (Tables 10.11 and 10.20, pp. 163, 170.)

Measuring Heredity vs. Environment: MAVA

Since measured traits may reflect both hereditary and environmental influences, Cattell has suggested that the best approach to predicting behavior is to determine the relative contributions of each influence. He has, therefore, developed a statistical approach called the Multiple Abstract Variance Analysis (*MAVA*). The MAVA technique (Cattell 1960) involves the collection of specific quantitative data concerned with environmental and genetic influences within and between families. The MAVA equations are then applied to indicate the nature-nurture ratio for each trait. For example, if the similarity of scores on a given personality trait is greater for related children (siblings) reared apart than for unrelated children reared together, this would constitute some evidence favoring a hereditary influence on the particular trait under consideration. A reversal of this result would suggest greater environmental influence.

Cattell and his colleagues have applied MAVA to a number of different personality traits in a variety of studies. They have found, for example, that intelligence (Factor B) is high in hereditary determination, with heredity contributing about 70 to 80 percent of the variance, whereas ego strength is more environmentally determined, with about 60 to 70 percent accounted for by environmental factors. Q-data factors that are more heavily influenced by environment are radicalism, surgency, and ergic tension. Those that are more dependent on genetics include parmia, coasthenia, and proneness to guilt. It should be noted that there are some inconsistencies in MAVA studies and that the nature–nurture ratios can be expected to alter somewhat with circumstances.

THE DETERMINANTS OF BEHAVIOR

Cattell has always been interested in being able to predict the behavior of the individual in specific situations. In fact, he defines personality as "those characteristics of the individual which contribute to behavior prediction" (Cattell 1965d, p. 25). We have already seen that much of what is theoretically involved in behavior prediction exists as a complex pattern of traits that characterize the individual at a given point in time. Cattell also believes, however, that other factors must be taken into account. A full understanding of Cattell's treatment of behavior determinants requires knowledge of three major sets of factors: (1) long-term traits of the individual, (2) short-term states and moods of the indivdual, and (3) situational factors external to but affecting the individual.

Traits: The Dynamic Lattice

In large part, behavior is determined by the complex interaction of ergs and sentiments. Since ergs and sentiments are quite stable long-term aspects of the personality, it should be possible to discover at least some of the relationships among these personality structures. The *dynamic lattice* represents this complex set of interrelationships for a given individual. Figure 12-1 is a hypothetical dynamic lattice for one person. Traits are shown as relevant to a series of goals and subgoals. Since the ultimate goals of behavior are innate, the ergs (right column of the diagram) are the major end goals. The individual works toward these instinctive goals through the use of sentiments and attitudes that contribute to goal accomplishment. The overall pattern of relationships in the dynamic lattice is one of *subsidiation,* reflecting the hierarchical nature of the lattice. In general, attitudes are subsidiary to sentiments, which in turn are subsidiary to ergs. As an example, in Figure 12-1 the protection erg has subsidiated to it the president of the United States, the country, the spouse, and the bank account. Other sentiments and attitudes are also less directly subsidiated to protection. A single erg is usually contributed to by a number of different attitudes and sentiments acting as subgoals. At the same time, most subgoals are subsidiated not to one erg or sentiment but to several.

Although the ergs and sentiments that constitute the dynamic lattice are stable personality characteristics, in time traits can change gradually. Cattell (1966e) has, therefore, specifically formulated a factor analytic approach to the study of change. Change occurs through interaction with the environment and, specifically, does so through learning. Because the learning process simultaneously affects a number of traits, learning is a multidimensional change in the behavior of an individual in response to a multidimensional situation. The factor analytic approach to complex personality change through learning is called *adjustment process analysis* (Cattell 1966).

States

Cattell was one of the first major theorists to hypothesize a *state* concept formally. The concept recognizes that not all characteristics are maximally stable. A given individual is likely over time to show a considerable variation in a wide variety of states, such as emotional states or moods, levels of autonomic activity, and fatigue. States are differentiated from traits in three ways. First, states are reversible,

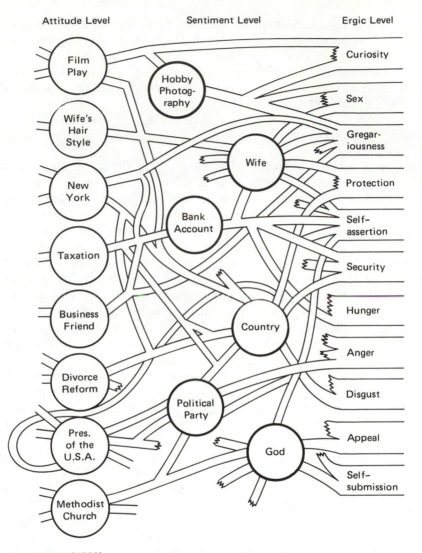

Attitude Level	Sentiment Level	Ergic Level

Film Play

Hobby Photography

Wife's Hair Style

Wife

New York

Bank Account

Taxation

Business Friend

Country

Divorce Reform

Political Party

Pres. of the U.S.A.

God

Methodist Church

Curiosity

Sex

Gregariousness

Protection

Self-assertion

Security

Hunger

Anger

Disgust

Appeal

Self-submission

From Cattell (1965).

Figure 12-1 A segment of a dynamic lattice.

whereas traits may change somewhat but are unlikely to reverse. An individual who is fairly high on a trait dimension of aggressiveness may frequently engage in assertive, forceful behavior. Summoned before a congressional committee, this person may be quite submissive during the hearing and become markedly more assertive immediately after leaving the committee room. This individual's state changes rapidly from aggressive to submissive and back to aggressive—but it is unlikely that the person's long-term trait of aggressiveness will change markedly or reverse through a single experience. A second difference is that changes in states occur much more rapidly than do changes in traits. Children who are unhappy because they must stay in and clean their room may quickly become virtually ecstatic upon learning that they are going to the circus, whereas children who have developed a trait of depression are unlikely to show a rapid change in that trait. A third differentiator is that states, when they change, tend to modify a pattern of variables which often cut across traits.

In some cases states affect momentary behavior in much the same way that a trait may affect behavior over a longer period of time. For example, the same anxious behaviors (such as nail biting, fidgeting, sweaty palms, and the like) that frequently characterize the individual high on trait anxiety (U.I.-24) may occasionally be seen in the person low on trait anxiety who is currently under considerable stress.

States cannot readily be taken into account in predicting behaviors unless we have systematic knowledge of the major state dimensions that characterize human functioning. According to Cattell, such state dimensions, like trait dimensions of personality, can be determined through factor analysis. This statistical technique determines the state dimensions relevant to an individual's particular behavioral variations and provides a basis for finding the point representing the person's state at a given time. For example, we may find a state dimension of anxiety representing potential variations in expressed anxiety and then determine the point at which a given individual stands on this dimension at a particular time. Cattell has applied P-technique, in which the same individual is measured repeatedly on a given set of variables, and the differential R-technique, in which a sample of individuals is measured twice and the differences on each variable is used as a basis for correlation across individuals. Research to date has typically revealed some eight to twelve major state dimensions. These internal states of the person are, to a substantial degree, affected by environmental factors.

Situational Factors

Cattell's theory of the role of environmental factors that affect states and influence behavior suggests that the environment can be broken up into a series of situations. Just as it is possible to determine state and trait dimensions or factors, it is also possible to develop an objective taxonomy of environments or situations according to their psychological meanings. A situation might, for example, be dangerous or safe, stressful or nonstressful, pleasant or unpleasant, and so on.

Situational factors may affect the person's immediate state on one or more dimensions and may also affect the level of ergic tension. For example, knowledge that a nuclear reactor core may soon melt down and release radioactivity (a dangerous situation) may increase the individual's level of state anxiety and arouse ergic tension in the security erg, which causes the person to orient some of his or her behavior towards dealing with the tension.

The Specification Equation

Cattell has not been content with simply breaking traits, states, and situations down into components or factors, but he has also been concerned with putting these pieces together again as a functioning organism. The central concept here is the *behavior specification equation,* which says that all traits of personality, that is, the total personality, enter into every behavioral act and that the influence of each trait is mediated by the nature of the situation. That is:

$$R = f(S. P.)$$

The specific response (R) of the individual, meaning what he or she does or thinks or verbalizes, is some unspecified function (f) of the stimulus situation (S) at a given moment in time and of the existing personality structure (P).

Expanding somewhat on the basic concepts contained in this behavioral equation, we have already seen that both the personality and the situation are multidimensional. The dimensions or factors of the personality are called *traits* and those of the situation are called *situational indices.* These considerations bring us to the general form of the behavioral specification equation:

$$R_j = b_{j1} T_{1i} + b_{j2} T_{2i} \ldots + B_{jk} T_{ki}$$

This equation may, on first glance, appear complex, but it is basically the elementary linear equation of high school algebra. It simply indicates that the individual's specific response to any given situation is a function of all the combined traits relevant to that situation, each trait interacting with situational factors which may affect it. More specifically, R is the individual's response or behavior in situation j. Each b in the equation has a subscript j to indicate that the behavioral or situational index involved is peculiar to the individual's response to situation j. Each b also has a number, corresponding to a given trait number, and indicating that the situation is appropriate to the particular trait involved. Each trait (T) has a subscript to indicate which specific one of k different traits it represents in the individual's personality and a subscript i to indicate that it is specific to a particular individual. The various traits form a *personality profile* for the individual, while the situational indices form a *situational profile* for the specific situation. Each behavioral or situational index thus indicates the extent to which a given trait is relevant to that situation and hence the extent to which the trait is involved in the response.

Let us take an example of how the specification equation can be applied. We might wish to predict how successful a person will be in solving a mathematical puzzle. There may be evidence that four traits measured by the 16-PF are likely to be involved: intelligence (Factor B), ego strength (Factor C) dominance (Factor E), and a form of anxiety (Factor O). We might write these factors as a specification equation:

$$Success\ in\ Situation = .6B + .3C + .3E - .4O$$

The weights, (such as .6 for B) show the extent to which a particular factor influences behavior in this situation. Thus, in our hypothetical example, intelligence has the most influence, then anxiety (which detracts from performance) and so on.

It is worth noting that Cattell's basic specification equation (R = F[S. P.]) is similar to that of Lewin (Chapter 14), who had, like Cattell, wanted to predict specific behavior occurring in specific situations. Cattell's expansion and application of the behavior specification equation goes well beyond the efforts originally made by Lewin, however, and incorporates a degree of mathematical statement not possible in the Lewin theory.

Overall, it can be seen that Cattell's treatment of the determinants of human behavior is both straightforward (if somewhat complex) and comprehensive. He takes into account the major factors which comprise the personality, the extent to which these factors are genetically and environmentally determined, and the ways in which environmental and genetic factors interact to determine attitudes. In addition, he systematically considers the influence of external situations and the temporary, internal states that these affect.

ORIGIN AND DEVELOPMENT

We have already seen that the personality of the individual contains both hereditary and environmental components and that it is possible, using the multiple abstract variance analysis (MAVA), to determine the proportions of heredity and environment involved in a given trait. Cattell's theory of personality development is simply an extension of this idea. For him, the individual is born with a number of ergs. By interacting with the environment, he or she develops sentiments and attitudes. The learned sentiments and attitudes are based on the innate ergs and subserve the latter throughout the individual's life. Both the expression of the ergs and the major expression of sentiments and attitudes can be changed gradually through a continuing process of environmental learning.

The Learning Process

In his earlier work Cattell distinguished among three basic types of learning. *Classical conditioning* is the development of associations between an existing response and a previously neutral stimulus. In *instrumental learning,* which Cattell prefers to call means-end learning, an emitted response is learned because it leads to a reward. Classical conditioning is seen as being essential to the development of associations between particular environmental cues and important emotional responses, whereas means-end learning is involved in the development of the dynamic lattice. The individual learns responses necessary for the achievement of energic goals. Cattell points out that this difference in perspective and terminology is a natural consequence of wedding personality structure research to learning theory. In the latter we can only say that a response is reinforced. But if we know the number and nature of ergs and can measure tension reduction in them, we can say by just what profile of ergic goal satisfactions a given act is reinforced and how the dynamic lattice is likely to be modified. A set of equations, called the *dynamic calculus,* has been developed as a part of Cattell's structured learning theory. The third form of learning, *integration learning,* is more important. It is the develop-ment of a hierarchy of responses that are involved in the enhancement of the entire personality and that tend to satisfy a number of ergic goals simultaneously. Integration learning is thus a form of multidimensional learning, and the concept emphasizes Cattell's point that the "old" learning theory idea of a single learned response satisfying a single learned drive is inadequate to an understanding of complex human functioning.

Cattell (1973a) has provided a careful treatment of the question of how learning affects personality development in his structured learning theory. In the theory Cattell views personality learning as a process in which a multidimensional person-ality consisting of multiple traits interacts with a multidimensional situation con-sisting of multiple situational indices to produce multidimensional change. *Struc-tured learning* requires three major changes from a classical (reflexological) learning theory, such as that of Dollard and Miller: (1) it argues that personality is not simply a conglomerate of conditioned reflexes but has ascertainable structures that must be taken into account; (2) it holds that reinforcement alone does not fully account for learning, since it can be shown that existing structures powerfully determine the rate and extent of learning that takes place; and (3) it suggests that without knowledge of ergic structure, the dynamics of reinforcement lack essential information, just as a black and white picture lacks the information provided by color. Applying structured learning theory, the factor analyst who has a measure-ment of a child's personality structure in terms of trait scores at the age of six may obtain measurements of the same traits at the age of twenty-five. A personality structure can be specified at each of the two ages, and the differences between the two structures constitute the overall change in personality and hence the individ-ual's structured learning. Structured learning takes place throughout the life-span, and some twenty curves, analogous to the standard curve for intelligence growth, have now been mapped for source trait development with age. Cattell has presented evidence that some factors increase or decrease, or rise or fall, over the entire measured range. As an example, ego strength, the capacity to subordinate emo-tional impulses to less immediate satisfactions, shows an increase with age.

Despite an emphasis on long-term personality change, Cattell has believed that the first few years of life are critical to the formation of personality. He has agreed with psychoanalytic theorists in arguing that basic personality formation is com-plete by the age of six or seven.

SOME EXTENSIONS

Group Membership

Recognizing the important influence of sociopsychological and sociocultural factors, Cattell has also developed a characteristically systematic model for understanding the effects of group membership on the individual. His theory applies a factor analytic model and suggests that groups have factors or attributes, collectively called *syntality,* that are similar to the traits of the individual personality. More generally, Cattell's group theory closely parallels his theory of individual personality, and, according to Cattell, may be applied to any group, ranging from a family to a nation. Recent work has focused on relating the cultural dimensions of nations to mean personality scores on the 16-PF over some seventeen cultures.

Beyondism: A Science of Morality

Concern for the influence of the larger society on the individual, and particularly for the importance of moral values, has recently led Cattell to seek a scientific approach to morality. In his book *A New Morality from Science: Beyondism* (1972) he notes that the morals and goals of society have generally been derived from religion and the arts. He proposes, instead, a scientific basis. The scientific goal of social progress would be the evolution of the society, and the goal of evolutionary progress would be met through the establishment of a social ethos involving an atmosphere of cooperative competition among groups. International goals and purposes for various groups would be established, and these groups would then move competitively in different social directions to achieve shared goals. Social scientists would establish and continually evaluate experimental societies having systematically varied biological and cultural characteristics. The structure of future societies would be determined on the basis of the results of these experiments.

Where does this experimental approach to society leave the individual? Cattell would answer that both the individual and society are important and interact with each other to the benefit of the individual and the progress of the society. In this context, he provides an eloquent statement on the role and potential impact of the individual. We provide here a lengthy quote from Cattell (pp. 437-38) not only because it provides a clear statement of his view of the individual but also because it demonstrates his capacity for beautiful prose.

> *The only immortality we know of is in our children, and in that unfinished story of the acts of lives, which, forever expanding, like waves from a pebble in the lake, have their immortality in the acts of future generations. The*

personal experience of consciousness, and of communication with one's loved ones, are vouchsafed to us as part of a strangely brief pilgrimage from oblivion to oblivion. Against this strange brevity the human heart has mourned in the language of a thousand mystified poets. There could well be scientific reasons utterly beyond our present imaginations for this brevity being an illusion. Meanwhile, we are compelled to puzzle over it as an insoluble mystery, incomprehensible except insofar as we can at least see that evolution and simple individual continuity are incompatible. But at least each soul is given his hour of contact with immortality. The individual may enjoy fully his hour of vision and his moment of illumination from the great minds which shine down the corridors of history. And perhaps there is some eternal consequence of his experience of the miraculous fire of life in his own being.

In any case brevity is not meaningless; and, indeed, perhaps all we need for complete peace of mind as we are borne on this flood of life is to learn to correct the powerful "optical illusion" of the self-contained and separate ego—an illusion necessitated in maintaining its very existence in an indifferent world. For plainly each is part of something far greater than himself. To each is given the opportunity to contribute, however humbly, his personal thoughts and acts to an eternal river of human understanding. It is a river that visibly gathers breadth and depth by the tributaries of our lives, though we do not know yet to what ocean it is bound. But while life is with us, the supreme delight is possible which Plato knew (and which he attributed as fit life for the Deity) of watching in rapture the perfect working of the laws of an amazing creation.

Psychopathology, Diagnosis, and Therapy

Cattell has extended his theory in an attempt to better understand the causes of psychopathology and to provide a system for psychiatric diagnosis as a basis for more effective psychotherapy. His concept of general causes and psychopathology is consistent with the theoretical view that the personality functioning of the individual is a result of the interaction of hereditary and environmental traits expressed in particular situations and modulated by the presence of short-term states. Within this framework Cattell believes that pathology is basically a result of conflict within the personality. Ergic tension is aroused and an ergic goal established, but the path to this goal is blocked, often by the presence of a contradictory goal. The result is frustration and anxiety. Attempts to reduce the anxiety and to achieve the ergic goals may lead to the development of neurotic symptoms.

In order to develop an approach to diagnosis, Cattell and his colleagues have used factor analytic techniques to compare normals with neurotic and psychotic groups (see, for example, Cattell, Schmidt, and Bjersedt 1972). Results show that compared with normals, neurotic subjects tend to be high on such 16-PF factors as guilt-proneness, tender mindedness, ergic tension, and a second order anxiety factor and low on ego strength. Psychotics also deviate from normals on certain factors. Now that the differentiating score patterns are known, *psychometric depth analysis* (Cattell 1967) can be applied to any given patient to determine both the pattern of source traits and the severity with which he or she manifests a given abnormal syndrome.

With the relevant data in hand, Cattell can now use a computer program called *taxonome* (Cattell and Coulter 1966) to match the score profile of the patient on the 16-PF with a variety of "standard" profiles to determine what syndrome the patient's score pattern most closely approximates. This, in effect, becomes the patient's diagnosis.

CATTELL'S THEORY IN EMPIRICAL CONTEXT

The nature of Cattell's basic research methods has already been described. Basically, his preference is for multivariate research, focusing primarily on factor analytic methodology. He has tended to work primarily with R-technique, comparing large groups of individuals on various measures taken on a single occasion, but has also worked with P-technique, Q-technique, and differential R-technique.

Over the years, Cattell's research has encompassed many areas. One of his principal activities has been the factor analytic development and validation of questionnaire and objective test instruments. This research interest is exemplified by the development of and subsequent work with the 16-Personality Factor Questionnaire (Cattell, Saunders, and Stice 1950; Cattell 1956; Cattell and Specht 1968), the IPAT Anxiety Scale (Cattell 1958), and the Objective-Analytic Battery (Cattell and Schwerger 1978; Hundleby, Pawlick, and Cattell 1965). Cattell's research efforts have also led him to apply his questionnaires and factor analytic methodology to a variety of psychological phenomena and problems. He has done work with creative artists (Cross, Cattell, and Butcher 1968; Drevdahl and Cattell 1958) and work on leader selection (Cattell and Stice 1954), prediction of school achievement (Cattell, Sealy, and Sweeney 1966; Cattell and Butcher 1967), the measurement of national morale and morality (Cattell and Gorsuch 1965; Cattell and Woliner 1975), the relationship of blood groups to personality traits (Cattell, Young, and Hundleby 1964), the differentiation of criminals and homosexuals from normals using test scores (Cattell and Morony 1962), child-rearing practices (Dielman, Barton, and Cattell 1973), dimensions of marital relationships (Barton and Cattell 1973), and questionnarie evaluation (Cattell 1973b, 1974). He has also done a number of studies oriented toward a better understanding of personality trait structure in abnormal groups. These include studies of depression (Cattell and Bjersted 1966, 1967), neurosis (Cattell and Scheier 1961), psychosis (Cattell and Latro 1966), and character disorders (Cattell and Killian 1967).

A third research area has reflected Cattell's continuing concern with the nature-nurture question as it relates to personality structure and function. Work in this area has focused on the development and application of the MAVA technique. It has ranged from the development and early application of the technique to a full-scale development of its equations and solutions (Cattell 1960) and recently to the extension of MAVA to include a separation of genetic and environmental contributions to both maturation and learning (Cattell 1973a).

Much of Cattell's remaining work has involved a long series of theoretical and empirical contributions to the development and revision of multivariate techniques, demonstrating his considerable accomplishment as a mathematical statistician. Included among these contributions have been a factor analytic index for the similarity of variables in a matching situation (Cattell and Baggaley 1960), the development of computer programs for specific types of factor rotation (Cattell and Muerle 1960; Cattell and Foster 1963), real base factor analysis (Cattell 1972), and the Scree test for determining the number of factors to extract in factor analysis (Cattell 1966d). Finally, Cattell has contributed considerably to the area of taxonomy (Cattell, Bolz, and Korth, 1973; Cattell, Coulter, and Tsujioka 1966; Cattell and Warburton 1967). It is quite possible that as psychology moves toward more detailed and precise taxonomies for factors, tests, variables, and abnormal syndromes, historians will dub Cattell the Linnaeus of modern psychology.

EVALUATION

A critique of Cattell's work must look at the factor analytic basis for his research, the theory he has developed, and at the specific research information he has contributed.

Major Assets

The application of nearly any reasonably objective criterion—prominence among psychologists, uniqueness and originality of theoretical contributions, skill in empirical research, quality of empirical contribution, number of publications, and so on—is likely to lead one to the conclusion that Raymond Cattell is a most accomplished individual. Indeed, the mass of empirical data he has collected and the careful integration provided by his theory makes his work a virtual tour de force in psychology.

To be more specific, he and only a few others have brought to psychology the considerable quantitative power of the major multivariate techniques. The careful empiricism which has often accompanied the multivariate approach has been a major asset to the growth of knowledge in the personality field. Careful operational definition, objective scientific procedure, and often a fresh inductive approach to the understanding of human personality have characterized the work of Cattell and his colleagues.

As a further asset, there is evidence that Cattell, despite his rigid insistence on the superiority of the multivariate technique, has provided one of the most flexible overall approaches to understanding personality functioning. He has, over the years, combined a sense of scientific purpose and rigor with a willingness to formulate theoretical ideas that go far beyond the data.

Problems and Difficulties

These solid contributions are, however, matched by some serious problems with the factor analytic approach and with Cattell's theory.

Factor Analytic Methodology. Cattell and other factor analysts have claimed, implicitly and sometimes explicitly, that through the appropriate application of factor analytic techniques we may be able to discover the most basic and essential dimensions of the human personality. Surely this is a worthwhile goal, but critics have long questioned the ability of factor analysis to reach it. More specifically, they have questioned particular assumptions and methodological aspects of factor analysis. One is that the factors determining behavior combine additively. It may be that in some instances an observed behavior is not the result of an additive combination of factors but of, say, a multiplicative combination. A second questionable assumption is that all variables have linear relationships to each other so that when one variable shows an increase, it always produces a corresponding increase (or decrease) in another variable. It is possible that some variables have curvilinear relationships, so that an increase in one variable would produce an increase in another only up to some maximal point, after which the second variable would show a decrease with continued increase in the first. A further difficulty is the claim that the factor analyst gets out of a factor analysis what he or she puts in. While this criticism is almost a cliché of factor analysis, it is an important one. It could mean, for example, that the carefully isolated factors represented in the 16-PF test, the Objective-Analytic Battery, and Cattell's other measures are by no means all or even a major portion of the important factors in personality functioning. Only those factors for which relevant variables are specifically available in a given experiment can be isolated in factor analysis. This point also applies to the simpler bivariate approaches.

Two further concerns with methodology have been the failure of factor analysis to agree on statistical points and the subjectivity with which the factor analyst interprets and names factors. Even a brief glance at the extensive literature in factor analysis will show that there are many major disagreements among factor analysts as to what the most appropriate quantitative procedures are for applying the technique to a given set of data. Questions asked throughout the literature are how many factors to extract from the data and how one knows when to stop factoring. Another question concerns the method of factor rotation. Should a rotation be orthogonal or oblique, and what particular type of orthogonal or oblique solution should be used? These and a number of other ongoing statistical arguments suggest that any given method in current use may change in the future, although it should be noted that Cattell has answered these critical points by factoring physical examples where the causes behind dimensions are known. Assuming, however, that the factor analysis is accomplished and yields a set of variables loading on a set of factors, how does one know the names of these factors? Is a given factor "anxiety," or would it be better called "arousal," "activation," or "fear?" The factor is whatever the factor analyst chooses to call it, and the decision, as we saw earlier, is a largely subjective one based on a careful, but nevertheless speculative, review of the variables loading on that factor. Cattell's answer has been that he follows accepted semantic conventions in arriving at his factor names (Cattell, personal communication 1979).

Conclusions. Certain conclusions of the factor analytic approach have also been seriously questioned. In particular, some critics have argued that the factors isolated through factor analysis may not be *meaningful* and, hence, will not be useful in explaining or understanding human behavior. A widely cited study by Overall (1964) appears to justify this criticism. Overall obtained a large number of books and recorded data on the physical dimensions of each. He then entered these data into a factor analysis to determine the dimensionality of books. Whereas most people would describe a book physically in terms of length, width, and thickness, the factor analysis yielded factors described as size, squareness, and obesity! Thus, the factor analysis yields factors that are quite different from those that we would usually consider to be meaningful in describing books. The factor analyst could argue that the analysis had indeed identified the basic physical dimensions of books, even through these may not be the ones generally recognized as descriptive. The point that the dimensions may not be meaningful is, nevertheless, an important one.

Two additional concerns are the number and similarity of factors identified in various studies. When different factor analyses involve basically the same sets of variables, should they not isolate at least the same number of factors in various studies? If so, how do we explain the fact that Cattell has isolated somewhat different numbers of factors in his Q-data and T-data analyses and that in both cases he has many more factors than the three that characterize Eysenck's (1967) system? Cattell has provided a partial answer by suggesting that the Eysenck dimensions may well represent higher order factors. Further explanations come from differences among the various factor analytic techniques applied.

A more serious question is whether factors derived by the same factor analytic methods show high degrees of similarity across the data types identified by Cattell and across different investigations. We have already seen that there is some matching of factors among the three Cattell data types but that this matching is by no means complete. Whether this means that the factors not matching across the Cattell types have little behavioral generality or whether matching simply awaits the addition of new tests and variables to permit the isolation of additional factors remains an open question. The related question of factor similarity across studies within the same data type but utilizing different subject samples is also unresolved. In one example of attempted factor matching, Cattell and Gibbons (1968) gave over three hundred undergraduate students sets of items representing fourteen of the 16-PF factors and fifteen factors taken from the Guilford-Zimmerman scales, which were developed independently in another laboratory. Results showed that the two sets of scales have eight dimensions in common. Some would suggest that these are close to "basic" dimensions of personality. On the other hand, some investigators, not using any objective test for the number of factors, have found that new factor analyses of the 16-PF itself do not yield the same factors found by the Cattell group (Howarth and Browne 1971a, 1971b; Sells, Demaree, and Will 1970, 1971). Factor analysts have countered the criticism by interpreting the results of repeated studies as indicating considerable matching of factors across various age groups and populations (Hundleby, Pawlick, and Cattell 1965).

The Theory. One reviewer has commented that many psychologists have considerable respect for Cattell's work, but the vast majority have chosen not to attend closely to his theoretical and practical messages to psychology (Gordon 1966). This should not imply, of course, that Cattell's work has had no impact. In fact, the instruments he has developed are widely used in research and practical settings. Moreover, Cattell is widely recognized as a major personality theorist. Nevertheless, Gordon is correct in saying that Cattell has not turned "mainstream psychology" in the direction of his multivariate approach.

One reason why psychologists have tended to ignore much of Cattell's work is that its massive volume and high level of complexity have obscured its potential for contribution. Part of the difficulty also lies in the fact that, at least until very recent years, many psychologists were not trained in multivariate statistical methods and thus were not equipped to understand an approach like Cattell's. Moreover, the multivariate approaches—particularly Cattell's—have appeared to some as radical departures from methods long established as effective. Cattell, well aware of this latter point, has commented that new discoveries and new approaches are often not adopted by a science until many years after their discovery. For example, penicillin was not used in clinical medicine until some thirteen years after Fleming discovered it, and Copernicus' calculations of the solar system were not accepted by professional astronomers for a century!

It is certainly not Cattell's fault that psychologists were not trained earlier in multivariate techniques or that it is often difficult to get new ideas accepted immediately. However, Cattell has perhaps tended to pile additional bricks on the wall that isolates him from much of psychology through his use of unnecessarily complex and unusual terminology. While appreciating Cattell's concern that common terms may not perfectly describe his factors, one can question whether he would communicate better with the professional community by using such terms as, say, dependence and self-reliance instead of premsia and harria; or whether parmia and threctia are so essential that they could not be replaced by bold and timid. In addition to modifying the complex terminology, it might be helpful for Cattell and his colleagues to bring together in one or perhaps two relatively brief works the essence of his theoretical and empirical contributions. Thus far, each of Cattell's major books has tended to deal in considerable detail with one or two relatively narrow aspects of his work without giving the reader any overall viewpoint. Even the *Scientific Analysis of Personality* (Cattell 1965d) does not accomplish the integration needed in such a work. An alternative possibility might be simply to stop and let the field catch up!

REFERENCES

Barton, K., & Cattell, R. B. Personality factors of husbands and wives as predictors of own and partners marital dimensions. *Canadian Journal of Behavioral Science,* 1973, *5*, 83-92.

Cattell, R. B. The ergic theory of aptitude and sentiment measurement. *Educational and Psychological Measurement,* 1947, *7*, 221-246.

Cattell, R. B. The scientific ethics of "beyond". *Journal of Social Issues,* 1950, *6*, 21-27.

Cattell, R. B. Validation and intensification of the sixteen personality factor questionnaire. *Journal of Clinical Psychology,* 1956, *12*, 205-214.

Cattell, R. B. *The IPAT anxiety scale.* Champaigne, Illinois: Institute of Personality and Ability Testing, 1958.

Cattell, R. B. The multiple abstract variance analysis equations and solutions: For nature-nurture research on continuous variables. *Psychological Review,* 1960, *67*, 353-372.

Cattell, R. B. Objective personality tests: A reply to Dr. Eysenck. *Occupational Psychology,* 1964, *38*, 69-86.

Cattell, R. B. Factor theory psychology: A statistical approach to personality. In W. S. Sahakian (Ed.), *Psychology of personality: Readings in theory.* Chicago: Rand McNally, 1965.

Cattell, R. B. The configurative method for surer identification of personality dimensions, notably in child study. *Psychological Report,* 1965, *16*, 269-270.

Cattell, R. B. Higher order structures: Reticular versus hierarchical formula for their interpretation. In C. Banks & P. L. Broadhurst (Eds.), *Studies in psychology presented to Cyril Burt.* London: University of London Press, 1965.

Cattell, R. B. *The scientific analysis of personality.* Baltimore: Penguin Books, 1965.

Cattell, R. B. *Evaluating therapy as total personality change: Theory and available* instruments. *American Journal of Psychotherapy,* 1966, *20*, 69-88.

Cattell, R. B. (Ed.). *Handbook of multivariate experimental psychology.* Chicago: Rand McNally, 1966.

Cattell, R. B. Multivariate behavioral research and the integrative challenge. *Multivariate Behavioral Research,* 1966, *1*, 4-23.

Cattell, R. B. The screen test for the number of factors. *Multivariate Behavioral Research,* 1966, *1*, 245-276.

Cattell, R. B. Personality structure: The larger dimensions. In B. Semeonoff (Ed.), *Personality Assessment.* Baltimore: Penguin Books, 1966.

Cattell, R. B. Personality theory and dynamic calculus from quantitative experimental methods. In A. M. Freedin & H. I. Kaplin (Eds.), *Comprehensive textbook of psychiatry.* Baltimore: Williams & Wilkins, 1967.

Cattell, R. B. *A new morality from science: Beyondism.* New York: Pergamon, 1972.

Cattell, R. B. Unraveling maturational and learning developments by the comparative MAVA and structured learning approaches. In J. R. Nesselroade & H. W. Reese (Eds.), *Life-span developmental psychology: Methodological issues.* New York: Academic Press, 1973.

Cattell, R. B. *Personality and mood by questionnaire.* San Francisco: Josey-Bass, 1973.

Cattell, R. B. How good is the modern questionnaire? General principles for evaluation. *Journal of Personality Assessment,* 1974, *38,* 115-129.

Cattell, R. B., & Baggaley, A. R. A conformation of ergic and engram structures in attitudes objectively measured. *Australian Journal of Psychology,* 1958, *10,* 287-318.

Cattell, R. B., & Baggaley, A. R. The salient variable similarity index for factor matching. *British Journal of Statistical Psychology,* 1960, *13,* 33-46.

Cattell, R. B., & Bjerstedt, A. The structure of depression, by factoring Q-data, in relation to general personality source traits, in normal and pathological subjects. *Educational and Psychological Interactions,* 1966, *16,* 13.

Cattell, R. B., & Bjerstedt, A. The structure of depression, by factoring Q-data, in relation to general personality source traits. *Scandinavian Journal of Psychology,* 1967, *8,* 17-24.

Cattell, R. B., & Bolton, L. S. What pathological dimensions lie beyond the normal dimensions of the 16 P.F.? A comparison of MMPI and 16 P.F. factor domains. *Journal of Consulting and Clinical Psychology,* 1969, *33,* 18-29.

Cattell, R. B., Bolz, C., & Korth, B. Behavioral types in purebreed dogs objectively determined by taxonome. *Behavior Genetics,* 1973, *3,* 205-216.

Cattell, R. B., & Butcher, H. J. *The prediction of achievement and creativity.* Indianapolis: Bobbs-Merrill, 1968.

Cattell, R. B., & Coulter, M. A. Principles of behavioral taxonomy and the mathematical basis of the taxonome computer program. *British Journal of Mathematical & Statistical Psychology,* 1966, *19,* 237-269.

Cattell, R. B., Coulter, M. A., & Tsujioka, B. The taxonometric recognition of types and functional emergents. *British Journal of Mathematical & Statistical Psychology,* 1966, *19,* 288-329.

Cattell, R. B., & Cross, K. P. Comparison of the ergic and self-sentiment structures found in dynamic traits by R- and P-techniques. *Journal of Personality,* 1952, *21,* 250-271.

Cattell, R. B., & Delhees, K. Seven missing normal personality factors in the questionnaire primaries. *Multivariate Behavioral Research,* 1973, *8,* 173-194.

Cattell, R. B., & Foster, M. J. The Rotoplot program for multiple, single-plane, visually guided rotation. *Behavioral Science,* 1963, *8,* 156-165.

Cattell, R. B., & Gibbons, B. D. Personality factor structure of the combined Guilford and Cattell personality questionnaire. *Journal of Personality and Social Psychology,* 1968, *9,* 107-120.

Cattell, R. B., & Gersuch, R. L. The definition and measurement of natural morale and morality. *Journal of Social Psychology,* 1965, *44,* 160-166.

Cattell, R. B., Kawash, G. F., & DeYoung, G. Validation of objective of ergic tension: Response of the sex erg to visual stimulation. *Journal of Experimental Research in Personality*, 1972, *6*, 76-83.

Cattell, R. B., & Killian, L. R. The pattern of objective test personality factor difference in schizophrenia and character disorders. *Journal of Clinical Psychology*, 1967, *23*, 342-348.

Cattell, R. B., & Morony, J. H. The use of the 16 P.F. in distinguishing homosexuals, normals, and general criminals. *Journal of Consulting Psychology*, 1962, *26*, 531-540.

Cattell, R. B., & Muerle, J. L. The "max plane" program for factor rotation to oblique simple structure. *Educational and Psychological Measurement*, 1960, *20*, 569-590.

Cattell, R. B., & Nichols, K. An improved definition, from 10 researchers, of second order personality factors in Q data (with cross cultural checks). *Journal of Social Psychology*, 1972, *86*, 187-203.

Cattell, R. B., Saunders, D. R., & Stice, G. F. *The 16 personality factor questionnaire.* Champaign, Ill.: Institute of Personality and Ability Testing, 1950.

Cattell, R.B., & Scheier, I. H. *The meaning and measurement of neuroticism and anxiety.* New York: Ronald Press, 1961.

Cattell, R. B., Schmidt, & Bjerstedt, A. Clinical diagnosis by the objective analytic personality batteries. *Journal of Clinical Psychology*, 1972, *28*, 239-312.

Cattell, R. B., Sealy, A. P., & Sweeney, A. B. What can personality and motivation source trait measurements add to the prediction of school achievement? *British Journal of Educational Psychology*, 1966, *36*, 280-295.

Cattell, R. B., & Specht, L. The dimensions of pathology: Proof of their projection beyond the normal 16-PF source traits. *Laboratory of Personality Analysis* (Advanced publication No. 12). Urbana: University of Illinois, 1968.

Cattell, R. B., & Stice, G. F. Four formulae for selecting leaders on the basis of personality. *Human Relations*, 1954, *7*, 493-507.

Cattell, R. B., & Tatvo, D. F. The personality factors, objectively measured, which distinguish psychotics from normals. *Behavior Research and Therapy*, 1966, *4*, 39-51.

Cattell, R. N., & Warburton, F. W. *Objective personality and motivation tests: A theoretical and practical compendium.* Urbana: University of Illinois Press, 1967.

Cattell, R. B., Young, H. B., & Hundleby, J. B. Blood groups and personality traits. *American Journal of Human Genetics*, 1964, *16*, 397-402.

Cross, P. G., Cattell, R. B., & Butcher, H. J. The personality pattern of creative artists. *British Journal of Educational Psychology*, 1967, *37*, 292-299.

Dielman, T. E., Barton, K., & Cattell, R. B. Cross-validational evidence on the structure of parental reports of child rearing practices. *Journal of Social Psychology*, 1973, *90*, 243-250.

Drevdahl, J. E., & Cattell, R. B. Personality and creativity in artists and writers. *Journal of Clinical Psychology*. 1958, *14*, 107-111.

Eysenck, H. J. *The biological basis of personality.* Springfield, Ill.: Promise, 1967.

Gordon, J. E. Review of R. B. Cattell's personality and social psychology. *Contemporary Psychology,* 1966, *11,* 236-238.

Howarth, E., & Browne, J. A. An item-factor analysis of the 16-P.F. Personality Questionnaire. *Personality: An International Journal,* 1971, *2,* 117-139.

Howarth, E., & Browne, J. A. Investigation of personality factors in a Canadian context, I: Marker structure in personality questionnaire items. *Canadian Journal of Behavioral Science,* 1971, *3,* 161-173.

Hundleby, J. D., Pawlick, K., & Cattell, R. B. *Personality factors in objective test devices: A critical integration of a quarter of a century's research.* San Diego, Calif.: Knapp, 1965.

Overall, J. E. Note on the scientific status of factors. *Psychological Bulletin,* 1964, *61,* 270-276.

Sells, S. B., Demaree, R.G., & Will, D. P., Jr. Dimensions of personality: I. Conjoint factor structure of Guilford and Cattell trait markers. *Multivariate Behavioral Research,* 1970, *5,* 391-422.

Sells, S. B., Demaree, R. G., & Will, D. P., Jr. Dimensions of personality: II. Separate factor structures in Guilford and Cattell trait markers. *Multivariate Behavioral Research,* 1971, *6,* 135-186.

Skinner, B. F. *Science and human behavior.* New York: Macmillan, 1953.

Sweeney, A. B. Faktorenanalytische methoden in der motivations-forschung Cattels. *Archiv gesamte Psychologie,* 1961, *8,* 136-147.

13

A Typological Theory:

Hans Jurgen Eysenck

Cattell defined traits as essentially broad determining tendencies that characterize the structure and dynamics of the human personality and influence behavior. As we have seen, he has viewed the personality as comprising a fairly large number of source traits, each interacting with the others and with situational influences to determine behavior. It can be argued that the most important level at which behavior analysis can take place is not at the trait level but at an even broader level of behavior determination called the *type*. For most theoretical purposes, a personality type consists of a set of related traits, and the total number of typological dimensions characterizing human personality is relatively small, typically ranging from two to four, depending upon the specific theory. Typological theories have not yet become particularly popular among American psychologists, although such theories have long been influential in Western Europe and the Soviet Union. Eysenck's theory, which is of British origin, is especially important. It is the only major typological theory of personality currently having some impact in American personality psychology and being widely studied in a number of other countries. In fact, with the partial exception of Jungian theory, it is the only typological theory that we will cover.

Historically, the formulation of typological theories can be traced to the writing of Hippocrates, who is credited with being the originator of medicine, in the fourth century B.C., and to the somewhat later work of Galen in the second century A.D. Both espoused humoral doctrines, which were essentially typological in nature. Galen specifically postulated four types of individuals based on the relative dominance of humors: choleric, characterized by irritability; phlegmatic, seen as behaviorally slow and apathetic; sanguine, described as energetic; and melancholic, characterized by depression.

The humoral doctrine continued to influence medical and psychological thinking about human temperament for many centuries, culminating in the work of the physiologist Von Haller, the early physiological psychologist Cabanis, and the German idealist philosopher Kant in the eighteenth century. Both Von Haller and Cabanis employed substantially modified versions of humoral theory, while Kant hypothesized the four major temperaments defined by Galen but went considerably further than the earlier writer in treating the four temperaments as totally independent—the factor analyst would say orthogonal—of one another and genetically determined. At the turn of the twentieth century, Wundt, who began experimental psychology, proposed that the same four temperaments employed by earlier writers are based on two major dimensions of human response. One is an affective reactivity dimension, with the individual who experiences strong emotions at one extreme and the weak reactor at the other extreme. The second dimension is a rate-of-change dimension, with very changeable individuals at one extreme and relatively unchanging persons at the other.

Twentieth-century typology began with the theoretical work of the Austrian psychiatrist, Gross. He described two basic types, the deep–narrow type, characterized by a high degree of emotionality and high level energy, and the shallow-broad type, who has low levels of emotional activity and energy.

Three other twentieth-century theorists who deserve mention here are Kretschmer, Sheldon, and Jung. Kretschmer (1921 and 1925) proposed a specific set of relationships between physique and psychiatric disorder. Sheldon (1940) also proposed a specific typology related to temperament. He engaged in extensive studies of physique-temperament relationships, and postulated four major physical types, each associated with a specific temperament. The third theorist, Carl Jung, is of even more direct interest, since his major personality dimension, introversion-extroversion, is the same as that of Eysenck. We have already seen the nature and impact of Jung's personality theory, including his introversion-extroversion dimension. Jungian theory also postulates, at least implicitly, a second dimension which Eysenck would later term *neuroticism*.

BIOGRAPHICAL SKETCH

Hans Jurgen Eysenck, the leading modern typologist, was born March 4, 1916, in Germany. Recognizing the destructive influence of Nazism, he left Germany in 1934. He studied in France and England and obtained both his B.A. and Ph.D. degrees, the latter in 1940, from the University of London. During World War II years from 1942 to 1946 he served as a research psychologist at the Mill Hill Emergency Hospital. Following this, he became, in 1946, a reader in psychology at the University of London and, simultaneously, director of the Psychological Department of Maudsley and Bethlehem hospitals in London. He has remained at the University of London, where he became professor of psychology in 1955. During his career, Eysenck has also held positions in the United States, serving as visiting professor at the University of Pennsylvania in 1949 and at the University of California at Berkeley in 1954.

STRUCTURAL PRINCIPLES

Eysenck has proposed that human personality can best be understood as comprising a hierarchy consisting of behaviors and sets of behaviors that vary in level of generality and importance in the personality. At the lowest level of the hierarchy are *specific responses.* These are particular, individual acts observed on at least a single occasion in a given individual. They may or may not be characteristic of that individual's behavior, and they serve as basic data for the experimental observer. At the second level of the hierarchy we encounter a set of *habitual responses* that are simply habits. These habits are specific responses which have developed a tendency to be repeated in similar situations. Learning theorists, such as Dollard and Miller, have tended to focus their theoretical efforts at the level of habitual response. However, Eysenck hypothesized a third level in the hierarchical organization of personality which he terms the *trait.* A number of traits, such as anxiety, persistence, and irritability, may characterize a given personality. Each of these traits consists of a set of intercorrelated habitual responses. A number of theorists, such as Allport and Cattell, have concentrated on the trait level of personality organization.

Eysenck formulated a fourth level of organization, the *type.* This, the broadest level of personality organization, constitutes a major determining tendency influencing broad segments of the individual's behavior. Basically, the type is an organization of intercorrelated traits. For example, introversion as a personality type may consist, in part, of the traits of persistence, accuracy, autonomic imbalance, and irritability. Each of these several traits, in turn, consists of a particular set of habitual responses, which constitute organizations of recurrent specific responses.

Where other investigators have chosen to concentrate on the habitual response or trait levels of the theoretical hierarchy, Eysenck has studied primarily the typological level. His focus on this level of influence reflects a desire to better understand the basic organization of the mind and to provide viable physiological bases for this organization as it affects individual behavior. It should be noted that in choosing to work at the typological level Eysenck may be sacrificing some ability to predict very specific behaviors. It would seem easier to predict a specific response if one knows the person's habitual response than if only general knowledge of the person's type is available. For example, if we have knowledge of the habitual responses of a particular political figure when faced with questions concerning certain issues, we can quite readily predict his or her specific responses to questions at an interview. We know that the politician is likely to respond in terms of a certain consistent position regarding the economy, foreign policy, or some other area. On the other hand, knowledge that the political figure is an introvert, while of great value in understanding the basic organization of the person's personality, might not seem to allow the precision of prediction achievable through knowledge of habitual responses. In fact, however, one recent study (Reynolds and Nichols 1977), suggests that knowledge of a person's type might be of great value in predicting specific behaviors. This and other relevant work is reviewed below.

A THREE-DIMENSIONAL TYPOLOGY

Eysenck's search for the basic dimensions of personality grew out of and is consistent with what may be called the London or British school, as opposed to the American school, of factor analysis. The latter, exemplified by Cattell and Guilford, emphasizes the trait level, while the London school has traditionally searched for the broadest levels of organization, such as types. The British approach to factor analysis grew basically out of the work of Charles Spearman and, in Eysenck's case, more directly out of the work of Burt, who conducted an early factor analytic study of personality types in children.

Eysenck's first factorial study (1947) involved psychiatric ratings on thirty-nine variables in seven hundred neurotic soldiers. The ratings were intercorrelated and factor analyzed, using an orthogonal rotation to yield uncorrelated factors. Eysenck focused on the first two factors extracted as the most general and most important factors in the study. The first factor was characterized by such items as badly organized personality, dependent, abnormal before illness, and poor in muscular tone. It appeared to be a general factor reflecting emotional stability, and Eysenck used the term *neuroticism* to denote the factor and also to describe its upper or unstable extreme. The opposite end of the bipolar continuum was termed *stability*. The second factor characterized at one extreme patients who showed hysterical conversion symptoms (the classic "glove" paralysis of one hand with no physiological basis is an example) and sexual anomalies, while patients at the other extreme showed such symptoms as obsessions, depression, and high anxiety. Using psychiatric terminology, Eysenck called the first (high-score) extreme of the dimension *hysteria* and the opposite extreme *dysthymia* (meaning disorder of mood). In more general terms, applicable to normal as well as abnormal personality, the second factor was seen as contrasting extraversion with introversion, and the dimension was termed *extraversion.*

The observation of major extraversion and neuroticism factors is not without historical precedent. As has been noted, Jung anticipated Eysenck, postulating a major extroversion factor and essentially suggesting a neuroticism factor as well. Certain empirical work is also of interest. In particular, an early study carried out by Heymans and Wiersma (1909) involved personality ratings of over twenty-five hundred individuals by four hundred physicians. The investigators interpreted the data as supportive of a three-dimensional system, consisting of emotionality, activity, and a "primary function–secondary function" factor, descriptively very similar to extroversion-introversion. Eysenck (1960) factor analyzed the Heymans-Wiersma data and found confirmation of emotionality as an independent dimension. The activity and extraversion dimensions were, however, highly correlated, and Eysenck concluded that two dimensions, extraversion and emotionality (neuroticism), adequately characterized the data.

While neuroticism and extraversion were the early concerns of Eysenck's further work, a third dimension, called *psychoticism,* has also been identified (Eysenck 1952a, 1952b), and Eysenck has developed a factorial scale for its measurement (Eysenck and Eysenck 1968; Eysenck, S. B. G. and Eysenck, H. J. 1975). The psychoticism dimension is seen as independent of neuroticism and extraversion. Its items are endorsed more frequently by psychotic patients than by normals or neurotics.

Inventories for Extraversion, Neuroticism, and Psychoticism

Following the initial studies which identified and confirmed the existence of major extraversion and neuroticism factors, Eysenck has concentrated his efforts primarily in three areas: (1) the development, validation, and revision of scales for the measurement of the three factors; (2) empirical studies of behaviors relating to neuroticism (N) and extraversion (E); and (3) further development of a theoretical position concerning physiological and psychological bases for E and N. We will take up the first of these here, holding the question of empirical and theoretical efforts for later treatment.

Eysenck felt that questionnaires were needed to measure his factors, and he and his wife, Sybil, set out to develop them. The first inventory developed was the Maudsley Medical Questionnaire (MMQ); (Eysenck 1952), which was constructed to measure the neuroticism factor as a personality dimension. The MMQ was then revised by adding new items, carrying out item analyses, and factor analyzing to yield the forty-eight-item Maudsley Personality Inventory (MPI), measuring the two major factors, N and E. Further revisions have led to the development of the Eysenck Personality Inventory (EPI), the Eysenck Personality Questionnaire (EPQ), and the Junior Eysenck Personality Inventory (JEPI).

The Independence of Extraversion and Neuroticism

Both Eysenck's empirical findings and his theoretical treatment of extraversion and neuroticism indicate that the two dimensions are independent (uncorrelated) personality factors, except when the sample is dominated by high N subjects, where the tendency is to find a substantial negative correlation between N and E (Eysenck 1961). Some have, however, doubted the independence of the dimensions. Carrigan (1960), in a major review of the extraversion literature, has seriously questioned the independence of E and N. Her point is supported by several studies which have found the two dimensions to be significantly correlated (Jensen 1958; Lynn and Gordon 1961; Spence and Spence 1954). On the other hand, additional investigations have found that the two dimensions are substantially independent. Included is a study by Farley (1967) in which data were obtained on seven different samples totalling over fourteen hundred subjects. He found that the E-N correlations were never significant and tended to approximate zero (no relationship). Standardization studies involved in the development of the EPI (S. B. G. Eysenck and H. J. Eysenck 1963) and the JEPI (Eysenck 1965b) have similarly found the E and N dimensions to be statistically independent. More generally, the literature suggests very small but nonsignificant negative relationships. One detailed factor analytic study was designed specifically to deal with the independence question (Eysenck, Hendrickson, and Eysenck 1969). Results quite clearly indicated that the E and N dimensions, which emerged as fourth order factors, were independent. Eysenck (personal communication, 1979) has suggested that the whole issue of E-N independence is a pseudo-question without real scientific meaning, since E and N are concepts, not real entities.

Whether or not E and N are definitively independent remains a question for further research. It is quite clear, however, that many investigators have found Eysenck's theoretical treatment of extraversion and neuroticism, as well has his EPI measure of these dimensions, acceptable for purposes of empirical study. As a result, there have been numerous investigations aimed at determining the relationships, of particular behaviors to the Eysenck dimensions. The most common approach has been to use the MPI or EPI (and now the EPQ) as a measure of one or both dimensions and to select subjects falling at the extremes of the dimension in question for further study on experimental tasks. For example, an investigator may administer the EPI to a group of five hundred college students, then ask those with very high and very low scores on the E scale to come to the experimental laboratory to participate in a conditioning study aimed at determining whether, under certain conditions, extraverts or introverts learn more rapidly. A majority of such studies have focused on the extraversion dimension, though a substantial number have also related to neuroticism.

EXTRAVERSION

Following his development of the extraversion and neuroticism dimensions and initial research to clarify the nature of these dimensions, Eysenck began to formulate a theoretical position concerning the bases for and nature of these major personality factors. His treatment of the extraversion dimension is built upon the concepts of excitation and inhibition. Excitation refers, in general, to a state of intensified or heightened activity of the cerebral cortex of the brain, while inhibition suggests the reduction or elimination of such activity. Care must be taken to note the kind or level of activity referred to in the Eysenck description. One type of activity we may think of is the overt behavior of the individual, and at that level we may tend to think in terms of behavioral excitation and inhibition. A more outgoing or behaviorally active person may be viewed as having a high level of behavioral excitation. At another level, activity is described in terms of excitation and inhibition of the cortex of the brain, in which case the focus is on cortical excitation and cortical inhibition. It is this latter level of activity in which Eysenck is primarily interested. The distinction is an important one, since cortical and behavioral excitation and inhibition are not always positively correlated. They may, in fact, be inversely related, such that a person with a high level of cortical excitation tends to be behaviorally inhibited or inactive. Neurophysiological theory suggests that one major function of the cortex is to control the functioning of lower or subcortical centers of the brain. As a result, a heightened level of cortical activity (that is, cortical excitation) may tend to *reduce* the influence of certain subcortical structures, leading to a reduction in behavioral excitation. Conversely, cortical inhibition may tend to cause *increased* activity in some subcortical centers, resulting in increased behavioral excitation.

The Early Theory

After studying the extraversion dimension empirically for some years, Eysenck put forth, in 1957, a major theoretical statement, using intervening variables to provide a hypothetical basis for extraversion and its effects on behavior. While the theory does rely on the balance between excitation and inhibition as the basis for behavioral differences between introverts and extraverts, it is largely an inhibition theory of extraversion–introversion, employing Hull's concept of *reactive inhibition*. Hull (1943) hypothesized that any response made by an organism tends to increase a state of inhibition which reduces the probability of that response occurring again. Reactive inhibition may be recognized as a state similar to that which is commonly described as fatigue.

Eysenck (1957) has stated two basic postulates relating to the Hullian concept. First, he hypothesized that there are differences among human beings in the rate at which excitation and inhibition are generated as well as in the strength of these states and the rate at which inhibition is dissipated or reduced. The second postulate holds that individuals in whom excitation develops relatively slowly and weakly but who are quick to develop strong reactive inhibitions tend to display extraverted behavior patterns. Conversely, individuals who generate excitation rapidly and strongly and inhibitions slowly and weakly are predisposed toward introverted behavior patterns. The theory goes on to suggest, and tends to emphasize, that differences between extraverted and introverted groups should be seen in the development of reactive inhibition, with extraverts characterized by high levels of rapidly developing inhibition and introverts by relatively low levels of slowly developing inhibition. Simply stated, extraverts tend to show more and introverts less reactive inhibition. This hypothesis may seem counterintuitive since it holds that introverts are more aroused than extraverts, but Eysenck's theory deals with cortical not behavioral excitation. It may be useful to think of the introvert in this theory as an individual who avoids external stimulation and, hence, is not outgoing because he or she is attempting to avoid any further increase in an already high cortical arousal level. The theory allows Eysenck to predict the differential performance of introverts and extraverts in a variety of areas, such as conditioning and the occurrence of involuntary rest pauses during an experimental task. Empirical findings concerned with these and other areas have been generally supportive of the theory and are taken up below, following the discussion of Eysenck's more recent theoretical statement.

The Revised Theory

Eysenck found that while his 1957 theory was successful in predicting a number of behavioral phenomena, it did not provide an adequate basis for predictions of other phenomena, such as the differences observed between introverts and extraverts in sensory thresholds. The revised theory (Eysenck 1967) incorporates the earlier theory but places it in a broader theoretical context, changes certain major emphases, and provides a neurophysiological basis for extraversion. The revised theory focuses more clearly on the excitation/inhibition (E/I) balance and changes the emphasis from inhibition to excitation. In making this change in emphasis, Eysenck adopts the term *arousal* to denote a continuum of excitation, ranging from a lower extreme, such as that characterizing a state of sleep, to an upper extreme, such as the arousal which would accompany a state of panic. The extravert is seen as functioning at a lower level of arousal than the introvert, and a variety of performance differences between the two groups, such as those seen in the conditioning and rest pause phenomena, are explained equally as well by the arousal theory as by the earlier reactive inhibition treatment. In addition, Eysenck has (1967) argued that the arousal theory is better able to explain certain other behavioral phenomena, such as differences in sensory thresholds (see below) between the extraverted and introverted groups. The hypothesis that extraverts develop inhibition more readily than introverts remains as an important part of the theory but is subtended to the more general arousal postulate.

Neurophysiological and Genetic Bases for Personality

The revised theory provides much more than a change in emphasis from inhibition to arousal. It provides specific theoretical postulates concering a neurological basis for the extraversion dimension. The postulated mechanism is the ascending reticular activating system (ARAS), which consists of the reticular formation in the brain stem and the pathways projecting from that structure to the cerebral cortex (Fig. 13-1). A substantial body of neurophysiological research has pointed to the

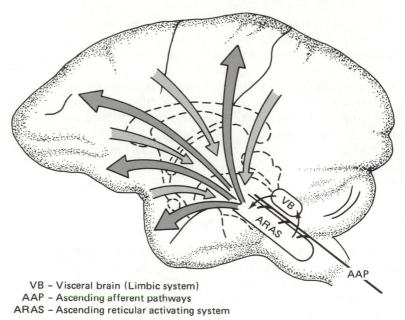

VB – Visceral brain (Limbic system)
AAP – Ascending afferent pathways
ARAS – Ascending reticular activating system

Figure 13-1 Diagrammatic representation of anatomical-physiological structures responsible for inherited differences in E (ARAS) and N (VB). Source: Eysenck, H. J. *The structure of human personality.* London: Methuen and Co., 1970, p. 434 (Fig. 61).

ARAS as the principal system in the brain responsible for integrating and controlling the arousal level of the individual.

Eysenck has further postulated that E/I balance differences, attributed to the ARAS, are largely genetic in origin. In a searching paper on the determinants of human behavior, Eysenck (1978) points out that twentieth-century psychologists to date have largely tended to ignore, if not deny, the possibility that genetic factors may play an important role in the determination of human behavior. Strongly environmental views have so dominated the field that many students of psychology have no training in genetics and many psychologists have no appreciation of the potential role of genetics in behavior. Eysenck has adopted the position that behavior is determined not by environmental factors alone, or by genetic factors alone, but by both environment and heredity. With regard to extraversion, he has postulated that the E/I balance differences, attributed to the ARAS, are largely genetic in origin. In support of his genetic hypothesis concerning extraversion, Eysenck has pointed to a large and growing body of evidence linking genetic factors with a variety of personality traits and functions (Eysenck 1976). The evidence for a genetic basis for extraversion comes from studies of twins. Investigations by Eysenck (1956) and Shields (1962) have shown a higher degree of concordance (agreement) on extraversion scores in identical than in fraternal twins, supporting genetic theory. A sophisticated, biometrical reanalysis of the Shields (1962) data by Jinks and Fulker (1970) also provides clear evidence of a genetic basis for extraversion, with the introvert genotype being somewhat more subject to environmental influence than the extravert genotype. Other evidence suggests greater effects of heredity at the extremes of the extraversion continuum, with environmental factors having more impact near the middle of the continuum (Eysenck 1976).

Eysenck (1967, 1968, 1970) has not proposed that extraversion-introversion differences and the behavioral effects of these differences are entirely inherited. Rather, he has suggested that individuals inherit certain neurological and physiological characteristics, such as those of the ARAS, which form the basis for the E/I balance. This genetically determined balance significantly influences a person's characteristic level of arousal, which in turn influences his or her performance in a variety of areas, such as conditioning and sensory threshold. The individual who conditions best at relatively low levels of environmental stimulation or stress, who has low sensory thresholds, and who is more sensitive to mild stimulation (that is, the introvert) is seen as quite likely to develop different patterns of behavior than the person who conditions best at high levels of environmental stimulation and is relatively insensitive to sensory stimuli (the extravert). It is thus the differences in conditioning, sensory threshold and other basic phenomena which cause the individual to interact differently with the environment, and this interaction, in turn, produces the behavioral traits differentially characterizing the extravert and the introvert. Figure 13-2 outlines this proposed theoretical structure in which the E/I balance acts as a *genotype,* functioning at the very core of the personality to influence basic aspects of the individual's interaction with the environment (laboratory phenomena). The interaction of these genetic and environmental components results in the traits that differentiate extraversion and introversion.

The fact that Eysenck attributes a significant role to the environment as a determinant of behavior should not be permitted to detract from the basic biological emphasis of the theory. Despite a substantial bow to environmental determinism, Eysenck has remained convinced that at least the extraversion-introversion dimension is determined largely by genetic factors. Citing correlations between the personality phenotype and the underlying genotype as "not likely to lie below .75" (Eysenck 1970, p. 454), he suggests that "we might be justified in saying that some three-quarters of individual differences in personality, insofar as these relate to E and N, are genetically determined" (Eysenck 1970, p. 454).

Empirical Studies of Extraversion

Experimental studies of the extraversion dimension have attempted to determine the differential characteristics of extraverts and introverts. Since the literature is extensive, we will provide here only some major examples of research areas and specific studies, then consider the characteristics of the two groups more generally.

Conditioning. Eysenck and Levey (1972) conditioned subjects using either a strong or a weak unconditioned stimulus (UCS). They found that introverts condition better when there is a weak (less arousing) UCS, extraverts when there is a

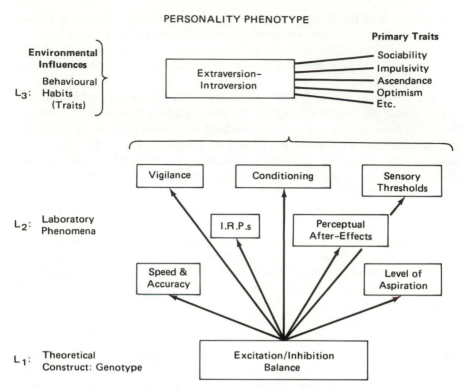

PERSONALITY PHENOTYPE

Primary Traits

Environmental
Influences

Behavioural
L₃: Habits
(Traits)

Extraversion–
Introversion

Sociability
Impulsivity
Ascendance
Optimism
Etc.

Vigilance   Conditioning   Sensory
Thresholds

L₂: Laboratory
Phenomena   I.R.P.s   Perceptual
After-Effects

Speed &
Accuracy   Level of
Aspiration

L₁: Theoretical
Construct: Genotype   Excitation/Inhibition
Balance

Figure 13-2 Diagrammatic representation of interplay between genotype and environment to produce phenotype of extravert-introvert personality. Source: Eysenck, H. J. *The structure of human personality*. London: Methuen and Co., 1979, p. 456 (Fig. 75). CJBS.

strong (more arousing) UCS. Eysenck (1966) reasoned that this result is consistent with a higher level of arousal in introverts if the classic Yerkes-Dodson arousal-performance relationship is invoked. This relationship and its relevance to extraversion are discussed below. Eysenck (1965a) has provided a more extensive review of the relevant conditioning literature.

Sensory Threshold Effects. Since the extraversion dimension is a typological dimension, it is expected to influence a wide variety of behaviors. In addition to conditioning, one of the major areas investigated by Eysenck has been that of sensory threshold. Eysenck (1967) has suggested that introverts, due to their high levels of cortical arousal, should display lower sensory thresholds (that is, respond at lower intensities of stimulation). This prediction arises, in part, from the observation that high levels of induced arousal have been found to produce lower thresholds (Gray 1964). For example, subjects can hear somewhat softer tones when placed under stress. Research has tended to support the Eysenck hypothesis. Haslam (1966) used radiant heat to induce pain and found lower pain thresholds in introverts than in extraverts.

Effects of Stimulation. If introverts have higher levels of cortical arousal, it would follow that under conditions of equal stimulation, effector output should be greater (that is, responses should be larger) for introverts than extraverts. Experiments have tended to confirm this observation. Two such investigations explored the amount of salivation exhibited by groups of introverted and extraverted subjects upon stimulation. Specifically, Corcoran (1964) found greater salivary output in introverts in response to stimulation by four drops of lemon juice placed on the tongue. In a later study, S. B. G. Eysenck and H. J. Eysenck (1967) confirmed this finding.

Involuntary Rest Pauses. Eysenck (1967) has argued that the theoretical and experimental concept most closely corresponding to the personality dimension of extraversion–introversion is fatigue, with extraverts behaving more and introverts less like a fatigued person. A direct measure of fatigue previously used in the learning literature is the involuntary rest pause (IRP), which is simply a momentary hesitation or cessation in performance. A more fatigued person, one who, in Hullian terms, has built up more reactive inhibition, should show more IRPs than a less fatigued one. Spielman (1963) tested this hypothesis by having extraverted and introverted subjects simply tap with a metal stylus on a metal plate. A recording system permitted precise measurement of the amount of time the stylus was in contact with the metal plate during each tap and the time away from the plate between taps. Treating the time between taps as an involuntary rest pause, Spielman found significantly more IRPs in extraverts than introverts. In fact, the extraverts displayed fifteen times as many IRPs. Eysenck (1964b) confirmed the result in a similar study.

Additional Characteristics. We have seen that extraverts condition less rapidly than introverts under conditions of low or moderate arousal but better under higher arousal, show more IRPs, display higher sensory thresholds and less effector output, and tend to learn and retain information better under some conditions but not under others. As was noted, these findings merely scratch the empirical surface of the Eysenck literature. To mention a few additional differences, research has shown that extraverts tend to overreact to relatively small doses of a depressant drug, extinguish learned responses more rapidly, smoke more than introverts and prefer cigarettes, hold their breath longer, and be less reactive to stimulant drugs.

Arousal and Performance

We have seen that Eysenck's theory attributes to arousal an important role in the determination of behavior and personality. More specifically, to the extent that extraversion influences a given area of behavior, it will be the level of arousal at the time that the behavior occurs which will directly influence the nature of the behavior. The level of arousal at any given time can be seen, from Eysenck's theory, as determined by three major factors. First, and perhaps most influential, is the genetically determined *excitation/inhibition balance,* mediated by the ARAS. This factor should tend to be highly consistent over a long period of time and perhaps throughout the individual's life. The second factor is the person's *prior exposure* to the environment, resulting in what might be termed learned arousal habits. This second factor recognizes that learning and environmental experiences more generally can interact with genetic determinants to modify arousal level. The final determinant of arousal is the environmental situation existing *at the time* that behavior takes place. Whether an individual is extraverted or introverted, introduction of significant stress from the environment may substantially raise his or her arousal level.

It is the addition of the third factor, current environmental influences on arousal, that makes simple predictions based on the postulated difference in arousal levels difficult. The reason for this difficulty is that arousal level does not appear to bear a simple, linear relationship to performance. That is, it is not true that performance consistently increases as arousal level increases. Rather, an inverted U-shaped function relating arousal to performance has been proposed (Yerkes and Dodson 1908; Hebb 1955; Broadhurst 1959). This relationship has been termed the *Yerkes-Dodson Law* and holds that performance tends to increase as arousal increases up to an optimal point. Further increases in arousal beyond this point tend to decrease performance. The result is the inverted U-shaped (curvi-linear) arousal-performance relationship (Fig. 13-3).

Applied to the extraversion theory, the Yerkes-Dodson Law would suggest that the more aroused introvert is likely to perform more efficiently than the extravert as long as environmental conditions are not stressful enough to raise arousal levels extremely high, since both introvert and extravert remain below or at the optimal level of arousal for maximal performance. Under stressful environmental conditions, however, the arousal levels of both introvert and extravert may be increased beyond the optimal point, such that the performance efficiency of the introvert will actually drop below that of the extravert. The results of the Eysenck and Levey (1972) experiment with an unconditioned stimulus, discussed above, can be clearly seen as supportive of Eysenck's theory.

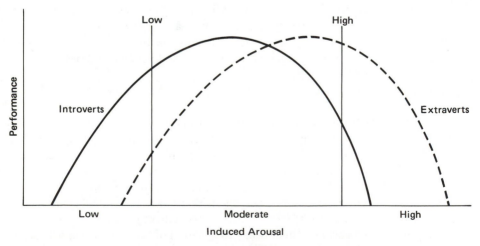

Figure 13-3 Under conditions of low induced arousal (relaxation), introverts show superior performance. Under high arousal (tension), extraverts are superior.

NEUROTICISM

Eysenck has done relatively little empirical work on neuroticism compared to his work on extraversion. He notes that the two reasons for the lesser emphasis in this area are: (1) the basic physiological and neurological bases for neuroticism are better understood; and (2) genuine emotional responses of the type that would be needed to study neuroticism are difficult to produce reliably in the laboratory, while cortical arousal, needed to study extraversion, can quite readily be manipulated (Eysenck, personal communication 1978).

The Eysenck theory of neuroticism, while less elaborate and less firm than that for extraversion, parallels the extraversion theory to a substantial degree. Neuroticism is seen essentially as an independent personality dimension with genetic origins and a neurophysiological basis and is hypothesized to affect certain aspects of both normal and abnormal behavior. With regard to this latter point, it seems essential to clarify at the outset Eysenck's use of the term *neuroticism*. The terms *neurosis* and *neurotic* are used in psychopathology to denote certain combinations of symptoms constituting abnormal behavior. In Eysenck's usage, however, the term neuroticism does not necessarily refer to abnormal behavior. Rather, it is a dimension reflecting the *emotionality* of the individual. Persons high on the emotionality dimension are termed emotionally *labile* and tend to be particularly sensitive to painful, novel, disturbing, or other emotional stimulation, while persons low on emotionality, termed emotionally *stable,* are relatively insensitive. Some have thought of the lability–stability differentiation as reflecting the intensity of the individual's reactivity to stimulation, the labile person being expected to exhibit extreme reactions, the highly stable person to exhibit very small reactions. Eysenck (1960b) and Duffy (1962), however, have contended that the differentiation should be in terms of the persistence of the reaction rather than its intensity. The labile person exhibits a more persistent emotional reaction than does the stable.

Arousal vs. Activation

Emotionality, like extraversion, has drive properties. Eysenck (1967) has hypothesized, however, that the drive properties associated with neuroticism are, at least in part, different from those associated with extraversion. We have already seen that arousal, the drive concept coupled theoretically with the extraversion dimension, is contributed to by external stimulation impinging upon the senses and by internal stimulation from the cerebral cortex. Eysenck has proposed that *activation,* which is the drive concept associated with the neuroticism dimension, is contributed to primarily or exclusively by *emotional* stimulation. The neurological basis for emotional activation is the limbic system or visceral brain (see Fig. 13-1, p. 318). This important brain system appears, after considerable research, to be involved in emotional functioning. It interacts with the cerebral cortex, stimulating the cortex to increase cortical arousal and receiving emotionally relevant stimulation from the cortex. The visceral brain is also the neural origin of the autonomic nervous system, which is also involved in emotional functioning. The visceral brain interacts, in addition, with the ARAS, contributing to the overall level of arousal controlled by that structure.

Eysenck has suggested that the neuroticism dimension, like extraversion, is basically genetic in nature. Results of a number of studies are consistent with this hypothesis. Eysenck and Prell (1951), in an early study, compared concordance for neuroticism in identical twins, supporting the genetic hypothesis. The Shields (1962) study discussed above examined neuroticism as well as extraversion in the identical and fraternal twin pairs involved in the study. Concordance for neuroticism was considerably greater in identical than in fraternal twins, and the Jinks-Fulker (1970) reanalysis of the Shields data also provides evidence of a genetic basis for neuroticism.

Performance and Activation. We have seen in relation to the extraversion dimension that the hypothesized relationship between performance and arousal is an inverted U-shaped curve. Eysenck (1967) has proposed that the same inverted U-shaped curve that characterizes the arousal-performance relationship also exists between performance and the activation dimension influenced by neuroticism. Under the influence of the Yerkes-Dodson Law, it is expected that increases in emotional activation will produce increased performance efficiency up to the point where activation reaches its optimal and performance its maximal point. Further increases in activation beyond this point should cause a decline in performance.

Empirical Studies of Neuroticism

We said in discussing the extraversion dimension that there have been a substantial number of empirical studies of the differential characteristics of extraverts and introverts and that many of these studies are based specifically on extraversion as measured by the EPI or MPI. The research story is quite different for neuroticism, where relatively few studies have been done, and much of the work completed to date has not operationally defined neuroticism specifically in terms of the MPI or EPI scales.

Eysenck (1967) has reviewed much of the research literature which is relevant to neuroticism as he defines it. Most of the studies considered are based on the somewhat tenuous assumption that Eysenck's neuroticism dimension is closely related to anxiety and to neurosis. Reviewing studies of heart rate, blood pressure, electroencephalographic (EEG) patterns, and other psychophysiological variables, Eysenck (1967) has concluded that anxious and neurotic subjects tend to show stronger, more variable responses to stimulation and take longer to return to prestimulation baselines of physiological activity. Jensen (1964) carried out a study of neuroticism, as well as extraversion, in relation to a variety of learning tasks. While extraversion correlated with various aspects of learning, neuroticism showed no relationship to learning. On the other hand, Shanmugam and Santhanam (1964) found subjects high on neuroticism to be superior in performance on a serial learning task. And Eysenck (1962) found the N dimension to be essentially uncorrelated with pursuit motor learning. No clear relationship has been found between N and the types of learning investigated thus far; the neuroticism-learning literature is, however, far from definitive.

Studies of recognition threshold, electrodermal response (EDR), and the electroencephalogram (EEG) may give some further insights into the differential characteristics of subjects high and low in neuroticism. Ehlers (1963) had subjects learn an association between a nonsense syllable and one of several stimuli. She then used a tachistoscope to present the nonsense syllables for very short periods of time. The recognition threshold, defined as the amount of time a stimulus had to remain on before the subject could respond to it, was found to be lower in subjects high on the N dimension. That is, neurotics required less time to recognize the stimulus than did stables. In another area, EDR studies show that neuroticism, though less clearly than extraversion, is related to this important measure of the activity of the autonomic nervous system (Mangan and O'Gorman 1969; Orlebecke 1973; Coles, Gale and Kline 1971; Wigglesworth and Smith 1976). In EEG work, Savage (1964) recorded the average size or amplitude of brain waves in the alpha frequency range. He found no differences between subjects high and low on the neuroticism dimension, though extraverts showed significantly higher alpha amplitudes than introverts, indicating higher levels of cortical inhibition (or lower levels of cortical arousal) in extraverts, as Eysenck has predicted.

The E-N Crossover

Although we have thus far considered extraversion and neuroticism separately, Eysenck (1970) has proposed that we can expect to predict many behaviors better, not from E or N alone but from the interaction or *crossover* of the two dimensions. The general method for studying the dimensional interaction is termed *zone analysis*. It will be recalled that Eysenck views extraversion and neuroticism as orthogonal dimensions, which can be pictured as two lines intersecting at right angles (Fig. 13-4). The crossing lines form four sectors or zones, each of which must be defined in terms of scores on both the N and E dimensions. Subjects who are high on both E and N fall in one zone, those high on N and low on E fall in a second zone, and so on. One can thus speak of neurotic extraverts (NE), neurotic introverts (NI), stable extraverts (SE), and stable introverts (SI). In practice, it is possible to create even more zones by establishing additional cutting points on the two dimensions. In particular, the establishment of a total of nine groups of subjects by including medium groups on both dimensions may be desirable.

An example of zone analysis is seen in the work of McLaughlin and Eysenck (1967), who divided their subjects into four personality groups formed by the E-N crossover. Some subjects in each of the four groups learned an easy paired-associate nonsense syllable list, while others learned a difficult list. Results showed

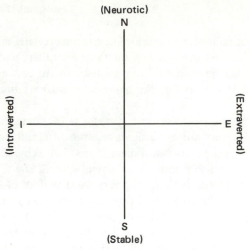

(Neurotic)
N

(Introverted) I ———————— E (Extraverted)

S
(Stable)

Figure 13-4 Eysenck view of extraversion and neuroticism as orthogonal dimensions.

that neurotic introverts learned less rapidly on the easy list and more rapidly on the difficult list than did stable introverts. The reverse pattern was true for extraverts. Neurotic extraverts outperformed stable extraverts on the easy list, with the reverse being true on the difficult list. The investigators interpreted these results as quite consistent with the Yerkes-Dodson arousal-performance relationship. Greater arousal or drive would be contributed in this particular study by the difficult as opposed to the easy list. It has been argued that, as a result, the NI group is at its optimal level of arousal under easy list conditions, with the relatively low-arousal SE group below its optimum, and the remaining two groups above optimum. The increase in arousal produced by the difficult list raises the SE group to its optimum, pushing the NE group over the top of the Yerkes-Dodson curve to join the two remaining groups at levels of arousal so high as to interfere with performance.

EXTENSIONS AND APPLICATIONS

Eysenck has applied his theory to and conducted research in a number of areas, ranging from education and vocational guidance to psychopathology and sex. Some of the major applications are considered here.

Psychopathology

It will be recalled that the original Eysenck (1947) study of seven hundred neurotic soldiers resulted in a major division of patients into two groups. One group displayed dsythymic symptoms, including anxiety, reactive depression, compulsivity, and phobia, while the other showed hysterical symptoms. Further empirical studies have supported the subdivision of neurosis into two major types, and Eysenck has maintained this theoretical distinction, which originated in the work of Jung and was in Janet's later work. Eysenck's theory holds, in essence, that all clinically neurotic subjects can be expected to exhibit high scores on the neuroticism dimension as measured by the EPI. Those with low extraversion scores (the NI group in a zone analysis) tend to show dysthymic symptoms, while those higher on the extraversion dimension tend to show the symptoms of hysteria.

Criminal Behavior

Psychopathy is a category of abnormal behavior characterized predominately by antisocial behaviors. The psychopath is the classic "con artist," the individual who has no apparent conscience, and who exploits others and society in general to gain his or her own ends. The psychopath has much in common with the criminal, and in fact, many psychopaths are criminals in the literal sense that they commit illegal acts and are convicted and sentenced to prison terms.

Eysenck (1964, 1977) has presented a controversial theory of criminal behavior in which he holds that the roots of criminality lie in the genetic makeup of the individual and in the interaction of that makeup with environmental factors. Specifically, Eysenck has suggested that the learned set of moral and ethical values held by the individual is a product of a virtual life-long process of conditioning. If the socially based conditioning which forms the conscience is lacking or inadequate for any reason, the conscience may not be fully or appropriately developed. Since a normal conscience is essential if moral and legal acts are to dominate the individual's behavior pattern, the person without adequate conscience development can be expected to engage in psychopathic and criminal activities.

Under what conditions would the moral value system not develop adequately? There are a variety of possible answers to this question, but Eysenck's is that extraversion and neuroticism play significant roles. Specifically, he has predicted and found that the emotionally reactive (high N) person, who is also extremely extraverted and thus falls in the NE group in zone analysis, is likely to be the psychopath or criminal. A number of studies have been supportive of this hypothesis (Eysenck 1977), although some have not (Buikhuisen & Hemmel 1972).

Eysenck's theory has been controversial because it postulates involvement, at least indirectly, of genetic factors in criminal behavior. That is, extraversion and neuroticism, both of which are in part genetically based, affect the conditioning process. This, in turn, leads to less effective conditioning of conscience in the neurotic extravert, hence increasing the likelihood that this individual will become a psychopath and perhaps a criminal. He does note that the neurotic and extraversive tendencies that are inherited only predispose the individual toward higher emotional reactivity and poor conditionability and thus toward criminality. Specific criminal behaviors themselves are conditioned. As a result, the theory leads to a proposal of treatment for criminal behavior that is based on the individual's relative position on the extraversion and neuroticism dimensions and previous history of reinforcement for criminal behavior. Eysenck has suggested that the criminal can be retrained through behavior therapy techniques that are individually tailored to each criminal depending upon the factors noted above. Details of the revised theory and a review of relevant evidence appear in Eysenck's 1977 book, *Crime and Personality*.

Sexual Behavior

Eysenck (1972) has applied the three dimensions of his system to the study of sexual attitudes and behavior. His work on sexual behavior is of particular interest in demonstrating the broad applicability of the typological dimensions with which he has worked. He reports a study involving four hundred male and four hundred female college students, all single and most under twenty-one years of age. Each student completed questionnaires measuring P (Psychoticism), E and N, an inventory of sexual attitudes and an inventory dealing with sexual behavior. The latter two inventories were analyzed to indicate percentages of males and females answering "yes" to each item. Results indicated, for example, that men are more interested than women in pornography, orgies, and voyeurism and are more in favor of legalizing prostitution. Premarital sex and promiscuity were also favored by more men than women, but women expressed more satisfaction in their sex life, while indicating more frequent guilt about sexual experiences.

The relationship of sexual attitudes and practices to E, N, and P is of particular interest, and of most importance are the results that indicate that these major typological dimensions relate to sexual behavior. Both extraverts and introverts, Eysenck has concluded, exhibit good sexual adjustments. The extravert, however, has less difficulty approaching members of the opposite sex and is not at all "prudish." The introvert is somewhat prudish and has difficulty in making the necessary social contacts. On the neuroticism dimension, the high N scorer is prudish, has high levels of both sexual excitement and sexual nervousness, and obtains only minimal satisfaction. High P scorers exhibit high levels of sexual hostility and promiscuity, and they are also somewhat prudish and show inhibitions. The work on sexual behavior has been extended and its genetic bases discussed in Eysenck's (1976) book, *Sex and Personality*.

Treatment

Eysenck (1952, 1966) reviewed empirical studies of psychotherapy and reached the conclusion that traditional psychotherapies are ineffective. This conclusion was viewed by many as controversial and has led to a long series of criticisms by others, replies by Eysenck, and, the consequence of most importance, to careful studies of the effectiveness of psychotherapy. After a careful review of the literature relating to the controversy, Bergin (1971) concluded that there is some evidence for weak positive effects of psychotherapy, suggesting that some methods of psychotherapy are effective in the hands of some therapists, but there are also many cases of failure.

Convinced of the ineffectiveness of psychotherapy, Eysenck turned to the use of behavior therapy techniques, some of which are consistent with his theory of psychological disorder. Eysenck's basic theoretical proposal for treatment is based on the observation that dysthymic disorders, such as anxiety states and depressive reactions, result from a high drive level and superior conditionability, resulting in disorders which arise from overconditioning. Psychopathic disorders reflect the poor conditionability seen in neurotic extraverts and are thus disorders based on underconditioning. This implies that the overconditioned dysthymic disorders require a therapy which will involve deconditioning, while the underconditioned psychopathic disorders require a therapy which will increase conditioning. *Desensitization* is a deconditioning procedure which involves substituting for a strong emotional (anxiety) response an incompatible relaxation response and is thus appropriate for dysthymic disorders. *Aversion therapy,* another form of behavioral treatment, is a conditioning procedure which involves the use of punishment to reduce the occurrence of undesirable behaviors and should thus be effective with psychopathic and related disorders.

THE THEORY IN EMPIRICAL CONTEXT

Much has already been said about Eysenck's research methods as well as about the specific research in which he has been involved and the research which his theory has generated. We will thus not go into the details of further research, restricting our discussion to a particular research method advocated by Eysenck.

The method referred to is termed *criterion analysis,* and it is more than a method in that it reflects much of Eysenck's philosophy concerning scientific method and its relationship to theory. Criterion analysis is basically a specific factor analytic application of the hypothesis-testing or hypothetico-deductive method. We have already discussed factor analytic approaches in the chapter on Cattell. The hypothetico-deductive method is a traditional approach of the experimental scientist and involves simply stating a specific proposition or hypothesis and then testing that hypothesis.

Criterion analysis begins with the theorist's proposal of a factor, hypothesized on the basis of previous research or theory. The entire remaining procedure of criterion analysis has the goal of determining a mathematically defined factor which represents the hypothetical factor and of finding the best measures of that factor. The interrelationships of the measuring instruments are examined through factor analysis to determine whether or not the hypothetical factor exists and what its relationship to the criterion is.

The development of measures of a dimension of neuroticism provides an example. A neuroticism factor would first be hypothesized and roughly described. The researcher would then obtain tests thought to be related to neuroticism and would identify two criterion groups, one a group of clinically diagnosed neurotics and the other a group of normals. The measures to be used would then be given to both the normal and neurotic groups, and the tests would be correlated with the dichotomy or discrepancy between the two groups. The neuroticism factor derived through this process would load most highly on those items or tests which best discriminated between groups. Thus, those items on which there is a greater response difference between neurotics and normals would most heavily determine the neuroticism factor.

EVALUATION

Some of the critical points concerning Eysenck's theory and associated research grow out of his emphasis on the need for scientific approaches in psychology, others relate to the factor analytic bases for his dimensions, still others reflect his membership in the community of behaviorists, and a final group is specific to Eysenck's own theory and methodology.

Contributions

Among Eysenck's greatest contributions over the years have been his emphasis on the need for science in psychology and the need for the acceptance by the society of a scientific approach to human social problems. He has thus joined, with loud voice, Skinner, Cattell and a few others in the quest for a science of human behavior. Some of the major criticisms of his work have grown out of his willingness to criticize severely other psychologists for their failure to provide adequate evidence for the effectiveness of their techniques.

A second area of contribution grows out of Eysenck's forceful and innovative use of factor analytic and other multivariate approaches to research. In this he has joined Cattell to lead virtually the entire field of multivariate research in personality psychology not only in England and the United States but throughout the world. While his particular use of factor analysis has been criticized, as will be seen below, he has demonstrated the viability of a particular factor analytic approach to personality and its use in conjunction with bivariate, experimental research. Where Cattell has criticized the extensive use of the traditional, bivariate experimental approach and others have criticized the use of multivariate techniques, Eysenck has shown that a combination of the two approaches can be fruitful in the expansion of scientific knowledge.

A further contribution lies in the continuing demonstration that a typological approach to human personality is feasible at both theoretical and empirical levels. The uniqueness of Eysenck's contributions in formulating a typological model has often not been fully appreciated. At the present time the only other major typology relevant to personality is that of the Russian investigators, Teplov (1964) and Nebylitsyn (1972), whose work is based on dimensions dealing with the properties of the nervous system.

Problems and Difficulties

Eysenck shares with Cattell and others the major criticisms of factor analysis that were discussed earlier. In addition, Eysenck has often been singled out by critics for his particular approach to the use of factor analysis. First, criterion analysis has been criticized by some as an approach which may tend to restrict the factor analytic treatment of the data in such a way as to increase the probability of confirming the investigator's hypothesis. Eysenck has held that this is not the case. Several technical criticisms of Eysenck's approach have been offered by Cattell. Of particular relevance is Cattell's contention that Eysenck's major factors, E and N, may not represent broad, typological dimensions, as he maintains. Cattell refers to Eysenck's position that a broad primary factor is comparable with a second order factor and suggests that this is probably not the case. The broad primary factors thus become "pseudo-second-order" factors, which may mislead the theorist in making inferences about personality. This is a somewhat elaborate way of saying that in studies where Eysenck's E and N factors have been first order or primary factors, rather than "true," higher order factors, the E and N dimensions do not, by definition, subsume sets of traits ordinarily represented by the primaries. If correct, this could be a telling criticism, since the Eysenck theory assumes that E and N are typological dimensions, each subsuming traits that exist at a lower level in the hierarchical organization of behavior, discussed earlier. Eysenck, Hendrickson and Eysenck (1969) have, however provided statistical evidence that the pseudo-second-order factors referred to by Cattell do bear a close similarity to the true second orders.

A further criticism of Eysenck's position has been that the important extraversion factor may not be unitary (Carrigan 1960). That is, rather than being a single dimension of personality, extraversion may contain at least two independent factors, termed *sociability* and *impulsiveness.*

S. B. G. Eysenck and H. J. Eysenck (1963) replied to the Carrigan criticism with an empirical study. Their analyses of data from a sample of three hundred subjects indicated that both sociability and impulsiveness are aspects of extraversion, but, since they are related to each other, they do not constitute an independent factor as the Carrigan criticism implies. More recent work has examined the predictive power of the sociability and impulsivity components in psychophysiological studies Revelle et al., 1980) and the relative genetic and environmental contributions to the determination of these components (Eaves and Eysenck 1975, 1977).

A further concern of some critics has been with the replicability of the Eysenck dimensions. While factor replication is, as we have seen, important for any factor analytic theory of personality, the failure to replicate would be particularly devastating to a theory like Eysenck's, which relies almost totally on only three dimensions. If even one of these, particularly E or N, were not found consistently across studies, Eysenck's entire theory would be in considerable jeopardy.

While there have been some failures to find clearcut E and N factors, Eysenck has amassed considerable evidence for the replicability of these two dimensions. Particularly relevant is a study of the combined factorial structures of the Cattell, Guilford, and Eysenck scales. The study is presented as a series of papers by Eysenck, White, and Soueif, all appearing in Eysenck and Eysenck (1969). The purpose of the study was to determine the extent to which factors contained in three major factorial personality inventories would replicate in a large subject sample and which factors would hold up when the factorial structure of the three inventories was tested. There was little evidence for replication of the Cattell and Guilford primary factors. However, E and N, extracted as higher order factors, did replicate both across inventories and across sexes. As a further indication of replicability, Sybil Eysenck has given the EPQ in translation to a number of national groups, including the Japanese, Nigerian, Indian, and Yugoslav. The results of her work show that the same three factors occur in all nationalities studied. Indices of factor comparison, which show the degree of similarity between factors in different samples, have usually been above .95, indicating that the factors are nearly identical (H. Eysenck, personal communication 1978).

An important additional consideration relevant to factor replication is that the E and N factors have not been found exclusively in Eysenck's laboratories. In particular, Cattell has reported some evidence for the existence of higher order E and N factors. In a recent cross-cultural study (Cattell and Nichols 1972) the Cattell 16-PF test was given to males and females in various age groups from several cultures, including the United States, West Germany, Brazil, Venezuela, and New Zealand. The partial replication of primary 16-PF factors found in this study is overshadowed by the impressive cross-cultural replication of the second order E and N factors. Cattell calls the latter "low anxiety-high anxiety," but it is quite similar to the neuroticism factor of Eysenck's work.

A final area of concern is Eysenck's use of only three factors—and in most of his work, only two—to describe and understand personality. How is it possible to deal with so complex a structure as the human personality with only two or three dimensions? Moreover, can we reasonably expect to predict on the basis of such a small number of very broad dimensions? These questions cannot, at the present time, be fully answered, for most answers must come in the form of statements of opinion reflecting particular theoretical biases. One recent study is, however, of considerable relevance to the question of whether a small number of factors can yield fairly specific predictions. This study (Reynolds and Nichols 1977) involved the California Personality Inventory (CPI). The CPI contains eighteen scales, and it has been found that two higher order factors (superfactors) account for much of the variance in the total CPI. The two factors, Adjustment and Extraversion, are similar to Eysenck's Neuroticism and Extraversion factors. The investigators found that the superfactors were much more predictive of a number of quite specific behaviors than were portions of the CPI scales not included in the superfactors, thus supporting Eysenck's contention.

Conclusions

Hans Eysenck has been among the most controversial of the major personality theorists whom we will study. The broad, typological dimensions he postulates as bases for behavior, the partial genetic origins that he hypothesizes for these dimensions, and his occasional attacks on traditional psychology have all been sources of controversy and criticism. He has, however, thrived on these controversies and on the not infrequent plaudits directed at his theory to become one of the most prolific researchers and writers among the major personality theorists. While typology more generally has not yet found its way into American psychology in a major way, it may well represent one of the trends of the future as psychologists learn more and more about the underlying factors that influence personality and behavior. If such a trend does develop, Eysenck will surely be regarded as a major historical figure for his pioneering efforts in this area; even if typology does not become a major force in American psychology, Eysenck has surely had a major impact on the field and is likely to continue to do so.

REFERENCES

Bergin, A. E. The evaluation of therapeutic outcomes. In A. E. Bergin & S. L. Garfield (Eds.), *Handbook of psychotherapy and behavior change.* New York: Wiley & Sons, 1971.

Broadhurst, P. L. The interaction of task difficulty and motivation: The Yerkes-Dodson law revived. *Acta Psychologia,* 1959, *16,* 321–338.

Buikhuisen, W., & Hemmel, J. J. Crime and conditioning. *British Journal of Criminology,* 1972, *12,* 147–157.

Carrigan, P. M. Extraversion-introversion as a dimension of personality: A reappraisal. *Psychological Bulletin,* 1960, *57,* 329–360.

Cattell, R. B., & Nichols, K. E. An improved definition, from ten researchers, of second order personality factors in Q data (with cross cultural checks). *Journal of Social Psychology,* 1972, *76,* 187–203.

Coles, M. G. H., Gale, A., & Kline, P. Personality and habituation of the orienting reaction tonic and response measures of electrodermal activity. *Psychophysiology,* 1971, *8,* 54–63.

Corcoran, D. W. J. The relation between introversion and salivation. *American Journal of Psychology,* 1964, *77,* 298–300.

Duffy, G. *Activation and behavior.* London: Wiley, 1962.

Eaves, L., & Eysenck, H. J. The nature of extraversion: A genetical analysis. *Journal of Personality and Social Psychology,* 1975, *32,* 102–112.

Eaves, L. J., & Eysenck, H. J. A genotype environmental model for psychoticism. *Advances in Behaviour Research and Therapy, 1977, 1,* 5–26.

Ehlers, B. *Eina eperimentelle, untersuchung ber wahremungshemmung und ihre peziehung zur extraversion.* Unpublished doctoral dissertation, Marburh, 1963.

Eysenck, H. J. *Dimensions of personality.* New York: Praeger, 1947.

Eysenck, H. J. Schizothymia-cyclothymia as a dimension of personality: II. Experimental. *Journal of Personality,* 1952, *20,* 345–384.

Eysenck, H. J. *The scientific study of personality.* New York: Macmillan, 1952.

Eysenck, H. J. The inheritance of extraversion-introversion. *Acta Psychologia,* 1956, *12,* 95–100.

Eysenck, H. J. *Dimensions of personality.* New York: Praeger, 1957.

Eysenck, H. J. (Ed.) *Behavior therapy and the neuroses.* New York: Pergamon, 1960.

Eysenck, H. J. Reminiscence, extraversion, and neuroticism. *Perception and Motor Skills,* 1960, *11,* 21–22.

Eysenck, H. J. (Ed.). *Handbook of abnormal psychology: An experimental approach.* New York: Basic Books, 1961.

Eysenck, H. J. Figural aftereffects, personality, and intersensory comparisons. *Perception and Motor Skills,* 1962, *12,* 161–162.

Eysenck, H. J. *Crime and personality.* London: Routledge and Kegan Paul, 1964.

Eysenck, H. J. Involuntary rest pauses in tapping as a function of drive and personality. *Perceptual and Motor Skills,* 1964, *18,* 173–174.

Eysenck, H. J. Extraversion and the acquisition of eye-blink and GSR conditioned responses. *Psychological Bulletin,* 1965, *63,* 258–270.

Eysenck, H. J. Factor theory psychology: A dimensional approach to personality. In W. S. Sahakian (Ed.), *Psychology of personality: Readings in theory.* Chicago: Rand McNally, 1965.

Eysenck, H. J. Personality and experimental psychology. *Bulletin of the Psychological Society,* 1966, *62,* 1–28.

Eysenck, H. J. *The biological basis of personality.* Springfield, Ill.: Charles C. Thomas, 1967.

Eysenck, H. J. An experimental study of aesthetic preference for polygonal figures. *Journal of General Psychology,* 1968, *79,* 3–17.

Eysenck, H. J. *Readings in extraversion-introversion: Bearings on basic psychological processes* (Vol. 3). New York: Wiley, 1970.

Eysenck, H. J. Personality and sexual behavior. *Journal of Psychosomatic Research,* 1972, *16,* 141–152.

Eysenck, H. J. Genetic factors in personality development. In A. R. Kaplan (Ed.), *Human behavior genetics.* Springfield, Mass.: Charles C. Thomas, 1976. (Pp. 198–229.)

Eysenck, H. J. *Sex and personality.* London: Open Books, 1976.

Eysenck, H. J. *Crime and personality* (3rd Ed.). London: Paladin, 1977.

Eysenck, H. J. Genetics and personality. In J. M. Thoday & A. S. Parkes (Eds.), *Genetic and environmental influences on behavior.* Edinburgh, 1978.

Eysenck, H. J., & Eysenck, S. B. G. A factorial study of psychoticism as a dimension of personality. *Multivariate Behavioral Research,* 1968, *Special Issue,* 15–31.

Eysenck, H. J., & Eysenck, S. B. G. *The structure and measurement of personality.* London: Routledge, 1969.

Eysenck, H. J., Hendrickson, A., & Eysenck, S. B. G. The orthogonality of personality structure. In H. J. Eysenck & S. B. G. Eysenck (Eds.), *Personality structure and measurement.* San Diego: R. R. Knapp, 1969.

Eysenck, H. J. & Levey, A. A. Conditioning, introversion-extraversion, and the strength of the nervous system. In V. D. Nebylitsyn & J. A. Gray (Eds.), *Biological bases of individual behavior.* New York Academic Press, 1972.

Eysenck, H. J., & Prell, D. B. The inheritance of neuroticism: An experimental study. *Journal of Mental Science,* 1951, *97,* 441-465.

Eysenck, S. B. G., & Eysenck, H. J. The validity of questionnaire and rating assessments of extraversion and neuroticism, and their factorial stability. *British Journal of Psychology,* 1963, *54,* 51-62.

Eysenck, S. B. G. & Eysenck, H. J. Salivary response to lemon juice as a measure of introversion. *Perceptual and Motor Skills,* 1967, *24,* 1047-1053.

Farley, F. H. The independence of extraversion and neuroticism. *Journal of Clinical Psychology,* 1967, *23,* 154-156.

Gray, J. A. *Pavlov's typology: Recent theoretical and experimental developments from the laboratory of B. M. Teplov.* New York: Pergamon, 1964.

Haslam, D. R. *Individual differences in pain threshold and the concept of arousal.* Unpublished doctoral dissertation, University of Bristol, 1966.

Hebb, D. O. Drives and the conceptual nervous system. *Psychological Review,* 1955, *62,* 243-254.

Heymans, G., & Wiersma, E. Beitrage zur apexiellen psychologie auf grund. Einer Massenunterfuchung. *Ztschr. F.,* 1909, *25,* 1-72.

Hull, C. L. *Principles of behavior.* New York: Appleton, 1943.

Jensen, A. *Individual differences in learning: Interference factor.* U.S. Department of Health, Education and Welfare Project Report 1867, 1964.

Jenson, A. R. The maudsley personality inventory. *Acta Psychologia,* 1958, *4,* 314, 325.

Jinks, J. L., & Fulker, D. W. Comparison of the biometrical, genetical, MAVA, and classical approaches to the analysis of human behavior. *Psychological Bulletin,* 1970, *73,* 311-349.

Kretschmer, E. [*Physique and character*] (W. J. H. Sprott, trans.). New York: Harcourt, Brace & World, 1925. (Originally published, 1921.)

Lynn, R., & Gordon, I. E. The relation of neuroticism and extraversion to intelligence and educational attainment. *British Journal of Educational Psychology,* 1961, *31,* 194-203.

Mangan, G. L., & O'Gorman, J. G. Initial amplitude and rate of habituation of orienting reaction in relation to extraversion and neuroticism. *Journal of Experimental Research in Personality,* 1969, *3,* 275-282.

McLaughlin, R. J., & Eysenck, H. J. Extraversion, neuroticism and paired-associates learning. *Journal of Experimental Research in Personality,* 1967, *2,* 128-132.

Nebylitsyn, V. D. *Fundamental properties of the human nervous system.* New York: Plenum Press, 1972.

Orlebeke, J. F.   Electrodermal, vasomotor, and heart rate correlates of extraversion and neuroticism. *Psychophysiology*, 1973, *6*, 716–721.

Revelle, W., Humphreys, M. S., Simon, L., & Gilliland, K.   The interactive effect of personality, time of day, and caffeine: A test of the arousal model. *Journal of Experimental Psychology: General*, 1980, *109*, 1–31.

Savage, R. D.   Electro-cerebral activity, extraversion and neuroticism. *British Journal of Psychiatry*, 1964, *110*, 98–100.

Shanmugam, T. E., & Santhanam, M. L.   Personality differences in serial learning when interference is presented at the marginal visual level. *Journal of the Indian Academy of Applied Psychology*, 1964, *1*, 25–28.

Sheldon, W. H.   *The varieties of human physique: An introduction to constitutional psychology*. New York: Harper & Row, 1940.

Shields, J.   *Monozygotic twins*. London: Oxford University Press, 1962.

Spence, K. W., & Spence, J. T.   The relation of eyelid conditioning to manifest anxiety, extraversion, and rigidity. *Journal of Abnormal Psychology*, 1964, *68*, 144–149.

Spielman, J.   *The relation between personality and the frequency and duration of involuntary rest pauses during mass practice*. Unpublished doctoral dissertation, University of London, 1963.

Teplov, B. M.   Problems in the study of general types of higher nervous activity in man and animals. In J. A. Gray (Ed.), *Pavlov's typology*. Oxford: Pergamon Press, 1964.

Wigglesworth, M. J., & Smith, B. D.   Habituation and dishabituation of the electrodermal orienting reflex in relation to extraversion and neuroticism. *Journal of Research in Personality*, 1976, *10*, 437–445.

Yerkes, R. M., & Dodson, J. D.   The relation of strength of stimulus to rapidity of habit-formation. *Journal of Comparative and Neurological Psychology*, 1908, *18*, 459–482.

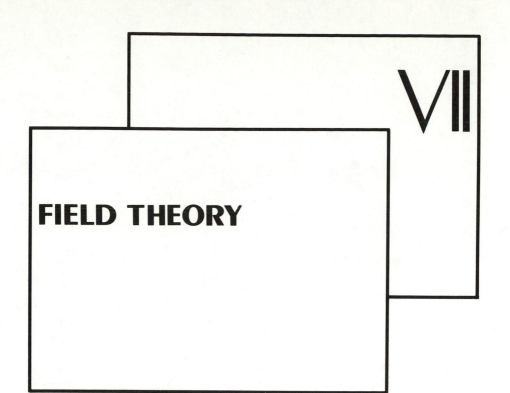

VII

FIELD THEORY

14

Field Theory:

Kurt Lewin

Kurt Lewin was born in Mongilno, Prussia, on September 9, 1890. He entered the University of Freiburg in 1908, moved to the University of Munich the following year, and finally enrolled in the University of Berlin, where he remained until he received his Ph.D. in 1914. When Germany went to war that same year, Lewin entered the army as a private and served until the Armistice, winning promotion to commissioned rank. After the war, he returned to the University of Berlin to take up the duties of instructor and research assistant in the Psychological Institute. It was during these years immediately following World War I that Lewin associated with, and was influenced by, the Gestalt theorists Max Wertheimer and Wolfgang Kohler. In 1926, he received an appointment as professor of philosophy and psychology. Two years later, he married Gertrud Weiss. At the time Hitler and the National Socialist Party came to power, Lewin obtained a visiting professorship at Stanford University. Attracted by the way of life he found in America and alarmed by the rising menace of anti-Semitism in Nazi Germany, Lewin joined the small but growing number of German expatriates who found a refuge and a home in the United States. He taught at Cornell University until 1935, when he accepted a position as professor of child psychology at the University of Iowa in the Child Welfare Station. In 1945, he became director of the Research Center for Group Dynamics at the Massachusetts Institute of Technology. He died in Newtonville, Massachusetts, on February 12, 1947 at the age of 56.

LEWIN AND FIELD THEORY

Lewin's field theoretical approach to the problems of psychology originated in the field theory concepts developed by scientists of the last century, like Maxwell, Hertz, and Faraday. Until the middle of the nineteenth century, the Newtonian assertion that all physical phenomena could be explained by assuming the existence of simple forces acting upon and between elementary particles had not been seriously challenged. According to this doctrine, if one knew the mass, velocity, direction, location, and the like, of particles of matter, it would be possible to predict accurately what would occur when a number of them interacted. Every change of motion was viewed as a consequence of a force which arose either through impact—the golf ball struck by a club—or through a mutual attraction of the bodies for each other, that is, Newton's law of gravity. The gravitational force between bodies (for instance, between the sun and the earth) was presumed to act instantaneously to produce action at a distance. Space and time were treated as the members of a fixed and immutable framework within which the movement of a particle occurred, but they were conceptualized as independent of the movement itself.

It required the brilliant experiments on electromagnetic phenomena by Oersted and Faraday to challenge the concept of simple forces acting instantaneously at a distance upon particles in an empty space. These experiments demonstrated that it was more valid to conceptualize regions or *fields* through which electromagnetic forces were distributed and to assume the existence of these forces even in the absence of particles of matter to which such forces applied. It was found that a knowledge of the properties of the electromagnetic field was sufficient to explain electromagnetic phenomena and, further, that given this information, knowledge about the source of the electromagnetic field was unnecessary. According to the field conception, the distribution of forces in a given environment determines how an object with particular properties will act within that environment.

The field concept provided Lewin with the beginnings of a frame of reference. He sought to conceptualize psychological phenomena as taking place within a field, that is, as part of a totality of elements which coexist in a mutually interdependent and dynamic relationship with one another. *Field theory,* as Lewin (1943) employed the term, refers to "a method of analyzing causal relations and of building scientific constructs." Lewin's applied field theory is analogous to physics in assuming that the properties of any event are determined by its relation to the system of events of which it is a component.

One of the earliest objections that was raised to Lewin's theorizing was his extensive reliance on the use of terms like force, vector, and tension, which already possess quite specific definitions within the realm of physics. Although such terms might imply a tendency toward reductionism, Lewin's intention was not reductionistic but quite consistently psychological. He employed terms of this kind simply to develop a "logic of dynamics" for psychology which is similar to that of other branches of science, emphasizing, however, that psychological phenomena must be explained in psychological terms, just as physical phenomena are explicable in physical terms.

Lewin's emphasis upon the psychological explanation of psychological events is one of a number of major assumptions and assertions which are interwoven in the fabric of Lewinian theory. One direct result of this first assumption is the Lewinian assertion of the reality of psychological phenomena, despite the fact that such phenomena cannot always be described in physical terms or located in physical space. According to Lewin, it is perfectly possible to investigate such concepts as hope, desire, and ability within a system which uses scientific methods related to those employed by the neurophysiologist or the physicist. A second result of the psychological explanation approach is that it leads, in Lewin's case, to avoidance of achievement concepts, that is, concepts which define behavior in terms of what it accomplishes (Lewin 1950). Lewin also objected to the use of simple external criteria to identify or define a psychological state or process. He maintained that it is poor psychological theorizing to conclude that a person who is exposed to a given external event (that is, being rewarded) will necessarily interpret or experience the event as it was intended (Lewin 1943). Lewin pointed out that in order to develop psychological laws we must be able to deal with psychological processes, such as the perception of an external event as opposed to the physical event itself.

A further assertion of the Lewin approach is that psychology is concerned with the individual's behavioral transactions with his or her internal and external environment. All behavioral transactions and psychological events (for example, thinking, hoping, dreaming) are conceived of as involving both the individual and the environment, viewed as a single constellation of interdependent and interacting factors. All psychological events are thus determined not by isolated properties and features of either the person or his or her environment but by mutual interrelationships among the properties and coexisting facts which comprise the person-environment complex. The facts arise from the momentary condition of the individual and the momentary structure of that individual's environment. Individual processes are "always to be derived from the relation of the concrete individual to the concrete situation, and, so far as internal forces are concerned, from the mutual relations of the various functional systems that make up the individual" (Lewin 1935, p. 41).

The importance of this approach to the study of behavior is best seen in historical perspective. Just as Newtonian theory had dominated physics, Aristotelian logic

had dominated much of psychological theory. According to this logic, psychological events are determined by inferred characteristics of the individual, such as instincts, heredity, intelligence, needs, and habits, all relatively independent of the situation in which the behavior takes place. Lewin (1935) promulgated an alternative logical approach that stresses mutual relations of factors in concrete whole situations to psychological events. Since Lewin, it has been meaningless to speak of behavior without referring to both the person and the environment.

Lewin emphasized that just as field theory in physics had destroyed the notion of action at a distance and replaced it with structural equations based upon the field at a given time, so must psychological events be explained in terms of the properties of the field that exists at the time those events occur. Past events can only play a role in the historical process which creates the present situation; they cannot directly influence present events. Lewin did not deny the significance of the past as an indirect source of influence upon current behavior. He merely insisted that the past affects behavior only by modifying the structure of the present field.

A final emphasis at the metatheoretical level is seen in Lewin's own reference to his conceptualization of personality as a dynamic theory of personality. Employing a relatively narrow definition, the term *dynamic* refers to the conception of living things as systems which tend to maintain a dynamic or changing equilibrium in relation to their environments. The individual is conceived of as comprising components that maintain a relative flexibility of interrelations so that variation in one aspect of the component system may induce compensatory changes in other aspects, thereby maintaining the integrity of the system. The Lewinian approach emloys an "equilibrium maintaining" system and concerns itself, as such an approach must, with the process by which equilibrium is restored when it is disturbed. The maintenance and restoration of equilibrium constitutes the major dynamic of Lewin's theory.

Just where the metatheory of the Lewinian approach stops and the psychological theory begins is a somewhat open question, and authorities have disagreed (Deutsch 1954; Henley 1965). For present purposes, however, we have chosen to present the foregoing discussion of metatheory theory and to treat as theory the major constructs and specific psychological postulates of the Lewinian approach.

STRUCTURAL PRINCIPLES

The structural aspect of Lewinian theory is directly concerned with the basic assumption that behavior is a function of the ongoing interaction of the person with his or her environment. The structural concepts of the field approach thus deal with the internal structure of the person, the external structure of the environment, and the structural relationships of the person and the environment.

The Life Space

In Lewinian theory, structure consists of a series of differentiated, yet interrelated and interacting, parts. Each part, each aspect, is differentiated from the totality of the person-environment complex, yet each aspect is included in a part-whole relationship with the totality and, therefore, interacts with that totality.

The first aspect of differentiation is the person and the environment or nonperson. The individual is viewed in this conceptualization as an entity apart from, but included in, the external environment. The picture of structural relationships is only slightly complicated by a further differentiation of the environment into the psychological environment and the nonpsychological environment.

Taken together, the person and the psychological environment constitute the *life space*, a postulate which can be represented by the simple equation $LS = P + E$, where P is the person, E is the psychological environment, and LS is the life space. The life space is the major structural construct of Lewinian theory, and it is important to note several properties of the life space. First, while it consists of the person and the psychological environment, the life space is itself a part of the greater totality comprising the universe. In Lewin's treatment, the universe outside the life space is divided into two major components, the foreign hull and the remainder of the universe. The more important aspect of the universe is the *foreign hull,* which is the area (physical and nonphysical) immediately adjacent to the boundaries of the life space. It is with this region that the life space primarily interacts.

A second major property of the life space is that it is the single determinant of all behavior. It is the psychological totality of the individual, containing all influences that can in any way possibly determine the behavior of the individual. This total determination of behavior by the life space can be expressed simply in the equation, $B = f(LS)$, where B is behavior, and the equation is read, "Behavior is a function of the life space." The implications of this equation for the explanation, understanding, and prediction of behavior are important. It says that if we can determine with some precision the elements constituting the life space, we can predict and understand the behavior of the concrete person in the concrete situation, Lewin's major goal. The precision with which we can predict and understand will depend on the degree of precision with which we can determine the life space, and we must, therefore, strive for mathematical precision.

A third consideration is the principle of *contemporaneity*, which states that any given behavior is dependent only upon the life space or psychological field at the time that behavior occurs. Put otherwise, behavior depends upon present, not past or future, situations. The principle can be expressed in the form of a simple equation: $B^t = F(S^t)$, where B^t is behavior at a given time and S is the situation at that time as it exists in the life space. The equation is thus read as, "Behavior at a given time is a function of the existing situation at that time and not a function of past or future situations." It is important to note that "at the present time" in this context does not refer to a specific moment with no time extension, but, in Lewin's usage, it refers to a time period. The length of this period depends upon the duration or scope of the psychological situation. We are dealing not merely in time units but in situation units, and the situation which exists in the life space and hence determines behavior may exist for a few minutes, a few hours, or a longer period of time. In addition, past or future considerations may influence the behavior of the individual if they exist in the life space at the time that behavior occurs. For example, a currently active memory of some past event or a current thought about some future goal may be a part of the present life space and hence influence present behavior.

A final characteristic of the life space is its permeability. As we have seen, the person is an entity, separated from the psychological environment by a boundary, and the psychological environment, in turn, is separated by a boundary from the foreign hull. In order for the person and the environment to influence each other directly as Lewinian theory specifies, it is necessary for the individual to communicate with the external environment. As a result, Lewin postulated that the boundary existing between person and environment is a penetrable or permeable boundary not a solid wall. Similarly, the boundary between life space and foreign hull is permeable. Functionally, this means that events outside the person or outside the foreign hull can intrude to influence behavior. For example, an important phone call, which originates in the foreign hull, may enter the life space and change one's entire day—or life.

Regions of the Life Space

During early childhood, the life space of the child is small and undifferentiated. At first, the infant may not even be able to differentiate clearly between his or her person or self and the external environment. Even when this differentiation comes, Lewin noted, the boundary between self and environment remains relatively vague throughout early childhood.

As a result of both physical maturation and the expansion of experiences with the environment, the life space of the growing child becomes increasingly larger and more differentiated into regions. A *region* is simply an area of the life space having properties which set it off conceptually from other areas of the life space and may be either physical or social in nature. Regions might include tables, chairs, or beds as well as friends, dogs, and parents. Some regions may be defined primarily in terms of physical appearance, but ordinarily most regions are identified on the basis of their functional possibilities. Any defined region that cannot be further divided into subregions is termed a *cell.*

During the course of development, differentiation occurs in both the person and the psychological environment. The major differentiation of person is into perceptual-motor (P-M) and inner-personal (I-P) regions. The *perceptual-motor* system interacts with the external environment, taking in the environment through the various senses and acting upon the environment through the operation of the muscular system. The *inner-personal* region lies, in Lewinian theory, completely within the perceptual-motor system, and Lewin notes that he would not object to an interpretation of the inner-personal region as representing various brain regions.

In early life both the P-M and I-P systems are relatively undifferentiated. With development, however, both undergo some degree of differentiation. Lewin has not detailed the nature of the differentiation of the perceptual-motor system. However, he has noted that the motoric is subdivided into the various muscle groups and individual muscles of the muscular system. This postulated differentiation does not, of course, mean that separate muscle groups must act in isolation from the remainder of the muscular system. Rather, the various muscles and muscle groups are coordinated and integrated for actions directed toward the environment. The inner-personal region likewise shows differentiation, dividing into central and peripheral cells (Fig. 14-1).

That Figure 14-1 shows the perceptual-motor system between the inner-personal system and the psychological environment is no accident. In fact, this schematic representation is an accurate, if oversimplified, picture of the relationships of the inner-personal and perceptual-motor systems and the psychological environment. The inner-personal region never acts directly upon the environment but serves as an area in which the needs of the person are conceptualized, the actual action upon the environment being carried out through the perceptual-motor system. In Lewin's

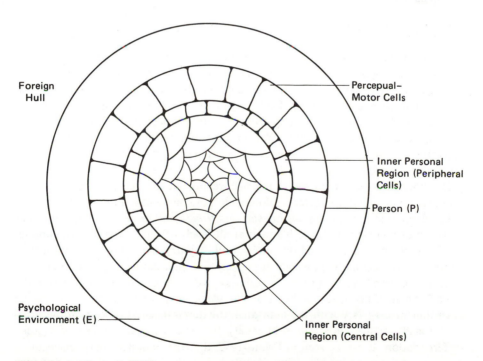

Figure 14-1 Life space (P+E).

theory the relationship of the two systems of the person is such that the P-M system acts primarily as a tool of the I-P system. The motoric, then, serves primarily to carry out the actions conceived by the inner-personal system. Lewin was careful to note, however, that the process is not conceived of as a mechanistic one. Rather, the P-M system is seen as a dynamic medium which serves to interconnect the inner-personal region with the psychological environment. The I-P system does not in some mechanistic way fire or trigger the P-M action but rather induces action by the medium. The inducing-medium relationship of the I-P and P-M systems increases in importance from infancy to adulthood.

While the person is differentiating developmentally into regions, subregions and cells, the psychological environment likewise shows conceptual differentiation for the individual. The differentiations that take place are defined primarily in terms of functions, and they are many and varied. While some similarities certainly exist, each person is expected to have a life space with regions quite different from those of other people. In addition, for a given individual some regions may be relatively permanent, other regions may show gradual change, and still others may change from moment to moment as situations change. It should be noted that despite the existence of some reasonably or permanently stable regions, the life space as a whole changes from moment to moment and situation to situation, and it is the life space existing at the moment a behavior occurs that determines the nature of that behavior.

Properties of Boundaries

The Lewinian conceptualization of person and environment as comprising a number of distinctive regions and cells implies that the individual is not totally free to move through the psychological environment and, indeed, that barriers, or *boundaries,* exist between separate regions. Each region of the life space is surrounded by boundary cells separating it from all other regions, although two neighboring regions may share a common boundary. The process of differentiation may be seen as consisting, in part, of the development of an increasingly larger number of boundaries within the life space.

The boundaries which surround regions are not all identical. In particular, the boundaries surrounding different regions and, from moment to moment, the boundaries surrounding any given region vary in *functional firmness.* This important variation in boundary firmness is found at all levels of differentiation. The boundary between the life space and the foreign hull may be firmer in one individual than another, may become increasingly firmer as the child develops and differentiates toward adulthood, and may vary in firmness from moment to moment within the same individual. Likewise, the boundary between the person and the psychological environment may vary with the individual, the developmental process, or the situation. Finally, similar variations in boundary firmness occur at the level of regional differentiation. It can be seen in Figure 14-2 that the boundary between region 1 and region 3 is considerably firmer (heavier) than the boundary between region 2 and region 3. Functionally, this means that movement from 1 to 3 would be con-

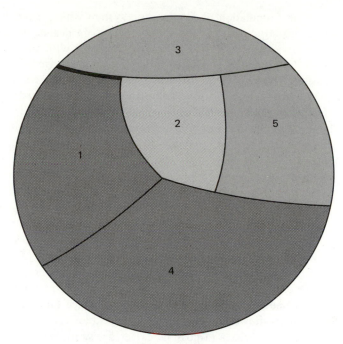

Figure 14-2 Boundaries and tension systems in the life space. Darker shading denotes regions of higher tension.

siderably more difficult than movement from 2 to 3. It also implies that the differentiation between regions 1 and 3 is more clear-cut than the differentiation between 2 and 3 or that 2 and 3 are more closely related than are 1 and 3. For example, a child might see the boundary between the region which he or she calls mother and the region called father as a relatively weak one, since both are parents and the child recognizes a relationship between the two; the perceived boundary between the father and a stranger would be relatively firm, since the child perceives no particular relationship between the two. If the child learned that the stranger was, in fact, a close associate or friend of his or her father, the perceived boundary would correspondingly weaken. A second example follows from the observation that boundaries, in general, can become firmer with the increased differentiation which accompanies development. The infant who is just beginning to verbalize meaningfully may thus refer to men quite indiscriminately as "da da." As differentiation occurs and boundaries become firmer, the child will come to attach the label only to his or her actual father.

Topological Concepts

In his concern with person-environment structure, Lewin was convinced that the determinants of behavior would have to be expressed in mathematical terms if psychology were ever to become a rigorous discipline. He, therefore, devoted a major effort to the formulation of a geometric system which could be used to express or depict his structural and dynamic concepts. In dealing with structure, Lewin employed *topology,* a branch of geometry that deals with nonmetric spatial relations, such as the properties of figures which remain unchanged under continuous transformation. Topology deals not with the size or shape of space but with such phenomena as part–whole relations, belongingness, and membership character, terms taken from the earlier Gestalt psychology from which Lewin's approach is partially derived. All of Lewin's structural concepts are treated topologically.

The Hodology of Locomotion

Despite the existence of boundaries and the consequent restriction of movement through the environment, the individual must move from region to region in order to function. Any movement from one region of the psychological environment to another is termed *locomotion.* In dealing with the concept of locomotion, we are concerned with what is essentially a part of the structural basis for a dynamic model. Thus, locomotions are neither entirely mechanistic nor primarily physical in nature. Of course, one may literally perform a physical locomotion by moving, for example, from one's home (one region) to one's office (another). The most important locomotions, however, are those of a psychological or social nature. A college student changes curricula (a possible career decision), becomes engaged, or joins a fraternity; the executive solves a complex financial problem, makes a business decision to produce one product rather than another, or promotes one subordinate or another. Each of these involves a form of locomotion, a movement from one region or state of the life space to another, but physical movement is not an important part of the locomotion in any one of these examples. Locomotions may also occur within the inner-personal region of the individual from one cell to another. Lewin termed this inner-personal locomotion *communication.*

Locomotion across regions may occur from one region to a neighboring region across a common boundary or it may involve crossing regions to reach a terminal point. If one is to consider carefully the nature of locomotion, then, it is necessary to take into account the questions of the distance of locomotion and, in addition, the direction in which the locomotion takes place. Lewin points out that direction and distance must ordinarily be expressed geometrically. The concept of direction in psychology, however, does not lend itself to existing geometries, including topology. As a result, Lewin developed a new geometry which he called *hodology.* In his treatment, hodological space is essentially the space within which and through which directed action takes place across a distance. Hodology is capable of taking into account both the direction and the distance of the behavior. In hodological space any locomotion takes place along a path which stretches from the initial to the terminal point of the locomotion. The path has, of course, both direction and distance. If the individual is located in a given region, *a,* and must reach another region, *d,* a number of possible directions or paths may exist. The path which is actually chosen and over which the locomotion eventually takes place is termed the *distinguished path*. The important question then becomes the factors which determine the selection of one path over another.

If all movements of the individual were physical and the space were Euclidean (the space we usually think of), rather than hodological, we might expect the determining characteristic of the distinguished path to be its length—the shortest path would simply be chosen. Lewin could not, however, use this simple explanation, since the determinants of psychological, and therefore hodological, functioning are clearly more complex than distance. Lewin proposed that it is not the distance between *a* and *b* (although this may be a factor) but something closer to the overall *attractiveness* of the path that is involved in the selection process.

It is probably not possible to specify clearly all the factors which enter into the selection of a distinguished path. Some of these may, however, be explored. If it is first noted that the path extends across some number or regions, it becomes clear that any factors relating to the relative ease or difficulty of crossing the intervening regions would potentially be factors in the determination of a distinguished path. We have already considered one such factor in another context, the functional firmness of boundaries. A second factor, also noted above, may be the *distance* between the initial and terminal regions. A third factor derives from the observation that the individual must choose not only the path to be taken but also the type of *locomotion* to be utilized. The latter choice may be at least partially independent of the selection of a path but may directly influence that selection. Thus, if the individual desires to cross from region *a* to region *b*, he or she may have the choice of walking, driving, or looking from *a* to *b*. Each of these is, of course, a quite different type or form of locomotion; the type of locomotion chosen may well influence the path taken.

Another factor which may enter into the selection of the distinguished path is the relative *fluidity* of regions intervening between the initial and terminal points of the locomotion. Fluidity is a concept referring to the quality or flexibility of a region, which Lewin referred to as the medium of the region. If the medium of a given region is relatively fluid, that medium will be fairly amenable to change and also relatively easy to traverse. If, for example, regions *a* and *b* are separated by only highly fluid regions, the path from *a* to *b* across these regions will be, in that respect at least, an easy one to follow. If, on the other hand, a region is relatively rigid, it will not be amenable to change and neither will it be easy to cross. One may consider a direct, if somewhat crude, example. The individual who must cross a region by swimming through water will (assuming ability to swim) have a fairly easy traverse. If, however, the medium is more viscous than water (for example, molasses or glue), the path will be a difficult one.

A final factor to be considered is the *level of reality* at which a locomotion takes place. At the level of maximal unreality stand the dream and the daydream, while reality is seen in the concrete behavior of the person in satisfying needs in the real environment. A continuum varying in degree of reality exists between these two extremes. Any given locomotion may occur on a relatively real or a relatively unreal level. For example, an individual may actually solve a problem or take a job. These locomotions occur at a high level of reality. On the other hand, a person may consider the possibility of solving a problem or plan to change jobs, a less real level of behavior. At the opposite extreme, one may merely daydream about the possibility of obtaining a solution to a problem or about holding some other job, very possibly one which that person could never realistically hold. Unreality is not limited to imaginal or thought processes but can involve action. Lewin (1935) provided the example of the kindergarten child who has been forbidden to draw, and, as a substitute, watches the other children draw or holds and strokes his or her own crayons. The reality dimension is a consideration in the selection of a distinguished path, since unreality presents, in Lewin's words, a "soft and easily moveable medium" (1935, p. 174). In the unreal world of imagination, lengthy paths can be traversed quickly and locomotions can occur with little interference. An unreal path of locomotion may thus, at times, be chosen over a real path.

MOTIVATIONAL DYNAMICS

A child develops a strong desire for a new game that is available at a nearby toy store. Counting the coins in a piggy bank, the child finds that there is not enough money for the game. The child then approaches his or her parent, asks for and receives the money, goes to the store and obtains the game, and feels very satisfied, happy and contented with the purchase.

What are the dynamics of the child's behavior? That is, how might we understand in theoretical terms the bases for the behavior, and what would we have to know about the child and about the child's environment in order to have predicted that behavior? Some theorists would refer to the influence of primary and secondary drives, to patterns of previous reinforcement of related behaviors, and to the development of habits which might be involved in controlling the behavior in question. Others might refer to the operation of basic instincts or drives, possibly modified through experience, to the modeling of behaviors seen in parents or older siblings, to the interaction of certain dynamic traits and situational factors, or to the actualization of the organism or of the self-concept.

Lewin (1951) felt that these varied views were inadequate in that they do not clearly differentiate between the energizing and directive properties of motives in their effects on behavior. In addition, he felt that most theories have tended to involve a formulation that classifies motives into a small number of groups rather than allow for the virtually unlimited range of possible motives that he felt represent reality. The Lewinian account of our hypothetical child's behavior thus takes a somewhat different approach from other theorists and revolves around the concepts of need, tension, valence, and vector. The first two of these constructs represent properties of the person, while the remaining two are properties of the psychological environment.

Needs

The child's desire to obtain the new game represents the operation of a *need* in Lewinian theory. A need is basically a motive and, as such, is fairly equivalent to the psychodynamic term, *instinct,* and the learning theory term, *drive.* For Lewin, a need occurs in an inner-personal region and may be either an unlearned physiological need, such as hunger or thirst, or a learned need, such as the child's desire for a new toy. Lewin felt, however, that most of the important needs that govern human behavior are subject to the influence of learning processes and are social in nature.

Beyond suggesting the broad differentiation between physiological and learned needs, Lewin refrained from categorizing or listing specific needs. This, of course, is consistent with his position that it is undesirable to limit a theory of needs to a few specific types or classes, since this limitation tends to stifle the investigation of needs and impede progress toward a full understanding of motivation. In short, he felt that little is gained and much is potentially lost by developing need lists. He did make one further distinction, namely, differentiating between needs and *quasi-needs.* A need involves the particular state of an inner-personal region of the personality, while a quasi-need involves a directed intention to satisfy a need in a particular way. Thus, thirst might arise as a need, while the desire to satisfy this thirst with a specific beverage obtained from a particular store, bar, or restaurant is a quasi-need.

When a need is aroused, it creates a state of *tension* within an inner-personal region. It is this tension which constitutes the motivating force driving the actions of the individual.

Tension

For purposes of understanding the motivation of human behavior, Lewin suggested that the inner-personal regions of the individual are basically *tension systems,* each having its own level of tension relative to currently aroused needs. The tension in a given region or tension system is determined by the existence of one or more needs, and the level of that tension is a function of the strength of the needs. The tension in any one system is relative to the tension in other adjacent systems.

The Entropy Principle. The major principle governing the ebb and flow of tension in the person is that of entropy or equilibrium. This principle holds that there will be a tendency for tension to flow from regions of greater to regions of lesser concentration, thus tending to equalize tension throughout the system. This means, in Figure 14-2, that tension tends to flow from regions 1 and 4 into region 2 and, to a lesser extent, regions 3 and 5. The child in our example has experienced an increase in tension in an inner-personal region relevant to the desired game. There is a tendency to equalize the tension in that system with the tensions in surrounding systems by creating a flow of tension from the "game" region to other regions.

The equalization of tension across regions occurs basically through the performance of behavior. That behavior may take the form of overt action, as in the case in which the child obtains money and goes to a store to purchase the desired game, or the behavior may be somewhat more covert. The experiencing and expression of emotions, the arousal of memory, and the activation of perceptual processes are examples of behaviors which may also serve to equalize tension.

It should be noted that the equilibrium principle as Lewin employs it is not entirely the same as the tension reduction principle employed by Freud, Dollard and Miller, and some other theorists. In those theories, the arousal of tension through the activation of instincts and drives causes behavior that ideally leads to a reduction of the specific tension in question and a consequent lowering of the overall tension level in the person. In the case of Lewinian theory, the tension level is not necessarily lowered. Rather, the tension moves from one inner-personal region to another without actually leaving the person. Functionally, this means that the person is always in a state of tension. At times, this tension may be heavily concentrated in certain inner-personal regions which have active needs, while at other times it may reach a state of equilibrium. Equilibrium may be achieved at either a relatively high or relatively low level of tension in the overall person; a person with equilibrium established at a relatively low tension level may appear to be relaxed and calm, while a person in a state of equilibrium at a high tension level may appear tense and restless.

Boundaries and Communication. In order to move toward a state of equilibrium, regions of higher energy concentration exert pressure on the boundaries of surrounding regions in order to create energy flow. At this point, the hodology of *communication*—the inner-personal region parallel to locomotion—takes over. The extent to which tension flows from one region to another is determined by the degree of communication between the two systems. Communication is determined by the strength or firmness of boundaries separating the systems and by the hodological distance between systems within the person. In Figure 14–2, pg. 347, it can be seen that region 1, an area of high tension concentration, borders on both regions 2 and 3. The firmness of the boundary between region 1 and region 3 is much greater than that between 1 and 2, so that tension should flow from region 1 into region 2. Tension is not likely to flow, to any substantial extent, from region 1 to region 4 because the latter is also an area of high concentration. Region 5, although having a somewhat lower tension than region 1 is separated from that region by a greater distance than is region 2, and, hence, it will receive energy from region 4 but little from region 1.

Tension as Psychic Energy. Lewin's concept of tension is basically an energy concept. He hypothesized that behavior dynamics occur as a function of an energy system, not unlike the energy system dealt with by physicists, except that the energy of the person is psychological or psychic energy. He contended that the inner-personal region functions as a fairly closed energy system in which energy flows from subregion to subregion, depending upon its relative concentrations. The state of disequilibrium that causes energy flow arises when needs create a state of increased tension in one region of the inner-person relative to other regions, and energy is released when the person is attempting, through behavior, to return to a state of equilibrium.

The Psychological Environment

In order to satisfy needs and release tension or energy, it is often essential for the person to interact with the psychological environment. Lewin felt that it was necessary to define the nature of goals or goal regions in the psychological environment relative to the active needs and to consider the forces which move the person toward these goals.

Valence. Any given region of the psychological environment may, at a particular moment in time, have a property known as a *valence*. The usual interpretation of the term valence suggests that it denotes a value attached to a region of the environment. The value may be either positive or negative, depending upon the active need within the person. When the child in our example experiences a need to obtain the desired game, a region of increased tension is established within the inner-personal sector, and the need imparts a positive valence to the game. It might be noted that, although Lewin agreed on the use of the English language term valence, his original German term, *Aufforderungscharacter,* suggests something more than a simple value. A more literal translation of the term is "demand character," suggesting that the valenced region may have a more active role in *eliciting* the behavior of the individual.

The valence of a given region of the psychological environment may vary from time to time in both sign and strength. The variation in sign of the valence is a function of the extent to which the relevant need is being satisfied. The valence of the needed object will be positive if the need is currently active and unsatisfied, neutral if the need is currently inactive, and negative if the need has been over satiated. For example, a child may experience a hunger or desire for a chocolate bar, activating the need and imparting a positive valence to the chocolate bar that exists in the psychological environment. Consuming the candy may lead to satiation, and the chocolate now has an essentially neutral valence. If the child, on the other hand, has rapidly consumed five chocolate bars, the candy may take on a negative valence for a time.

It is worth noting the consistency of the valence construct with Lewin's principle of contemporaneity. Behavior occurs as a function of a *current* state of the life space. Any previously existing or future valence that an object may take on is irrelevant to behavior at that particular time. Only present valences matter. The strength of a valance is also variable over time and depends largely upon the strength of the need at a given moment. Similar to the psychoanalytic concept of the impetus of an instinct and the learning theory concept of drive strength, the idea of variable valence strength recognizes differences in the degree of motivation from one occasion to another and from one need to another. The child may be extremely hungry on one occasion, moderately hungry on another, and only slightly hungry on the third.

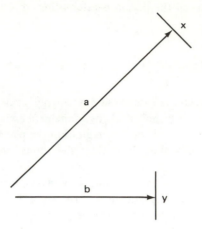

Figure 14-3 Two Vectors. They differ in direction, strength (a is stronger, as shown by its longer shaft), and point of application (point X for Vector a, point Y for Vector b).

Vectors. Needs provide tension and energize the behavior of the individual, and valences provide goals or regions toward or away from which locomotion might occur; but for Lewin, the actual occurrence of locomotion requires an additional concept, that of *force* or *vector*. The force is created by the need. Where the need and its associated tension exists within the person, however, the force exists outside the person in the psychological environment.

Any given force or vector has three major properties, those of strength, direction, and point of application. Graphically, a vector is represented simply as an arrow (Figure 14-3), in which the strength of the vector is denoted by the length of the shaft on the arrow, the direction is represented by the direction of the arrow, and the point of application in a specific area on the boundary of the person who will move through the psychological environment in relationship to a valenced region. If the valence of the region is positive, the force, and hence the locomotion, will be toward that region. Recognizing the complexities of real human behavior, Lewin noted that there are often many vectors acting upon a person at a given moment. The actual locomotion that takes place in response to these multiple forces is a result of all the combined vectors.

Returning, for purposes of illustration, to our example of the girl purchasing a game, we can diagram the child's behavior as in Figures 14-4a and 14-4b. In Figure 14-3, it can be seen that the vector acting on the child is directed toward the bank. Both the bank and the game have positive valences. Watching television and the child's parents both have neutral valences, while taking a nap, which would interfere with buying the game, has a negative valence. The bank is shown, how-

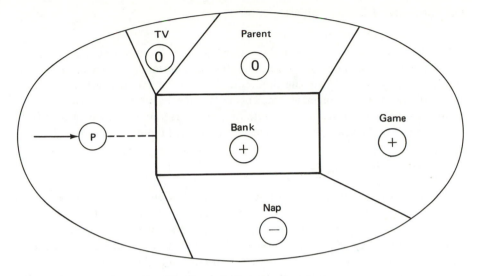

Figure 14-4a Movement in a changing psychological environment.

ever, with heavy boundaries to illustrate that the needed money is not available there. In Figure 14-4b, the direction of the vector has changed toward the parent, and the parent has taken on a positive valence, while the bank now has a negative valence. The dashed line shows the direction of the child's movement, first to the parent, then to the store where the game is bought.

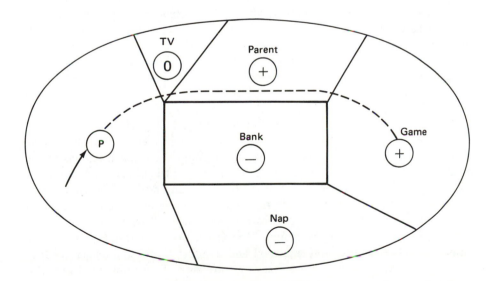

Figure 14-4b Movement in a changing psychological environment.

Like many theorists, Lewin basically conceptualized development as a process in which the individual moves from the undifferentiated totality that exists in infancy, through a process of increasing differentiation, to the eventual attainment of a state of a relatively integrated wholeness. Lewin's particular approach to conceptualizing the processes of differentiation and integration is a function of the structure and dynamics of the personality as seen in his theory more broadly.

Differentiation

The Lewinian infant is seen as existing in a state of *simple dynamic unity.* This is essentially a global state in which the life space is, at first, an undifferentiated totality. There are few or no separate regions either within the inner-personal sphere or in the psychological environment. The infant acts and reacts as a whole. There is initially no awareness of the differentiated functions of body parts, such that the infant does not know that an object can be obtained by extending the arm and hand. Similarly, there is no perceptual differentiation of the psychological environment so that the infant may not, for example, differentiate between his or her mother and other people in the environment.

Differentiation comes with physiological maturation and, more important, with environmental experience. It involves the separation of both the inner-personal region and the psychological environment into identifiable subregions. The longer the child has lived and the more experience the child has had, the greater will be the degree of regional differentiation both in the person and in the environment. The young child may come to recognize, for example, some of the differential functions of arms and legs. The somewhat older child may begin to use one hand in preference to the other, an indication of further differentiation. Similarly, the young child learned to differentiate his or her own mother from other adult humans and, somewhat more specifically, other adult women. The older child will further differentiate among adult women in the environment.

The simple dynamic unity that characterizes the infant gradually gives way to a more clearly and firmly differentiated life space in which communication among regions within the inner-personal sector and locomotion through regions in the psychological environment may become increasingly difficult. This is because the process of differentiation is accomplished by increasing not only the number of boundaries in the life space but also the strength of some of these boundaries. In the infant and young child, boundaries are few and weak, resulting in easy and rapid communication and locomotion. The infant does not readily perceive the difference between needs for, say, food and comfort (as when a diaper needs to be changed). As a result, one need may be substituted for another, and the satisfaction of one need may, to some extent, result in the perceived satisfaction of another. Similarly, there is little differentiation between reality and irreality, as

Freud had noted, possibly resulting in fantasy need satisfaction to a greater degree than would be true in the older child or adult. As boundaries become more numerous, some regions of the life space become more widely separated, and, according to the rules of *hodology*, communication and locomotion between regions become more difficult. Added to this is the fact that boundaries become firmer with experience, again increasing the difficulty of movement through the environment.

Integration

Differentiation leads to a better knowledge and understanding of the external environment and of the inner person and also increases the *variety* of needs, social activities, and emotions experienced by the person. It often, in addition, produces a relative isolation of activities, such that the older child may function in a somewhat "scattered" way, rather than in a manner that would indicate a high degree of organization of the life space. The adult does tend to display such organization. The increasingly complex and skilled interpersonal relationships and coordinated activities in which the adult engages are indicative of a high level of integration and interdependence among the regions of the life space. Lewin thus referred to the organization of the adult life space as representing a *complex dynamic unity*. By this he means that the adult, like the infant, is functioning much more as a whole than as a collection of separate parts. The unity of the adult personality, however, is not simply based on the lack of differentiating boundaries but rather on a systematic and complex integration of the many and varied regions that constitute the adult life space. There is, to use another Lewinian term, a high degree of *organizational interdependence* in the adult life space.

THE THEORY IN EMPIRICAL CONTEXT

Tolman (1948) placed Kurt Lewin alongside Sigmund Freud as one of the geniuses of early twentieth-century psychology. Both men achieved greatness in part because of their integrative theories, but Freud was basically a clinician, while Lewin was an experimentalist. Lewin himself conducted a number of important experiments demonstrating the validity of various elements of his theory, and, more important, he influenced scores of others to carry on experimental investigations related to his theory. His influence on these psychologists seems to have been achieved as much through the active magnetism of his dynamic personality as through the genius of his theory. When he spoke to groups or held conferences, audiences seemed spellbound, and a series of annual conferences, at which he was always the central figure, attracted the loyal, the curious, and the suspicious, nearly all of whom seemed to leave the conferences with reluctance, enthusiastically ready to return the next year.

Lewin's influence has resulted quite directly in literally thousands of experiments over the years. We will review here a small number of studies representing each of five major areas of investigation which grow directly out of Lewinian theory: (1) behavior interruption; (2) psychological satiation; (3) substitution; (4) level of aspiration; and (5) conflict.

The early work on interruption of activity is classic. It is based on Lewin's postulate that needs create tensions that must be discharged. This leads to the hypothesis that when an individual accepts and begins a task, this creates a need, quasi-need, or intention to carry the task through to its final completion. The hypothesis was tested in experiments which examined the effects of task performance interruption on the memory of the subject for the task, resumption of the task, and the satisfaction of the need through use of a substitute task.

An anecdote about Lewin relates to memory of completed and uncompleted, or interrupted, tasks. Lewin and his colleagues were in a restaurant in Berlin and were engaged in a lengthy theoretical conversation. A considerable amount of time had passed since the waiter had totaled their bill. Lewin, on an insightful impulse, called the waiter over, asked and was immediately told the total amount of the bill, and paid the waiter. Much later, the conversation having gone on at length, Lewin again called the waiter and asked the total of the bill. The waiter had forgotten. The satisfaction of the waiter's need and the consequent reduction of his tension when the bill was paid had erased the memory.

The first major study dealing with a subject's memory for completed and uncompleted tasks was done by Zeigarnik (1927). She followed up on Lewin's insight by having subjects carry out a series of tasks. Half of the tasks were continued to completion, the other half were interrupted before completion. Zeigarnik then asked the subjects to recall the names of all the tasks. Name retention was better for uncompleted than for completed tasks, theoretically because the tension of the unresolved need in the case of the uncompleted task supported better recall.

Ovsiankina (1928) showed that subjects whose past performance had been interrupted usually resumed their interrupted work without further instructions when given a free opportunity to do so. In a follow-up study, Nowlis (1941) found that task resumption occurred primarily under a neutral condition, with either praise or failure for incomplete performances tending to reduce resumption. Mahler (1933), Lissner (1933), and others have taken the work on task interruption further to show that the process is more complex than initially imagined, with the relevant behavior being affected by such variables as ego involvement in the task and the extent to which task interruption is perceived as threatening.

Related to the work on interruption is that on *satiation* (Lewin 1951). Lewin held that repeated performance of a task should, theoretically, reduce the tension corresponding to that task and cause the subject to leave the activity and turn to some other task. The choice of a new task and the direction of locomotion should be determined by the relative strengths of the tension systems and similarity of the new task to the one the subject has left. Lewin hypothesized that the person would tend to move toward a relatively unrelated task. Acting on this idea, Karsten (1928) used mechanical, repetitive tasks, such as placing thimbles in holes and repeatedly drawing vertical lines. She instructed subjects to work as long as possible but to stop when they wanted to. After varying lengths of time, subjects showed evidence of satiation. They attempted to vary the nature of the task, became inattentive and fatigued, expressed anger toward the experimenter, and daydreamed of other activities in which they would prefer to engage. In addition, Karsten showed that satiation transferred to tasks that were related to but were somewhat different from the task on which the subject achieved satiation.

Conceptually related to the work on interruption and satiation is a body of research dealing with the *substitution* phenomenon. Lewin (1935) provided the basic experimental design for the substitution experiments. In his design, a child is interrupted in the midst of a task, leaving the involved inner-personal region in a state of tension. The child is then given a second task, setting up a second state of tension in a different inner-personal region. The child completes the second task and is then given an opportunity to return to the first task. If the child does not, that is taken as an indication that the second task has substituted for the first and served as a basis for the discharge of tension from the first inner-personal region. If, however, the child resumes the interrupted task, this demonstrates that the second task did not have adequate substitute value to discharge the tension of the first. A control group, also used in Lewin's design, is interrupted in its first task, given no substitute task, then given an opportunity to return to the interrupted task. The fact that these children do return to the task demonstrates that there is some tension left over in the first task region.

The most important of the relatively early substitution studies were those done by Henle (1942). In her first experiment, she gave subjects a series of five homogeneous tasks (for example, all mosaic designs), interrupting the subject during the fourth task, allowing completion of the fifth task, then permitting a return to the uncompleted fourth task. She confirmed her prediction that subjects would resume work on the interrupted task because the last two tasks formed elements of a homogeneous series. Her later studies confirmed and extended the early substitution findings.

Another important area of Lewinian research has been that dealing with *level of aspiration.* This work, in and of itself, is so voluminous as to have insured the heuristic value of Lewin's efforts, even if he had done no other theoretical or experimental work. Lewin proposed that a person's level of aspiration or expectation is an important determinant of performance on a task and is systematically influenced by prior experiences with that task and related situations. As an example, a subject may be asked to throw a number of darts at a target and, before throwing the first dart, to state his or her expectation as to how good the performance will be. After throwing the darts, the subject may again be asked to state a level of aspiration for the next trial, and so on. Experiments by the Lewin group (Lewin and others, 1944) and others have shown that successful performance generally produces an increase in aspiration level, while unsuccessful performance leads to a decrease. Additional research has shown that a number of factors other than success on the task influence importantly both the level of aspiration and performance. Included are age, the pattern and regularity of previous successes, individual differences relating to past success and failure in activities other than the task in question, and knowledge of achievements on the task by groups of people similar to or different from the subject in specific respects. In addition, it has been found that the subject's estimate of the probability that he or she can obtain a desired goal significantly influences the value that the subject attaches to the goal. In Lewin's formulation, the greater the subject's expectancy (subjective probability) of obtaining a goal, the less will be the perceived value of the goal.

A final area of research initiated by Lewin is that on *cognitive-motor conflict*. Lewin noted that whenever two goals are present in the life space, the subject may be placed in a state of conflict. There are three major types of conflict to be considered. The first, *approach-approach* conflict, is the simplest form and occurs when the individual is faced with two goals having positive valences and, therefore, with two approach tendencies. The child given a choice of two kinds of candy and enough money to purchase only one kind would be in an approach-approach conflict situation. A second major conflict, *approach-avoidance,* occurs when there is a single goal which has both positive and negative valence qualities. This is exemplified by the child who is asked to weed the garden. Doing so will gain the child some money which can be used to purchase a desirable toy but will take him or her away from playing with other children. The *avoidance-avoidance* conflict occurs when the child must either go shopping with mother or take a nap. A fourth type of conflict was introduced by Miller (1944) as an extension of the Lewin model. Miller referred to a *double approach-avoidance* conflict as occurring when two or more goals each has both positive and negative valences.

The work on conflict following from the basic Lewin model has been extensive, involving both animal and human subjects and a variety of goal situations and combinations of conflict types. The classic human study was done by Hovland and Sears (1938). More recent work (Epstein and Smith 1967; Smith and Epstein 1967; Smith and Gehl 1974) has confirmed some of the original Hovland-Sears findings and extended the work on human conflict to provide further tests of the Lewinian model. In these studies, human subjects were presented with a Lewinian field consisting of a simple maze and told that whenever a light was turned on they must leave the starting point of the maze and move in relationship to goals. Each goal contained one red light and one white light, and subjects were told to approach white lights and avoid red lights, moving as rapidly as possible and without touching the sides of the maze. Subjects were then given a series of simple trials in which there was no conflict. A white light would be turned on at one goal, instructing the subject to move toward that goal, or a red light would be turned on at the goal, instructing the subject to move away from that goal and thus toward the opposite goal. Interspersed among these nonconflict trials, however, were random trials involving the four major conflict types. An approach-approach conflict occurred when white lights were turned on at both goals, approach-avoidance occurred when the red and white light at one goal were turned on, avoidance-avoidance involved the two red lights, one at each goal, and double approach-avoidance occurred when all four lights appeared.

It was found that, despite the simple nature of the conflict task, the subjects, normal college students, had considerable difficulty resolving the conflicts in a correct or meaningful way. The speed with which subjects moved through the maze was greatly reduced by any conflict except approach-approach; the avoidance-avoidance and double approach-avoidance conflicts produced the greatest reduction in speed. In addition, error rates increased with increasing conflict difficulty, again the avoidance-avoidance and double approach-avoidance conflicts producing the greatest difficulty for subjects. It was also found that response speed increased and error rate decreased with repeated practice on the conflicts, even though they were interspersed among nonconflict trials. Further, it was found that the subjects varied in their correct or erroneous responses to the conflicts, showing different response modes as a function of the type of conflict being experienced. Thus, for example, on an approach-approach conflict, many subjects would go first to one goal, then to the other and on approach-avoidance, a common response was to approach the opposite (neutral) goal, though a surprisingly large proportion of subjects went directly to the conflicted goal. Finally, it was found that many subjects, responding to avoidance-avoidance or double approach-avoidance conflicts, either blocked (remained inappropriately at the starting point) or went directly to one or the other of the two negative or conflicted goals.

These experiments with conflict in human subjects provide considerable support for some of Lewin's conflict hypotheses. In addition, they demonstrate the powerful behavioral impact of conflict and, in this regard, support some of the hypotheses of both Lewin and Freud. The latter, in particular, had suggested that conflict is a major and important basis for anxiety and neurosis.

We have attempted here to give only a sense of the scope and types of empirical research generated by Lewin and his theoretical model. For more detailed and intensive reviews of Lewinian research, the reader is referred to summary chapters by Lewin and his colleagues (Lewin 1954; Lewin and others, 1944), by Deutsch (1968), and by Cartwright (1959).

EVALUATION

It has, no doubt, already become apparent that Lewin's point of view has been influential in guiding the thinking and work of many psychologists. In this broad sense, the theory has passed the test of time and professional influence to become one of the major theories of twentieth-century psychology. At the same time, Lewinian theory has often been controversial and has been criticized by a number of psychologists from various schools of thought.

Positive Qualities and Contributions

First among its contributions is that Lewin's theory brought to psychology its first thoroughly developed, systematic field theory of human behavior. Unlike the psychoanalytic and behavioral approaches, field theory formally and fully recognizes the importance of the individual's psychological surroundings, or field, in the determination of human behavior. It accounts for both simple and complex behaviors through an understanding of both the qualities and actions of the person and those of the external environment as perceived. The Lewinian theory thus brings to psychology a systematic wholism, which seems to insist that behavior is neither as simple as the behaviorist might like to consider it nor as complex and remotely determined as the psychoanalyst would hypothesize.

A second value of the Lewinian theory is that it focused from the start on the normal person and, hence, on the vast majority of human beings. Other theories, such as psychoanalysis, have often been developed primarily on the basis of observations of individuals defined as psychopathological and then generalized in an attempt to predict the behaviors of all humans. This is not to say that theories dealing with psychopathological behavior are not valuable, but, rather, that a theorist whose data base consists of information about normal people is, at least initially, better equipped to predict the behavior of normal people.

A further contribution lies in the tremendous heuristic value of the theory. We have already seen that the scope of Lewin's influence on empirical research in psychology is so broad that it spans to the very horizons of the field. Lewin's theory has also been responsible for the development of additional theories in psychology. Festinger (1957) developed a theory of cognitive dissonance, which represents a quite direct extension of Lewin's ideas on the relationship of decision-making processes and situational characteristics. McClelland, Atkinson, Clark, and Lowell (1953) and Atkinson (1964) have developed theories of achievement motivation that rely substantially on Lewin's ideas, particularly those concerned with level of aspiration. Heider (1958), a major social psychological theorist, has developed a widely subscribed theory of interpersonal perception and interaction based in large part on Lewin's concepts. Finally, some important aspects of the phenomenological-humanistic theories of Carl Rogers and others are quite clearly anticipated in Lewin's treatment. The Lewinian conceptualization of the life space, containing the person and the surrounding psychological environment, is seen in a somewhat different form in the Rogerian theory of personality. There, the person, differentiated principally into the total organism and the self-concept, is seen as surrounded by a phenomenal field. The organism and the self interact with the field to determine the nature of specific human behaviors.

Difficulties and Criticisms

While many were and are awed by the scope and power of the Lewinian theoretical system, others have not been as positively impressed with Lewin, and his theory has frequently been the center of controversy and criticism. Among his major critics, from whose critiques we draw, have been Leeper (1943), Tolman (1948), Spence (1944), London (1944), and Garrett (1939).

Some of these critics have argued that Lewin's theory ignores important factors that may be determinants of human behavior. Among the seemingly ignored factors are the individual's past history and possible future goals. The full and firm application of the principle of contemporaneity, which is so central to the Lewinian position, seems to exclude both past and future, and such potentially important factors as previous learning, social experience, heredity, and long-term goals, therefore, seem to be ignored. Lewin (1951) answered his critics by pointing out that the principle of contemporaneity suggests only that there is no direct impact of past and future. The person's thoughts about and perceptions relating to the past, as well as to future goals, are expected to influence current behavior. Thus, if thoughts about a future goal are currently active at the time behavior is occurring, they may well influence the person's behavior.

Similarly omitted from consideration as a major determinant of behavior is the objective external environment. Lewin acknowledged that objects do exist in the external environment, but it is the individual's perception and interpretation of these objects relevant to internal needs that actually determine behavior. The factual external environment has no direct effect on behavior. Some of the critics noted above have pointed out that this is a serious shortcoming in the Lewinian theory, since there is no way for the experimenter (or the clinician) to know the effects actual factors in the external environment have on particular kinds of behavior.

Another area of criticism focuses on the observation that Lewin's theory explains, but does not help us to predict or understand, human behavior. To appreciate the thrust of this criticism, we return to the example of the child who has a need to obtain a new game from a store. Lewin's system allows us to explain the nature of the child's behavior conveniently. The child's needs and tensions and resultant locomotion through the environment can be neatly described in terms of the topology and hodology of field theory. That is to say, knowing that the child first went to the piggy bank, then to the parent to obtain money, and finally to the store to obtain the desired toy, we can diagrammatically picture the sequence of behavior and verbally explain it in field theoretical terms. Could we, however, have *predicted* the behavior before seeing what the child actually did? Some of Lewin's critics would argue that we could not. Lewin (1951) tended to agree, in part, with the criticism, since he had found that his own early goals of predicting very specific behavior in very specific situations seemed unattainable within the context of his theoretical system.

Another criticism often made of Lewinian theory is that it makes inappropriate and inaccurate use of certain mathematical and physical concepts. The mathematical equations that Lewin utilized were developed after data had been collected, rather than used to provide a mathematical basis for specific prediction. A more serious criticism is that Lewin's topology may represent an inaccurate application of some possibly inappropriate constructs and terms drawn from a quite exact mathematical discipline. Lewin's response to his critics regarding these issues suggested that he had been careful and selective in using topological concepts, avoiding use of those aspects of topology that are not appropriate to a psychology of personality.

A final criticism of the Lewinian approach is that its experiments do not relate to its theory. Experiments on level of aspiration, psychological conflict, frustration, and the like, may, it has been argued, be interesting and of some importance in their own right. However, most of Lewin's empirical work does not directly and specifically test his theory, and some of it seems to bear very little relationship to the theory. This particular criticism may well be more a matter of viewpoint than of fact. Most theorists—and Lewin is no exception—have tended to see their theories as widely applicable to a broad range of human behavior. Given this orientation, it is a fairly small step for the theorist to believe that any of a wide variety of experiments will test his or her theory. At the same time, it can also be argued that at least some of Lewin's research quite clearly, even in the views of those outside the Lewinian movement, relates directly to the theory. Clearcut examples would be the work on interruption and substitution discussed above.

Conclusion

Taken in historical perspective, it seems clear that the criticisms of Lewin's theory have done little to detract from the heuristic power of the orientation. Lewin's introduction of the concepts of psychological field and contemporaneous motivation were unique at the time he made them and, as we have seen, his work has influenced that of many other psychologists. He is also among the relatively few theorists to have clearly spanned the fields of social and personality psychology. While his name is perhaps not invoked as often in discussion of theory as are those of Freud, Rogers, or Skinner, Lewin's influence is by now deeply imbedded in personality and social psychology and will no doubt be clearly felt well into the future.

REFERENCES

Atkinson, J. W. *An introduction to motivation.* New York: Van Nostrand-Reinhold, 1964.

Cartwright, D. Lewinian theory as a contemporary systematic framework. In S. Koch (Ed.), *Psychology: A study of a science* (Vol. 2). New York: McGraw-Hill, 1959.

Deutsch, M. Field theory in social psychology. In G. Lindzey (Ed.), *Handbook of social psychology.* Cambridge, Mass.: Addison-Wesley Press, 1954. (Pp. 181–222.)

Deutsch, M. Field theory in social psychology. In G. Lindzey & E. Aronson (Eds.), *Handbook of social psychology* (Vol. 1). Cambridge, Mass.: Addison-Wesley, 1968.

Epstein, S., & Smith, B. D. Modes and adequacy of resolution of three basic types of cognitive motor conflict. *Journal of Experimental Psychology,* 1967, *74,* 264–271.

Festinger, L. *A theory of cognitive dissonance.* Palo Alto, Calif.: Stanford University Press, 1957.

Garrett, H. E. Lewin's "topological" psychology: An evaluation. *Psychological Review,* 1939, *46,* 517-524.

Heider, F. *The psychology of interpersonal relations.* New York: Wiley, 1958.

Henle, M. An experimental investigation of dynamic and structural determinants of substitution. *Contributions to Psychological Theory,* 1942, *2,* (No. 3).

Henle, M. On Gestalt psychology. In B. B. Wolman (Ed.), *Scientific psychology: Principles and approaches.* London: Basic Books, 1965.

Hovland, C. I., & Sears, R. R. Experiments on motor conflict. Types of conflict and modes of resolution. *Journal of Experimental Psychology,* 1938, *23,* 477-503.

Karsten, A. Psychische Sättigung. *Psychologische Forschung,* 1928, *10,* 142-254.

Leeper, R. W. *Lewin's topographical and vector psychology: A digest and a critique.* Eugene, Ore.: University of Oregon Press, 1943.

Lewin, K. *A dynamic theory of personality: Selected papers* (D. K. Adams & K. E. Zener, trans.). New York: McGraw-Hill, 1935.

Lewin, K. Defining the "field at a given time." *Psychological Review,* 1943, *50,* 292-310.

Lewin, K. Will and need. In W. D. Ellis (Ed.), *A sourcebook of Gestalt psychology.* New York: Humanities Press, 1950.

Lewin, K. *Field theory in social science: Selected theoretical papers.* New York: Harper & Brothers, 1951.

Lewin, K. Behavior and development as a function of the total situation. In L. Carmichael (Ed.), *Manual of child psychology.* New York: Wiley, 1954.

Lewin, K., Dembo, T., Festinger, L., & Sears, P. S. Level of aspiration. In J. McV. Hunt (Ed.), *Personality and the behavior disorders* (Vol. 1). New York: Ronald Press, 1944. (Pp. 333-378.)

Lissner, K. Die Entspannung von Bedürfnissen durch Ersatzhandlungen. *Psychologische Forschung,* 1933, *18,* 218-250.

London, I. D. Psychologists' misuse of the auxiliary concepts of physics and mathematics. *Psychological Review,* 1944, *51,* 266-291.

Mahler, W. Ersatzhandlungen verschiedener Realitatgrades. *Psychologische Forschung,* 1933, *18,* 27-89.

McClelland, D. C., Atkinson, J. W., Clark, R. A., & Lowell, E. L. *The achievement motive.* New York: Appleton-Century-Crofts, 1953.

Miller, N.E. Experimental studies of conflict. In J. McV. Hunt (Ed.), *Personality and the behavior disorders.* New York: Ronald Press, 1944.

Nowlis, H. The influence of success and failure on the resumption of an interrupted task. *Journal of Experimental Psychology,* 1941, *28,* 304-325.

Ovsiankina, M. Die Wiederaufnahme von unterbrochener Handlungen. *Psychologische Forschung,* 1928, *11,* 302-379.

Smith, B. D., & Epstein, S. Influence of incentive on adequacy and mode of conflict resolution. *Journal of Experimental Psychology,* 1967, *75,* 175-179.

Smith, B. D., & Gehl, L. Multiple-exposure effects of resolutions of four basic conflict types. *Journal of Experimental Psychology*, 1974, *102*, 50-55.

Spence, K. W. The nature of theory construction in contemporary psychology. *Psychological Review*, 1944, *51*, 47-68.

Tolman, E. C. Kurt Lewin. *Psychological Review*, 1948, *55*, 1-4.

Zeigarnik, B. Über das Behalten von erledigten und unerledigten Handlungen. *Psychologische forschung*, 1927, *9*, 1-85.

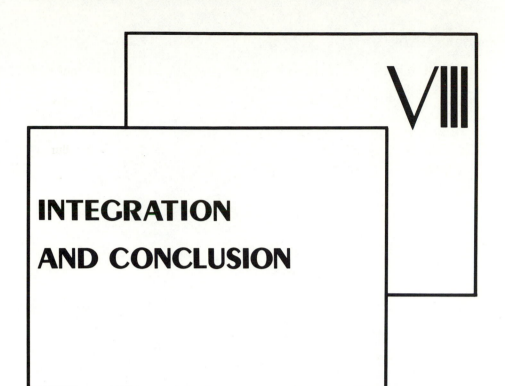

INTEGRATION
AND CONCLUSION

15

An Overview of Personality Theory:

The progress of scientific understanding has often followed a slow and tedious path, and the influence of great theorists and great theories has often extended well beyond both the lifetimes of the theorists and the utility of their theories. On his death in 370 B.C., Hippocrates left his eighty-seven great treatises, constituting the first major theory of medicine. While insightful in some respects, his work greatly lacked accuracy and depth, due partially to the ban on human dissection. It was not until the second century A.D. that the physician and medical theorist, Galen, drew together the body of medical research that had accumulated since Hippocrates and updated medical knowledge and theory. He was able to locate the mind in the brain—Aristotle had located it in the heart—and he drew an important distinction between sensory and motor nerves. At the same time, however, Galen created a medical theory that was at once incomplete, unverified, and often inaccurate. Nevertheless, his theory was followed as medical dogma for fully thirteen hundred years after his death. In fact, it was not until Andreas Vesilus published *De Fabrica Corporis*

Humani that Galen's ideas began to lose their influence. Vesilus studied the human body carefully and in great detail, practicing careful and extensive dissection, and arrived at a far more accurate understanding of human anatomy than had been approached in the Galenistic doctrine. That was in 1543. It was in that same scientifically crucial year that Copernicus published his heliocentric theory, stating that the earth is not the center of the universe. His theory, later verified, rejected the geocentric theory which had been held as truth for centuries.

Given these and other examples of how slowly science has often progressed, we are faced with the observation that formal psychological theories of personality, and the research associated with these theories, have been under way for less than one century. When Sigmund Freud published his first book, *The Interpretation of Dreams,* in 1900, he had no prior psychological theories of personality upon which to draw. This did not, of course, mean that Freud's theory developed out of a vacuum. There were medical theories of psychopathological human functioning at the time of Freud's early work. Most of these theories held that psychopathology is based on brain dysfunction; the work of Krafft-Ebbing, Kraepelin, Griesinger, and others all pointed in that direction. Philosophers had also long been interested in human behavior but had approached it through casual observation, speculation, and logic, not through scientific study. The philosophies of Leibnitz, Locke, Kant, John Stewart Mill, and others are certainly relevant to the development of modern theories of personality, but they were philosophies, not psychologies of personality.

All of this is not to say that the scientific understanding of human personality and behavior has not advanced during the twentieth century. On the contrary, there have been remarkable advances in our ability to predict and understand human functioning, both normal and psychopathological. Moreover, much of this advanced knowledge has come about through the development and application of the major personality theories.

THE GREAT THEORETICAL THRUSTS

We have seen the development, during the twentieth century, of what Maslow (1954) has termed three great forces in personality psychology. The first force is that of psychodynamic theory, originally in the form of Freudian psychoanalytic theory. This insightful school of thought has captured the imaginations and theoretical interests of a great many psychiatrists and psychologists and certainly remains one of the primary forces in modern psychology. Though modified somewhat in its modern form, classic Freudian theory views conscious man as but a feather buffeted by the winds of the unconscious, on the one hand, and by the environment, on the other. Unable to cope, man defends by forcing more and more of his conscious anxieties into the dark abyss of the unconscious. This defense merely fans the flames beneath a seething cauldron of unrealistic and antisocial urges and anxieties that seek to bubble over into consciousness. The overall result

Human Motivation

A second major set of issues is concerned with the dynamics of huma[n]. We have seen that neither the clinical nor the experimental literature in p[?] allows the theorist to make a simple choice in postulating one type of mo[tive] tem or another. In fact, motivation varies on several major dimensions, and th[ey] differ substantially in their positions on some of these dimensions.

The Time Base. Is motivation largely a function of the past, the present, or [the] future? Some theorists, in discussing the dynamics of current human behavio[r,] have emphasized motives developed in the past. Included here would be primarily the learning theorists, Eysenck, and, in some ways, Freud. Among the learning theorists, Dollard and Miller have emphasized the need to refer secondary motives back to primary drives, Skinner has noted that the individual's current behavior is a function of the history of reinforcement, and Bandura has been somewhat more mixed on this issue, suggesting that behaviors modeled in the past may be expressed in the presence of current reinforcements. Eysenck has noted the important role of heredity in predisposing the individual toward extraversion or introversion and toward neuroticism or stability and has shown how the person's hereditary position on these dimensions is modified through past experience to control present behavior. Freud has suggested that all human behavior can be traced back to the influence of the instincts, has noted that many adult behaviors are based on identifications formed during childhood, and has emphasized the role of early developmental experiences in determining adult personality functioning. He also noted, however, the role of the ego ideal as a function of the superego in causing the individual to strive toward more effective functioning in a somewhat teleological fashion.

Another sizeable group of theorists call for varying degrees of teleological motivation in their theories, often emphasizing that this goal-oriented, purposive, or growth motivation is central. Perhaps most obvious here is Rogers's concept of actualization, Maslow's concept of self-actualization, and Allport's propriate striving. Other theorists with purposive aspects to their theories include Jung and the social analytic theorists.

A third logical possibility would be to emphasize that motivation comes neither from the past nor from the future, but rather exists in the present. Lewin, in his field theoretical orientation, adopted this viewpoint. While past experience and future goals may, through memory and thought processes, enter the life space, the actual motivation of behavior takes place in the present.

Number and Centrality. Some theorists postulate that the number of motives governing human behavior is large but indefinite, others propose a fairly large set of specific motives, and still others suggest that only one or two motive systems are present. Clearly included in the first group is Lewin, who postulated the possibility of virtually innumerable needs which serve to motivate behavior; Jung, who proposed that many motivators are involved; and Allport, who has been somewhat more definite in proposing that a large number of dynamic traits may exist to drive

is a personality at best conflicted, largely unconscious, and, all too often, anxious and neurotic.

Objections to the psychoanalytic view of man were rife, and there arose two great counterposing forces. The first began with Watson and continued in the works of such theorists as Skinner, Dollard and Miller, and Bandura. Broadly viewed as behavioral approaches, these theories became nearly as diverse and varied as those within the psychodynamic movement. Basically, though, the behavioral approaches share the almost certain conviction that only a scientific, objective approach to human behavior will permit people to understand it. The result of this metatheoretical orientation has been a set of theories involving relatively few constructs and postulates, which is at once praised for its scientific rigor and damned as overly simplistic.

The third great force comprises a group of psychologists who were happy neither with the Freudian view of man as dominated largely by biological, nonrational, unconscious forces nor with the mechanistic simplicity of behavioral laws. These psychologists—the humanists and phenomenologists—saw a pressing need to give the individual's evaluative conception of his or her own characteristics a central role in behavior determination. Only by establishing the self as a major aspect of the personality and principal determinant of behavior could we hope to predict important human behavior or treat important human problems effectively. Classic Freudian theory had no phenomenological concept of self, though Hartmann later introduced one, and behaviorism seemed not to need such a complex construct. The humanistic movement also asserted the importance of viewing man as having a direct hand in determining his own destiny and held that the individual is motivated to strive for future goals and for the realization of potentials, not merely to satisfy the biological requirements of the organism and the sociopsychological requirements of the environment.

Not all major personality theories fall clearly within the three principal schools of thought, and some defy classification within any one approach. Carl Jung, while developing a basically psychodynamic theory, was also strongly typological in his orientation in the tradition of Wundt and his philosophical and physiological predecessors, Galen, Kant, Gross, and Hippocrates. Eysenck, also a typologist, has emphasized the physiological underpinnings of personality, quite possibly ushering in a new era of concern with genetic and other biological factors in human behavior. Eysenck is also a factor analyst, but in that domain he is surpassed by Raymond Cattell, whose work has constituted a tour de force in psychology. While its value is only beginning to be recognized, it may well become the cornerstone of a new and powerful movement, quite possibly the fourth major force in psychology. As a trait theorist, Cattell was anticipated by Allport, whose thorough treatment of human traits emphasized the idiographic approach as strongly as Cattell's work has stressed the nomothetic line of research. Finally, we must note the theory of Kurt Lewin, which stands nearly alone as the major representative of field theory, having broad influence on both theory and research in social psychology as well as personality psychology.

SUBSTANTIVE COMPARISONS AMONG THEORIES

We have seen, in reviewing the various theoretical treatments of personality, both important similarities and major differences among the theories covered. It should be carefully noted that a given theorist's position on a particular substantive issue is in part a matter of what the theorist intends to say on that issue and in part "in the eyes of the beholder." Thus, our comparative comments regarding the positions of various theories on particular issues are somewhat a function of how we perceive the theory. The reader may choose to disagree.

Origins of Personality

Theories differ, as we have seen, on several issues relevant to the origin and development of human personality. The first major issue is the classic nature–nurture question. What are the relative roles of heredity and learning in personality development? It is of some interest to note that every major theorist discussed indicates that both nature and nurture underlie human personality development and functioning. There are, however, major differences in emphasis among the theorists. Freud, Jung, and, most recently, Eysenck have placed heavy emphasis on the importance of hereditary factors in personality. Freud emphasized the importance of the inherited physiological instincts or drives and of a motivational process which governs much of personality development. Jung, for his part, suggested the inheritance of predispositions to respond to environmental objects or stimuli and called for psychologists and psychiatrists to recognize the possibility of a cultural inheritance of such predispositions. Eysenck saw an important role for heredity in the form of neurophysiological bases for his major typological dimensions of personality. At the opposite pole on the heredity-environment issue are the major behavioral theorists. Of these, Skinner adopted perhaps the strongest antiheredity position, giving no specific role to inherited factors in his treatment of the origins of behavior. All behaviors are learned through repeated reinforcement of emitted responses, and heredity need not be taken into account. Dollard and Miller also emphasized the learning process but allowed for the inheritance of reflexes and primary drives. Lewin and the social analytic theorists have also tended to deemphasize heredity.

Most other theorists have given heredity and environment a somewhat more balanced treatment. Rogers, for example, placed heavy emphasis on learning but opted for the inheritance of his major motive system, actualization. Allport and Murray both discussed the role of heredity in the context of their primarily environmental theories. Perhaps the most balanced and sophisticated treatment of the heredity-learning issue has been given by Cattell. He not only incorporated both heredity and environment into his theory of factors in personality functioning but has taken the approach of examining the differential portions of variance contributed by heredity and environment to his various factor analytic traits.

The Developmental Process. Theorists have also differed on the basic issue of ether personality development is a smooth, continuous path or whether i occur in a series of discrete stages. Among the major "stage" theorists are , ullivan, and Dollard and Miller. It might be noted that although each of heorists postulated a discrete series of steps in the developmental process, the for staging vary from one position to another. Freud proposed that staging is for staging on a physiological maturational process. Sullivan, on the other hand, point on a physiological maturational process. Sullivan, on the other hand, point the occurrence of certain developments and events relevant to interpersonal tions as the bases for moving from one stage to the next. And Dollard and M pointed to the occurrence of certain significant learning situations as providing bases for staging. Most other theorists have either explicitly or implicitly opted a smoother developmental process, rather than one that takes place in disc steps. Rogers, for example, has been quite explicit in his belief that the devel ment of the personality, based upon the hereditary actualization motive, is a c tinuous and smooth one, beginning with the first day of life and continui throughout childhood and adulthood.

Continuity of Development. Does the mature, adult personality represent tl culmination of continuous development from early childhood? Psychoanalytic an behavioral theorists contend that it does in that one major set of developmenta principles accounts for the continuous development of the personality from birtl throughout adulthood. Freud, Hartmann, Bandura, Skinner, and Dollard and Mille have been explicit in postulating developmental continuity. Somewhat less clearly, Eysenck, Sullivan, and Adler also adopted continuity positions. A mixture of theorists, cutting across several major schools of thought, have proposed discontinuity, seeing the adult personality as relatively independent of the developmental processes of childhood. Included in this group would be Jung, Rogers, Allport, and Lewin.

Significance of the Early Developmental Process. Freud greatly emphasized the significance of the first few years of life, postulating that both normal adult personality traits and psychopathological functioning in adulthood are largely a function of these early years of development. A number of theorists who have borrowed from Freud more generally in developing their theories have also emphasized the essential importance of early development. Included here are, certainly, Dollard and Miller, whose learning theory represented essentially a Hullian reinterpretation of Freud's theory, and Adler, one of Freud's major early disciples. Most other theorists have deemphasized the importance of early development, either explicitly noting that personality development is ongoing and that the personality remains malleable even into adulthood, or, alternatively, by not emphasizing early development. Lewin, for example, has made it quite clear that the most important determinants of behavior lie in the present and, therefore, certainly not in early childhood. Allport and Sullivan, in somewhat different ways, have talked specifically of the significance of the developmental process that extends into adulthood. Eysenck and Skinner, likewise, have placed no special emphasis on early development, and Bandura, though he has done much of his modeling research with children, has not overly emphasized early childhood.

human behavior. Only Cattell has thus far been able to specify more precisely the relatively large number of motives in his theoretical system. Somewhat more limited sets of motives are postulated by Freud, Hartmann, and the social analytic theorists. Eysenck's theory also appears to fall in this latter group, while Skinner's has no specific concept of motivation, and the other behavioral theories, as well as Maslow's, fall in the middle of the continuum in terms of the number of motives postulated. Rogers's theory is at the opposite extreme, postulating that only one major motive system, that is, actualization, or two systems if self-actualization is considered to be a separate motive, govern behavior.

It is important to note, that, in general, the lesser the number of motives postulated by a theorist, the more there tends to be an emphasis in the theory on the centrality of a few motivational systems. Freud, from the psychodynamic group, and Rogers from the phenomenological-humanistic group, exemplify theorists who consider their major motives to be central to personality functioning. Freud proposed that the life and death instincts underlie all or much of behavior, while Rogers has explicitly noted that all behavior is motivated by actualization and self-actualization.

Level of Consciousness. Freud's hypothesis that most important human behavior is governed by unconscious motives was, when he proposed it and continues to be, a most controversial issue. On the one hand, many have praised Freud as the first person to develop a systematic theory of unconscious motivation; on the other hand, he has been faulted for not giving conscious motivation an appropriately substantial role. As the initial controversy died down and research programs in such areas as word association, selective remembering and forgetting, and perceptual defense, all generally supportive of the psychoanalytic concept of unconscious motivation, got under way, the deep significance of Freud's contribution became increasingly clear to larger and larger numbers of psychologists and psychiatrists. The long-term result of this realization was that many theorists, across all three major schools of thought, began to develop personality theories that included a concept of unconscious motivation. Within the psychodynamic movement most theorists praised Freud for his "discovery" of the unconscious and incorporated concepts of unconscious motivation in their theories. Among behavioral theorists we see in Dollard and Miller a concept of unconscious motivation in which repression is seen as a learned response and unconscious conflicts are seen as the bases for neurosis. In Roger's phenomenological-humanistic theory we also see a concept of unconscious behavior determination in which those experiences not consistent with the existing self-concept may be kept out of awareness or consciousness, yet continue to influence behavior by causing the individual to have an inaccurate self-concept.

Although we do see unconscious motivation across schools of thought, there are certainly differences in the degree to which this concept is emphasized. Rogers has placed less emphasis on unconscious motivation than do many of the psychodynamic theorists, although his theory relies more heavily on this concept than do those of Lewin, Skinner, or Allport. At the other end of the emphasis continuum are those theorists placing greater stress on the unconscious determinants of behavior. Hartmann, although he certainly gave more weight to conscious motivation than did Freud, still heavily emphasized the influence of unconscious determinants. Similarly, Jung, to a great extent, and Horney and Murray, to somewhat lesser degrees, postulated that unconscious motives are far more important than those of which the individual is aware.

Determinism and Free Will. Even as Freud rejected the idea of behavior determined entirely or largely by conscious motivations, he insisted that all behavior must be and is causally determined. The concept of a free will not subject to scientific laws was immediately disposed of in psychoanalysis, and all behaviors, both consciously and unconsciously motivated, were seen as governed by principles that could be hypothesized in scientific theory and verified through scientific research. This approach separates Freud from many of the philosophers of earlier centuries, such as Kant, and allies him with the scientific psychology of the twentieth century to come. On this one point at least—the deterministic nature of human behavior—virtually all later personality theorists would explicitly or implicitly agree with Freud. With a single exception, there is no free will in twentieth-century personality theory. The exception is in existential theory, which rejects the basic tenet of determinism, that all human behaviors are causally based and subject to scientific principles.

Environmental Influences

Personality theorists are in general agreement that cultural learning has some influence on the development and functioning of the human personality but are somewhat less agreed on the roles of the interpersonal environment and the psychological environment. Even though no theorist has openly rejected the idea that the culture is involved in shaping the individual personality, there are great variations in the degree to which this type of environmental influence is emphasized. Freud, Jung, and Fromm are among the major theorists to have given cultural learning a specific and well-defined role within their theories. Freud's treatment emphasized the childhood inculcation of cultural values taught by the parents and others as agents of the society and learned by the child as the content of the superego. Jung emphasized not so much cultural learning as cultural transmission in the form of genetic predispositions to respond to identifiable objects and persons in the external environment. Fromm, of course, has focused much of his theoretical effort on dealing in depth with the multitude of cultural determinants seen as crucial to personality functioning. Though with somewhat less emphasis, Hartmann and Adler have clearly given culture a major role in personality functioning, and Allport, who has emphasized that the personality is within the individual, also postulated that cultural influences interact with this inner personality structure in determining behavior. Horney has also placed considerable emphasis on the role of culture but focused her treatment primarily on the family and its influence on the child as the major acculturative, and potentially neurotogenic, influence. Dollard and Miller have also focused on the family as a social training agent and, within that context, emphasized the role of cultural determinants.

The influence of the interpersonal environment through dyadic and small group interaction is seen most clearly in Sullivan's theory. Interestingly enough, most other theorists have not followed up systematically on this line of thought, though interpersonal interaction is central to Berne's treatment, somewhat less central in Rogers's, and a major factor in many social psychological theories of human behavior.

The concept of a psychological environment suggests, in its fullest treatment, that the individual's behavior is controlled, to a substantial extent, by his or her immediate perceptual surroundings. The psychological environment is thus the environment as perceived by the individual, and the idea of an objective reality is deemphasized in favor of perceptual reality. Lewin has formulated the most thorough and clear-cut concept of the psychological environment as a major determinant of human behavior. Rogers has also emphasized the importance of the psychological environment, as have the major existential theorists.

A final possibility is that the immediate situation, in a somewhat more objective sense, may influence behavior. This theoretical theme is seen most explicitly in Mischel's proposal that situations may be more important than traits in determining human behavior. His view is allied with that of Bandura, who has maintained that behaviors previously learned through modeling may be expressed in the presence of immediately available reinforcements. Many other theorists have noted the role of immediate situations in behavior determination but have deemphasized this role in favor of more trait-like structures.

Not all theories fall neatly into our system for categorizing environmental influence. Cattell and Skinner, in particular, defy classification within this scheme. Cattell's theory postulates a complex set of traits, termed *sentiments,* which are the result of environmental experience, but these sentiments are influenced by genetically determined ergs and interact with the immediate situation to produce actual behavior. In contrast to Cattell's conceptually complex treatment, in his theory Skinner offers the parsimonious suggestion that all behavior is a function of its reinforcement history, with many of the reinforcements presumably coming from cultural agents, some in the context of interpersonal interactions and some existing in the immediate situational context.

A somewhat broader issue with regard to environmental influences is the question of whether interaction with the environment tends to enhance or impede the development and functioning of the personality. Society may, on the one hand, be seen as imposing on man a set of standards, requirements, and stresses, which have a largely negative or, at best, neutral influence on the personality. On the other hand, the theorist may give the society a predominantly positive role, proposing that the culture provides a basis not only for the satisfaction of essential needs and drives but also a basis for psychological growth, thus helping man to enhance his own personality functioning.

The more negative role of society is one in which the culture takes an active role in socializing the person, insisting that he or she inculcate social norms, mores, and skills. The normal person, following this socialization process, is basically a conformist. The molten wax has been poured into the mold of the society and has hardened in the prescribed shape. Freud suggested that such social molding represents a significant blow to the biological nature of man, insisting that some essential drives can be satisfied only in narrowly defined, socially acceptable ways, while others may have to go unsatisfied for long periods of time or permanently. From a quite different perspective, Rogers pointed out that the conditions of worth, developed as a set of cultural values through a socialization process, may have the negative effect of inhibiting the realization of organismic potentialities, thus stopping or slowing the process of actualization. Other theorists have been more positive about the role of society. Fromm, while noting the negative role often played by society, has stated that the ideal function of the culture is to enhance the functioning of the individual. Maslow, similarly, has depicted the society as providing a systematic means for the satisfaction of many human needs, thus allowing people to move up the hierarchy toward self-actualization. Hartmann, Jung, Horney, and Allport, among others, have all been quite clear in viewing societal influences as both inhibiting and enhancing, depending upon the individual and the particular social structures and processes to which he or she is exposed.

Individuality and Integrity of the Organism

Allport most clearly emphasized that each person is a unique individual, with characteristics and qualities not found in any other person. Dollard and Miller, on the other hand, have formulated a theory in which the person operates according to a broad set of principles which do not readily lend themselves to an emphasis on individual uniqueness. These theories represent the opposite extremes on the issue of the need to recognize the significance of individuality. Falling in line with Allport, though with less emphasis on the importance of the uniqueness postulate, are Adler and Lewin. Joining Dollard and Miller in deemphasizing the importance of uniqueness are Skinner and Bandura.

On the related issue of the integrity of the organism, theorists divide into those who emphasize the need for a wholistic understanding of behavior and those who believe that the person must be dissected into a number of component parts or segments in order to study the causes of behavior scientifically. The major wholist we have studied is Lewin, whose field theory stresses the interrelation of the organism and its environment in behavior determination. Rogers and Adler have also tended to adopt a more wholistic emphasis, though perhaps not as thoroughly as Lewin. Cattell, Eysenck, and the behavioral theorists have most clearly relied on separate component behaviors and behavior determinants in order to understand human functioning.

Traits and Situations

Behavior may, on the one hand, be determined predominately by stable, long-term characteristics of the individual personality, termed *traits,* or, on the other hand, it may be largely a function of situations facing the individual at the time behavior occurs. As we have seen, the roles of traits and situations have been hotly debated in recent years, and the split between traditional trait theorists and recent situational theorists has formed the basis for a major controversy. Most of the major theorists we have studied, including psychodynamic, behavioral, and humanistic theorists, have agreed that the principal determinants of behavior are the stable traits of the personality. When Mischel (1968) strongly suggested that this is not the case and that situational factors are preeminent in behavior determination, all of these major traditional theories were implicitly threatened. The result was a strong reaction against a predominantly situational approach to understanding behavior, then a partial resolution of the controversy and the suggestion that traits and situations actually interact to determine behavior. In fact, it is important to recognize that the interactionist position, like the trait position and the situational position, is a theoretical orientation. Although interactionism would appear to be the obvious resolution of the trait-situation controversy, it is no more factual (as opposed to theoretical) than either of the seemingly more extreme positions. It is reasonable to anticipate that the trait-situation-interaction controversy will go on and that more theorists will be forced to state and restate their positions regarding this controversy.

Self-Evaluation

To what extent is behavior determined by the individual's evaluation of his or her own characteristics? Here, the self-concept as an evaluation and control center in the personality has been the primary focus of theorists choosing to emphasize this behavior determinant. Rogers most clearly and adequately has formulated a concept of the evaluative self, which oversees and influences most of the person's behavior. Allport's proprium, Cattell's self-sentiment, and Hartmann's self, though somewhat less central in their respective theories than the Rogerian self-concept, are closely related constructs. The self-efficacy concept of Bandura's recent writings represents a somewhat different treatment of the self-construct, and the self-system of Sullivan's theory is basically an anxiety-reduction mechanism and not closely related to the Rogerian form of the self-concept. The remaining theorists have largely ignored self-conceptualization as a determinant of behavior.

Applicable Populations

Some theorists, as they developed their theoretical approaches, observed clinically or did research with primarily neurotic populations. Other theorists have focused their observational efforts to some extent on psychotic patients. And still others have been concerned largely with observation of normal individuals. Freud, for example, made his principal observations on the basis of clinical work with neurotic patients, Sullivan worked with both neurotic and psychotic patients, and Jung was most interested in psychosis. Rogers dealt primarily with mildly disturbed clients, often college students, and Allport and Cattell have based most of their research on

normal individuals, although Cattell has also done research with patient populations. The major point here is that care must be taken in generalizing the theory
beyond the population on which it is based. In some cases, the basis for such generalizations, though not seen in the theorist's original observations, is available in
literature developed by others. Psychoanalytic theory, for example, has been
studied as to its applicability to psychotics and normals. In other cases, generalization must be much more tenuous, and it has sometimes been found that generalizing
a particular theory beyond its original population is difficult. A good example of
this latter situation occurred when Rogers and his colleagues applied client-centered
therapy, based on Rogerian theory, to a group of schizophrenics with minimal
success.

The Nature of Man

The question of which theorists are most optimistic and positive about the nature
and possibilities of humans and which the most pessimistic and negative is a difficult one to answer except in certain of the more extreme cases. Freud quite clearly
took the more negative view, emphasizing the impulsive, regressive, anxious, abnormal, destructive side of human behavior. Fromm joined Freud in a basically
negative view, emphasizing the sociocultural context in which personality develops
and the often desperate, isolated loneliness of persons in that context. At the
opposite pole, we see the positive strivings that grow out of the actualizing tendency in Rogers and the self-actualizing motive in Maslow, and we see the relatively
optimistic personology of Allport. Within the psychodynamic group, Hartmann and
Erikson have led modern psychoanalysis into a much more optimistic view of
human nature, emphasizing the relatively substantial roles of awareness, external
reality, and rationality and the possibility of a conflict-free sphere within which
much of human behavior operates. And Horney, while giving conflict a central role
in her theory of neurotic behavior, also emphasized that conflict and its effects can
be avoided if social conditions, particularly within the family, are right.

A GAZE INTO THE CRYSTAL BALL

What does the future of the personality field hold in store for us? A glance into the
crystal ball reveals, first, a sea of swirling clouds, giving little hope that we can
accurately assess the future of a currently very active field. Nevertheless, some
small openings in the cloud cover will permit us to speculate concerning several
possible future directions.

Research and Research Methodology

The need for, and possibility of, carefully controlled research has been realized only
in recent years. It seems likely that the current widespread concern with the refinement of relevant research methodologies, the development of new research tech-

nologies, and the ongoing conduct of increasing numbers of careful empirical studies will continue. This means that the reasonably near future may see the rapid accumulation of an important body of empirical information that will be relevant to the development and modification of personality theories in the future.

As an important part of the increased interest in careful research in recent years, there is an increasing emphasis on the need to evaluate carefully both the process and outcome of psychotherapy. The individual therapist is increasingly being encouraged to conduct programmatic and systematic evaluations of his or her own therapeutic interventions and, in addition, to contribute more generally to broader research efforts which are attempting to determine the variables relevant to the successful conduct of psychotherapy. Since therapies, and the observations of patients or clients that are so central to the work of the therapist, are closely tied to the development of many personality theories, it is likely that the increased emphasis on therapy evaluation will provide a particularly important body of knowledge for the personality theorist.

Modification of Existing Theories

The major schools of thought in personality that we have discussed, and most of the individual theories within those schools, will probably continue for some time to be major forces in psychology. History would suggest, however, that many of these theories will not remain in precisely their current form and that some will be quite substantially modified as new observations and empirical evidence become available. We have seen, for example, the very substantial modifications of Freudian theory that are present in modern ego psychology and the ongoing modifications of behavioral theory, particularly in recent years. It is thus reasonable to predict that whatever else might happen in the personality field within the reasonably near future, the three major schools of thought will continue, with some modifications, to be influential.

Physiological Factors in Behavior

In 1890, William James theorized that much of human behavior, including social behavior, is based on physiological, inherited instincts. In a theory focused more centrally on this point, William McDougall, in 1908, provided a list of human instincts which included self-assertion, gregariousness, and self-abasement, among others.

The reaction against the instinct concept as applied to humans was deep and profound. The behaviorists under Watson's direction, anthropologists, such as Franz Boas, and many others launched an all-out attack on the concept of human instincts. The attack culminated in a paper by Bernard (1924), who pointed out that literally thousands of human actions had been designated as instinctive by one theorist or another and that evidence pointed to environmental bases for most of these actions. As a result, the instinct concept died, and with it went most of the interest of psychologists in the possibility of genetic or other physiological factors that might underlie human behavior. It should perhaps be recalled that Freud's theory, which became a major force even as the instinct concept was declining in favor, did not employ the term instinct in the same sense as it was used by James or McDougall, but rather defined instincts as drives.

Following the demise of the instinct concept, most psychologists tended to largely ignore genetic factors. The social analysts moved away from even Freud's relatively acceptable view of biological factors underlying personality, while the behaviorists, like Dollard and Miller, tended to relegate such factors to species-wide reflexes and primary drives, or, like Skinner, to having no role at all. Similarly, phenomenological theorists have seen little need to postulate physiological bases for behavior other than at the broad, general level of the actualization drive.

Relatively recent years have seen some research interest in possible genetic and other physiological factors that might underlie human behavior. We have reviewed Eysenck's theory and some related evidence regarding the probable genetic and neurophysiological bases for extraversion and neuroticism as major personality dimensions and have also noted Cattell's interesting work with the multiple abstract variance analysis technique for determining the relative contributions of genetics and environment to his personality trait dimensions. Related developments have been seen in the area of psychopathology, where a growing body of evidence strongly suggests that genetic factors are likely to be involved in at least some cases of schizophrenia and of affective psychosis (Rosenthal 1970). In addition, a smaller, and, therefore, more tentative, body of evidence suggests the possible involvement of important genetic factors in at least some instances of neurotic disorder (Shields 1962).

It should be cautioned that none of this research suggests that personality is largely or entirely inherited or that there is a need to revive ethological instinct concepts, such as those of McDougall and James. What does seem likely is that personality theorists will find it increasingly essential to take genetic research into account and focus on the possibility that much of human behavior is determined by an interaction of genetic and environmental factors. In the long run we will need to assess for each of a number of areas of human behavior and personality factors the relative influence of genetic variables, environmental variables, and the interaction of these two.

Multivariate Approaches

Raymond Cattell and Hans Eysenck are major representatives of an approach to personality theory not yet pursued by most psychologists. They have used multivariate—primarily factor analytic—statistical approaches in attempts to determine the most important dimensions of human personality functioning and the ways in which behavior is dependent upon and affected by the position of the individual on these dimensions. Despite the fact that both of these theorists, and a number of other psychologists, have been pursuing multivariate approaches for over thirty years, it is only recently that interest in the broader application of multivariate techniques has developed. More and more psychologists are currently being trained in multivariate analysis, and, with the increased concern over the refinement of research methodology, it is likely that the future will see more and more researchers and theorists turning to multidimensional approaches to understanding human behavior.

Cognitive Variables

There has also been in recent years an increased interest in the study of cognitive variables and their influence on behavior. Cognitive variables are those which specify the process through which the person obtains information from the external environment, interprets that information in an individualistic fashion, then makes a response based on the information. Such processes as thinking, memory, sensation, perception, and problem solving are seen as cognitive processes. George Kelly (1955), as we have seen, has developed a personal construct theory of human behavior, which holds that the individual's personality is a system of constructs. A construct is an approach to interpreting or construing the world, and many constructs are cognitive in nature. Finally, such learning theorists as Bandura and Mischel have placed considerable stress on cognitive variables, emphasizing the need to understand the roles and functions of these variables in determining behavior.

It appears that cognitive variables have already begun to take a substantial place alongside the drives and emotions of the better-established personality theories and that future theories—and future modifications of current theories—will have to take into account the growing body of theory and research dealing with these variables.

More Specific Theories

Another trend in the general area of personality theory in recent years has been toward the development of "mini-theories" dealing with relatively specific aspects of human behavior rather than with the entire domain of personality. We have not dealt with such theories in previous chapters, but some examples may be useful. Witkin's 1962 work, dealing with cognitive styles and psychological differentiation, is one such example. It does not attempt to account for all human behavior but rather focuses on the way in which the individual perceives and interprets the environment along certain dimensions. A second example of such a specific-area theory is the achievement motivation theory of David McClelland (1951). In his theoretical work, McClelland focused on one specific need hypothesized by Henry Murray, the need for achievement. He elaborated a theory of need for achievement and achievement motivation and conducted a program of research relating to this construct. Along similar lines, Leon Festinger (1957) dealt with the effects of discrepancies or inconsistencies in an individual's perceptions or cognitions. Such cognitive dissonance leads to certain theoretical effects which may result, for example, from making a decision, and the individual may strive to reduce the dissonance. Finally, a number of specific-area theories have dealt with particular forms of psychopathology. Examples are theories of schizophrenia, such as those developed by Epstein (1967) and Broen and Storms (1966).

Interactionism

We reviewed, in discussing the work of Bandura, Mischel, Bowers, and others, the controversy regarding the relative influence of traits and situations on behavior. It is clear that this controversy has moved toward at least temporary resolution in favor of an interactionist position, which emphasizes the role of trait-situation interaction in determining behavior. Both traits and situations, independently, can influence behavior, but from a strong interactionist position, it is a third factor, the interaction of traits and situations, that is most important. Cattell, as we have seen, proposed the need to take into account both traits and situations in a formal way many years ago, and it is clear that this is one direction in which the field has moved and probably will continue to move in at least the near future. If traits are relatively stable characteristics of the person and situations are the current environmental conditions to which the individual is exposed, we may have to also include at least a third variable in an extended interactionist scheme, namely states. These are relatively temporary conditions of the individual, such as fatigue or emotional mood. They change much more readily than traits and may be based on the interaction of a number of dimensions or traits. As an example, a given individual may ordinarily be quite happy (perhaps displaying a trait of happiness) but at the time of entering a particular situation may be temporarily in a state of unhappiness. The state, as well as the trait and the situation, may have an important influence on behavior.

The more sophisticated theories of the future may have to deal with a dual form of interactionism in which not only the trait-state-situation interaction is taken into consideration but also the genetic-environment interaction. Such a theory would have to recognize formally that the trait-state-situation interaction, as well as the separate influence of each of these three, is important in determining current behavior. It would also have to consider that the hypothesized traits, and perhaps also states, are determined in part by biogenetic factors and in part by environmental-learning factors. Thus, it would become important to determine the relative amount of influence or proportion of variance attributable to genetics, environment, and their interaction in relationship to each trait and state and the portions of variance attributable to traits, states, situations, and their interactions in determining current behavior.

Whatever the fate of our specific predictions about directions for the future, we can be certain that personality theory, begun in the early 1900s, is yet in its youth and shows much promise for a long and fruitful life. It is, after all, one of the most complex and fascinating areas of study ever undertaken, for it deals not with the behavior of atoms or chemicals, not with the behavior of plants or "lower" animals, but with the behavior of humans—with *our* behavior. And now that we have sipped from this clouded fountain of knowledge about ourselves and found its taste to be sweet, though escaping full description, we can hardly cease to drink.

REFERENCES

Bernard, L. L. *Instinct, a study of social psychology*. New York: Holt, Rinehart, & Winston, 1924.

Broen, W. E., & Storms, L. H. Lawful disorganization: The process underlying a schizophrenic. *Psychological Review*, 1966, *73*, 229–248.

Epstein, S. Toward a unified theory of anxiety. In B. A. Maher (Ed.), *Progress in experimental personality research* (Vol. 4). New York: Academic Press, 1967.

Festinger, L. *A theory of cognitive dissonance*. Stanford, Calif.: Stanford University Press, 1957.

Gottesman, I. I. Heritability of personality: A demonstration. *Psychological Monographs*, 1963, *77*, (9, Whole No. 572).

Jackson, S. *The Lottery*. New York: Farrar, Straus, 1949.

Kelly, G. A. *The psychology of personal constructs*. New York: Norton, 1955.

Maslow, A. H. *Motivation and personality*. New York: Harper & Row, 1954.

McClelland, D. C. *Personality*. New York: Holt, 1951.

Mischel, W. *Personality and assessment*. New York: Wiley & Sons, 1968.

Rogers, C. *Client-centered therapy: Its current practice, implication, and theory*. Boston: Houghton Mifflin, 1951.

Rosenthal, D. *Genetic theory and abnormal behavior*. New York: McGraw-Hill, 1970.

Shields, E. Comparison of children's guessing ability (ESP) with personality characteristics. *Journal of Parapsychology*, 1962, *26*, 200–210.

Witkin, H. A., Dyk, R. B., Faterson, H. F., Goodenough, D. R., & Karps, S. A. *Psychological differentiation*. New York: Wiley, 1962.

Author Index

Subject Index